STRANGERS TO NEIGHBOURS

MCGILL-QUEEN'S REFUGEE AND FORCED MIGRATION STUDIES

Series editors: Megan Bradley and James Milner

Forced migration is a local, national, regional, and global challenge with profound political and social implications. Understanding the causes and consequences of, and possible responses to, forced migration requires careful analysis from a range of disciplinary perspectives, as well as interdisciplinary dialogue.

The purpose of the McGill-Queen's Refugee and Forced Migration Studies series is to advance in-depth examination of diverse forms, dimensions, and experiences of displacement, including in the context of conflict and violence, repression and persecution, and disasters and environmental change. The series will explore responses to refugees, internal displacement, and other forms of forced migration to illuminate the dynamics surrounding forced migration in global, national, and local contexts, including Canada, the perspectives of displaced individuals and communities, and the connections to broader patterns of human mobility. Featuring research from fields including politics, international relations, law, anthropology, sociology, geography, and history, the series highlights new and critical areas of enquiry within the field, especially conversations across disciplines and from the perspective of researchers in the global South, where the majority of forced migration unfolds. The series benefits from an international advisory board made up of leading scholars in refugee and forced migration studies.

1 The Criminalization of Migration
   Context and Consequences
   Edited by Idil Atak and James C. Simeon

2 A National Project
   Syrian Refugee Resettlement in Canada
   Edited by Leah K. Hamilton, Luisa Veronis, and Margaret Walton-Roberts

3 Strangers to Neighbours
   Refugee Sponsorship in Context
   Edited by Shauna Labman and Geoffrey Cameron

Strangers to Neighbours

Refugee Sponsorship in Context

Edited by

SHAUNA LABMAN AND
GEOFFREY CAMERON

McGill-Queen's University Press
Montreal & Kingston · London · Chicago

© McGill-Queen's University Press 2020

ISBN 978-0-2280-0136-2 (cloth)
ISBN 978-0-2280-0137-9 (paper)
ISBN 978-0-2280-0275-8 (ePDF)
ISBN 978-0-2280-0276-5 (ePUB)

Legal deposit third quarter 2020
Bibliothèque nationale du Québec

Printed in Canada on acid-free paper that is 100% ancient forest free (100% post-consumer recycled), processed chlorine free

This book has been published with the help of a grant from the Canadian Federation for the Humanities and Social Sciences, through the Awards to Scholarly Publications Program, using funds provided by the Social Sciences and Humanities Research Council of Canada.

Funded by the Government of Canada   Financé par le gouvernement du Canada   Canada   Canada Council for the Arts   Conseil des arts du Canada

We acknowledge the support of the Canada Council for the Arts.

Nous remercions le Conseil des arts du Canada de son soutien.

Library and Archives Canada Cataloguing in Publication

Title: Strangers to neighbours: refugee sponsorship in context / edited by Shauna Labman and Geoffrey Cameron.

Names: Labman, Shauna, 1977– editor. | Cameron, Geoffrey, editor.

Series: McGill-Queen's refugee and forced migration studies; 3.

Description: Series statement: McGill-Queen's refugee and forced migration studies; 3 | Includes bibliographical references and index.

Identifiers: Canadiana (print) 20200243209 | Canadiana (ebook) 20200243675 | ISBN 9780228001362 (cloth) | ISBN 9780228001379 (paper) | ISBN 9780228002758 (ePDF) | ISBN 9780228002765 (ePUB)

Subjects: LCSH: Private Sponsorship of Refugees Program (Canada) | LCSH: Refugees—Government policy—Canada. | LCSH: Refugees—Canada.

Classification: LCC JV7282 .S77 2020 | DDC 325/.210971—dc23

This book was typeset by Marquis Interscript in 10.5/13 Sabon.

Contents

Figure and Tables ix

Acknowledgments xi

Introduction: Private Refugee Sponsorship: An Evolving Framework for Refugee Resettlement 3
Geoffrey Cameron and Shauna Labman

PART ONE CONTEXT

1 Reluctant Partnership: A Political History of Private Sponsorship in Canada (1947–1980) 19
Geoffrey Cameron

2 "Naming" Refugees in the Canadian Private Sponsorship of Refugees Program: Diverse Intentions and Consequences 42
Sabine Lehr and Brian Dyck

3 How *Should* We Think about Private Sponsorship of Refugees? 61
Patti Tamara Lenard

4 A Port in the Storm: Resettlement and Private Sponsorship in the Broader Context of the Refugee Regime 74
Megan Bradley and Cate Duin

PART TWO CASES

5 Religious Heritage, Institutionalized Ethos, and Synergies: The Mennonite Central Committee and Canada's Private Sponsorship of Refugees Program 95
Thea Enns, Luann Good Gingrich, and Kaylee Perez

6 Operation Ezra: A New Way Forward   112
  Madison Pearlman

7 The Blended Visa Office-Referred Program: Perspectives and Experiences from Rural Nova Scotia   134
  Rachel McNally

8 Refugee Sponsorship in the Age of Social Media: Canada and the Syrian Refugee Program   152
  Elizabeth Coffin-Karlin

PART THREE CHALLENGES

9 Kindred Spirits? Links between Refugee Sponsorship and Family Sponsorship   177
  Audrey Macklin, Kathryn Barber, Luin Goldring, Jennifer Hyndman, Anna Korteweg, and Jona Zyfi

10 Transactions of Worth in Refugee–Host Relations   198
  Christopher Kyriakides, Arthur McLuhan, Karen Anderson, and Lubna Bajjali

11 Mobilization of the Legal Community to Support PSR Applications through the Refugee Sponsorship Support Program   212
  Kelsey Lange

12 Judicial Review in Canada's Refugee Resettlement Program   227
  Pierre-André Thériault

PART FOUR COMPARISON

13 "Doing Something to Fight Injustice": Voluntarism and Refugee Resettlement as Political Engagement in the United States   247
  Scott Harding and Kathryn Libal

14 Private Humanitarian Sponsorship: Searching for the Community in Australia's Community Refugee Sponsorship Program   264
  Anthea Vogl, Khanh Hoang, and Asher Hirsch

15 A Model for the World? Policy Transfer Theory and the Challenges to "Exporting" Private Sponsorship to Europe   286
  Craig Damian Smith

Conclusion: Sponsorship's Success and Sustainability?   303
Shauna Labman

Contributors 319

Index 325

Figure and Tables

FIGURE

8.1 Reddit screenshot 164

TABLES

1.1 Religious groups in Canada 23
9.1 Comparison of the text of the family class sponsorship and the refugee sponsorship undertaking 189
12.1 Resettlement applications approval rates (2011–2018) 230
12.2 Overview of judicial review applications (2011–2015) 233
12.3 Summary of judicial review outcomes (2011–2015) 234

Acknowledgments

We both began our research on refugee resettlement at a time when political interest in this aspect of refugee policy was relatively minimal. This quickly changed in the wake of the 2015 Canadian election, when the new Liberal government committed to resettling 25,000 Syrian refugees and promoted the use of private refugee sponsorship. Many Canadians knew little about this unique aspect of refugee policy at the time, but just a few years later about one quarter of Canadians know someone who has participated in sponsorship. The world also knows more about the Canadian program, owing to the federal government's efforts to promote it as a model for other countries to adopt.

When we saw each other at a Pierre Elliott Trudeau Foundation Summer Institute in May 2017, we began to talk about these changing realities and the need for a volume that would bring together a cross-disciplinary group of scholars who could enhance academic and public understanding of the program. This idea took shape with the support of a grant from the PETF's Public Interaction Program and the partnership of the Global Migration Lab at the Munk School of Global Affairs and Public Policy. Jennifer Petrela at the PETF and Randall Hansen at the Munk School both supported the initiative in its early stages.

A call for papers was distributed, abstracts were selected, and authors were invited to present at a two-day workshop in October 2018, held at the Munk School. That event, "Private Refugee Sponsorship: Concepts, Cases, and Consequences," came together with the phenomenal support of Joseph Hawker and Olga Kesarchuk, who managed logistics and the administration of our grant. We also benefited from the assistance of two volunteer rapporteur-participants, Ian Van Haren and Enbal Singer. Through the Legal Research Institute at the University of Manitoba, the final details of the book came together with the support and careful research of Jonathan Andrews.

Jacqueline Mason at McGill-Queen's University Press has supported the idea of this book from the outset and worked with us throughout the process to swiftly bring it into print.

Of course, we would not have a complete book without the chapter authors. We put out an open call for papers setting out our ideas and questions on private refugee sponsorship with the hope we could gather some people to work with us. The response was outstanding; there are many great ideas and papers that we could not include in this volume but that we hope to read elsewhere. We selected authors with a range of experiences, expertise, and perspectives. In addition to writing their own papers, these authors committed to reviewing one another's drafts in advance of our workshop, coming to Toronto to sit with us for two days to discuss themes and connections, and responding to our detailed edits and tight timelines. We feel fortunate and grateful as editors to have worked with such insightful and responsive authors, and we are proud of the community of diverse scholars that has generated this project.

As this book goes to print, we are in a much different reality than where we began. The coronavirus pandemic has grounded most international travel and closed borders. The IOM and UNHCR temporarily suspended resettlement in March 2020, and the Canadian government cancelled all imminent refugee arrivals. Sponsors in Canada are now working to support arrived refugees to navigate the uncertainty, while the future of further resettlement and private sponsorship waits in the distance. As we plan to rebuild and recover, we are confident the insights in this book will be invaluable.

Shauna Labman – Winnipeg, MB
Geoffrey Cameron – Hamilton, ON

STRANGERS TO NEIGHBOURS

Introduction:
Private Refugee Sponsorship:
An Evolving Framework
for Refugee Resettlement

Geoffrey Cameron and Shauna Labman

Canada's framework of private refugee sponsorship has generated heightened interest among policy-makers, scholars, and advocates in recent years. This has been related to a broader return to consideration of resettlement as a durable solution to refugee crises.[1] The reasons for this are complex. On one hand, they include the disproportionate burden placed on certain countries by spontaneous arrivals. Resettlement is a necessary component of any system of responsibility-sharing in the context of a large influx of refugees, such as the one experienced by Europe following the Syrian war.[2] Another dimension of this interest in resettlement has been the cross-pressures faced by leaders of liberal democratic countries, who often face compelling foreign policy reasons for increasing the numbers of refugees they admit for resettlement, while also encountering reactionary domestic opponents.[3] The rising threat of far-right nationalism in Western democracies has raised sensitivities to inflaming anti-immigrant sentiment, which has in turn had a strong deterrent effect on resettlement policy.

In this evolving international policy environment, Canada's framework of private refugee sponsorship has received (indeed, actively sought) growing international attention.[4] Unique among other countries of resettlement, Canada operates a program that allows small groups of individuals and established charitable organizations to sponsor refugee families. The precise terms of this sponsorship have evolved in ways that chapters in this volume will explain; however, at its core, private sponsorship entails a financial and social relationship between sponsors and refugees. Sponsors commit to providing the funds for the first year of the sponsored refugee(s) resettlement while accompanying the refugee(s) in the process of settlement. The government covers health care, education, language training, and some other costs. Refugees, who become permanent residents upon landing, qualify for social welfare benefits in their second year of residence. Sponsors are also allowed to select, or "name," the refugees they are resettling. Private sponsors have resettled more than 300,000 refugees since the formal program commenced in the late 1970s.[5] Since private sponsorship is intended to be complementary, and additional, to the government-funded resettlement program, it is viewed as a way to increase refugee resettlement numbers while controlling the burden on the public purse and stimulating favourable public opinion.[6]

Canada has employed a form of private refugee sponsorship since the postwar period. In 2016, it began to promote its policy framework among other states. Announcing a new Global Refugee Sponsorship Initiative (GRSI), immigration minister John McCallum said, "I think one aspect of this crisis today is that there are not enough countries receiving enough refugees to solve the problem, to put it mildly ... So I do believe this initiative, which is essentially to export to interested countries in the rest of the world our privately sponsored refugees [program], could make a significant impact on the refugee crisis."[7] The GRSI was supported by the Government of Canada, the UN High Commissioner for Refugees, and the Open Society Foundations, for the purpose of replicating Canada's private sponsorship program in some nineteen countries. Canada has also sought to promote the study and diffusion of its program through other channels, including the deliberations leading to the Global Refugee Compact as well as by funding academic research.[8]

While private sponsorship has a long history in Canada, it is relatively understudied[9] beyond limited and dated attention to particular groups.[10] This lack of research is swiftly changing with the surge in academic interest in the Syrian resettlement program,[11] but there remains a need for a more expansive understanding of the sponsorship framework. The purpose of this volume is to contribute a cross-disciplinary body of knowledge to the academic and policy discourse around private refugee sponsorship in particular, and refugee policy more generally. It aims to elucidate and evaluate Canada's practice of private refugee sponsorship in a historical and comparative context in order to draw out some implications of Canada's experience both for Canadian policy and for other countries. The contributors to this volume include scholars, practitioners, and scholar-practitioners, who draw upon the theoretical and analytical tools of law, social science, and philosophy. Together, they add a more robust and objective perspective on Canada's experience with private refugee sponsorship to these wider conversations. The intention of this volume is not to present a critical view of either Canada's framework or its efforts to export it, but to contribute a more comprehensive perspective and greater depth of analysis than that which can accompany the enthusiasm of policy entrepreneurs and evangelists.

Before the chapter authors launch into their particular discussions, this introduction summarizes the legislative framework and historical trajectory of Canada's PSR program. We describe the main elements of the program's institutional framework as well as some of its key characteristics. Finally, we briefly introduce each of the main chapters that follow and set out some of the themes that connect them.

BACKGROUND AND FRAMEWORK

What we now call "refugee resettlement" emerged from the post–Second World War crisis of displaced people. While refugees were an enduring product of an international state system several centuries in the making, it was not until after the war that states devised laws and policies that explicitly targeted recognized classes of people facing the threat of persecution. Previous refugee admissions had been made by states using normal immigration policy; refugee resettlement emerged as a new pathway of admissions, one that included a stronger dimension of foreign policy. After the war, millions of displaced people were residing in camps, and those who refused repatriation remained in them to insist upon resettlement in third countries. The International Refugee Organization (IRO) was founded in 1948 for the explicit purpose of coordinating international resettlement efforts. Between 1947 and 1951, around one million refugees were resettled in the United States, Australia, Israel, Canada, and various European states.[12] The 1951 Refugee Convention created an international legal definition of a refugee. The IRO's functions were assumed in 1952 by the UN High Commissioner for Refugees (UNHCR). Resettlement is defined by the UNHCR as "the selection and transfer of refugees from a State in which they have sought protection to a third State which has agreed to admit them – as refugees – with permanent residence status."[13] Resettlement is one of three durable solutions for refugees, alongside voluntary repatriation and local integration, promoted by the UNHCR.

Within this emerging field, a number of humanitarian and religious groups that had acquired significant experience in relief work and immigrant aid began to advocate for resettlement of displaced people. This advocacy was initially framed in sectarian or ethnic terms, but in both the United States and Canada, interfaith coalitions gradually became a prominent feature of the postwar refugee policy scene.[14] Early resettlement programs in the countries that emerged as some of the primary destinations for refugees – such as Australia, Canada, and the United States – were facilitated in no small part by the participation of these religious groups at various stages in the resettlement process. Thus, at an early period in the evolution of refugee resettlement, non-governmental groups found themselves woven into a system of international migration for refugee populations.

As refugee policies evolved in response to changing political conditions throughout the Cold War period, most countries gradually constrained or actively excluded these groups. In Canada, however, they retained an active – albeit contested – role in resettlement. That contestation typically revolved around a number of issues, such as whether voluntary groups could select the refugees they were bringing over; what criteria would be applied in the selection process; how long these groups would be responsible for the care of incoming refugees; and the extent of financial liability for the refugees. These programs were active throughout the 1950s but became less prevalent in Canada's resettlement programs throughout the 1960s.[15] These programs were primarily the result of bureaucratic negotiation with religious groups, with no real foundation in legislation.

Canada became a state party to the 1951 Refugee Convention in 1969, a move that required Canada to enshrine its international obligations to refugees in domestic law. The legislative review to design new immigration laws began in the early 1970s with the intent of including specific provisions for the selection and processing of refugees.[16] The Immigration Act, 1976, put Canada's refugee policy into statutory form. The new law included a provision for private refugee sponsorship:

> I.6.(4.) Any body corporate incorporated by or under any Act of Parliament or the legislature of a province, and any group of

Canadian citizens or permanent residents, may, where authorized by the regulations, sponsor the application for admission of [a recognized refugee].[17]

This private sponsorship provision was unspecific, and lawmakers left it to be elaborated through future policy development led by immigration program managers. The Immigration Department sought out test cases of private sponsorship, first approaching the Jewish human rights group B'nai B'rith and the Jewish Immigrant Aid Society, which had advocated for the inclusion of the sponsorship provision, and then the Catholic Church's Migration Commission. Then, as the Indochinese refugee crisis unfolded, the Mennonite Central Committee of Canada negotiated the first Master Agreement with the Immigration Department.[18] Master Agreements allowed corporate bodies to assume the liabilities associated with sponsorship, which would be undertaken by their local Constituent Groups. Most early Master Agreements were signed with religious groups. Under these agreements, sponsoring groups were responsible for paying first-year settlement costs, and the government would "provide an overall structure that included language training and allowances and a willingness to take over from the sponsors any cases that were exceptionally costly or requiring unusual professional services."[19] These agreements clarified a number of long-standing questions and disputes around the terms of private sponsorship by establishing a clearer and more equitable set of responsibilities between sponsoring groups and the Government of Canada. From this period onward, private sponsors have asserted that the principles of naming and additionality guide their contribution to Canada's resettlement efforts.

Canadian sponsorship took off with the sponsorship of around 35,000 Indochinese refugees. The Indochinese were resettled mainly by sponsoring groups to whom they were effectively strangers.[20] This dynamic, however, has shifted over time. A 1990 government review of the private sponsorship program found that outside of periods of "crisis," the program was primarily used as a tool for family reunification. Canadians who had themselves arrived as refugees could form "Groups of Five" to name and sponsor members of their extended families who were refugees, or they could work with Sponsorship Agreement Holders (SAHs) to bring in known refugees. By 2003 there were suggestions that between 95 and 99 percent of private sponsorship applications were for extended family or close friends.[21] About half the sponsor-referred names were rejected by immigration managers between 1998 and 2007.[22] The outcomes of private refugee sponsorship appeared to have drifted from the original policy goal, and this was leading to significant inefficiencies.[23]

In response, the government sought to redirect private sponsorship to particular refugee populations not necessarily known by sponsors. A number of initiatives were undertaken for the purpose of blending public priorities with private resources within the refugee sponsorship program. In Project FOCUS Afghanistan in the 1990s, the government funded the first three months of settlement support for sponsored refugees, after which sponsors would assume responsibility for the remaining nine months of the first year. Sponsors were given some authority to select refugees for participation in the program. Similar programs were designed for particular groups of refugees, including those from the former Yugoslavia, Iraq, Sierra Leone, and those fleeing gender and sexuality-based violence.[24] In each of these programs, the practice of "naming" was restricted to high-vulnerability populations, and the government shared in some of the financial costs of resettlement normally borne by private sponsors. In 2012 the government began placing a cap on sponsorship applications to reduce wait times and control the "inventory" where each SAH receives an annual allotment from the cap. In 2013 the government introduced the Blended Visa Office–Referred (BVOR) program, in which sponsors and the government share equally the cost of the first year of settlement. As the name of the program suggests, sponsors effectively give up their authority over "naming" in exchange for cost-sharing with the government. BVOR applications do not fall within the caps.

Three distinct programs now exist within the Canadian refugee resettlement scheme: the Government Assisted Refugee (GAR) program, the Private Sponsorship of Refugees (PSR) program, and the BVOR program. The focus of this volume is the PSR program, although this will necessitate some discussion of the GAR and BVOR programs. Government-assisted resettlement has long accounted for most refugee resettlement to Canada, with private refugee sponsorship averaging 25 to 40 percent between 1994 and 2018.[25] The BVOR program accounts for the smallest number of resettled refugees. The 2019–21 Immigration Levels Plan published by the Government of Canada in 2018 projects that in 2021, 10,000 GARS, 1,000 BVORS, and 20,000 PSRS will be resettled in Canada.[26] This marks a significant increase in Canada's yearly resettlement commitments, which averaged a yearly combined total of 12,000 GARs and PSRs from 2005 to 2015, with GAR numbers consistently outnumbering – tending to more than double – PSR admissions.[27] The numbers moving forward reverse focus, with PSR numbers doubling GARs. This is a further reason for this volume to focus on the PSR program.

Within the institutional framework for private refugee sponsorship, sponsorship is permitted through three types of sponsorship groups: "Groups of Five," "Community Sponsors," and "Constituent Groups" (CGs), which belong to an organization that is a SAH. SAHs are the evolution of early Master Agreement holders. As of August 2019, there were 120 SAHs across Canada.[28] Many of these SAHs are linked with religious communities (around 75%, as of 2014).[29] About 65 percent of refugees privately resettled are sponsored or co-sponsored by a SAH.[30] SAHs must be incorporated, whereas Community Sponsor groups do not have to be incorporated and simply need to be based in the community where refugees are expected to settle. Co-sponsorships permit an individual to partner with a SAH, a CG, or a Community Sponsor. A Group of Five is, as the name suggests, any group of five or more Canadians and permanent residents formed for the purpose of sponsoring refugees. In 2018 the government estimated the cost of sponsoring a single individual at $16,500, and a family of four at $28,700.[31]

The particulars of Canada's resettlement program are found in the *Immigration and Refugee Protection Regulations*.[32] As set out in the regulations, resettlement in Canada is open to Convention refugees who fall within the "Convention Refugees Abroad Class" but expands beyond the refugee definition in the "Country of Asylum Class" to others outside their countries of nationality and habitual residence who have been, and continue to be, seriously and personally affected by civil war, armed conflict, or massive violation of human rights.[33] UNHCR referrals of Convention refugees are the primary source for GAR and BVOR resettlement to Canada.[34] The criteria used by UNHCR to assess resettlement need are as follows: legal and physical protection needs, survivors of violence and torture, medical needs, women and girls at risk, family reunification, children and adolescents at risk, and the lack of foreseeable alternative durable solutions.[35] Privately sponsored refugees can be, and often are, more broadly selected under the "Country of Asylum Class." Until 2011, Canada further permitted resettlement of individuals who had not crossed an international border through a "Source Country Class" that by its end operated mainly out of Colombia.[36]

There is no single model of private refugee sponsorship in Canada, as the framework within which Canadians work has evolved over time. Even in a volume of this size it is impossible to capture the entirety of a program that has operated for more than forty years and that has been moulded by government program managers, changes in political leadership, the sponsors who come together, and the refugees they resettle in communities large and small across Canada.

OVERVIEW

The chapters that follow are organized into four sections. The first section is for stage-setting. Cameron's chapter traces the origins of the program from the end of the Second World War to the introduction of legislation in the 1970s. Lehr and Dyck then move the narrative forward by examining the principle of "naming" refugees. From here the lens widens to the global refugee regime. Lenard's chapter raises normative questions on refugee selection. Bradley and Duin's chapter closes the section with a discussion of the risks and unintended consequences of resettlement in relation to broader global protection goals.

The second section brings context to many of the questions raised in the initial chapters, providing case studies to help readers understand private sponsorship as it is practised. The chapter by Enns, Good Gingrich, and Perez examines the Mennonite Central Committee's sustained sponsorship efforts since signing the first Master Agreement. In contrast, Pearlman's chapter discusses the recent and distinct approach to sponsorship taken by Operation Ezra in Winnipeg. McNally's chapter looks at the use of the BVOR model of sponsorship in a rural context. The chapter by Coffin-Karlin turns to social media and internet culture as it relates to the experience and training of new Canadian sponsors.

The third section addresses the challenges of sponsorship. Exploring responses to a national survey of private sponsors, the chapter by Macklin, Barber, Goldring, Hyndman, Korteweg, and Zyfi argues that elements of kinship are embedded in sponsorship relationships. Kyriakides, McLuhan, Anderson, and Bajjali's chapter details how the refugee–host relationship influences settlement success. Lange's chapter details how the legal community mobilized to support private sponsorship applications as interest in the program surged with the Syrian conflict. Thériault's chapter steps beyond this to the legal framework of resettlement and private sponsorship that comes into play when sponsorship applications are rejected.

In the fourth section, the authors look both beyond and out from the Canadian context. Harding and Libal's chapter examines volunteerism and community mobilization in support of refugees in the United States in a political context of diminished government support for refugees. Vogl, Hoang, and Hirsch's chapter critiques Australia's Community Sponsorship Program, which includes elements of private sponsorship. Canada's Global Refugee Sponsorship Initiative is surveyed in Smith's chapter through the lens of policy transfer to understand the barriers to the uptake of private sponsorship in Europe.

Labman's concluding chapter attempts to bring the ideas of the volume together around the idea of sustainable and successful sponsorship.

CONCLUSION

It is our hope that readers will approach this volume as a coherent whole, one that examines a number of key dimensions of a policy framework that is often oversimplified in public and academic discourse. The contributors have worked to converse with one another so that the volume reflects a process of learning among some of the leading researchers and practitioners in the field. This effort began with a workshop hosted by the Global Migration Lab at the University of Toronto's Munk School of Global Affairs and Public Policy, with the support of the Pierre Elliott Trudeau Foundation. Several themes connect the chapters, but there are also conflicting interpretations and approaches. These are the realities of a program that is valued and propelled by individual Canadians (albeit sometimes in tension with government goals), that is currently celebrated, and that is bringing thousands to a safe future in Canada; yet that is also minimally contributory to the reduction of global refugee numbers and dependent on personal relations between refugees and sponsors for its success. Finally, it is a program that both operates along a long-standing continuum and has been newly undertaken by many Canadians in moments of crisis.

NOTES

1 See Idean Salehyan, *The Strategic Case for Refugee Resettlement* (Washington, DC: Niskanen Center, 2018); Randall Hansen, "The Comprehensive Refugee Response Framework: A Commentary," *Journal*

of *Refugee Studies* 31, no. 2 (June 2018): 131–51; Adèle Garnier, Liliana Lyra Jubilut, and Kristin Bergtora Sandvik, eds, *Refugee Resettlement: Power, Politics, and Humanitarian Governance* (Oxford: Berghahn, 2018); Marion Couldrey and Maurice Herson, eds, "Resettlement," *Forced Migration Review* 54 (February 2017).
2 Astri Suhrke, "Burden-Sharing during Refugee Emergencies: The Logic of Collective versus National Action," *Journal of Refugee Studies* 11, no. 4 (1998): 396–415.
3 James Hampshire, *The Politics of Immigration: Contradictions of the Liberal State* (Washington, DC: Polity, 2013).
4 Hansen, "The Comprehensive Refugee Response Framework"; Judith Kumin, "Welcoming Engagement: How Private Sponsorship Can Strengthen Refugee Resettlement in the European Union," *Migration Policy Institute Europe* (December 2015); Susan Fratzke, "Engaging Communities in Refugee Protection: The Potential of Private Sponsorship in Europe," *Migration Policy Institute Europe* (September 2017); Global Refugee Sponsorship Initiative, http://refugeesponsorship.org.
5 The government gives the number as 288,000 sponsored refugees as of fall 2016. Government of Canada, "Canada's Private Sponsorship of Refugees Program," 19 September 2016, https://www.canada.ca/en/immigration-refugees-citizenship/news/2016/09/canada-private-sponsorship-refugees-program.html. In 2017, 16,873 privately sponsored refugees were admitted to Canada. Immigration, Refugees, and Citizenship Canada, "2018 Annual Report to Parliament on Immigration," https://www.canada.ca/en/immigration-refugees-citizenship/corporate/publications-manuals/annual-report-parliament-immigration-2018/report.html.
6 Jennifer Hyndman, William Payne, and Shauna Jimenez, "Private Refugee Sponsorship in Canada," *Forced Migration Review* 54 (2017): 56–9; Audrey Macklin, Kathryn Barber, Luin Goldring, Jennifer Hyndman, Anna Korteweg, Shauna Labman, and Jona Zyfi, "A Preliminary Investigation into Private Refugee Sponsors," *Canadian Ethnic Studies* 50, no. 2 (2018): 35–57.
7 Kathleen Harris, "'Extraordinary Initiative': Canada's Private Refugee Sponsorship System Exported as Model for the World," CBC *News*, 14 December 2016, https://www.cbc.ca/news/politics/canada-refugees-privately-sponsored-global-initiative-1.3895704.
8 Hansen, "The Comprehensive Refugee Response Framework." See also Social Sciences and Humanities Research Council, "Targeted Research: Syrian Refugee Arrival, Resettlement, and Integration," 9 October 2018, http://www.sshrc-crsh.gc.ca/funding-financement/programs-programmes/syrian_refugee-refugie_syrien-eng.aspx.

9 Shauna Labman, "Private Sponsorship: Complementary or Conflicting Interests?" *Refuge* 32, no. 2 (2016): 67–80; Ashley Chapman, "Private Sponsorship and Public Policy: Political Barriers to Church-Connected Resettlement in Canada," *Citizens for Public Justice* (September 2014): 1–14; Hyndman et al., "Private Refugee Sponsorship in Canada"; Jennifer Hyndman, "Research Summary on Resettled Refugee Integration in Canada" (2011), accessed 3 September 2019, https://www.unhcr.ca/wp-content/uploads/2014/10/RPT-2011-02-resettled-refugee-e.pdf; Barbara Treviranus and Michael Casasola, "Canada's Private Sponsorship of Refugees Program: A Practitioner's Perspective of Its Past and Future," *Journal of International Migration and Integration* 4, no. 2 (2003): 177–202.

10 Howard Adelman, *Canada and the Indochinese Refugees* (Canada: L.A. Weigl Education Associates, 1982); Michael Lamphier, "Sponsorship: Organizations, Sponsor and Refugee Perspectives," *Journal of International Migration and Integration* 4, no.2 (2003): 237–56; Tracey Derwing and Marlene Mulder, "The Kosovar Sponsoring Experience in Northern Alberta," *Journal of International Migration and Integration* 4, no.2 (2003): 217–37; Thomas Denton, "Understanding Private Sponsorship in Manitoba," *Journal of International Migration and Integration* 4, no.2 (2003): 257–71. Shauna Labman and Madison Pearlman, "Blending, Bargaining, and Burden-Sharing: Canada's Resettlement Programs," *International Migration and Integration* 19, no. 2 (May 2018): 439–49.

11 Julie Drolet, Richard Enns, Linda Kreitzer, Janki Shankar, and Anne-Marie McLaughlin, "Supporting the Resettlement of a Syrian family in Canada: The Social Work Resettlement Practice Experience of Social Justice Matters," *International Social Work* 61, no. 5 (2018): 627–33; Hyndman et al., "Private Refugee Sponsorship in Canada."

12 Michael R. Marrus, *The Unwanted: European Refugees in the Twentieth Century* (Philadelphia: Temple University Press, 1985), 344–5.

13 UNHCR, *Resettlement Handbook* (2011), 9, https://www.unhcr.org/protection/resettlement/4a2ccf4c6/unhcr-resettlement-handbook-country-chapters.html.

14 Gerald E. Dirks, *Canada's Refugee Policy: Indifference or Opportunism?* (Montreal and Kingston: McGill-Queen's University Press, 1977); J. Bruce Nichols, *The Uneasy Alliance: Religion, Refugee Work, and U.S. Foreign Policy* (Oxford: Oxford University Press, 1988).

15 Dirks, *Canada's Refugee Policy*.

16 Department of Manpower and Immigration, "A Report of the Canadian Immigration and Population Study" (Ottawa: Information Canada, 1974).

17 *Canada: Immigration Act*, 1976–77, c. 52, s. 1.
18 See William Janzen, "The 1979 MCC Canada Master Agreement for the Sponsorship of Refugees in Historical Perspective," *Journal of Mennonite Studies* 24 (2006): 211–22.
19 Gordon Barnett, in Michael J. Molloy, Peter Duschinsky, Kurt F. Jansen, and Robert Shalka, *Running on Empty: Canada and the Indochinese Refugees, 1975–1980* (Montreal and Kingston: McGill-Queen's University Press, 2017), 75–6.
20 Molloy et al., *Running on Empty*, 3–4.
21 Labman, "Private Sponsorship: Complementary or Conflicting Interests?," 69.
22 Ibid.
23 Jacob S. Hacker, Paul Pierson, and Kathleen Thelen, "Drift and Conversion: Hidden Faces of Institutional Change," in *Advances in Comparative-Historical Analysis*, ed. James Mahoney and Kathleen Thelen (New York: Cambridge University Press, 2015), 180–210.
24 Labman, "Private Sponsorship: Complementary or Conflicting Interests?"
25 Macklin et al., "A Preliminary Investigation into Private Refugee Sponsors."
26 Government of Canada, "Notice – Supplementary Information 2019–2021 Immigration Levels Plans," 11 January 2019, https://www.canada.ca/en/immigration-refugees-citizenship/news/notices/supplementary-immigration-levels-2019.html.
27 The only exception is 2013, when GAR numbers sat at 5,781 and PSR numbers reached 6,392. Calculations based on Immigration, Refugees, and Citizenship Canada, and previously Citizenship and Immigration Canada, "Annual Report to Parliament on Immigration."
28 Government of Canada, "Private Sponsorship of Refugees Program – Sponsorship Agreement Holders," 27 August 2019, https://www.canada.ca/en/immigration-refugees-citizenship/services/refugees/help-outside-canada/private-sponsorship-program/agreement-holders/holders-list.html.
29 Kumin, "Welcoming Engagement."
30 Ibid.
31 Canada, Immigration, Refugees, and Citizenship Canada, "Guide for Groups of Five to privately sponsor refugees (IMM 2200)," 5 October 2018, https://www.canada.ca/en/immigration-refugees-citizenship/services/application/application-forms-guides/guide-sponsor-refugee-groups-five.html#costtables.
32 Immigration and Refugee Protection Regulations, SOR/2002–227 [IRPR].
33 Ibid., ss.144–147.

34 Michael Casasola, "UNHCR updates on resettlement activities for 2015–2016," *Canadian Orientation Abroad,* 18 January 18, 2016, www.coa-oce.ca/unhcr-updates-on-resettlement-activities-for-2015-2016.
35 UNHCR, *Handbook and Guidelines on Procedures and Criteria for Determining Refugee Status* (December 2011), 245.
36 Immigration and Refugee Protection Regulations, SOR/2002–227, Section 148 repealed, SOR/2011–222, s.6; Citizenship and Immigration Canada, "Regulations Amending the Immigration and Refugee Protection Regulations and Regulatory Impact Analysis Statement," *Canada Gazette* 145, no. 2, 19 March 2011, http://www.gazette.gc.ca/rp-pr/p1/2011/2011-03-19/html/reg3-eng.html.

PART ONE

Context

1

Reluctant Partnership: A Political History of Private Sponsorship in Canada (1947–1980)

Geoffrey Cameron

This chapter traces the evolution of Canada's private refugee sponsorship program from its origins in 1947 to the passage and implementation of the 1976 Immigration Act. It argues that private refugee sponsorship started as a partnership between religious groups and Canadian immigration officials and that there was a great deal of continuity over the evolution of the program before it was formalized in law. A close examination of this developmental path reveals that many contemporary issues related to private sponsorship have characterized the program since its inception. These include questions related to selection processes (who identifies, or "names," the refugees to be sponsored), selection criteria (whether humanitarian, economic, or strategic criteria should be applied), and financial responsibility (the distribution of costs and liabilities shared by sponsors and the state). Negotiations over these issues between sponsoring groups and immigration officials have made for the development of a reluctant partnership within a relatively durable institutional framework.

The research in this chapter expands upon histories of Canadian immigration policy that narrate the period between the 1940s and the mid-1970s as a series of disconnected ad hoc responses to refugee crises in the context of the Cold War and expanding immigration. The "standard" history of Canadian immigration policy appears to suggest that the private sponsorship provision of the 1976 Immigration Act appeared out of nowhere – perhaps on the whim of a legislator who introduced language that was a placeholder for something to be determined later.[1] A more recent historical treatment of the period proposes that it was a product of an essentially Canadian value system.[2] Shauna Labman has identified the key role played by the Canadian Jewish Congress following its advocacy to admit Soviet Jews under terms of private sponsorship during the late 1960s.[3]

In fact, the genesis of private sponsorship can be traced to a contingent period of policy change after the Second World War, after which a set of institutional arrangements became path dependent over time. Paul Pierson uses the analogy of a branching tree to describe the process of path dependency, where each step in one direction makes it more difficult to reverse course.[4] Because of positive feedback, "the probability of further steps along the same path increases with each move down that path."[5] The modalities of private sponsorship by religious groups adopted following the Second World War became replicated over time, as learning and coordination effects locked in those initial responses.[6] As religious groups defined a role for themselves in the field of refugee resettlement, they made an effort to retain their position as sponsors of refugees who failed to meet the labour market criteria established by government refugee programs. Iterative negotiations between these groups and government officials, in the context of episodic refugee crises, elaborated a framework of private refugee sponsorship that created the basic template for the provisions included in the 1976 Immigration Act and later Master Agreements with sponsorship groups.

POSTWAR ORIGINS

After the formal end of hostilities in Europe in 1945, some 30 million people were left stateless as refugees and displaced people. The early Allied military effort to facilitate repatriation succeeded at relocating 11 million refugees, while many others integrated locally or returned home on their own. By 1946, more than one million refugees had refused repatriation outright and remained in refugee camps in Germany, Italy, and Austria, awaiting emigration to third countries.[7] Other returnees returned to the Allied zone as refugees after experiencing persecution when they returned home. The problem of displaced people became a leading international issue of the postwar period as the Allied powers struggled to resolve a growing humanitarian crisis.[8]

In Canada, decision-making on refugee admissions was concentrated within the Department of Mines and Resources, where the Immigration

Branch maintained a restrictive immigration policy. As early as January 1946, the Department of External Affairs wrote to the immigration director to advocate for the admission of refugees from Europe.[9] The foreign policy rationale was clear: Canada had been granted greater autonomy over its affairs by the British Parliament in 1931, and resettling refugees presented an opportunity to show leadership in the construction of an emerging postwar order. The Immigration Branch resisted these entreaties, explaining that "the problem just bristles with difficulties."[10] In response to repeated interventions, however (including from civil society groups like the Canadian National Committee on Refugees), the Departments of Labour, Health, and External Affairs and the Immigration Branch convened a small interdepartmental committee in March 1946 to begin generating recommendations to Cabinet.

Foreign policy arguments for admitting refugees were buttressed by the increasingly influential view of interest groups representing business leaders and railway companies that Canada needed to expand its economy by attracting workers to build its population. Europe's refugees were identified as a primary means for meeting this goal. When C.D. Howe – an energetic and powerful member of Mackenzie King's Cabinet – assumed responsibility for the Ministry of Reconstruction and Supply, he acquired temporary jurisdiction over the Immigration Branch and proceeded to push the idea that the government could admit refugees from DP camps to meet the need for unskilled labour on Canadian farms and in other economic sectors experiencing shortages of workers. He viewed DPs as "the simplest, cheapest and quickest way to find labour."[11]

Cabinet approved two refugee resettlement programs in 1946 and 1947 respectively: a "close relatives" scheme and a "bulk labour" movement. The bulk labour program was designed to meet particular labour demands of the Canadian economy while also demonstrating Canada's commitment to the international effort to clear the refugee camps in Europe. The close relatives scheme began as a narrow immigration program but quickly expanded to include refugees. Tens of thousands of applications poured in from relatives and from religious groups in the months following the announcement.[12] However, many of these applicants found that their nominated relatives were ineligible for sponsorship because ethnic Germans who were not German citizens were considered to be enemy aliens under Canadian regulations. They also were outside the mandate of the International Refugee Organization (IRO), the intergovernmental organization set up in

1946 to coordinate the resettlement of displaced people from Europe. The policy looked like a failure.

The initiative of an entrepreneurial Lutheran layman, T.O.F. Herzer, brought together a coalition of church groups to meet with immigration officials to determine how to overcome these obstacles to the resettlement of relatives. In June 1947, the Canadian Mennonite Board of Colonization, Canadian Lutheran World Relief, German Baptist Union, and Catholic Immigration Aid Society met with the government and transportation agencies to determine how to facilitate the movement of those among these refugees who qualified under the close relatives scheme. This meeting led to the founding of the Canadian Christian Council for the Resettlement of Refugees (CCCRR).[13]

The CCCRR would play a key role in the close relatives scheme. Transatlantic affiliates of CCCRR members were to find refugees outside the mandate of the IRO with Canadian relatives and assemble them for screening by Canadian authorities. As the number of relatives brought to Canada by the CCCRR gradually diminished, it sought from the Immigration Branch an expanded role in Canada's resettlement effort for the purpose of sponsoring refugees without Canadian family members. Already, the Canadian Jewish Congress had lobbied for and been permitted to resettle 1,000 orphan children, and the Catholic Immigration Aid Society had likewise been permitted to sponsor 1,000 refugees, who would arrive under its care.[14] In January 1949, the CCCRR was authorized to assume responsibility for resettling five hundred farm- and wood-workers as a trial program. The success of this initiative opened the door to the CCCRR receiving permission to bring to Canada refugees who were co-religionists of its member churches.

The CCCRR parlayed its relationship with the Immigration Branch into a new church sponsorship program that permitted sponsorship of non-family members. It recognized the change in its role from a voluntary agency assisting government programs for family sponsorship to one that had a broader mandate to help resettle refugees from Europe: "At the last meeting, official recognition was given to the change and status of the CCCRR ... It has now become the official agency for groups interested in relief and immigration, appointed and recognized in the participating church bodies ... The CCCRR [is] ... pledged to process all refugee immigrants eligible for admission to Canada, regardless of creed and race."[15]

The approval given to the CCCRR to expand the category of people who were eligible for its sponsorship would later be extended to other

Table 1.1
Religious groups in Canada

Group	Denomination	Dates active
Canadian Jewish Congress (CJC)	Jewish	1919–2011
Jewish Immigrant Aid Society (JIAS)	Jewish	1922–present
Canadian Mennonite Board of Colonization*	Mennonite	1923–1959
German Baptist Immigration and Colonization Society*	Baptist	1929–1954
Catholic Immigrant Aid Society*	Catholic	1928–1957
Canadian National Committee on Refugees (CNCR)	Interfaith Coalition	1938–1948
United Jewish Relief Agencies (UJRA)	Jewish	1938–1974
Canadian Council of Churches	Ecumenical Protestant	1944–present
Canadian Lutheran World Relief (CLWR)*	Lutheran	1946–present
Rural Settlement Society	Catholic	1946–1957
Canadian Christian Council for Refugee Resettlement (CCCRR)	Ecumenical Coalition	1947–1957

*Members of the CCCRR

religious groups. This marked the first appearance after the war of an ongoing program of private sponsorship of refugees nominated for resettlement in Canada. About 60,000 of the 163,984 displaced people who resettled in Canada between April 1947 and March 1952 arrived through the evolving sponsorship program.[16]

In 1949, the Canadian Council of Churches, a Protestant ecumenical group affiliated with the World Council of Churches, took steps to initiate its own refugee sponsorship program. Until this time, the CCC had advocated for refugee admissions but had not yet entered into the field of resettlement alongside the denominational groups of the CCCRR. Many members of the council were also part of the CCCRR.[17] However, at the urging of the World Council of Churches (WCC), which recognized new openings for resettlement in Canada through the sponsorship of religious groups, the CCC started its own refugee assistance project.

In September 1949, the Council of Churches wrote to the deputy minister responsible for immigration requesting authorization to "take advantage of arrangements now allowed by the Canadian government" for church congregations to sponsor displaced people.[18] In

January 1951, the Immigration Branch decided to encourage the WCC and CCC to sponsor refugees in Germany and Austria as a means to help resolve the refugee problem in Europe. The immigration director informed field officers that "where the application is made under the sponsorship of the World Council of Churches or the Canadian Council of Churches, as long as employment is guaranteed for one year and settlement arrangements are in order for that period, such applications should be approved."[19] This marked the beginning of a key element of Canada's private refugee sponsorship program – that sponsors assume responsibility for the care of refugees in their first year of arrival.

The Canadian Jewish Congress launched a similar program in collaboration with its European counterparts affiliated with the Jewish Joint Distribution Committee (JDC). Despite the support for their applications provided by the Canadian Jewish Congress, Jewish refugees continued to face obstacles with obtaining visas. The JDC wrote to Saul Hayes, head of the CJC, asking that someone from the Congress come to Austria to help Jewish refugees pass their selection interviews. They would often be told by immigration officers that Canadian employers "don't want this type of person."[20] The Canadian Jewish Congress was urged to assume greater responsibility for sponsoring refugees so that they didn't have to pass through the more selective bulk labour movement. The CJC helped accompany and resettle thousands of Jewish refugees from Europe through the bulk labour and sponsorship schemes.

When the IRO mandate ended in December 1951, so did Canada's refugee program for displaced people. However, there remained a "hard core" of refugees in Europe who were difficult to resettle, because of old age or illness. The Canadian Council of Churches urged the government to continue the arrangement it had developed in the latter years of its refugee program through cooperation with religious groups: "We feel deeply that there should be a place in Canada for a Christian enterprise like ours. May we not hope that in your general immigration scheme, this Church Sponsorship Plan of the Canadian Council of Churches may continue to find a place? We think this attitude could be accompanied by a return to the cooperative attitude which prevailed prior to the demise of the IRO."[21]

Just two months after receiving this letter, the Immigration Branch rescinded its cancellation of the church sponsorship program. The CCC agreed to guarantee employment for one year and to ensure other settlement requirements for sponsored refugees. They were relieved of the requirement to guarantee that sponsored refugees would not become public charges for an indefinite period of time. A directive to field officers from the immigration director noted that sponsorship would be given for refugees, and not standard immigrants, and that refugee files should "be given first degree of priority in examination."[22] Initially, the Canadian Council of Churches was restricted to sponsoring forty cases a month, but this limitation was later lifted provided that employment and housing were guaranteed.[23]

Decision-making in bureaucracies can be relatively insulated from group pressure, but it is not entirely closed off to advocacy. The policy failure of the close relatives scheme opened the door for religious groups to present themselves as government partners in successfully implementing the program. By associating themselves with the implementation process, these groups succeeded at generating "policy conversion" – a mode of institutional change that tends to occur when the "status quo bias" of the political environment is high (as it was in the Immigration Branch in the 1950s).[24] As Hacker, Pierson, and Thelen note, conversion happens when "political actors are able to redirect institutions or policies toward purposes beyond their original intent."[25] In this case, the relevant political actors were not bureaucrats or politicians but policy entrepreneurs representing Protestant, Catholic, and Jewish groups. They successfully redirected a family sponsorship scheme into a religious sponsorship scheme.

In 1953, the Department of Citizenship and Immigration sought to rationalize a number of practices that had developed through their ongoing sponsorship programs with different religious groups. A memo was sent to four religious groups[26] informing them that they would henceforth be considered members of a new Approved Church Program. The memo explained: "to ensure closer coordination between the activities of recognized agencies of the Protestant, Catholic and Jewish faiths and this Department with respect to immigration, it is desirable that such activities be governed by uniform procedures."[27] They were given authority to sponsor refugees for admission to Canada without having to demonstrate any prearranged employment or accommodation.

Although the program developed relatively quickly in response to demands from these voluntary groups, the bureaucrats in the Immigration Department were uneasy about the program because of the authority it gave the groups over the selection of immigrants to

Canada. The tension between religious groups and immigration officials related mainly to the criteria used for selecting refugees. The government remained focused on selecting immigrants who met labour demand in specific sectors of the Canadian economy, whereas groups wanted to select refugees based on humanitarian need.[28]

Notwithstanding the instrumental role played by religious groups in Canada's response to Europe's displaced people, the government was reticent to commemorate or applaud their humanitarian work publicly. Their very inclusion in Canadian efforts to identify, transport, and settle refugees was a reluctant concession of the government – one that religious agencies were compelled to defend repeatedly and to protect from bureaucratic jealousy. They forged a cooperative relationship with the government that was guided by policy directives, but there ultimately existed an unresolved tension over the scope of authority and freedom given to those agencies to play their part in Canada's response to Europe's refugee crisis. By 1955, this struggle had reached a stalemate of sorts as the DP problem wound down – only to rev up again for the next major refugee crisis, when millions of Hungarians fled to Austria in response to a Soviet crackdown. The resettlement of Hungarian refugees helped consolidate the practice of private refugee sponsorship by Christian and Jewish groups.

POLICY EVOLUTION (1956–1976)

As a result of the displaced persons resettlement program, religious groups linked up with immigration officials in a loose and informal issue network.[29] As Jordan notes, an issue network is "the politics of the ad hoc and irregular" and the "loose-jointed play of influence."[30] Such networks can appear to consolidate during particular windows of opportunity but can scatter when the moment passes. These networks are unstable in part because they are not well institutionalized and do not share a refugee policy framework with the bureaucracy. In 1950s Canada, religious groups viewed themselves as humanitarian actors in the refugee field and were critical of immigration officials' more instrumental view of refugees as contributors to the Canadian economy. Nevertheless, they had access to immigration officials and political leaders by virtue of their established role in refugee resettlement, and they used these spaces to advocate for policy changes. These relationships played a key role in the program to resettle Hungarian refugees; however, they were increasingly tense and adversarial in the late 1950s and '60s.

On 4 November 1956, the Soviet army entered Hungary to overthrow the new government of Imre Nagy, which had been formed with the support of a popular uprising against Soviet-imposed policies. About 180,000 Hungarians fled across the Austrian border, and some 20,000 escaped into Yugoslavia, until both borders were closed in early 1957. With the support of the International Committee for European Migration (ICEM) and the UN High Commissioner for Refugees (UNHCR), many of these Hungarian refugees were resettled in Western countries.[31] Canada accepted 37,565 refugees, more than any other country except the United States.[32]

The Canadian government initially resisted pressure from the UNHCR, religious groups, and the opposition parties in Parliament to resettle Hungarian refugees.[33] In the meantime, the department was receiving a flood of offers from across the country to assist Hungarian refugees. These offers came from organized groups, as well as from citizens who were sending "chain telegrams" to the government.[34] Faced with organized pressure to resettle Hungarian refugees, immigration officials recommended that Canada expand its existing program of cooperation with religious groups.[35] They suggested that religious groups and their affiliates in Europe could "present to us refugees who would be sponsored by the Canadian voluntary agencies."[36]

By early December 1956, the government estimated that more than 30,000 refugees could arrive in Canada within four or five months under a cooperative resettlement program.[37] The Department of Citizenship and Immigration instructed its district offices to identify the local affiliates of the agencies "regularly associated with immigrant movements: RSS, CJC, CCC, CCCRR" to coordinate settlement in Canada. As the minister commented, he viewed the role of the department as simply to "recruit immigrants" and not to "handle social problems" – that responsibility would fall to "social agencies and organizations."[38]

By the time the program concluded, 37,565 Hungarian refugees had arrived in Canada. Virtually all of the refugees had arrived under the sponsorship of one of the four religious groups, establishing the resettlement scheme that Dirks describes as "a useful precedent for those who pressed the government in later years for equally generous programs and policies."[39] Troper adds that this was "a watershed event" and "a model for a series of Canadian refugee initiatives during the next twenty years."[40]

After the Hungarian program, the immigration director continued to seek a formal end to the Approved Church Program – something the department had pursued repeatedly since 1954. These requests were finally approved in 1958.[41] However, when Ellen Fairclough became Minister of Citizenship and Immigration that same year, she encountered international and domestic pressure for Canada to play a role in the upcoming World Refugee Year. The four religious groups seized this opportunity to push for the reinstatement of the Approved Church Program. They wrote to Fairclough, advocating for the creation of a sponsorship program that would allow them to select refugees from abroad without consideration for employment prospects.[42] The groups were invited to meet with Fairclough and other senior immigration officials about their requests. Following the meeting with the minister, all four groups submitted proposals to resurrect the Approved Church Program. In their proposals, they reserved a role for themselves in selecting refugees to resettle; they also committed to taking responsibility for travel, reception, accommodation, and employment.

The government decided on a private sponsorship scheme that would resurrect many features of the church sponsorship program and the Approved Church Program. Internal memos from within the Department of Citizenship and Immigration reveal a great deal of frustration with the groups, which were criticizing government policy even while resisting the sponsorship terms they were offered. The Canadian Council of Churches, in particular, voiced its displeasure that the government would not allow refugees to access welfare services for their first year, calling it "an amazing suggestion and one which we cannot accept."[43] This did not stop the minister from publicizing the new private sponsorship program. In one public address, she identified the recognized voluntary agencies,[44] noting that the government would accept as part of its WRY commitment any number of privately sponsored sick or handicapped refugees. "It would be difficult to find a more rewarding project for a church group or private agency than the sponsorship of a refugee during Refugee Year," she added. "Action by government agencies alone will not solve our refugee problem – there must be in addition a multitude of individual efforts which spring from the deep roots of our religious and democratic faith."[45]

Between 1956 and 1960, the relationship between the handful of religious groups concerned with refugee policy and the Department of Citizenship and Immigration became more routinized, yet also increasingly adversarial. It became routinized in the sense that regular meetings and exchanges between the leaders of the CCC, CCCRR, CJC-JIAS, and the Catholic groups, and senior officials in the department became a part of the normal policy discourse. However, these relationships also grew more contested over time. Although the department had broken out of its highly restrictive policy stance of the interwar years, it remained reluctant to cede control over admissions of refugees who did not present tangible benefits to the Canadian economy. The cooperative arrangements with religious groups led to the admission of a greater number of "humanitarian" cases. Religious groups also exerted pressure (often unsuccessfully) to accept refugees from non-European countries such as China – who, although no longer blocked by law, were still viewed as undesirable by bureaucrats steeped in early-twentieth-century race thinking.[46]

As the terms of the Approved Church Program were repeatedly renegotiated, frustration mounted on both sides. The religious groups – especially the Canadian Council of Churches – wanted a liberal refugee policy that would enable them to select and resettle refugees while allowing them access to welfare support from the government. The Department of Citizenship and Immigration saw things differently. It valued the role of religious groups in "reception and integration" but sought to exclude them from "selection and movement processes."[47] The department thought if groups were to have a role in selection, they should provide guarantees that the refugees they were bringing into the country would not become an immediate burden on public finances.

Under the new private sponsorship scheme, one of the major religious groups could sponsor refugees who would not ordinarily be approved for immigration to Canada, provided the costs of their first year of accommodation and maintenance were paid.[48] The groups protested these new terms, arguing that they unduly shifted the "full burden of risks" onto the churches.[49] By 1960, the relationship between the religious groups and the Department of Citizenship and Immigration was evolving away from its early mode of close cooperation. Many of these groups would distance themselves from cooperation with government in the decade to come.

Religious groups largely abandoned refugee resettlement during the 1960s, retreating to an outsider stance of advocacy against government policy. The loose issue network that had formed around postwar refugee resettlement and the Approved Church Program broke down soon after the program was terminated in 1959. Although religious groups remained engaged with some specific refugee issues during this time (Jewish groups with Soviet Jews, and Christian groups with Chinese refugees in Hong Kong, among others),[50] they dramatically reduced refugee sponsorship.[51] They were virtually absent from the policy discourse around the Czech refugee program in 1968 and the Ugandan program in 1972, both of which were government-led initiatives that were (at least initially) undertaken principally for more utilitarian reasons of selecting talent and skilled labour, in the context of Cold War politics.[52] The Christian groups re-engaged more strongly with public refugee advocacy in 1973, however, following the coup in Chile against Salvador Allende.[53] Their adversarial, "outsider" advocacy tactics generated sufficient pressure to provoke a policy change, leading to the resettlement of thousands of Chilean refugees, many of them with church sponsorship.[54]

The mobilization of religious groups in response to the coup in Chile re-formed issue networks that had become weakened during the 1960s and reignited a political discourse about the role of voluntary groups in refugee resettlement in Canada. As debate over the Chilean program was wrapping up, Parliament was presented with a new Green Paper on immigration policy that was intended to inform major immigration and refugee legislative change. The role of voluntary groups and private sponsorship arose as a key question in this period of public debate. Although the Canadian Jewish Congress was one of the main advocates for including private sponsorship in the new legislation, the experience of the Chilean program was also significant. Several retired civil servants note: "The prolonged and intensive controversy accompanying Canada's response to the Chilean refugees led policy-makers in Ottawa to consider reintroducing a refugee sponsorship option to channel public concern into direct action."[55] These recollections are corroborated by more oblique references in later internal memos to the need to take steps to channel the interest of religious groups in refugee policy because their relationship with the government "has not always been as productive and mutually beneficial as [it] should be."[56]

Thus between 1960 and 1973, the issue network connecting religious groups and immigration officials went through a period of disintegration and reconstruction. It had collapsed because of divergent beliefs about the purpose of refugee policy and the roles to be played by religious groups. And in this context, refugee resettlement became more anemic, despite a growing economy, low unemployment, and increasing immigration. Except through the Czechoslovakian program in 1967 – which was effectively carried out within the parameters of immigration policy – relatively few refugees were resettled in Canada. This changed with the public debate over Chilean refugees, which was driven by church and solidarity groups. The resettlement of Chileans in 1973 re-formed cooperative ties with immigration officials (albeit in a relationship that remained quite adversarial) and laid the groundwork for the revitalization and formalization of the private sponsorship program in the years ahead.

THE 1976 ACT AND INDOCHINESE PROGRAM

The Immigration Act of 1976 was passed with near unanimous support in Parliament. It received Royal Assent in August 1977 and took effect on 10 April 1978. The private sponsorship provision in the Act was not specific – lawmakers left it to be elaborated through future policy development. The concept of private sponsorship was formally introduced as such in 1960 but has been little used since. One of the only exceptions was the use of private sponsorship by the Jewish Immigrant Aid Services of Canada to facilitate the resettlement of Soviet Jews in the late 1960s and early 1970s.[57]

Private sponsorship was included in the 1976 Act because it had been established as a practice in Canadian refugee resettlement. The new law was not going to create a policy framework on a blank slate; it looked to the past. As Janzen recalls, "officials who worked in the Immigration Department at that time said they had not known what to expect from the private sponsorship provision. They had just felt that it would be good to have [in] the Act, to be used if necessary."[58]

After the passage of the 1976 Act, the Immigration Department looked for a test case to develop the new private sponsorship program. It found one in the Jewish human rights group, B'nai Brith.[59] Jack Manion, the deputy immigration minister, recommended that the private sponsorship scheme "rely on national organizations responsible for the identification of needy groups of refugees and displaced persons but that the actual sponsorship ... come from local groups providing services directly to the immigrant or refugee."[60] In this pilot program, B'nai Brith's planned sponsorship of some fifty Soviet Jews required their local chapters to arrange accommodation, provide initial food and clothing, and offer reception and resettlement assistance. The program was eventually carried out by JIAS after B'nai Brith backed out, but the experience was sufficiently instructive to be described in an internal departmental memo, "Sponsorship Provisions for Refugee and Humanitarian Cases," which set out its main elements.

Following the program for Soviet Jews, department officials began to meet with religious groups to develop the private sponsorship program. One early meeting was with bishops of the Catholic Church's Migration Commission. The commission was initially reluctant to cooperate with the government, for it had been one of the groups that campaigned in favour of admitting Chilean refugees. This adversarial history coloured the tone of the first meeting, at which the bishops initially resisted assuming the costs and responsibility of a program that was viewed as a government duty.[61] However, the bishops eventually endorsed the program as measure to complement government resettlement efforts. Soon after this initial meeting, the deputy minister wrote to the leaders of the major religious denominations in Canada to outline a process for securing refugee sponsorships.[62] Local Catholic groups responded most positively, along with Mennonite groups, and articles began to appear in church bulletins and newsletters outlining the program.

Private sponsorship did not finally expand in a significant way, however, until the Indochinese refugee crisis. Despite an unfolding refugee emergency in Indochina since 1975, Canada was initially on the periphery of the US-led international resettlement effort. Canada agreed to nominal admissions of refugees in 1976 and 1977, in response to pressure from the United States.[63] In 1978, the Liberal government under Prime Minister Pierre Elliott Trudeau agreed to take fifty families per month.[64] The objective was to make minimum commitments that would help support wider international burden-sharing.[65] However, growing public concern with a deteriorating situation in Southeast Asia coincided with a change of government, when Joe Clark's Progressive Conservatives defeated Trudeau's Liberals.

Soon after Clark's government came to power it was exposed to growing domestic and international agitation over the continuing humanitarian disaster in Indochina. Within several months, the new Cabinet decided to resettle up to 50,000 Indochinese refugees before the end of 1980.[66] Flora MacDonald, the Secretary of State for External Affairs, described the program as "one of partnership between the Canadian Government and private citizens and organizations."[67]

It committed to a one-for-one matching scheme, where the government would match private sponsorship for up to 50,000 refugees, a number later pushed to 60,000 because of unexpectedly high numbers of sponsorships.

This resettlement program would not have reached anywhere near the scale it did without private sponsorship as well as collaboration between bureaucrats and religious groups that preceded the July 1979 announcement. The 1976 Immigration Act came into force in April 1978, creating private sponsorship as a formal refugee program in law. However, it took the initiative of the Mennonite Central Committee of Canada (MCC Canada), meeting with senior immigration officials in January 1979, to create the policy framework to implement private sponsorship on a larger scale. This first meeting was held seven months before Canada's massive expansion of refugee resettlement. It led to the creation of a policy framework whereby the government assumed more risk and cost for privately sponsored refugees, compared to private sponsorship of the 1960s, which had placed all responsibility on sponsors and had led to the disengagement of religious groups from the program.

The result of these negotiations was the creation of "Master Agreements," whereby a national corporate body could accept responsibility for sponsored refugees, releasing local groups from liabilities required by the government. The Master Agreements resembled earlier arrangements made under the Approved Church Program, although they made available more government-funded services for refugees. These agreements also enabled the program to operate at a larger scale than would have been possible otherwise. After the government signed its Master Agreements with the MCC Canada on 5 March 1979, it quickly proceeded to sign agreements with four other religious groups before the government made its July 1979 announcement. After that announcement, eight other national groups signed agreements, alongside twenty-one Roman Catholic dioceses and five Anglican dioceses. All forty Master Agreements signed in 1979 were with religious organizations.[68]

Private sponsorship during the Indochinese movement was organized along two lines, following the 1976 Act and associated regulations: organized groups affiliated with a Master Agreement holder, and groups of five or more private citizens. Of the roughly 7,000 sponsorship groups, about 70 percent were organized groups, and 30 percent were citizen groups. Ninety-nine percent of organized groups were affiliated with churches and synagogues, whereas most citizen groups were classified by the government as "secular."[69] Notwithstanding the important role played by citizen mobilization outside of religious structures, coming out of the Indochinese movement the organized groups established a tighter policy network that become more closely connected with government decision-making. The Immigration Department began at this time to introduce annual planning into its refugee resettlement program, alongside immigration levels planning.[70] This process engaged the leaders of the major sponsorship groups in a number of "extensive consultations," including "face to face discussions and written exchanges."[71] The reinvigoration of private sponsorship also had the effect of rebuilding the issue network connecting religious groups and immigration officials.

Although the landmark Immigration Act was passed in 1976, its full implications for refugee resettlement were not realized until the conclusion of the Indochinese program, which saw private sponsorship more fully elaborated and exploited. What the legislation produced as a placeholder for cooperation between the government and private groups was elaborated through negotiations between senior bureaucrats and organized religious groups. This was a well-established pattern in Canadian refugee policy-making: political leaders made broad commitments in response to lobbying and other domestic and international sources of pressure, and these commitments provided a framework for practical deliberation between civil servants and organized groups. As civil servants who observed these negotiations up close have noted in published recollections, the "emergence of a forceful advocacy community" often "pushed us in the direction we wished to go."[72]

CONCLUSION

The sentiment of common cause between bureaucrats and voluntary groups was an exception largely confined to the Indochinese program. For most of the preceding decades, the relationship between bureaucrats and refugee groups had been a reluctant one. Political leaders were sensitive to the pressure that organized groups could generate through their constituencies and media, but bureaucrats often saw those groups as naive, inexpert, or hostile – and sometimes all three – in relation to their policy goals. However, when it came to implementing the private sponsorship provisions of the 1976 Act, cooperation came more easily. Molloy and Madokoro contend that policy innovation was "driven" by civil servants during the late 1970s, but this may be overstating their singular role.[73] The way in which the Immigration Act reframed an active refugee policy aligned the government position more closely with those of organized groups and enabled a cooperative relationship within the framework of private sponsorship. Cooperation was also supported by the shared view that refugees needed humanitarian protection, which was a significant change from the more pragmatic view of immigration officials in the past.

This chapter has analyzed and narrated the history of Canada's private refugee sponsorship program as a developmental process of negotiation and partnership between organized religious groups and immigration officials. It was not driven entirely by civil society actors seeking policy concessions from the government, nor did it amount to an opportunistic off-loading of government responsibilities onto the private sector. Rather, at its origins it was developed as a partnership between a handful of religious groups and a government that lacked the capacity to fully implement its policy of family reunification. This initial cooperative enterprise created an issue network within which the terms of private sponsorship could be gradually defined in the context of evolving immigration policy in the years to come.

Today, religious groups continue to play a central role in private refugee sponsorship in Canada. An estimated 90 of the 120 Sponsorship Agreement Holders are affiliated with a religious community. However, the declining resource and membership bases in many of the communities that initially forged this partnership raise questions about the future of the program in its current form. The terms of the program were negotiated by groups that had institutional capacity, social networks, community support, and a resource base independent from the government. Private sponsorship is an institutional legacy of government cooperation with Canada's religious groups as they existed in the mid- to late twentieth century. However, it remains to be seen what its future will be. That may, to some extent, depend on the future role of religion in Canadian society.

NOTES

The author gratefully acknowledges support for this research by the Social Sciences and Humanities Research Council of Canada and the Pierre Elliott Trudeau Foundation.

1 Ninette Kelley and Michael Trebilcock, *The Making of the Mosaic: A History of Canadian Immigration Policy* (Toronto: University of Toronto Press, 2010), 367–79.
2 Michael J. Molloy, Peter Duschinsky, Kurt F. Jensen, and Robert Shalka, *Running on Empty: Canada and the Indochinese Refugees, 1975–1980* (Montreal and Kingston: McGill-Queen's University Press, 2017), 81.
3 Shauna Labman, *Crossing Law's Border: Canada's Refugee Resettlement Program* (Vancouver: UBC Press, 2019), 83.
4 Paul Pierson, *Politics in Time: History, Institutions, and Social Analysis* (Princeton: Princeton University Press, 2004), 21.
5 Ibid.
6 Paul Pierson, "Increasing Returns, Path Dependence, and the Study of Politics," *American Political Science Review* 94, no. 2 (2000): 251–67; Paul Pierson, "Review: When Effect Becomes Cause: Policy Feedback and Political Change," *World Politics* 45, no. 4 (July 1993): 595–628.
7 Gil Loescher and John A. Scanlan, *Calculated Kindness: Refugees and America's Half-Open Door, 1945–Present* (New York: Simon and Schuster, 1998), 1.
8 Mark Wyman, *DPs: Europe's Displaced Persons, 1945–51* (Ithaca: Cornell University Press, 1998); Gerard Daniel Cohen, *In War's Wake: Europe's Displaced Persons in the Postwar Order* (Oxford: Oxford University Press, 2011).
9 Gerald E. Dirks, *Canada's Refugee Policy: Indifference or Opportunism?* (Montreal and Kingston: McGill-Queen's University Press, 1977), 138.
10 Ibid.
11 Irving Abella and Harold Troper, *None Is Too Many: Canada and the Jews of Europe, 1933–1948* (New York: Random House, 1983), 242.
12 Dirks, *Canada's Refugee Policy*, 158.
13 Ibid., 161.
14 Kelley and Trebilcock, *The Making of the Mosaic*, 343.
15 Dirks, *Canada's Refugee Policy*, 163.
16 Annual Report of the Department of Citizenship and Immigration, Fiscal Year ending 31 March 1952.
17 When the CCCRR finally disbanded in 1955, it turned its operations over to the CCC.
18 Letter from Rev. Canon Judd, General Secretary, to Dr. H.L. Keenleyside, Deputy Minister, Ministry of Mines and Resources, re: Personal sponsorship of displaced persons and other immigrants, 27 September 1949, file 3-24-20, vol. 115, RG 26, LAC.

19 Memo from Laval Fortier, Deputy Minister, to the Director of Immigration, Department of Mines and Resources, 18 July 1951, file 3-24-20, vol. 115, RG 26, LAC.
20 Letter from Charles Jordan, JDC, to Saul Hayes, CJC, 23 July 1951, file 1951, box 30, series CA, Canadian Jewish Congress Archives.
21 Letter from W.J. Gallagher, General Secretary of the Canadian Council of Churches, to Walter Harris, Minister of Citizenship and Immigration, 15 May 1952, file 3-24-20, vol. 115, RG 26, LAC.
22 Directive no. 25 re: Sponsorship of immigrants by the Canadian Council of Churches, 13 July 1952, file 3-24-20, vol. 115, RG 26, LAC.
23 Memorandum for file, re: Meeting between Col. Fortier and Dr. W.J. Gallagher and Alex Maclaren, CCC, 16 March 1953, file 3-24-20, vol. 115, RG 26, LAC.
24 Jacob S. Hacker, Paul Pierson, and Kathleen Thelen, "Drift and Conversion: Hidden Faces of Institutional Change," in *Advances in Comparative-Historical Analysis*, ed. James Mahoney and Kathleen Thelen (New York: Cambridge University Press, 2015), 180–210 at 187–8.
25 Ibid., 180.
26 The Canadian Jewish Congress (with JIAS, the Jewish Immigrant Aid Service), the Canadian Council of Churches, the CCCRR, and the Rural Settlement Society (the Catholic group based in Montreal).
27 Letter from Laval Fortier to T.F. Herzer, Chairman, CCCRR, 8 April 1953, file 3-24-20, vol. 115, RG 26, LAC.
28 Field officers complained about the refugees to whom they were required to issue visas under the sponsorship of members of the Approved Church Program, which often targeted the "hard core" refugees. One such complaint read as follows: "[They] appeared almost to specialize in undesirable immigrants of this kind. 'Hard core' means just that; the final, ultimate dregs, the scrapings of the very bottom of the barrel. I do not wish to be and am not inhumane, but have never regarded our work in any other light than that the interests of our country must be paramount; which means that every immigrant should possess some desirable qualification, at the very least." Letter from a visa officer in Rome to the Director of Immigration, Department of Citizenship and Immigration, 14 January 1954, file 567-81, vol. 893, RG 76, LAC.
29 Hugh Heclo, "Issue Networks and the Executive Establishment," in *The New American Political System*, ed. Anthony King (Washington, DC: AEI Press, 1978), 87–107.
30 Grant Jordan, "Sub-Governments, Policy Communities and Networks: Refilling Old Bottles?," *Journal of Theoretical Politics* 2, no. 3 (1990): 1–20.

31 Gil Loescher, Alexander Betts, and James Milner, UNHCR: *The Politics and Practice of Refugee Protection into the 21st Century* (Abingdon: Routledge, 2008), 21.
32 Loescher and Scanlan, *Calculated Kindness*, 52; Dirks, *Canada's Refugee Policy*, 203. Other countries accepting Hungarian refugees for resettlement were as follows: Great Britain (21,000), West Germany (15,000), Switzerland (13,000), France (13,000), Australia (11,000), Sweden (7,000), Belgium (6,000), and Israel (2,000).
33 Michael J. Molloy and Laura Madokoro, "Effecting Change: Civil Servants and Refugee Policy in 1970s Canada," *Refuge: Canada's Journal on Refugees* 33, no. 1 (2017): 52–61 at 54.
34 Ibid.
35 Memo from the Director of Immigration to the Deputy Minister, re: Hungarian Refugees, Department of Citizenship and Immigration, 22 November 1956, file 3-24-34-1, volume 117, RG 26, LAC.
36 Ibid.
37 Confidential Memorandum to all District Superintendents re: Hungarian Refugee Movement, 10 December 1956, file 3-24-34-1, vol. 117, RG 26, LAC.
38 Dirks, *Canada's Refugee Policy*; Andrew S. Thompson and Stephanie Bangarth, "Transnational Christian Charity: The Canadian Council of Churches, the World Council of Churches, and the Hungarian Refugee Crisis, 1956–1957," *American Review of Canadian Studies* 38, no. 3 (October 2008): 295–316.
39 Dirks, Canada's Refugee Policy, 213.
40 Harold Troper, "Canada and Hungarian Refugees: The Historical Context," in *The 1956 Hungarian Revolution: Hungarian and Canadian Perspectives*, ed. Christopher Adam et al. (Ottawa: University of Ottawa Press, 2010), 176–93 at 191.
41 Memo for the Acting Minister from the Deputy Minister re: Approved Church Program, 7 May 1958, file 3-24-20, vol. 15, RG 26, LAC.
42 Memo from the CCC, CCCRR, CJC, and Catholic Immigrant Services to Minister Fairclough, 28 January 1959, file 3-24-20, vol. 115, RG 26, LAC.
43 Letter to Laval Fortier, Deputy Minister of Citizenship and Immigration, from Fred Poulton, Secretary, Department of Social Relations, Canadian Council of Churches, 20 August 1959, file 3-24-20, vol. 115, RG 26, LAC.
44 Canadian Christian Council for the Resettlement of Refugees, Canadian Council of Churches, Rural Settlement Society of Canada-Catholic

Immigrant Services, Canadian Jewish Congress-Jewish Immigrant Aid Services.
45 Address by Hon. Ellen Fairclough at the Hamilton Council of Women, 6 November 1959, file 566-10-1, vol. 886, RG 76, LAC.
46 Laura Madokoro, *Elusive Refuge: Chinese Migrants in the Cold War* (Cambridge, MA: Harvard University Press, 2016); Laura Madokoro, "'Slotting' Chinese Families and Refugees, 1947–1967," *The Canadian Historical Review* 93, no. 1 (2011): 25–56.
47 Memo to the Minister re: Approved Church Program, 3 June 1959.
48 Letter from Laval Fortier, Deputy Minister, to J. B. Lanctot, Catholic Immigrant Services, 3 July 1959.
49 Letter from Clifton L. Monk to Laval Fortier, Department of Citizenship and Immigration, 28 August 1959, file 3-24-20, vol. 115, RG 26, LAC.
50 See: Madokoro, "'Slotting' Chinese Families and Refugees," 50.
51 Dirks, Canada's Refugee Policy, 231.
52 Laura Madokoro, "Good Material: Canada and the Prague Spring Refugees," *Refuge: Canada's Journal on Refugees* 26, no. 1 (8 October 2010): 161–71; Dirks, *Canada's Refugee Policy*; Louis Parai, "Canada's Immigration Policy, 1962–1974," *International Migration Review* 9, no. 4 (1975): 449–77.
53 Kathleen Ptolemy, "Canadian Refugee Policies," *International Review of Mission* 71, no. 283 (1982): 362–67; Ptolemy, "From Oppression to Promise: Journeying Together with the Refugee," in *Canadian Churches and Foreign Policy*, ed. Bonnie Greene (Toronto: James Lorimer, 1990), 143–60; Robert O. Matthews, "The Christian Churches and Foreign Policy: An Assessment," in *Canadian Churches and Foreign Policy*, ed. Bonnie Greene (Toronto: James Lorimer, 1990), 161–79.
54 Suha Diab, "Fear and (in)Security: The Canadian Government's Response to the Chilean Refugees," *Refuge* 31, no. 2 (28 November 2015): 51–62.
55 Molloy et al., *Running on Empty*, 69–70.
56 Memo from W.K. Bell to J. Cross, Department of Citizenship and Immigration, 14 September 1978, file 8620-8, vol. 1815, RG 76, LAC.
57 Labman, *Crossing Law's Border*, 84.
58 Molloy and Madokoro, "Effecting Change"; Molloy et al., *Running on Empty*; William Janzen, "The 1979 MCC Canada Master Agreement for the Sponsorship of Refugees in Historical Perspective," *Journal of Mennonite Studies* 24 (2006): 211–22 at 217.
59 Molloy et al., *Running on Empty*, 71.
60 Ibid., 72.
61 Ibid., 74–5.

62 Ibid., 75.
63 Memorandum to the Minister of Employment and Immigration from J.L. Manion (Deputy Minister), 10 November 1977, file 8700-15, vol. 1838, RG 76, LAC.
64 Employment and Immigration Canada, The Indochinese Refugees: The Canadian *Response, 1979 and 1980* (Ottawa: Minister of Supply and Services Canada, 1980), 8.
65 Letter from Minister of Foreign Affairs Don Jamieson to Minister of Employment and Immigration Bud Cullen, 20 December 1977, file 8700-15, vol. 2838, RG 76, LAC.
66 Dirks, Canada's Refugee Policy, 120.
67 Secretary of State for External Affairs, "Notes for a Speech by the Secretary of State for External Affairs, Flora MacDonald, the United Nations Conference on Refugees, Geneva," 20 July 1979. Quoted in Molloy et al., *Running on Empty*, 506.
68 Master Agreements signed include the following: Mennonite Central Committee (5 March 1979); Presbyterian Church of Canada (9 March 1979); Council of Canadian Reformed Churches of Canada (5 April 1979); Canadian Lutheran World Relief (11 May 1979); World Vision of Canada (6 July 1979); United Church of Canada (23 July 1979); Baptist Convention of Ontario and Quebec (27 July 1979); National Council of YMCAs of Canada (1 August 1979); twenty-one Roman Catholic dioceses and five Anglican dioceses (August 1979); Baptist Union of Western Canada (10 August 1979); Ukrainian Canadian Committee (20 September 1979); Ontario Conference of Seventh-day Adventist Church (24 September 1979); United Baptist Convention Council of the Atlantic Provinces (25 September 1979); Seventh-day Adventist Church of Canada (26 October 1979); Christian and Missionary Alliance (31 October 1979). "Refugee and Humanitarian Programs," 5 December 1979, file 8620-1, vol. 1811, RG 76, LAC.
69 "The Experiences of Sponsors of Indochinese Refugees: A Statistical Analysis," Immigration Program Division, 8 December 1981, file 8703-1, vol. 1839, RG 76, LAC.
70 Molloy and Madokoro, "Effecting Change," 58.
71 "Canada's 1981 Refugee Resettlement Programs and the Prospects for 1982," 20 May 1981, file 8620-8, vol. 1815, RG 76, LAC. "A further, welcome result of the active partnership between government and the voluntary sector which characterized the special Indochinese program, has been the broadening of the consultation process leading to the preparation of the Annual Refugee Plan. For example, in the spring and summer of 1980,

extensive consultations concerning 1981 programs took place, both through face to face discussions and written exchanges, with the leadership of all the major voluntary groups who wished to do so ... This process of consultation on a wide range of refugee issues is being continued and further developed in 1981 to reflect those factors identified by the groups concerned."

72 Molloy and Madokoro, "Effecting Change," 60. The latter quotation is from Kirk Bell.
73 Ibid.

2

"Naming" Refugees in the Canadian Private Sponsorship of Refugees Program: Diverse Intentions and Consequences

Sabine Lehr and Brian Dyck

Ever since the 1976 Immigration Act came into effect, sponsors' ability to select the refugees they resettle has been a feature of Canada's PSR program. This has become known as "the naming principle," reflecting a core principle of Canada's PSR program. In recent years, private or community sponsorship of refugees (PSR/CSR) initiatives have emerged in other countries, yet only a few of these seem to have adopted the naming principle. In most emerging PSR/CSR initiatives, both states and NGOs assert their commitment to humanitarian selection of refugees, with selection carried out through the UN Refugee Agency or other referral organizations. Some countries, such as Australia[1] and Germany,[2] have recently adopted naming-type schemes. However, the scope of private citizens' involvement in identifying refugees for permanent resettlement to Canada is unparalleled in other parts of the world.

In this chapter, we explore "naming" as a characteristic of private refugee sponsorship. Throughout the evolution of Canada's PSR program, there has been a continuous debate over the role of "naming." The ability to name refugees is an attractive aspect of the program for many sponsors and has sustained their involvement in a program that produces positive outcomes for refugees. Naming has allowed ordinary Canadians to participate directly in refugee selection and in that way impact public policy and Canada's international focus in a small way. In practice, however, "naming" in Canada's PSR program has served to make family reunification the only possible pathway for refugees with relatives in Canada. Critics have argued that this practice has transformed private refugee sponsorship into a family reunification program – something that can conflict with other refugee resettlement priorities. We explore some of the implications of this phenomenon.

On the one hand, the principle has been hailed as a mechanism for handling the "echo effect" (the desire of resettled refugees to reunite with other displaced family members once the government has moved on to other resettlement commitments). More diversity in resettled populations and successful settlement outcomes are repeatedly cited. On the other hand, critics have argued that the naming principle can erode a state's commitment to resettling the most vulnerable refugees based on strategic resettlement in a global context of insufficient resettlement spaces (for further discussion on private refugee sponsorship in the broader international context, see the chapter by Bradley and Duin in this volume).

With ever-increasing global refugee numbers, states in different parts of the world have launched PSR/CSR schemes to provide additional pathways for refugee protection.[3] Canada, through the Global Refugee Sponsorship Initiative (explored by Smith later in this volume), has been called upon to assist some states in conceptualizing these programs. The question of how much autonomy to give to sponsors over choosing which refugees to sponsor is a crucial part of such programs. Given that only a small minority of all refugees worldwide get access to resettlement – whether through traditional, state-led programs or through complementary programs such as PSR/CSR schemes – the criteria applied to the selection process warrant careful consideration. Without ultimately offering any prescription, this chapter explores a complex question: If citizens and permanent residents engage PSR/CSR and thus support a responsibility of states under international law and conventions, should these citizens have the right to select refugees for resettlement, or should governments reserve this responsibility for themselves? What factors ought to be considered? In no way are we attempting to make a normative statement regarding the desirability or undesirability of naming in PSR/CSR schemes. Rather, it is our intention to trace the principle in historic perspective; unpack some of the controversies around sponsor selection of refugees for resettlement; and offer an outlook on what this may mean for countries that are launching sponsorship schemes.

The question of who should choose refugees for resettlement is not purely philosophical. Equally important are legal, practical, and financial considerations. In Canada, both the legal framework and the global infrastructure for refugee processing facilitate naming of refugees by sponsors. States currently designing PSR/CSR programs must consider how such programs fit into their legislative frameworks. From a practical perspective, naming refugees for sponsorship who may be located anywhere in the world requires a broad network of visa offices that can reach refugees in remote parts of the globe. Not all states have such an infrastructure or are willing to build one. Canada is in an unusual position, given its sheltered geographic location. The resulting focus on overseas selection has always been Canada's preferred *modus operandi* for immigration policy.[4] From a financial point of view, it has historically been advantageous for Canada to give sponsors the power to select refugees. This privilege is linked to the sponsors' obligation to assume financial responsibility for the resettled refugees during their first year in Canada, which reduces – but does not eliminate – the cost to the Canadian government of resettling these refugees.

BACKGROUND TO NAMING REFUGEES FOR RESETTLEMENT IN CANADA

In 2003, Treviranus and Casasola noted that "the Private Sponsorship Program ... [has] evolved from being initially largely driven by the identification of cases by visa officers, to a program largely driven by the demands for sponsorship of refugee applicants with connections to Canada."[5] This development has not followed a linear trajectory, however. From the beginning of Canada's codified PSR program until today, the program has had two subcomponents: visa office-referred, or sponsor-referred,[6] with the latter more frequently labelled "named sponsorships." Within the ten years following the program's official launch in 1978–79, the majority of sponsorships were sponsor-referred. Canada's multi-year immigration levels plan, published on 31 October 2018, predicts that arrivals from named sponsorships are expected to continue to outnumber arrivals from visa office-referred sponsorships by a ratio of approximately 2:1 (PSR:GAR/BVOR).[7]

The strong position of the PSR program and its associated naming principle in Canada goes back to the program's legal and historical origins. Legally grounded in the 1976 Immigration Act, the program experienced its first major – and still biggest – test with the Southeast Asian crisis in 1979–80. With the Canadian government struggling to fulfill its resettlement promises through a period of federal elections and changes in political power, it relied on highly motivated and capable private sponsorship groups to help resettle the 50,000 refugees it had promised to bring to Canada.[8] The goal was achieved only by skewing the formula that had been agreed upon to match one-on-one government assistance and private sponsorship as well as by substituting government-assisted refugees for privately sponsored refugees.[9] As a consequence, the sponsorship community developed considerable influence over governmental resettlement policies from the outset. The sponsorship community's involvement in this large-scale effort on behalf of Southeast Asian refugees was made possible by regulations regarding designated classes (i.e., persons who did not meet the Convention refugee definition but who found themselves in refugee-like situations), which had come into force on 1 January 1979,[10] and for which the legal basis was embedded in the 1976 Immigration Act.[11] The motivation for establishing all three designated classes in 1979 (Self-Exiled Persons, Indochinese, and Political Prisoners and Oppressed Persons) was arguably political and linked to the Cold War mindset. These designated classes were important for the future of the PSR program, though, in that the Immigration and Refugee Protection Act (IRPA) Regulations in 2002 broadened and codified these classes for application across a range of situations. This was done through the new Humanitarian Protected Persons Abroad Class, which encompassed the Country of Asylum Class of persons "who did not meet the refugee definition ... because they did not meet the definition's requirement of a nexus to persecution" as well as the Source Country Class of persons who "had not fled across an international border."[12] The Source Country Class was abandoned in 2011; however, the Country of Asylum Class is still in place and has significantly broadened the pool of persons who can be sponsored.

It is also important to note that in the early years of the program, private sponsorships operated as true complements or additions; that is, they were not part of the government's annual resettlement plan, which meant that the only limitations on them related to the availability of sponsors and visa officers' processing capacity.[13] Because private sponsorships operated outside the government's immigration-levels planning, and because sponsors were able to name refugees in refugee-like situations for resettlement, conditions were ideal for a rapid increase in sponsorships of refugees with family links.

HISTORY OF NAMING IN THE CONTEXT OF CANADA'S PSR PROGRAM

As Cameron has discussed in this volume, the PSR program originated not in the Southeast Asian crisis, as is widely believed, but rather in the population displacements that immediately followed the Second World War. During the thirty years following that war, civil society organizations (mostly faith-based) gained increasing influence over refugee resettlement to Canada. They lobbied for a broadening of the parameters for refugee admission, and this led gradually to more selections being made on humanitarian grounds as opposed to ideological and labour-market-linked grounds.[14]

The 1976 Immigration Act, which came into effect in 1978, brought refugee sponsorship into Canada's immigration law for the first time; however, the Act was not specific about what this would look like. The procedures for sponsoring refugees and humanitarian cases that were subsequently proposed explicitly allowed sponsors to name an individual or a member of a specified affinity group (e.g., religious or ethnic) for sponsorship. This provision correlated with the perception that private groups would help ensure the successful establishment of admitted refugees or humanitarian cases, as ability to establish themselves in Canada was still a prime criterion for admission of refugees and humanitarian cases under the new Act.

As the Southeast Asian crisis intensified, interest in named sponsorships waned as several religious groups began showing interest in sponsoring refugees from Southeast Asia. In April 1979, the first Master Agreement with the Mennonite Central Committee was signed, and by the end of the year, forty groups (all faith-based) had signed Master Agreements with the government to sponsor refugees. These agreements contained provisions for named sponsorships; however, many of those sponsored were unnamed. The period of private sponsorship of refugees from Southeast Asia was short and intense. Over the course of 1979 and 1980, 34,000 privately sponsored refugees arrived in Canada.[15]

After this surge, private refugee sponsorship declined to between 4,000 and 6,000 persons annually.[16] Sponsorship moved from the unnamed "sponsorship of a stranger" to the family reunification that the Approved Church Program sponsorship had focused on and that the government envisioned in its procedures for operationalizing the PSR program under the 1976 Immigration Act. Gradually, however, government staff became concerned that the humanitarian program had evolved into a family reunification program. To move back toward unnamed sponsorships, a series of blended sponsorship programs have been tried, which have provided financial incentives for sponsorship of refugees selected by the government. The current Blended Visa Office-Referred (BVOR) program is the latest example; earlier versions included a 3/9 incentive program for refugees from the former Yugoslavia and a 4/8 blended program for refugees from Sierra Leone.[17]

Following a review of the PSR program in the early 1990s, the government expressed concerns about the high number of named sponsorships, which visa officers saw as undermining the program's humanitarian intent.[18] In a 1992 discussion paper, Employment and Immigration Canada (EIC) highlighted the increasing tendency of sponsorship groups to identify refugees for resettlement based on ties to relatives in Canada. EIC questioned the appropriateness of this practice but concluded that a varied approach to refugee selection was worthwhile and recommended that sponsorship groups continue to have the right to name refugees. EIC included a soft ask that sponsorship groups "remain open to receiving names from the Government, UNHCR, Amnesty International, International NGOs and other international agencies, etc., and passing them back to private sponsorship groups for sponsorship."[19]

The Canadian government's 1995 study report on a process for matching refugees with sponsors provides some insights into the thinking at the time.[20] The report concluded that in the absence of a formal matching process, naming had come to serve as an unofficial matching mechanism. At that time, it was estimated that about 90 percent of all sponsorships were named.[21] The study identified that the "principal reason for the current heavy emphasis on named refugees appears to be the pressure on sponsors by previously sponsored refugees to help bring other family members to Canada."[22] The study also concluded that a significant promotional effort, involving multiple stakeholders, would be required to increase the sponsorship of unnamed refugees.[23]

The report acknowledged that naming was important to sponsors but cautioned that it was failing to ensure that the refugees most in need were included in the sponsorship program. The report suggested that an effective matching process for unnamed refugees would likely resolve this matter by making unnamed sponsorships an attractive option for sponsors. At the same time, it was recommended to continue to allow named referrals without restrictions, for essentially two reasons: (1) to ensure ongoing cooperation from NGOs that demanded the right to named sponsorships; and (2) to account for the fact that not all named sponsorships were deemed to be family linked and could be high-priority humanitarian cases.[24] In hindsight, it appears that the report mistook a philosophical issue for an operational problem. The report identified a need for communications with sponsors to convince them of the importance of sponsoring unnamed refugees on humanitarian and compassionate grounds, suggesting that the speed of a new effective matching process would increase sponsorship of unnamed refugees. As the next two decades would show, Citizenship and Immigration Canada (CIC) had severely underestimated sponsors' interest in responding to the pleas of previously sponsored refugees to help them reunite with family members. To this day, that factor has had much stronger persuasive power than the government's argument for unnamed/visa office-referred refugees.

By the end of the 1990s, another major shift had occurred. During the consultation process in the run-up to IRPA taking effect in 2002, CIC proposed shifting the balance in refugee selection toward protection rather than ability to settle successfully. At the same time, CIC proposed to establish "procedures that will allow members of an extended refugee family to be processed together overseas and, where this is not possible, providing a mechanism for the speedy reunion of families."[25] Even though the document did not explicitly mention sponsor-referred refugees, sponsors' ability to name the relatives of resettled refugees for sponsorship provided an important vehicle for the reunification of extended families.

In 2007, the Government of Canada conducted a summative evaluation of the PSR program, and in 2016, it carried out a full evaluation of Canada's refugee resettlement programs, including the PSR program for named refugees and the BVOR program. The 2007 evaluation highlighted the links between the PSR program and the UNHCR's Agenda for Protection, in particular the program's alignment with two of that agenda's objectives: (1) "strengthened partnerships for protection with civil society, including NGOs,"[26] and (2) "provision of complementary forms of protection to those who might not fall within the scope of the 1951 Convention [Relating to the Status of Refugees], but require international protection."[27] The evaluation further confirmed that the PSR program was aligned with the government's refugee protection mandate under IRPA, as well as with the strategic outcome of successful integration of newcomers. In this way, the 2007 evaluation reaffirmed the PSR program's link to humanitarian protection without any criticism of sponsor referral. The report noted that visa office–referred cases accounted for less than 2 percent of all sponsored resettled refugees between 2002 and 2005, but this concern was viewed as problematic only in light of high refusal rates for sponsor-referred cases and the need for better training of sponsors regarding refugee eligibility.

As with the report on matching sponsors with refugees twenty years earlier, the 2016 evaluation called for the development of "an engagement strategy for SAHs to increase uptake of the BVOR program."[28] However, the evaluation simply concluded that "at this time, activities to increase sponsorship uptake are not part of the strategy as they are not currently required."[29] Even though the evaluation explicitly stated that the "2015 Syrian Refugee Initiative was not taken into consideration for the Evaluation,"[30] it appears that the conclusion about there being no need for an engagement strategy was based on sponsor behaviour during the Syria Initiative, when uptake was abnormally high. In the years since publication of the evaluation, sponsor interest in the BVOR program has dwindled, and it has become clear that it was incorrect to assume that a strategy to increase uptake of unnamed sponsorships was unnecessary.[31]

The evaluation recommended that Canada's "refugee resettlement programs align with Government of Canada and IRCC priorities to support humanitarian policy objectives."[32] It presented the link between the PSR program and family reunification in a positive light and as aligned with a key objective of Canada's resettlement program as outlined in IRPA. The evaluation noted that about 35 percent of refugees surveyed who had arrived in Canada under the Government-Assisted Refugees (GAR) program had family members in Canada and that 62 percent of PSRs surveyed had been sponsored by a family member.[33]

DIVERSE MOTIVATIONS, INTENDED AND UNINTENDED CONSEQUENCES OF NAMING

As the discussion so far has demonstrated, the motivations for incorporating naming into Canada's PSR program cannot be easily delineated. It is likewise not easy to distinguish between intended and unintended consequences of naming because they frequently constitute two aspects – policy, and practice – of the same underlying issue. What in more mature programs like the Canadian program may seem like serendipitous outcomes (e.g., faster integration and more diversity in the resettled refugee population) may well form the basis for the intentional design of newer programs. In this section, we therefore examine the consequences of naming without preoccupying ourselves with the question of whether these consequences are intended or unintended. We also refrain from making any value judgment on these consequences, because there are numerous reasons why states engage in refugee resettlement generally and in PSR/CSR programs more specifically, and why they may or may not allow naming. This chapter's purpose is simply to explore this concept toward an informed discussion.

As was outlined in the 2016 evaluation of Canada's resettlement programs, IRPA's Section 3.2f states that one of the Act's objectives is to "support the self-sufficiency and the social and economic well-being of refugees by facilitating reunification with their family members in Canada."[34] As such, the naming of refugees fulfills a domestic Canadian obligation toward refugees. The ability to name refugees for sponsorship allows civil society to respond to the so-called echo effect – the demand for resettlement of additional (family) members of a particular refugee population following a state-led resettlement effort. As the Canadian Council for Refugees has noted, naming in sponsorships "responds to situations around the world and to refugees who have been forgotten or who do not fit the priorities of governments or the UN."[35] Providing reunification avenues for extended refugee families is important: extended refugee families often live and flee together, and rigid state-led resettlement criteria break families apart.

Civil society has long been recognized as a vital partner in refugee integration. At a recent conference on Social Innovation for Refugee Inclusion, the need for a whole-of-society approach grounded in local community empowerment and cultivation of trust and relationships at the local level was repeatedly stressed.[36] Refugees' family members who are already established in the host communities act as brokers in the settlement and integration of the more recently arrived and in the development of social capital among the larger community toward establishing a welcoming environment. A fundamental trade-off faced by any resettlement program is between the frequently cited desire to resettle the most vulnerable, on the one hand, and the desire to facilitate successful integration within a reasonably short time, on the other – a trade-off that has been characterized as "particularly challenging."[37] Beirens and Fratzke have discussed a number of reasons why states engage in resettlement, and the idea of strategically using PSR/CSR schemes to build a "much needed integration and diversity management infrastructure"[38] seems to be gaining traction in light of large, irregular arrivals and rising anti-refugee sentiment in several countries. In Canada, there is evidence of fairly stable and sustained support for refugees at the community level, in large part because diversified communities are hardly new to Canada. Overall, Canadian society appears to be at ease with in-migration and has maintained a positive public consensus around immigration.[39] It has been rightly noted, though, that Canada's geographical isolation has sheltered the country from large, irregular arrivals of the kind that European countries have recently experienced.[40] A recent survey by the Environics Institute found that "multiculturalism and the acceptance of immigrants and refugees now stand out as the best way Canadians feel their country can be a role model for others."[41] The survey research reported a connection between this perspective and the fact that one in three Canadians had a direct or indirect link to refugee sponsorship in the preceding two years.

This potential for a positive connection between refugee sponsorship and a favourable public consensus on refugees has now been recognized in European countries that have recently had to integrate large numbers of refugees arriving irregularly. Migration experts contend that the close relationships created between refugees and sponsors will enhance trust-building between these groups and become a "key ingredient in cohesive communities."[42] Fratzke further noted the important role of "a sense of ownership of refugee protection efforts among community members."[43] Naming has the potential to enhance the sense of ownership sponsors feel, relative to a sponsorship model under which sponsors have little or no input into whom they sponsor.

One significant consequence of naming is that it can help ensure complementarity or additionality vis-à-vis a country's traditional resettlement program, thus providing additional protection spaces for refugees. Given that named refugees do not come from the same pool of resettlement candidates as those referred to the state by referral agencies, there is a higher likelihood that privately sponsored refugees are not simply substituting for state resettlement. However, the Canadian example shows that, even with naming, additionality may come under attack: since 2017, named PSR resettlement has outnumbered state-led resettlement by a ratio of about 2:1, with Canada's Multi-Year Immigration Levels Plan up to 2021 cementing this ratio into the coming years.[44] With numbers skewed in this way, some refugee advocates are asking whether the PSR program amounts to a privatization model of resettlement. Another aspect of the additionality question in a naming model pertains to the possibility that sponsors who want to see family members resettled may lobby the government to provide significantly more spaces for privately sponsored refugees than for traditional state resettlement, thus themselves contributing to the violation of the additionality principle. It is even conceivable that the ability to name refugees for sponsorship creates a pull factor among persons who are under some duress in their home country, and who may leave that country to create the necessary conditions that enable their sponsorship.

In a system of referral by private individuals, the person who makes the referral must know the refugees they wish to sponsor. This interaction typically comes about in one of two ways: (1) the private person who wants to sponsor has met the refugees in their country of first asylum during a leisure or work-related trip; or (2) a family member of the refugees proposes them for sponsorship. In either case, the main selection criterion is the existence of a personal relationship. Labman has noted that "social capital tends to guide sponsor selections."[45] Therefore, irrespective of the extent to which naming is aligned with humanitarian selection – a question that is beyond the scope of this chapter – an equity and fairness issue is embedded in naming: resettlement through named sponsorship is available only to those with connections to Canada where sponsors or family members have the necessary funds. As a result, the economic capacity of sponsors/family members becomes the primary selection factor rather than factors pertaining to the refugees themselves.

There are ways in which humanitarian selection based on clearly defined criteria and sponsor referral can be creatively combined. The Canadian Rainbow Refugee Assistance Program offers such an example.[46] The program ensures a certain level of humanitarian selection by offering protection to refugees fleeing persecution because of their sexual orientation or gender identity; yet sponsors are allowed to identify the specific refugees they wish to sponsor. Similar models that were developed earlier – albeit with a population focus rather than a protection focus – include the resettlement of Afghan Ismaili refugees between 1994 and 1998,[47] and the resettlement of Sierra Leonean refugees in 2001.[48]

THE PERSISTENCE OF NAMING IN CANADA'S PSR RESETTLEMENT PROGRAM DESPITE CRITICISM

As we have shown, criticisms of naming have repeatedly been raised over the past forty years. Yet naming continues to be a feature of the PSR; indeed, the PSR program has become the dominant refugee resettlement program in Canada. As Labman aptly noted, "the government has sent out mixed messages as it negotiates its role in facilitating sponsorship."[49] Labman has argued that the government ultimately seems content with continuing a sponsorship model that links public and private support because it enables "the government to appear responsive to refugee issues while relegating the majority of responsibility to the private sector."[50] Even though Labman made this comment in the context of blended refugee projects, the same can be said about the main Canadian sponsorship model, the PSR program. As has already been mentioned, ever since the significant Syrian resettlement project in 2015–16, the Canadian government has increasingly relied on private sponsorship for the majority of resettlement to Canada.

The earlier discussion of the history of naming points to several main reasons why the government has continued to permit naming of refugees with family links for sponsorship:

- to allow groups and private individuals to influence refugee policy;
- to make room for diversity by allowing the private sector to select refugees based on different priorities than those applied to government-assisted refugees; and
- to improve the adaptation process.[51]

As this last point demonstrates, the perception that privately sponsored refugees with family or community connections in Canada may have less difficulty adapting and integrating has been part of the thinking and the narrative around Canada's PSR program for more than twenty-five years. But this narrative neglects differences at the selection stage: GARs since IRPA have been selected for their protection needs and tend, on average, to be more vulnerable than PSRs named by family members or friends, for whom ability to establish may be a criterion applied by those doing the naming. IRCC's Rapid Impact Evaluation of the Syrian Initiative[52] identified considerable differences between privately sponsored and UN-referred refugees when it came to official language proficiency, educational background, and other integration-enabling factors upon arrival in Canada.

The positive link between reuniting refugees with family members in Canada and the refugees' integration outcomes has also been highlighted in the 2016 Evaluation of Resettlement Programs. IRCC found that since the introduction of IRPA, which largely eliminated the ability to establish as a selection factor for refugees and focused instead on protection needs, "GARs tended to have lower economic performance compared to PSRs. Specifically, they had lower incidence of employment, lower employment earnings and higher social assistance reliance."[53] Only after about ten years in Canada did the economic performance of GAR and PSR refugees converge.

As the previous section showed, the 2007 evaluation marked an important departure from earlier concerns about the PSR program's fixation with family-linked sponsorship in that it acknowledged the links between the PSR program, and the UNHCR's Agenda for Protection, and its alignment with the Canadian government's refugee protection mandate under IRPA. In this way, the 2007 evaluation reaffirmed the PSR program's link to humanitarian protection and weakened earlier criticism of family-linked sponsorships.

LESSONS LEARNED AND ISSUES TO CONSIDER FOR COUNTRIES STARTING PSR/CSR PROGRAMS

Notwithstanding Smith's critical account in this volume regarding the prospect for "exporting" the Canadian private sponsorship model to other jurisdictions, the last two years have shown that there is scope for introducing or expanding emerging PSR/CSR schemes in several countries, in particular those of Western Europe.[54] A key question in the design of such programs is whether to allow sponsors to name the refugees they wish to sponsor. As Canada's example shows, named refugees are predominantly those related to persons already established in Canada, and the question of naming can therefore also be framed in Kumin's words as "invariably [overlapping] with refugee family reunion ... Private sponsorship programmes expand refugee family reunion, making it possible for relatives beyond the nuclear family to be resettled."[55] Fundamentally, countries may then need to decide on the principal objectives of their PSR/CSR program: Is it supposed to provide established immigrant and refugee communities with a mechanism to assist their displaced extended family members? Is it supposed to provide the UNHCR and other referral agencies with an additional mechanism beyond state-led resettlement for finding durable solutions for those whom these agencies have assessed as being most in need? Should the program provide a mix of these two basic models?

A scoping study conducted by the International Catholic Migration Commission Europe in fall 2017[56] examined existing and emerging sponsorship schemes in Europe based on a range of criteria, including identification. They found a number of models, including two where sponsors made referrals based on family links (Germany and Ireland), one where referrals were made by the UNHCR (UK), and two where primary sponsoring organizations worked with local development organizations and with the UNHCR and the International Organization for Migration to make referrals (France and Italy). Over the past year, some of these states have undertaken more extensive consultations around PSR/CSR and, as a result, are now considering models that would rely more heavily on UNHCR referrals than on named sponsorships.

As Kumin noted, if naming is part of a PSR/CSR program, the interest in such programs and the number of applications can be expected to be high, regardless of which specific criteria are attached to the program design. Conversely, one may question the sustainability of a PSR/CSR program that does not allow some level of naming and that relies entirely on the altruism of private individuals or charitable organizations toward complete strangers. In PSR/CSR programs, the government counts on the goodwill of civil society. Without some level of control or input by civil society over the refugee populations or identity of the refugees they are asked to sponsor, programs risk losing their initial attractiveness and novelty over time, and public interest may fluctuate in unpredictable ways. Much will likely depend on the extent to which states that launch PSR/CSR programs rely on their private citizens to not only provide the necessary psychosocial settlement supports and community connections to refugees but also take on full or partial financial responsibility for their settlement. Canada's experience shows that sponsors who take on such financial responsibility during the first twelve months after the refugees' arrival also want to have input into whom they bring to Canada. States embarking on PSR/CSR programs have to find ways to address the tension between "encouraging private sector involvement [and] maintaining control."[57]

There are also practical considerations. A PSR/CSR program that allows little or no naming has to design an effective mechanism for matching sponsors to refugees. Some infrastructure is needed to operate such a system.[58] Moreover, if sponsors can name refugees for sponsorship who are located in various parts of the world, an effective processing infrastructure is necessary that may overstretch a country's current visa-processing capabilities. That, too, comes with costs that may be significant.

Emerging PSR/CSR program designers must decide to what extent they want protection to remain the core criterion for sponsorship and to what extent avenues for family reunification through refugee sponsorship meet this criterion. Labman has argued that in Canada, "the sponsorship community has played a powerful role in influencing the expansion of Canada's protection criteria ... [which risks] losing sight of the refugee definition."[59] However, the issue is not quite so black and white. The UNHCR has recognized the important role of family reunification "for the integration of beneficiaries of international protection in their host societies."[60] This dimension of sponsorship is also mentioned by Smith in this volume when he argues that refugees sponsored for family reunification may find it easier to integrate due to the existence of social networks and the resulting social capital – an argument that European countries preoccupied with the integration question may find appealing. Also, as Italy's example shows, models already exist that allow for sponsor referral of refugees selected by the sponsor using humanitarian selection criteria.[61] However, such models are only possible where the sponsor is an organization with substantial infrastructure in refugee-hosting countries. When private individuals are allowed to propose refugees for sponsorship, humanitarian selection criteria inevitably become tied up with additional considerations such as family or other links to sponsors. Preserving the notion of "objective" humanitarian selection criteria that refer those "most in need" of international protection for resettlement then becomes even more difficult than it already is in the absence of sponsor selection.

Therefore, protection and family reunification aspects of PSR/CSR programs are best understood not as a trade-off but rather as a balance of these two important principles. Whichever route a state in collaboration with civil society decides to pursue, pressure for naming is a reality – if not initially from sponsors, then certainly from the resettled refugees themselves. When Canada introduced a sponsorship model in the 1976 Immigration Act, it gave resettled refugees a powerful advocate – the sponsors – for bringing the family members of the resettled refugees to Canada as well. As other states look to the PSR/CSR model, they will need to find a constructive way to respond to this pressure or face a possible backlash from sponsors and find themselves with a program that lacks longevity.

NOTES

1 Australian Government, Department of Home Affairs, "Community Support Program (CSP)," 11 December 2018, https://immi.homeaffairs.gov.au/what-we-do/refugee-and-humanitarian-program/community-support-program.
2 UN High Commissioner for Refugees, "UNHCR Resettlement Handbook – Country Chapter Germany" (UNHCR, April 2013, revised August 2018), www.unhcr.org/5162b3bc9.pdf.
3 Global Refugee Sponsorship Initiative, "Joint Statement – Ministers from Canada, the United Kingdom, Ireland, Argentina, Spain, and New Zealand," 16 July 2018, http://refugeesponsorship.org/_uploads/5b4ca01e5c883.pdf.
4 Shauna Labman, *Crossing Law's Border: Canada's Refugee Resettlement Program* (Vancouver: UBC Press, 2019), 40.
5 Barbara Treviranus and Michael Casasola, "Canada's Private Sponsorship of Refugees Program: A Practitioners Perspective of its Past and Future," *JIMI/RIMI* 4, no. 2 (Spring 2003): 183.
6 Immigration, Refugees, and Citizenship Canada, "Guide to the Private Sponsorship of Refugees Program – 2. Private sponsorship of refugees-program," Government of Canada, 17 May 2017, https://www.canada.ca/en/immigration-refugees-citizenship/corporate/publications-manuals/guide-private-sponsorship-refugees-program/section-2.html#a2.1.
7 Immigration, Refugees, and Citizenship Canada, "Notice – Supplementary Information 2019–2021 Immigration Levels Plan," 31 October 2018, https://www.canada.ca/en/immigration-refugees-citizenship/news/notices/supplementary-immigration-levels-2019.html.
8 Labman, *Crossing Law's Border*, 91.
9 Ibid., 157.
10 James Hathaway, "Selective Concern: An Overview of Refugee Law in Canada," *McGill Law Journal* 33, no. 4 (1988): 693.
11 Labman, *Crossing Law's Border*, 126.
12 Ibid., 199.

13 Ibid., 158–9.
14 Marlene Epp, ed., *Refugees in Canada: A Brief History* (Ottawa: Canadian Historical Association, 2017), 13–16.
15 Labman, *Crossing Law's Border*, 90.
16 Ibid., 93.
17 Ibid., 98–9.
18 Treviranus and Casasola, "Canada's Private Sponsorship of Refugees Program," 186.
19 Employment and Immigration Canada, "Discussion Paper: Private Sponsorship of Refugees Program," *Refuge* 12, no. 3 (September 1992): 5.
20 Citizenship and Immigration Canada, Corporate Review, Planning, Review, and Renewal, "Study Report on the Review and Development of a Process for Matching Refugees and Sponsors" (Ottawa: CIC, February 1995).
21 Ibid., 2.
22 Ibid.
23 Ibid., 6.
24 Ibid.
25 Citizenship and Immigration Canada, *Building on a Strong Foundation for the 21st Century: New Directions for Immigration and Refugee Policy and Legislation* (Ottawa: Minister of Public Works and Government Services, 1998), 43, http://publications.gc.ca/site/eng/9.695621/publication.html
26 UN High Commissioner for Refugees, *Agenda for Protection*, 3rd ed. (Geneva: UNHCR, 2003), 59.
27 UNHCR, *Agenda for Protection*, 34.
28 Immigration, Refugees, and Citizenship Canada, *Evaluation of the Resettlement Programs (GAR, PSR, BVOR and RAP)* (Ottawa: IRCC, 2016), v.
29 Ibid., viii.
30 Ibid., 7.
31 The target for BVOR admissions in IRCC's Immigration Levels Plans for both 2017 and 2018 was 1,500. Canada admitted 1,285 BVOR refugees in 2017, and by 31 August 2018, Canada had only admitted 320 BVOR refugees and was on track to missing the target for the second year in a row (IRCC Open Government Data: Permanent Residents).
32 IRCC, *Evaluation of Resettlement*, 9.
33 Ibid., 21.
34 Immigration and Refugee Protection Act, S.C. 2001, c. 27, s. 3.2f.

35 Canadian Council for Refugees, *Renewing Canada's Private Sponsorship of Refugees Program* (n.p.: CCR, 2016), http://ccrweb.ca/en/renewing-private-sponsorship-refugees-program.
36 Liam Patuzzi and Alexandra Embiricos, *Social Innovation for Refugee Inclusion Conference Report: Maintaining Momentum and Creating Lasting Change* (Brussels: Migration Policy Institute, 2018), https://www.migrationpolicy.org/research/social-innovation-refugee-inclusion-conference-report.
37 Hanne Beirens and Susan Fratzke, *Taking Stock of Refugee Resettlement: Policy Objectives, Practical Tradeoffs, and the Evidence Base* (Brussels: Migration Policy Institute Europe, 2017), 18, https://www.migrationpolicy.org/research/taking-stock-refugee-resettlement-policy-objectives-practical-tradeoffs-and-evidence-base.
38 Ibid., 13.
39 Environics Institute for Survey Research, "Canadian Public Opinion about Immigration and Minority Groups" (Toronto: Environics, 2018), https://www.environicsinstitute.org/projects/project-details/focus-canada-winter-2018---canadian-public-opinion-on-immigration-and-minority-groups; Daniel Hiebert, *What's So Special about Canada? Understanding the Resilience of Immigration and Multiculturalism* (Washington, DC: Migration Policy Institute, 2016), https://www.migrationpolicy.org/research/whats-so-special-about-canada-understanding-resilience-immigration-and-multiculturalism.
40 Ibid.
41 Environics Institute for Survey Research, "Canada's World Survey 2018" (Toronto: Environics, 2018), https://www.environicsinstitute.org/projects/project-details/canada's-world-2017-survey.
42 Susan Fratzke, *Engaging Communities in Refugee Protection: The Potential of Private Sponsorship in Europe* (Brussels: Migration Policy Institute Europe, 2017), 5.
43 Ibid., 5.
44 IRCC, "Immigration Levels Plan."
45 Labman, *Crossing Law's Border*, 94.
46 Immigration, Refugees and Citizenship Canada, "Rainbow Refugee Assistance Pilot Program Extended," Government of Canada, March 23, 2018, https://www.canada.ca/en/immigration-refugees-citizenship/news/2018/03/rainbow-refugee-assistance-pilot-program-extended.html.
47 Labman, *Crossing Law's Border*, 98.
48 Ibid., 99.

49 Ibid., 106.
50 Shauna Labman, *At Law's Border: Unsettling Refugee Resettlement* (PhD diss., University of British Columbia, 2012), 179.
51 Employment and Immigration Canada, "Refugees Program," 10.
52 Immigration, Refugees, and Citizenship Canada, "Rapid Impact Evaluation of the Syrian Refugee Initiative" (Ottawa: IRCC, 2016), https://www.canada.ca/en/immigration-refugees-citizenship/corporate/reports-statistics/evaluations/rapid-impact-evaluation-syrian-refugee-initiative.html.
53 IRCC, *Evaluation of Resettlement*, 32.
54 International Catholic Migration Commission Europe, *Private Sponsorship in Europe: Expanding Complementary Pathways for Refugee Resettlement* (Brussels: ICMC Europe, 2017); Judith Kumin, *Welcoming Engagement: How Private Sponsorship Can Strengthen Refugee Resettlement in the European Union* (Brussels: Migration Policy Institute, 2015), https://www.migrationpolicy.org/research/welcoming-engagement-how-private-sponsorship-can-strengthen-refugee-resettlement-european.
55 Ibid., 4.
56 ICMC Europe, *Private Sponsorship*.
57 Labman, *At Law's Border*, 179.
58 See Citizenship and Immigration Canada, "Study Report on the Review and Development of a Process for Matching Refugees and Sponsors" (Ottawa: CIC, February 1995).
59 Labman, *Crossing Law's Border*, 109.
60 UN High Commissioner for Refugees, *Refugee Family Reunification: UNHCR's Response to the European Commission Green Paper on the Right to Family Reunification of Third Country Nationals Living in the European Union (Directive 2003/86/EC)* (n.p.: UNHCR, 2012), http://www.refworld.org/docid/4f55e1cf2.html.
61 ICMC Europe, *Private Sponsorship*.

3

How *Should* We Think about Private Sponsorship of Refugees?

Patti Tamara Lenard

The Private Sponsorship of Refugees Program in Canada is unique in the world. It allows private citizens to "name" specific refugees for admission to Canada; it allows private citizens to cover the financial and emotional costs of refugee resettlement for one year; and in its best moments, it permits private citizens committed to refugee justice to raise the bar for refugee admission to Canada, by supporting the admission of refugees over and above the numbers the government has committed to admit. Equally, there are many criticisms of the program. Not all sponsors do a good job of supporting refugees admitted to Canada, and the oversight mechanisms are imperfect; sponsors (in spite of the heroic efforts of the Refugee Sponsorship Training Program) are not always well-trained in how best to support newcomers; settlement services that operate around private sponsorship are not always efficient and cannot always handle the load demanded of them; and, according to some critics, such programs offload responsibility for supporting refugees from the state onto citizen volunteers.

In this chapter, I step away from the details of the program to consider broader normative questions about how to think about the selection of refugees by citizens. I consider three interrelated questions: (1) When a country like Canada evaluates its resettlement program as successful or otherwise, what is the benchmark for success? (2) Is "naming" justified? (3) What kind of task are citizens who engage in sponsorship engaging in – that is, are they engaging in charity or in the pursuit of justice? And, armed with an account of what kind of moral task citizens are engaging in, what constraints should be imposed on them, especially with respect to the choices they make about whom to sponsor? In what follows, I move between the principles of normative political theory of immigration and the actual workings of the private sponsorship scheme in Canada; in engaging with question 3, I rely on data I have collected via interviews with sixty sponsors in Ottawa.[1] I ultimately argue that the selection of refugees can be a job carried out by state and citizens, who share a duty of *justice* (not charity) to support the admission and integration of refugees.

CANADIAN EXCEPTIONALISM IN THE REFUGEE SPACE

The number of refugees globally is increasingly daily.[2] To set the stage, consider two facts: (1) of the nearly 20 million refugees in need (excluding Palestinians), the UN High Commission on Refugees (UNHCR) prioritizes around one million of them for resettlement, at any one moment; and (2) of these, only 125,000 (give or take) are resettled into third countries each year. Of these, a significant proportion are resettled to Canada, and that proportion is increasing as the United States reduces its total refugee intake. Canada therefore appears to be a major player in global refugee resettlement. How major a player it is depends on how many other countries are contributing resettlement spaces and how many refugees the Canadian government chooses to admit. These numbers all vary on a yearly basis, in response to a range of factors, but however they vary, they do not belie the fact that if the relevant comparator is "other countries" in general, or even "other resettlement countries," Canada does well in refugee admission for resettlement.[3] How, morally, should we respond to Canada's response? Canada was applauded for its work in admitting fleeing Syrians – did it deserve these accolades?[4]

The answer to this question depends on what the moral metric is for acting in the refugee resettlement space, so let me outline several options before I defend one of them. One option is to compare Canada's actions in refugee resettlement space to the actions taken by other countries, globally. If Canada's actions in this space are compared to the actions of the rest of the world, it is unambiguously praiseworthy. Indeed, Canada's actions remain praiseworthy even if the comparison is to other self-identified refugee resettlement states (of which, last I checked, there were thirty-seven, which included

Hungary). Only the United States has consistently ranked higher (historically) in terms of number of refugees admitted for resettlement.

However, if our actions are assessed against the *need* that is going unmet; or if they are being assessed according to our capacity to support resettled refugees; or indeed if they are being assessed in comparison to the work carried out by the global South countries to "temporarily" offer refuge to millions of refugees (countries like Jordan and Turkey), and compare this to the small number of resettled refugees that Canada admits each year, the response we should take to what now looks like Canada's relatively minor contribution to alleviating the suffering of refugees is less obvious. We do what we do well, and we may even do it well compared to other "like" countries that do the same thing, but that is perhaps fainter praise than we might like. And that still doesn't tell us what we *should* do.

An alternative answer is drawn from attempts by scholars to develop and promote "burden-sharing" regimes, which would more fairly distribute roles associated with supporting refugees globally. On this view, the aim is to identify Canada's *fair share* of refugee admissions. Such an assessment demands, first, the careful consideration of Canada's capacity for admission and resettlement,[5] alongside the capacity of others to do the same. Any fair assessment of capacity is additionally challenged by the normative question of whether Canada should be "credited" (morally and with respect to calculating its fair share) in some relevant way for having created an environment – both socially and bureaucratically – in which it is possible to resettle refugees effectively. Let's say, for the sake of argument, that it is possible to generate an algorithm that spits out a justified "fair share" number of refugees, which, because it is a fair share, should be understood as Canada's duty of justice to resettle.

None of what I have so far written answers the question with which this section began, which is, is Canada deserving of praise for its resettlement work? It should now be clear that the answer to the question depends on whether Canada's actions are compared to what other *resettlement* countries are doing, and how well they are doing it; or to its "fair share" allocation of refugee resettlement work; or to the unmet need for resettlement. Comparing Canada to other resettlement countries is problematic for at least two reasons: (1) it is biased in favour of the status quo (a status quo that permits all kinds of injustices against refugees to persist); and (2) it appears to let states that are refusing to engage in resettlement off the moral hook. But proposing that Canada's choices be measured against a fair share assessment, or unmet need, can be justified; to put this differently, Canada's actions should be praised if they fall between meeting our "fair share" obligations and meeting unmet need.

WHO IS RESPONSIBLE FOR SELECTING REFUGEES FOR ADMISSION?

Conventionally, we think of admission of migrants of all kinds as a matter of central government responsibility. When political theorists define state sovereignty, the right and ability of a state to control admission to its territory is one of its central features.[6] It is therefore noteworthy that in Canada some portion of this job is offered to private sponsors. Private sponsors are permitted to *name* individuals who fit the criteria of admission to Canada and, also, to make the case that they deserve to be admitted over others who are also making admission requests, implicitly or explicitly.[7] The power is not absolute, certainly, and any person proposed for admission following the rules of the private sponsorship program must meet a range of criteria, including that he or she is a genuine refugee and does not pose a security risk. Is this justified, or is there a reason to be sceptical of the power granted to Canadians? The reason to be sceptical is this: given the real unmet need with respect to resettlement spaces for refugees, the connection to a Canadian citizen or permanent resident gives refugees in need a significant advantage in the tragic competition to find a safe and permanent home. Maybe this introduces an unfairness into the distribution of resettlement spots.

Let me say something about the political theoretic framework that shapes the distribution of resources, to articulate the precise moral question here. Political theorists are often focused on the *fair* distribution of *scarce* resources.[8] The thought is generally that in many cases the things that people find valuable — money, certainly, but also educational or job opportunities and so on — are in some sense scarce. Given the assumption that these are goods that everyone desires, there is not enough to go around; so the question is, what sorts of distribution mechanisms are fair, given the scarcity? How can we decide who gets to go to medical school, or who gets which highly desirable job? Political theorists debate these kinds of questions — sometimes the distribution principle is "need," and other times it is "merit" — and the general thought is that once the right distribution principle and an associated distribution procedure have been identified, the resulting distribution is thereby *fair*. Correspondingly, it is understood by everyone, even those who have "lost," as legitimate in some fundamental way.[9]

More complicated theoretical questions, about fair distribution principles, emerge when the focus is not simply on scarce resources but on *highly* scarce resources. What distinguishes conditions of scarce resources from those of *highly* scarce resources is a matter of dispute. But going forward, let's say that a resource is highly scarce when the need for it far surpasses what is available, and where receiving it or not is often (if not always) a matter of life or death. These are the conditions that pertain in disaster situations, and a reading of disaster ethics in particular generates a whole set of principles and strategies that mainly medical personnel can use to determine whom to treat and when, knowing that these kinds of choices are matters of (immediate) life and death for those who are offered or denied treatment. Maybe those who "lose" in these kinds of situations would be able conceptually to treat the choice to prioritize others as legitimate, or maybe not. But the point is that even in conditions of highly scarce resources, it is reasonable to engage in questions about the normative criteria that guide choices, even if the specific criteria differ.

I think it is reasonable to treat the small number of resettlement spaces as highly scarce. What then are the proper distribution mechanisms for allocating the highly scarce resource that is resettlement spots?[10] I have written elsewhere that I believe the appropriate distribution principle is vulnerability. Vulnerability is a term of art in political theory, and here I use the term to mean the relative absence of agency over the conditions that shape one's life; vulnerability is therefore a matter of degree.[11] On my view, refugee resettlement spots should be allocated according to the vulnerability refugees face in their places of refuge, as well the vulnerability they can predictably be understood to face were they to return home (after the cessation of hostilities that, in some cases, propelled their flight in the first place, for example). In what follows, I leave aside the question of whether the UNHCR's priority mechanisms for allocating spots track vulnerability well, which is the subject of considerable controversy[12], and ask readers to permit me, simply, to assume that it does, so that I can focus on the following question: is having a connection to Canadians, which significantly improves one's chances of being resettled, *fair* in the context of the highly scarce resource that is global resettlement spots? Put slightly differently, assuming that the UNHCR process for allocating resettlement spots is fair, does the connection to a Canadian undermine fairness, or it is a legitimate criterion to include in allocating highly scarce resettlement spots?

Let me start by noting that it is presumed to be legitimate to prioritize connections to citizens/residents when considering immigration, and requests for admission, in general: when migrants request admission, temporarily or permanently, to a specific territory, the reason "I want to be with my family" is taken very seriously, at least in part because the right to be with one's family is a basic human right.[13] There is, in other words, a strong reason to permit certain, especially familial, *connections* between sponsors and refugees to matter – that is, to permit family members to be prioritized for admission for highly scarce resettlement spots.

What of broader, non-familial, connections, though? Of course, private sponsors in Canada select refugees to support for admission for all kinds of reasons, including a perception of shared religious, cultural, and ethnic identities. Rejecting or defending these connections as fair criteria for allocating resettlement spots demands consideration in general of these as reasons for admission preference,[14] and then asking whether they are also good reasons for allocating highly scarce resettlement spots extended by private sponsorship. In very general terms, democratic states have chosen to *reject* admission strategies that prioritize shared identities, such as race and ethnic background, on the grounds that they are discriminatory;[15] they would, if permitted, distribute goods on the basis of characteristics that are, as John Rawls famously described them, "arbitrary from a moral point of view."[16] Correspondingly, it seems to me, private sponsors should be at least discouraged, if not prevented, from selecting refugees for admission on these bases, which ought not to be relevant when determining whether one has access to a life-saving resettlement spot.

In summary, whereas I think it is reasonable to give Canadians the ability to "name" refugees for resettlement, in particular when those being named are family members, Canadians should otherwise be encouraged to select refugees for sponsorship from those who are listed on the UNHCR priority list, and they should be discouraged from selecting on the basis of discriminatory connections.[17]

ARE SPONSORS DOING JUSTICE OR CHARITY?

In the political theory of duties, there is a distinction that is frequently made between justice duties and humanitarian duties. The distinction is sometimes hard to capture, but the general thought is that justice duties are obligatory in some fundamental way and that humanitarian duties, though duties, are more like charity. For many, of course, we have charitable duties – the idea of "obligatory charitable giving"[18] is central to many religious world views, for example. But when we say that we have duties of justice, and compare the extent to which we are bound by them with the extent to which we are bound to carry out charitable duties, at least for some, the force of the former is greater than the force of the latter. Duties of charity are meant to be *additional* to our duties of justice. The ability to distinguish them, in the case of refugee resettlement and other domains of global inequality, is reduced because so often "charities" respond to the desperate need of others, in the face of all kinds of state failures. Put differently, charities, and charitable work, too often take up the work that states ought to do to make sure that people are treated justly, one key dimension of which is that their basic needs are met.

What does this distinction look like in the refugee space? The standard legal view is that states have an obligation to admit asylum-seekers who arrive at their borders and to consider their claims fairly. In particular, asylum-seekers cannot be returned "home" if there is any reason to believe that, there, their basic human rights would be violated – this is the well-established duty of non-refoulement. For many theorists of refugees, the duties owed to refugees extend beyond this basic duty to include the duty to permit refuges to stay permanently if, indeed, they are found to be refugees. What renders this view normatively *challenging* is that it interferes with state sovereignty, that is, it is a view that says states may choose whom to admit and who can stay permanently in general terms, but not with respect to refugees, where the rights of refugees take precedence over the rights of state sovereignty. An alternative view treats refugees as individuals in need of help, which some states are in the position to give, at no or low cost to themselves. This principle of humanitarianism, which draws on the parable of the good Samaritan, proposes that states should offer asylum to refugees where they can do so, that is, where the costs of doing so are low, but leaves states with considerable discretion to decide when they can do so and when they cannot. To the extent that it is a duty at all, it gives the admitting state discretion to interpret the costs that would thereby be borne as a result of carrying it out. It is, says Matthew Gibney in defending something like this view, "cautious in the demands it makes of states, and so treats the admission of refugees more like charity than justice."[19]

So the question is, is resettlement required by justice, or is it more like charity, and so a voluntary action taken on the part of a state (or its citizens, in the case of private sponsorship)? In research conducted in Ottawa in 2018, my research team asked sponsors why they chose to become involved in sponsoring refugees,[20] and both of the general views outlined above were reflected in the answers they gave. One cluster of respondents emphasized the duties they had to those who were in need, observing that since they were in a position to help, they had thereby incurred the duty to do so. A second spoke of the organizations of which they were members, which had proposed embarking on sponsorship as a collective project. Usually these organizations were faith communities, whose members felt directed by their religious beliefs to engage in charity in general; many cited faith leaders, who specified that the general requirement to help people in need, especially in 2015 at the height of international concern for Syrians, extended to refugees.[21]

Another interesting observation emerged, as well: When sponsors reflect on the work they are doing, they do not think that what they are doing is interfering with an existing selection mechanism for admitting refugees. They think of what they are doing in terms of the resettlement tasks with which they are charged, which range from practical support in finding housing, health care, education, and employment, to emotional support associated with being friends and "chosen family" to newcomers. These tasks are more amenable to interpretation as charitable, especially for sponsors who are attentive to the differences between the experiences of privately and government-sponsored refugees; these sponsors are often critical of the welcome that government-sponsored refugees receive, and consider the personal attention offered by private sponsors to be a charitable alternative to the paltry (and inadequately welcoming) attention offered to government-assisted refugees, rather than something that newcomers to Canada are owed as a matter of justice.

Why does this matter? Well, one reason it matters is merely pragmatic, which is that it is best to understand why sponsors do the hard work of resettlement, so that they can best be supported and encouraged in their work (e.g., by a government that might like to encourage more Canadians to participate in private sponsorship). Another is that it can inform how we respond to the flip side of the question I posed above. Above I asked, should it matter that a refugee has connections to Canadian citizens and residents, for whether he or she is prioritized for admission to Canada as a resettled refugee, and if so, does it matter what kind of connections those are? The flip question considers how we should respond to Canadians who express preferences for *specific* refugees for admission, and especially whether there are moral questions to ask about why Canadians prefer some over others.

Here is the challenge: If we believe that Canadians who sponsor and resettle refugees are doing so as a matter of justice, and that in doing so they are carrying out duties of justice, then we have strong reasons to constrain their choices so that justice is done. When people have rights – in this case to be granted asylum and perhaps resettled in some way – others possess duties to protect and fulfill those rights.[22] If this is the right way to interpret Canadian action in the field of refugee space, then Canadians can and should be constrained in ways that maximize justice, in the form of making sure that as many rights as possible are respected and protected. This also means that, to the extent that connections to Canadians (on the refugee side), or the expressed preferences of Canadians for certain refugees over others (on the Canadian side), undermine the just distribution of highly scarce resettlement spots, they should not be given moral relevance in allocating these spots, since they do not respond to the most urgent of unprotected rights.

If what we believe, however, is that Canadians who are sponsoring and resettling refugees are engaging in charitable action, as many sponsors do seem to believe they are doing, then we may be less worried about permitting what may seem like idiosyncratic preferences to sponsor and resettle certain refugees over others. That is, speaking more generally, there is a tendency to be more hands-off in our evaluation of charitable actions that people undertake. Charitable actions are undertaken on a voluntary basis, and whereas, as I described above, we may believe that we have duties of charity in general, no one has specific charitable duties toward specific others unless they adopt them as their own. With respect to charity, we might think, any person who chooses to engage in charity may also direct their charitable work toward specific recipients, including toward co-religionists, or co-ethnics, or teammates, or neighbours. If, in other words, sponsorship and resettling refugees is a matter of charity (rather than justice), it may be legitimate to permit private sponsors to make selections among refugees according to their personal preferences or felt identity connections. Indeed, it might be prudent and efficient (as a matter of public policy with respect to refugees) to foster the sense that charitable organizations have identity connections to refugees, as a way to encourage them to choose sponsorship and resettlement as their charitable action of choice. Certainly, the thought that capitalizing on identity connections is central to sponsorship is at the heart of recent work by Jewish organizations to sponsor asylum-seekers denied the right to stay and settle in Israel.[23]

I believe, however, that this is not the right way to characterize this work, and let me here gesture to why that is. Although sponsors self-characterize as engaging in resettlement rather than admission work, the moral impact of their work is precisely in their impact on admission. If sponsors were responsible only for resettlement, perhaps there would be a case to describe their work in exclusively or mainly charitable terms. But they have the ability to influence *admission*, and once they contribute in meaningful ways to admission, they are operating in the domain of justice and are thereby constrained by principles of justice. In this case, they should be constrained in two ways, which brings together the views I am defending in this section and in the earlier section: they should be constrained to selecting among those who are most vulnerable (especially because we already know that even most of those who are prioritized for resettlement by the UNCHR will not find resettlement spaces), and they should (as much as possible) be required to avoid using discriminatory preferences in selecting among those who are most vulnerable.

CONCLUSION

In sum: the proposal I am aiming to defend is a modified private sponsorship scheme, according to which sponsors are permitted to "name" refugees, but where this naming is limited to selecting among those who are most vulnerable for resettlement, and according to which sponsors are as much as possible limited in the ways that their discriminatory preferences can be exercised in selecting refugees for admission to resettlement. I outlined an exception, here, with respect to the sponsoring of family members of Canadian citizens and permanent residents, who can permissibly be prioritized for admission and resettlement alongside those who are most vulnerable.

Elsewhere I have argued that where family reunification is the claimed reason for a resettlement request, it should not "count" as taking a resettlement spot; citizens and residents of any country, including Canada, have a right to be with family, so when this right is claimed by Canadian citizens and residents as the basis for prioritizing a refugee for admission, it seems to me that it is normatively problematic that other refugees are penalized by having access to fewer resettlement spots as a result. In other words, although the private sponsorship scheme is well-known to be used by Canadian citizens and residents to resettle family members, I believe we should (a) protect the private sponsorship scheme for non-family members, and (b) set up a system that, as a matter of course, admits family members of Canadian citizens and permanent residents.

Ultimately, in my view, in participating in the sponsorship of refugees, Canadian citizens and residents are carrying out duties of justice, to open resettlement spaces for the highly vulnerable, and in so doing are supporting Canada's "fair share" obligations toward refugees (as well as unmet needs). Their actions should thus be constrained by the need to distribute highly scarce resources – in this case, resettlement spots – according to principles of justice that can reasonably be expected to gain acceptance from "winners" and "losers." As I have argued, the operative principle is *vulnerability*, and this principle should guide the admission of refugees for resettlement to Canada, as much as is reasonably possible.

As I indicated in the first section, the Canadian Private Sponsorship of Refugees Program should be commended, because it permits and encourages Canadians to contribute actively to the duties of justice we possess as a state. We can, and should, be proud of our work. But we must also be cognizant of the real impact that work has on the lives of the most vulnerable in the world, so we ought to consider how better to make it address the constraints that duties of justice impose on all of us. My proposals, above, are intended to do just that.

NOTES

[1] The study "Success and Failure in Supporting Agency among Refugees," supported by the SSHRC, interviewed sixty private sponsors in Ottawa, as well as twenty-five privately sponsored refugees and twenty government-assisted refugees. Ravi Pendakur, Emily Regan Wills, and I worked in collaboration with Refugee613, the Anglican Diocese, and Jewish Family Services. Our research assistants were Dania Dajani, Stacey Haugen, and Ula Abu Rashed.

2 Matthew Gibney, "*A Thousand Little Guantanamos*: Western States and Measures to Prevent the Arrival of Refugees," in *Migration, Displacement, Asylum: The Oxford Amnesty Lectures 2004*, ed. K. Tunstall (Oxford: Oxford University Press, 2006), 139–69.
3 I am being deliberately careful in using the language of resettlement. Many, many countries host refugees in much greater numbers for temporary stays that are not accompanied by the right to transition to citizenship and the rights and privileges that status grants.
4 UNHCR, "Global Refugee Sponsorship Initiative Promotes Canada's Private Refugee Sponsorship Model," 16 December 2016, http://www.unhcr.org/news/press/2016/12/58539e524/global-refugee-sponsorship-initiative-promotes-canadas-private-refugee.html.
5 And I assume that an objective is to sustain the high quality of resettlement on offer in Canada.
6 A. John Simmons, "On the Territorial Rights of States," *Noûs* 35 (2001): 300–26.
7 I take those who are on the priority list for resettlement to be making implicit requests, since they are requesting admission to any state that is willing to admit them for resettlement.
8 This way of thinking about justice is usually found in John Rawls, *A Theory of Justice*, rev. ed. (Cambridge, MA: Belknap Press of Harvard University Press, 1999).
9 David Miller, *Principles of Social Justice* (Cambridge, MA: Harvard University Press, 1999).
10 I should say, I treat resettlement spaces as highly scarce with some hesitation, given that their scarcity is so obviously constructed by states' active resistance to refugee admission.
11 For more discussion about the meaning of vulnerability, see the contributions to Christine Straehle, ed., *Vulnerability, Autonomy, and Applied Ethics* (New York: Routledge, 2017).
12 For example, Michael Kagan, "The Beleaguered Gatekeeper: Protection Challenges Posed by UNHCR Refugee Status Determination," *International Journal of Refugee Law* 18, no. 1 (2006): 1–29; Kristin Bergtora Sandik, "Legal History: The Emergence of the African Resettlement Candidate in International Refugee Management," *International Journal of Refugee Law* 22, no. 1 (2010): 20–47.
13 Notwithstanding complicated legal and contextual questions of who "counts" as family for the purposes of recognizing and exercising this right.

14 For an account of how to rank various claims for admission, see Rainer Bauböck, "Free Movement and the Asymmetry between Exit and Entry," *Ethics and Economics* 4, no. 1 (2006): 1–7.
15 For example, see Sarah Fine, "Immigration and Discrimination," in *Migration in Political Theory: The Ethics of Movement and Membership*, ed. Sarah Fine and Lea Ypi (Oxford: Oxford University Press, 2016), 125–50.
16 Rawls, *A Theory of Justice*, rev. ed.
17 The precise format of these "encouragements" and "discouragements" is beyond the scope of this chapter.
18 Michael Walzer, "On Humanitarianism: Is Helping Others Charity, or Duty, or Both?," *Foreign Affairs* 90, no. 4 (August 2011): 69–72, 73–6, 77–80.
19 Matthew J. Gibney, "Liberal Democratic States and Responsibilities to Refugees," *American Political Science Review* 93, no. 1 (1999): 169–81.
20 We specifically asked, "Why did you choose to become a private sponsor"?
21 For more on the Canadian response to Syrian refugees, see the contributions to *Canadian Ethnic Studies* 58, no. 2, "Special issue: Canada's Syrian Refugee Program, Intergroup Relationships and Identities" (2018).
22 Joseph Raz, "On the Nature of Rights," *Mind* 93, no. 370 (1 April 1984): 194–214.
23 Paul Lungen, "Jewish and Church Groups Sponsor Eritrean Refugee from Israel," *Canadian Jewish News*, 26 June 2018, https://www.cjnews.com/news/canada/jewish-and-church-groups-sponsor-eritrean-refugee-from-israel.

4

A Port in the Storm: Resettlement and Private Sponsorship in the Broader Context of the Refugee Regime

Megan Bradley and Cate Duin

Nationally and internationally, the private sponsorship system is perhaps the best-known aspect of Canada's response to refugee crises, and it attracts significant levels of financial, political, and popular support. However, the system directly benefits only a small and select pool of refugees each year. Canada and UNHCR's cooperative efforts to "export" the private sponsorship model to other interested states raise important questions about the relationship between the private sponsorship system and responses to the millions of refugees and internally displaced persons (IDPs) who are not assisted by such efforts. The private sponsorship system has greatly benefited not only resettled refugees but also communities across Canada. Yet exporting and scaling up this system could have unintended consequences for the operation of the international refugee regime and the protection of the majority of forced migrants who remain in the global South.[1] This issue demands closer examination as other states begin piloting their own private sponsorship programs.

A growing body of literature explores the intricacies of resettlement and the Canadian private sponsorship system in particular, but comparatively little attention has been paid to the role of resettlement in the wider refugee regime, and how states' resettlement policies relate to their broader response to forced migration as a global challenge. This chapter seeks to advance the conversation by situating private refugee resettlement systems and their potential consequences in an international political context. Resettlement, including through private sponsorship systems, serves as a crucial "port in the storm" for those refugees able to access it; preserving and expanding this opportunity is essential to contemporary refugee protection. Yet the promotion of private refugee sponsorship may – however inadvertently and counterintuitively – weaken the international refugee regime.[2] The relationship between countries' involvement in resettlement and private sponsorship and their broader engagement in the international refugee regime needs to be more thoroughly explored, and the risks more forthrightly acknowledged and addressed.

This chapter explores two connected risks that major investments in resettlement, and private sponsorship of refugees (PSR) in particular, may raise vis-à-vis the broader refugee regime. First, states may use resettlement as a way of shirking their responsibilities toward other forced migrants. Second, major investments in resettlement may exacerbate misalignment between resource allocation practices and refugee protection priorities. We examine these risks in relation to Canadian government policy and discourse on resettlement and support for the international refugee regime, particularly since the election of the Trudeau government in October 2015.

Preliminary evidence from Canada provides a measure of reassurance but also reasons for concern for those who hope to see the wider adoption of PSR strengthen the international refugee regime. In some ways these risks have not fully materialized; for instance, since 2015 the Canadian government has maintained or increased support for the international refugee regime, for including forced migrants in the global South, at the same time as it has expanded and encouraged the exporting of the private sponsorship system. However, Canada's support for resettlement has provided cover for more restrictive responses to asylum-seekers, particularly those who have entered Canada by land from the United States – a dynamic that is also apparent in some of the countries that are experimenting with the private sponsorship model.[3] These risks therefore need to be closely analyzed and mitigated. They are particularly concerning as the aims of resettlement in relation to broader responses to forced migration and efforts to resolve displacement remain underspecified, even though resettlement processes benefiting a small minority of refugees now represent a major proportion of public and private Canadian support for refugees.

We begin by providing a brief review of resettlement's role in the international refugee regime and Canada's resettlement system. Then we explore potential risks associated with resettlement in relation to recent Canadian policy and practice.

RESETTLEMENT GOALS, CHALLENGES, AND DEVELOPMENTS: A BRIEF INTRODUCTION

Resettlement is the process of moving refugees from a country of first asylum to a country where they may be permanently settled. Resettled refugees are selected in advance by the state accepting them, often with support from UNHCR.[4] Resettlement's popularity as a "durable solution" to displacement, alongside local integration and voluntary repatriation, has surged and dipped throughout the decades.[5] Recent years have seen increased state interest in resettlement in some quarters, but also dramatic cuts to resettlement quotas in the aftermath of 9/11 and more recently by the United States under the Trump administration. Alongside these developments, there has been increased recognition in forced migration scholarship of the potential, but also the limitations and risks, of this approach to supporting the resolution of refugees' displacement.

One major critique of resettlement is that states may use it as a foil to shirk their broader responsibilities to other forced migrants, including asylum-seekers. Many resettlement states such as Australia, Canada, and the United States prefer the more controlled nature of resettlement to the unpredictable arrival of asylum-seekers. Resettlement thus has a migration management function: it allows states to select refugees who fit their interests and ideals, while denigrating those who take it upon themselves to move to the global North and seek asylum there as "queue-jumpers."[6] At the same time, resettled refugees are a comparatively visible population; by celebrating their support for a limited number of selected refugees, states can paper over their negligible support for even more marginalized populations, such as IDPs.

A second, related critique centres on resettlement's costliness, particularly relative to the modest number of refugees involved. Despite a clear and pressing need for resettlement spaces, in 2017 and 2018 only 0.4 percent of refugees worldwide were able to access this option. Expenditures on resettlement far outstrip the funds dedicated to support voluntary returns and local integration in the global South, avenues accessed by larger numbers of refugees.[7] While it is extremely difficult to comparatively analyze spending in support of different refugee populations and durable solutions, by some estimates

USD$135 per refugee is spent on resettlement for every $1 spent on support for refugees who remain in the global South.[8] Particularly if states scale back their spending on refugees and IDPs who remain in the global South in order to increase funds for resettlement, this may have concerning implications in terms of equity.[9] These concerns are exacerbated by the fact that the decision to invest significantly in resettlement in support of particular populations does not always seem to be guided by clear goals and even-handed needs assessments, which raises concerns about misaligned priorities and spending decisions, as well as potential arbitrariness in allocation of the benefits resettlement offers.

In the midst of the recent increased focus on resettlement, UNHCR and its member states have worked to address these critiques, particularly by trying to find ways in which resettlement may translate into improved conditions for those refugees who are not resettled. One major component of this discussion centred on the concept of the "strategic use of resettlement" (SUR). Introduced as part of the 2003 Global Consultations on International Protection, SUR was defined as the use of resettlement to benefit, directly or indirectly, other refugees, host countries, or the international refugee regime at large in addition to the small number of refugees being directly resettled.[10] It cast resettlement as a tool for protection, as a way to open up durable solutions – particularly in protracted refugee situations – and as a means for countries in the global North to demonstrate responsibility-sharing to Southern host countries. Despite the widespread agreement on the sentiment behind SUR, attempts to implement it have been largely unsuccessful.[11]

Against this backdrop of contributions to and challenges and critiques of resettlement, states began negotiating the 2016 New York Declaration on Refugees and Migrants and a new Global Compact on Refugees. The Declaration and Compact, with its Comprehensive Refugee Response Framework (CRRF) and accompanying program of action, aimed in part to reinvigorate resettlement's role in the international refugee regime, calling for increased resettlement numbers.[12] The Government of Canada's effort to "export" the PSR model is situated in the compact process, but the CRRF has been criticized as unrealistic in terms of the role that resettlement will play in responding to the vast numbers displaced worldwide.[13] Indeed, the Global Compact on Refugees, finalized in late 2018, did not succeed in revitalizing support for resettlement. There was a surge in resettlement spots in 2016, but by 2018 those gains had disappeared, partly as a result of the US retreat from leadership on resettlement, with little reason for optimism that the implementation of the refugee compact would meaningfully move the needle on the number of resettlement places available.[14] In this sense the CRRF arguably falls into the same well-meaning but half-implemented space that SUR has occupied for the past two decades.

EXPORTING THE CANADIAN PRIVATE SPONSORSHIP MODEL: DISTINCTIVE OPPORTUNITIES AND RISKS FOR THE REFUGEE REGIME

While UNHCR struggles to shape states' use of resettlement, Canada has offered to provide assistance to fellow states looking to strengthen or diversify resettlement efforts through the introduction of private sponsorship.[15] PSR involves the provision of financial but also social and emotional support to resettling refugees by private groups, including but not limited to faith communities and ethnically based community organizations. In Canada, the placement of refugees through private sponsorship has historically been carried out above and beyond state commitments to assist quotas of refugees identified by UNHCR (so-called government-assisted refugees, or GARs). The intended upshot is a larger total number of refugees resettled each year. Some argue that private sponsorship also translates into improved integration outcomes, more welcoming attitudes toward newcomers, and a more positive environment for both domestic and international policy-making related to refugees, as citizens are more directly engaged with and sympathetic to refugees' predicament.[16] Canada and UNHCR responded to increased interest in supporting refugees through resettlement in the context of the Syrian displacement crisis, and began marketing the model to other states through the Global Refugee Sponsorship Initiative (GRSI).

Beyond the general risks or tensions associated with resettlement, discussed above, there has also been a significant discussion in the literature on the specific challenges and risks associated with this privatized model. However, this conversation has focused mainly on issues such as the relationship between private sponsors and the state. PSR functions on the cornerstone principle of "additionality," the idea that those who are sponsored are above and beyond the number of already available resettlement placements as determined by the state. Perhaps the most discussed risk is that the state might not respect additionality and instead use private sponsorship as a means of privatizing resettlement – that is, it might simply "substitute and subsidize" the refugees they would otherwise resettle through publicly funded programs.[17] Another concern is that by increasing the numbers of privately sponsored refugees, there could be an eventual backlash or burn-out from the expense in time and resources, instead of a groundswell of support leading to a more positive policy environment.[18] Frustrations in the sponsor community with the slow, delay-ridden resettlement bureaucracy could prove detrimental to the state's resettlement program as citizens become disenchanted with the process and lose their motivation.[19] These concerns raise important questions for proponents of exporting the PSR model and for those countries experimenting with this approach.

However, the risks or challenges the promotion of PSR may pose for states' engagement with the international refugee regime more broadly have yet to be fully unpacked. PSR creates a unique dynamic by connecting citizens to the international refugee regime in ways that were previously managed mainly by the state itself.[20] The conversation is incomplete without further discussion of how this dynamic could create challenges for states' ability and willingness to meet their responsibilities to other refugees, and also to IDPs. Investing in PSR instead of, or in addition to, other means of supporting refugees presents a wide range of opportunities and risks, but this conversation will build on the two overarching risks associated with resettlement more generally, discussed above: the risk of enabling states to shirk their responsibilities to other groups of forced migrants, and the risk of misalignment of priorities and support for different populations with pressing protection needs.

If private sponsorship models encourage public support for and commitment to refugees, they may foster a strong base for progressive policies toward refugees across the board, locally, domestically, and internationally. However, the sense of support for refugees that is inculcated through these models may be more selective, pertaining more narrowly to the minority of refugees chosen for resettlement. Public support for refugees fostered through PSR programs may also be unable to serve as an effective counterbalance to states' complex and competing interests vis-à-vis refugees: at the same time as states may want to reap praise for morally laudable actions such as (carefully controlled) refugee resettlement, they also want to exercise tight control over other forms of movement and limit their obligations toward other groups. Thus private sponsorship models may in fact play into or further strengthen states' efforts to avoid serious obligations toward the vast numbers unable to access resettlement. Because PSR allows states to go above and beyond the numbers they would have normally resettled, it creates an image of increased support for refugees, although much of the responsibility for this increase is, of course, shouldered by private citizens. The increase in resettlement placement numbers through PSR could in theory be used to obscure or explicitly justify decreases in commitments to respond to forced migration situations abroad.

PSR may also exacerbate the risk, discussed above, of misalignment between ostensible policy priorities, decision-making, and spending patterns surrounding resettlement. The grassroots, sponsor-shaped structure of PSR is part of the strength of the system, but it may not jibe with the aims of resettlement, particularly as articulated by UNHCR. According to UNHCR, resettlement is first and foremost a protection tool, although it may also serve as a durable solution to displacement and an expression of "responsibility sharing." UNHCR urges the prioritization for resettlement of refugees with legal and physical protection needs. Other priority categories include survivors of torture or violence; refugees with severe medical needs; women, adolescents, and children "at risk"; those in need of family reunification; and refugees for whom there is no other foreseeable durable solution.[21]

Allowing sponsors to choose who they will support may increase their drive to participate in the process but simultaneously reduce the extent to which private sponsorship supports the broader goals of resettlement in the context of the international refugee regime. Larger-scale, privately supported resettlement efforts may be more likely in cases of highly visible emergencies that grip the public imagination, such as in Canada after the publication of the image of Alan Kurdi, the three-year-old Syrian refugee boy who drowned off the coast of Turkey. In contrast, those coming from less well-known or protracted refugee situations may be less likely to secure private sympathies and support. Private sponsors may be unaware of or unconvinced by the priorities and approach favoured by UNHCR. They may for example be daunted by the prospect of sponsoring refugees with serious medical needs or those who are grappling with the consequences of torture, and may instead prefer to sponsor those with family connections or other groups with whom they feel more closely connected.[22] Family members and other refugees with personal connections to potential sponsors may of course themselves be in urgent need of resettlement, and there are often undeniably arbitrary aspects to decision-making by UNHCR and government agencies regarding resettlement priorities. Yet if, in theory, scarce resettlement places should go as a matter of priority to those in particularly pressing need, then private sponsorship may not necessarily be the most effective route to achieve this goal.

RISKS AND REWARDS: PSR'S RELATIONSHIP WITH THE WIDER CANADIAN RESPONSE TO FORCED MIGRATION

The risks posed by the exportation and "scaling up" of Canada's PSR model are dynamic. The ways in which these risks materialize, and to what effect, depend significantly on which countries take up the model, for what reasons, and in what ways. Canada's recent experience expanding engagement in PSR presents an opportunity to examine how these risks may unfold.

Avoiding Responsibilities to Other Forced Migrants

Analysis of Canadian policy and practice on refugees and forced migration since 2015 suggests that in some senses, the increased focus on resettling refugees to Canada under the Trudeau government has not come at the expense of support to forced migrants who remain in the global South. Though there were signs of decreased Canadian commitment to the refugee regime in the early 2010s, the early years of the Trudeau government saw some signs of increased commitment, including in financial terms. Though a very rough indicator, donations to UNHCR reflect state commitment to the refugee regime; at the same time as resettlement places in Canada and expenditures on resettlement increased, Canada modestly increased its financial contributions to UNHCR in support of displaced populations in the global South. In the early 2010s, Canada's donations to UNHCR hovered in the range of USD$70 million per year. With the change in government in late 2015, there was an unprecedented increase in 2016, with a donation of more than $117 million. In 2017, however, Canadian contributions decreased to some $81 million, and fell to $72.9 million in 2018.[23] These contributions must be interpreted not only in relation to changes in government in Canada and an expanded domestic focus on resettlement, but also in light of growing demand, as the number of displaced persons in need of assistance increased steadily in this period.

Although these numbers suggest that Canada's increased focus on resettlement, including PSR, has not necessarily undercut its commitment to other displaced populations, this remains a palpable concern in the Canadian case, and a pertinent risk for other states that might implement private sponsorship systems inspired by the Canadian model. Management of this risk depends greatly on a government's broad stance on refugees. For example, Australia, which is experimenting with the private sponsorship model, has been explicit in nurturing the perception that there are "good" refugees who wait patiently in the South to be resettled, and "bad" refugees who move without authorization to countries in the global North to seek asylum. The possibility, however minuscule, of a refugee being selected for resettlement is used to legitimize harsh and even draconian policies to curtail unorderly movements.[24] While the Trudeau government has cultivated a reputation for welcoming refugees, this restrictive logic is also apparent in the Canadian context: Many Canadians are wary of the rising numbers of asylum-seekers arriving in Canada from across the US border since the election of US president Donald Trump in 2016, a sentiment fanned by politicians arguing that Canada already does its part for refugees through the resettlement system. Reliance on the Safe Third Country Agreement between the United States and Canada, and recent moves to further reduce or remove the eligibility of asylum claimants who enter the country across the southern border, bring into question the "pro-refugee" branding advanced through the PSR system. The emphasis on supporting refugees through resettlement, including PSR, may foster the view that responding to refugees is more a matter of charity than obligation – setting the stage for the government to shirk its legal responsibilities toward inland asylum claimants.

More broadly, in its public statements and policy interventions on forced migration, Canada has made its unique contributions to resettlement particularly prominent, instead of pressing for improved responses to, for example, the vast numbers of IDPs without the resources or opportunities to flee their countries and access resettlement channels. This further shows that the risk that a strong focus on resettlement may substitute for leadership in support of other forced migrants is all too real.

Misaligned Priorities

The Canadian government's management of the misaligned priorities risk has also been a concern. Resettlement, particularly PSR, continues to be focused on particular, high-profile populations (often in emergency contexts) and shaped by personal networks, rather than a clearly strategized contribution to meeting clear aims in the international refugee regime, such as ensuring that resettlement places are allocated first and foremost to those with pressing protection needs, and achieving SUR goals.

For example, in a four-month period between November 2015 and February 2016, Canada welcomed over 25,000 Syrian refugees, more than the roughly 24,000 refugees resettled to Canada throughout 2014. Between 4 November 2015 and 29 January 2017, more than 40,000 Syrians were resettled compared to the nearly 19,000 resettled from all other locations during all of 2016.[25] Syrians thus received many more placements than other groups, and it is not clear that those selected by private sponsorship groups were those facing particularly pronounced protection concerns (a factor that is certainly very difficult to measure).[26] The introduction of the "Blended Visa Office-Referred" (BVOR) program, discussed by McNally in this volume, has made important contributions toward mitigating this risk. The BVOR program links refugees with significant protection concerns who have been identified by UNHCR as in need of resettlement, with Canadian private sponsors; the Canadian government and the private sponsors split the costs of financially supporting the refugees in their first year in Canada. In this way, the program has expanded access to resettlement in Canada for those refugees with pressing protection needs but without family and personal connections that would help them access PSR. Scaling up the BVOR model, and integrating it with efforts to "export" private sponsorship approaches to resettlement, will be integral to ensuring that PSR is well harmonized with the goals of refugee protection and the resolution of protracted refugee situations.

Governmental Discourse on Resettlement and Private Sponsorship

In order to deepen this analysis and better understand how the Government of Canada perceives and articulates the goals of the PSR system and its relationship to Canada's engagement in the international refugee regime more broadly, we conducted a discourse analysis of speeches and statements related to refugees delivered by senior officials in Global Affairs Canada and Immigration, Refugees and Citizenship Canada from 4 November 2015 to 1 June 2018.[27] We found that while Canadian government officials verbalized a commitment to responsibility-sharing with host countries, in its public discourse there was no clear articulation of Canadian policies and practices related to forced migration. Instead, the government's discourse as it related to refugees and resettlement was most strongly characterized by affirmations of Canadian identity as compassionate and pro-diversity. Rhetoric around refugee resettlement was a vehicle for Canada to assert its identity and leadership in the international community, particularly as the government changed from a long-standing Conservative government to the leadership of Liberal Prime Minister Justin Trudeau. In line with previous appraisals of how resettlement was portrayed throughout the 2000s and 2010s,[28] these discursive choices underspecified the role of resettlement within the government's overall approach to forced migration, domestically and internationally.

Although the connection between resettlement and the other durable solutions is not clearly communicated, it is not entirely missing from the government's discourse. There is consistent messaging that Canada intends to share responsibility for forced migration with host countries. Government officials repeatedly acknowledge the burden placed on Southern host countries arising from their proximity to countries in conflict. In their official remarks, after recognizing the difficulties faced by host countries, officials often discuss concrete policies to alleviate the burden, or more fairly share responsibilities to refugees. For instance, at the Trudeau government's first UNHCR Executive Committee meeting, the Canadian representative stated: "Canada recognizes the immense challenges faced by states in close proximity to significant displacement crises, and commends the generosity of states hosting large numbers of refugees. It is not for them to bear the responsibility alone."[29] This statement prioritizing responsibility-sharing was echoed repeatedly in subsequent government discourse.

While the government does state its support for responsibility-sharing, the *means* by which it intends to do so are not completely apparent, particularly in relation to PSR. Responsibility sharing through funding international humanitarian responses to refugees is the most clearly articulated aspect of the government's approach. This was reflected, for example, in the announcement by Marie-Claude Bibeau, Canada's Minister of International Development, of the government's strategy for addressing the crisis in the Middle East: "[Host countries for Syrian refugees] need help. That is why Canada is making a multi-year commitment to provide over $1 billion in humanitarian and development assistance as part of our comprehensive, whole-of-government strategy, which also balances security and stability."[30] Although the government frequently and explicitly links resettlement and the provision of donor funds with responsibility-sharing, there are few details regarding *how* resettlement will meaningfully lighten the load of host countries, given that resettlement quotas remain infinitesimal compared to the scale of the challenge. In her address to the Syria Donors Conference in February 2016, Minister Bibeau said:

> Jordan has welcomed 1.4 million Syrian refugees ... Lebanon is also facing huge challenges, with over a million Syrian refugees in a country of 4 million people. And let's not forget the millions of Palestinian, Iraqi and other refugees throughout the region. Syria's neighbours are responding to the crisis. But we, as members of the broader international community, also have a shared responsibility to act. Last November, Canada put in place a special operation to admit 25,000 Syrian refugees in three months. This was in addition to our usual level of 14,000 refugees per year.[31]

It is clear that Minister Bibeau is saying that Canada will provide resettlement placements well above and beyond previous levels, but these numbers are almost farcically low in comparison to the numbers hosted by Lebanon and Jordan. Beyond simply stating the number of refugees resettled, official public discourse generally fails to specifically articulate how resettlement generally, and PSR in particular, will enhance responsibility-sharing or address the issue of protracted displacement.

Although Canada was an early proponent of SUR, and of broader efforts to support the resolution of protracted displacement, in recent discourse there is little or no connection made between SUR and Canada's resettlement policies. In the materials analyzed, SUR is rarely mentioned. In an exception to this trend, Canada's 2016 statement to the UNHCR Executive Committee flags SUR as a part of the country's support for UNHCR: "Canada will support UNHCR in maintaining a strong focus on solutions programming, using innovative and practical approaches, and promoting the strategic use of refugee resettlement."[32]

There is also little to no clear discussion of why some individuals and groups are offered resettlement while others are meant to access other durable solutions. The only resettling groups explicitly mentioned in public discourse in this period are the Syrian refugees and, to a much lesser extent, the Yazidis. The resettlement of both groups is portrayed as an emergency measure rather than as part of a strategic plan for resettlement to Canada. Such an emergency response is arguably entirely appropriate, given the scale of Syrians' need and the value of seizing opportunities to tap into general public support for refugees. However, it also sits in tension with attempts to shape resettlement into a more strategic and less ad hoc response to forced migration. The lack of communication about which refugees become the focus of major resettlement initiatives and why leads to the perception that the Canadian resettlement system is fundamentally ad hoc. Why, for example, has there been no major resettlement push for the Rohingya refugees forced out of Myanmar? The prioritization of some groups over others raises complex ethical and political concerns, but because Canada has failed to broach the issue at all – despite positioning itself as a leading proponent of resettlement – the discussion does not evolve.

In contrast to the discursive murkiness surrounding the strategic positioning of Canada's resettlement program in relation to its broader engagement in the refugee regime, recent government discourse is remarkably direct regarding the proposed connection between resettlement on the one hand, and Canadian identity and values and its role in the international community, on the other. Three consistent themes emerge in relation to this aspect of the discourse. First, compassion is central to Canadian identity. Second, diversity is a key component of Canada's strength as a country. Third, Canada can serve as an example for the world at this point in history. These three themes thread through government discourse aimed at the international community as well as at the general Canadian public. Critically, in this discourse the private sponsorship system is positioned as the pinnacle of Canadian leadership and the values that undergird it. Throughout the government's discourse on refugees between November 2015 and November 2018, the private sponsorship of Syrian refugees was pointed to as the foremost concrete example of how Canada "walks the walk," matching words with action. In an address at the Canadian Immigration Summit, for example, Liberal MP Minister Hussen stated:

> Canadian private sponsorship of refugees ... is now being sought after by many, many countries in the world. They're saying teach us how you do this. They really love our PSR model ... So through our leadership, we're not only setting an example for the world but we're actually encouraging other countries to resettle more refugees and explore different models that we have tested over decades.[33]

In short, the discourse we analyzed does not communicate how resettlement and private sponsorship programs in particular strategically link up with the overarching refugee regime, beyond general platitudes about responsibility sharing. There is also no open articulation of why some populations are left out of resettlement efforts, nor is there discussion of the role of resettlement in protracted displacement situations. Instead, much of the discourse portrays three strong messages pertaining to the relationship between resettlement, particularly PSR, and Canadian national identity. These claims may not appear immediately pertinent to contemporary debates about the refugee regime, yet they point to the role that resettlement can play as a staging ground for identity politics. Notwithstanding the risks discussed above, one of the most significant contributions PSR may make vis-à-vis the refugee regime writ large may be in fostering more supportive sentiments toward refugees among the citizenries of states in the global North, inculcating the idea that assisting refugees is part of the national character, and positioning governments to take stronger leadership roles in the refugee regime – an all too pressing challenge given the United States' post-2016 retreat from leadership in the refugee regime, and the rise of ever-fiercer anti-refugee sentiment across much of the global North.

CONCLUSION

If Canada is to continue to market PSR internationally, there is a clear need for more discussion of the envisioned relationship between resettlement and the broader international refugee regime. This chapter sought to advance such a discussion through the consideration of two broad, interrelated risks associated with the expansion of private sponsorship systems: it might inadvertently enable states to shirk their responsibilities toward other groups of forced migrants; and it might perpetuate misalignment between priorities and action in support of refugee protection and assistance. We examined these risks in relation to recent Canadian experiences, concluding that while some aspects of these risks have been mitigated, in other senses these risks have been borne out in troubling policies and practices that eschew responsibilities toward asylum-seekers arriving in Canada from the United States, and that perpetuate the marginalization of the majority of forced migrants who remain in the global South, unable to access resettlement opportunities. Depending on the motivations and approaches of other states experimenting with private sponsorship, these risks may be amplified, and bring into question the wisdom of exporting the PSR model. If, however, these risks are forthrightly acknowledged and addressed, the promotion of private sponsorship may help ensure that resettlement serves as a port in the storm for more refugees.

NOTES

1 Broadly, the term "global North" denotes countries in Europe and North America as well as Australia and New Zealand, while "global South" refers to those typically less affluent states outside these regions.
2 Roughly, regimes entail the establishment of explicit or implicit norms and international organizations focused on particular global governance issues. The key elements of the international refugee regime are the international laws states have negotiated on refugees, including the 1951 Refugee Convention, and the international organizations they have created to address this challenge, particularly UNHCR. Alongside these foundational institutions, a broader range of norms and organizations have emerged pertaining to other, related forms of forced migration, such as internal displacement. See James Milner and Krystyna Wojnarowicz, "Power in the Global Refugee Regime," *Refuge* 33, no. 1 (2017): 8–9.
3 On these dynamics, see for example the chapter in this volume by Vogl, Hoang, and Hirsch.
4 Joanne van Selm, "Refugee Resettlement," in *The Oxford Handbook of Refugee and Forced Migration Studies*, ed. Elena Fiddian-Qasmiyeh, Gil Loescher, Katy Long, and Nando Sigona (Oxford: Oxford University Press, 2014), 2–4.
5 Shauna Labman, "Resettlement's Renaissance: A Cautionary Advocacy," *Refuge: Canada's Journal on Refugees* 24, no. 2 (2007): 35–47.
6 Joanne van Selm, "The Strategic Use of Resettlement: Changing the Face of Protection?," *Refuge: Canada's Journal on Refugees* 22, no. 1 (2004): 39–48; Alexander Betts, "Resettlement: Where's the Evidence, What's

the Strategy?" *Forced Migration Review* 54 (2017): 73–5 at 74; Labman, "Resettlement's Renaissance," 439–40; Jennifer Hyndman and Wenona Giles, *Refugees in Extended Exile: Living on the Edge* (London: Routledge, 2017).

7 Betts, "Resettlement"; van Selm, "The Strategic Use of Resettlement"; Randall Hansen, "The Comprehensive Refugee Response Framework: A Commentary," *Journal of Refugee Studies* 31, no. 2 (2018): 131–51.

8 Betts, "Resettlement," 73.

9 Michael Lanphier, "Sponsorship: Organizational, Sponsor, and Refugee Perspectives," *Journal of International Migration and Integration* 4, no. 2 (2003): 244.

10 UNHCR, *The Strategic Use of Resettlement: A Discussion Paper Prepared by the Working Group on Resettlement*, 3 June 2003, accessed 1 June 2018, http://www.refworld.org/docid/41597a824.html; Debra Pressé and Jessie Thomson, "The Resettlement Challenge: Integration of Refugees from Protracted Refugee Situations," *Refuge: Canada's Journal on Refugees* 25, no. 1 (2008): 95.

11 Joanne van Selm, *Great Expectations: A Review of the Strategic Use of Resettlement* (Geneva: UNHCR, 2013), 14–26.

12 United Nations, *New York Declaration*, 2016, http://www.unhcr.org/57e39d987.

13 Hansen, "The Comprehensive Refugee Response Framework," 15.

14 Ibid., 6–7.

15 Global Refugee Sponsorship Initiative, 1 June 2018, http://www.refugeesponsorship.org.

16 Thais Bessa, "From Political Instrument to Protection Tool? Resettlement of Refugees and North-South Relations," *Refuge* 26, no. 1 (2009): 91–100.

17 Shauna Labman and Madison Pearlman, "Blending, Bargaining, and Burden-Sharing: Canada's Resettlement Programs," *Journal of International Migration and Integration* 19, no. 1 (2018): 441–5.

18 Lanphier, "Sponsorship: Organizational, Sponsor, and Refugee Perspectives," 243–4.

19 Barbara Treviranus and Michael Casasola, "Canada's Private Sponsorship of Refugees Program: A Practitioners Perspective of Its Past and Future," *Journal of International Migration and Integration* 4, no. 2 (2003): 178–85; Labman and Pearlman, "Blending, Bargaining, and Burden-Sharing," 445–6.

20 Ekaterina Yahyaoui Krivenko, "Hospitality and Sovereignty: What Can We Learn From the Canadian Private Sponsorship of Refugees Program?," *International Journal of Refugee Law* 24, no. 3 (2012): 594.

21 UNHCR, *UNHCR Resettlement Handbook* (Geneva: UNHCR, 2004).

22 Labman and Pearlman, "Blending, Bargaining, and Burden-Sharing," 445–6.
23 *Contributions to UNHCR for Budget Year 2010*, accessed 20 May 2018, http://www.unhcr.org/partners/donors/4c0e031b9/contributions-unhcr-budget-year-2010-31-december-2010.html; *Contributions to UNHCR for Budget Year 2011*, accessed 20 May 2018, http://www.unhcr.org/4ffc0a609.pdf; *Contributions to UNHCR for Budget Year 2012*, accessed 20 May 2018, http://www.unhcr.org/partners/donors/4df1d0449/contributions-unhcr-budget-year-2012-31-december-2012.html; *Contributions to UNHCR for Budget Year 2013*, accessed 20 May 2018, http://www.unhcr.org/partners/donors/51c991a79/contributions-unhcr-budget-year-2013-31-december-2013.html; *Contributions to UNHCR for Budget Year 2014*, accessed 20 May 2018, http://www.unhcr.org/partners/donors/536c960a9/contributions-unhcr-budget-year-2014-07-april-2015.html?query=contributions%202015; *Contributions to UNHCR for Budget Year 2015*, accessed 20 May 2018, http://www.unhcr.org/partners/donors/558a639f9/contributions-unhcr-budget-year-2015-31-december-2015.html; *Contributions to UNHCR for Budget Year 2016*, accessed 20 May 2018, http://www.unhcr.org/partners/donors/575e74567/contributions-unhcr-budget-year-2016-30-september-2016.html; *Contributions to UNHCR for Budget Year 2017*, accessed 20 May 2018, http://www.unhcr.org/en-us/partners/donors/5954c4257/contributions-unhcr-budget-year-2017.html.
24 Hyndman and Giles, Refugees in Extended Exile.
25 For total resettlement numbers in 2014 and 2016, see "Facts and Figures 2016: Immigration Overview – Permanent Residents – Annual IRCC Updates: 02. Canada - Permanent Residents by Category, 2007–2016," 30 November 2017, accessed 20 May 2018, http://www.cic.gc.ca/opendata-donneesouvertes/data/IRCC_FF_PR_2016_02_E.xls; for Syrian resettlement numbers between November 2015 and February 2016 as well as November 2015 and January 2017, see Citizenship Canada, "#WelcomeRefugees: Key Figures," 27 February 2017, accessed 20 May 2018, https://www.canada.ca/en/immigration-refugees-citizenship/services/refugees/welcome-syrian-refugees/key-figures.html.
26 On the possibility that resettlement places are not necessarily allocated to those facing pronounced protection risks, see Cameron and Labman's introduction to this volume, where they discuss the category of generalized risk in the Country of Asylum class as opposed to the Convention Refugee class.
27 Our discourse analysis was completed through a scan of the current government's Web-archived statements and speeches as available from the

prime minister's office, IRCC, and GAC. Out of all the materials available between 4 November 2015 and 1 June 2018, we catalogued eighty-four speeches and statements containing references to refugees, resettlement, and protracted conflicts made by PM Justin Trudeau; IRCC Minister John McCallum; IRCC Minister Ahmed Hussen; GAC Minister Marie-Claude Bibeau; GAC Minister Stéphane Dion; GAC Minister Chrystia Freeland; Ambassador Michael Grant; Michael Bonser of the Permanent Mission of Canada to the UN; Permanent Representative of Canada to UN Marc-André Blanchard; Catherine Boucher, Counsellor to the Permanent Mission to the United Nations; Minister Harji Sajjran; and Ambassador Louise Blake, Deputy Permanent Representative of Canada to the UN. The speeches were made in front of international audiences at the UN and domestically at press conferences as well as public events. We then completed an inductive discourse analysis of these speeches and statements, with particular focus on discourse around PSR.

28 See Sharryn Aiken, "Of Gods and Monsters: National Security and Canadian Refugee Policy," *Revue Québécoise de droit international* 14, no. 2 (2001): 1–51; Catherine Dauvergne, *Humanitarianism, Identity, and Nation: Migration Laws in Canada and Australia* (Vancouver: UBC Press, 2000); Labman and Pearlman, "Blending, Bargaining, and Burden-Sharing"; Michael Lanphier, "Sponsorship: Organizational, Sponsor, and Refugee Perspectives," 237–56; Patti Tamara Lenard, "Resettling Refugees: Is Private Sponsorship a Just Way Forward?," *Journal of Global Ethics* 12, no. 3 (2016): 300–10; Alexandra Mann, "Refugees Who Arrive By Boat and Canada's Commitment to the Refugee Convention: A Discursive Analysis," *Refuge: Canada's Journal on Refugees* 26, no. 2 (2009): 191–206; Pressé and Thomson, "The Resettlement Challenge."

29 "Protection Statement," Speech, Government of Canada Intervention to the 67th Session of the UNHCR Executive Committee, United Nations, Geneva, Switzerland, 3–7 March 2016, accessed 20 May 2018, http://www.international.gc.ca/genev/statements-declarations/protection_statement2016.aspx?lang=eng

30 Marie-Claude Bibeau, "Press Conference to Announce Canada's New Strategy to Respond to Middle East Crisis," 8 February 2016, accessed 1 June 2018, https://www.canada.ca/en/global-affairs/news/2016/02/address-by-minister-bibeau-at-press-conference-to-announce-canada-s-new-strategy-to-respond-to-middle-east-crisis.html.

31 Marie-Claude Bibeau, "Address to Syria Donor's Conference," 4 February 2016, accessed 1 June 2018, https://www.canada.ca/en/global-affairs/news/2016/02/address-by-minister-bibeau-to-the-syria-donors-conference.html.

32 Marie-Claude Bibeau, "Press Conference to Announce Canada's New Strategy."
33 Ahmed Hussen, "Speech at Canadian Immigration Summit," 9 May 2017, accessed 1 June 2018, https://www.canada.ca/en/news/advanced-news-search/news-results.html?typ=speeches&dprtmnt=departmentofcitizenshipandimmigration&start=2017-01-01&end=&.

PART TWO

Cases

5

Religious Heritage, Institutionalized Ethos, and Synergies: The Mennonite Central Committee and Canada's Private Sponsorship of Refugees Program

Thea Enns, Luann Good Gingrich, and Kaylee Perez

Mennonite Central Committee (MCC) was founded in 1920 when famine and the decimation of Mennonite communities during the Russian Revolution stirred Mennonites in North America to respond to the need of their co-religionists.[1] In addition to aid, resettlement in Canada was an important aspect of the work of the newly formed organization.[2] Between 1923 and 1930, Canada accepted more than 21,000 Mennonites from the Soviet Union.[3] According to William Janzen, a long-time director of MCC Canada's Ottawa office, the historical experience of MCC in refugee resettlement served as a precedent for Canada's Private Sponsorship of Refugees (PSR) program, which was established more than fifty years later.[4] Janzen also served as one of the negotiators of Canada's original Master Agreement, which MCC signed in 1979. This agreement with the federal government provided the legal basis for MCC to work with local congregations, which in turn offered organizational and logistical support for groups of citizens to privately sponsor refugees. Although some provincial programs have intermittently faced periods of decreased capacity,[5] MCC has successfully sustained a vibrant refugee sponsorship program among Mennonite churches for more than forty years.

This chapter examines how and why MCC has maintained a commitment to refugee sponsorship for forty years. We argue that this is largely due to its historical beginnings, which were steeped in refugee resettlement; to its credibility as a Sponsorship Agreement Holder (SAH); and to its long history and substantial presence in international development work. Equally important are its structure and its grassroots connections with Mennonite and related congregations in North America. This has resulted in unique synergies between MCC as an organization and the congregations that comprise its base of support, many of which have engaged in multiple sponsorships over many years. Using MCC Ontario as a case example, we report on a community-based qualitative study of its constituent groups (CGs; in the main, Mennonite congregations), examining MCC's model of sponsorship, which has its roots in a specific religious tradition and refugee history. A guiding question for this research is: What are the specific features of MCC and its CGs that have motivated, anchored, and sustained refugee sponsorship?[6]

A comment about terminology: for the purposes of this chapter, when necessary, the various MCC entities will be clearly differentiated, for example, MCC Canada and MCC Ontario. However, it is important to note that "MCC" in most cases is not a specific legal entity; rather, it is a designation used for the organization as a whole or some combination of its parts. We discuss the structure of MCC in more detail below.

METHODOLOGY

Our research was conducted within a community-based framework. The research purpose, question, and design were collectively formulated, and the data generation was collectively conducted, through a partnership comprising researchers at York University, the MCC Ontario Refugee Sponsorship and Settlement Associate, and the MCC Ontario Refugee Program Coordinator. The research reported in this chapter is part of a larger project that aims to measure processes and outcomes of social exclusion and inclusion for immigrant and refugee newcomers in Canada.

Qualitative data were gathered in 2018 through focus groups with CGs of MCC Ontario and interviews with previously sponsored refugee newcomers.[7] Focus group discussions and interviews were audio-recorded and transcribed. Discussions with sponsors centred on the following topics: expectations or goals of sponsorship, values and guiding principles of sponsorship, shifting and growing relationships between sponsor and sponsored refugees over time, best practices, and personal experiences of sponsorship. Demographic information for each focus group participant was collected prior to each focus group. Thematic analysis of the focus group data was conducted through a collaborative and iterative approach that combined independent analyses by authors Enns and Good Gingrich with analysis consultation with MCC Ontario program coordinators.

Seven focus groups were conducted with five to eight individuals each, totalling forty-nine participants from twenty-one churches. One sponsoring church was affiliated with the Evangelical Missionary Church of Canada; all other congregations in the sample were members of Mennonite denominations that are formal contributing constituents of MCC, with the majority belonging to the Mennonite Church.[8] Within these CGs, most respondents were ethnically Mennonite, with primarily Dutch-Russian or Swiss-German Mennonite backgrounds.[9] Through its database, MCC Ontario identified sponsors across Ontario and provided formal invitations on behalf of the organization. Because a primary objective of the research was to understand the nature and development of sponsorship roles and relationships over time, the sample of CGs was limited to those that had sponsored a family or individual prior to the 2015–16 Syrian resettlement efforts. Contact information for CGs before 2007 was limited, thus our sample captured sponsors between 2007 and 2015. However, as the data reveal, several congregations had by then been sponsoring for decades, even since 1979. A purposive sample of groups that had engaged in multiple sponsorships prior to 2015 was selected from regions in Ontario with the largest representation of these groups: Waterloo Region, Stratford, Niagara, and the Greater Toronto Area. With the aim being multiplicity of perspectives, purposive sampling was further employed to add three additional focus groups: (1) sponsors from the Leamington area, to gather a rural perspective; (2) sponsors from Ottawa Mennonite Church, to gather the experiences of the longest-standing CG with the most completed sponsorships; and (3) a CG comprising individuals who had attended two different Mennonite churches and sponsored through MCC but independent of either congregation. We also interviewed MCC's National Migration and Resettlement Program Coordinator, Brian Dyck (co-author of another chapter in this volume), who provided information on MCC and its sponsorship program. Direct quotations from members of sponsorship focus groups are identified by the order in which the focus groups were conducted (e.g., FG#3).

MCC AND CANADA'S PRIVATE SPONSORSHIP OF REFUGEES PROGRAM

MCC defines itself as "a worldwide ministry of Anabaptist churches."[10] It has national offices in both Winnipeg, Manitoba (MCC Canada) and Akron, Pennsylvania (MCC US). Six distinct Canadian Mennonite denominations are the sponsoring denominations of MCC, the largest being Mennonite Church Canada and the Canadian Conference of Mennonite Brethren Churches. A key achievement of MCC since its inception in 1920 was negotiating with the Canadian government to accept Mennonites fleeing war and famine in the Soviet Union, with the understanding that Canadian Mennonite communities would provide for and resettle these newcomers. Over the following decades, MCC expanded its relief and international development work well beyond assistance to fellow Mennonites.

In 1963, MCC was formed, in part to access funding from the Canadian International Development Agency (CIDA) for MCC's expanding international development programs.[11] Provincial entities (and in the United States, regional offices) were also established, and they are the principal means by which MCC connects to its local supporting congregations. While MCC is the SAH, provincial staff work with the federal government (now Immigration, Refugees, and Citizenship Canada, or IRCC) and local congregations to match refugee newcomers with sponsors, facilitate the necessary paperwork, train and support congregations in this endeavour, and connect them to local refugee services.

The 1960s saw increasing concern among Mennonites over the Vietnam War and the displacement of Vietnamese. MCC had workers in Vietnam since 1954 following the First Indochina War,[12] and as media coverage of the Vietnam War grew, many Mennonites felt a "sense of conscientious responsibility."[13] The plight of refugees was viewed by many Mennonites, who identified with a religious commitment to pacifism and non-violent resistance, as a horrific outcome of the injustice of war.[14] It was in this context that MCC recognized the potential of private sponsorship. Furthermore, in practical terms, MCC was prepared to assist in the Indochinese crisis because of its on-the-ground presence in Vietnam.[15]

At its January 1979 annual meeting, MCC expressed its desire to increase the resettlement of refugees through a mechanism that would lighten the personal liability placed on individuals and groups that sought to sponsor refugees.[16] Janzen, then director of MCC's Ottawa office, and other MCC leaders initiated conversations with senior immigration officials to negotiate possible approaches. Subsequently, Janzen and ministry staff drafted a Master Agreement that enabled MCC to claim liability for constituent groups sponsoring refugees through their organization.[17] MCC became the first Master Agreement Holder (a term later changed to "Sponsorship Agreement Holder," signing the document on 5 March 1979. MCC's leadership in negotiating the Master Agreement was pivotal. As Janzen writes, "within weeks most of the other national church bodies had signed virtually identical M.A.s [sic]."[18]

MCC's commitment to Canada's private sponsorship program has not waned since this time. In terms of both commitment and capacity, MCC is one of the largest and most active of the 120 SAHs in Canada; estimates are that more than 12,500 refugees arrived in Canada through MCC's sponsorship program between 1979 and 1 July, 2018.[19] Since 2014, MCC constituent groups have sponsored between 3 and 4 percent of annual landings through the PSR and Blended Visa Office-Referred (BVOR) programs in Canada, reaching a high of 8 percent (or 1,824 of 22,796 arrivals) in 2016.[20] On a national level, MCC has played a leading role in supporting and promoting Canada's private sponsorship program on the SAH Council and in UNHCR consultations.[21] Governments in other countries have turned to MCC for advice and support on piloting and growing private refugee sponsorship programs.[22]

Some SAHs select refugees to sponsor through named cases; MCC, by contrast, is committed to meeting the resettlement needs of any refugee, regardless of religion or culture.[23] This was a deliberate decision made after a review of the sponsorship program in 2008, when MCC stipulated that at least 60 percent of all cases were to be referred by UNHCR or the Canada Visa Office so as to prioritize those who had been identified as most in need. Further demonstrating this commitment, MCC resettled approximately one third of all BVOR cases (refugees identified for resettlement by UNHCR) in 2017.[24]

LOCAL SYNERGY: A CHURCH CULTURE OF SPONSORSHIP ROOTED IN MCC'S REPUTATION

A prominent theme in focus group discussions was institutional synergy – a mutually supportive and constitutive relationship – between

MCC and affiliated churches. Congregations that have maintained long-term engagement in private sponsorship are heavily reliant on MCC – on its structure, reputation, and staff support. Conversely, the stability of MCC's refugee program is owed to the sustained engagement of individual congregations.

As the "active arm" of its constituent Mennonite churches, MCC enables congregations and their members to become engaged in "relief, development and peace in the name of Christ"[25] at home and abroad. The tight connection between Mennonite churches and MCC was articulated by a focus group member: "Our churches are all part of MCC, we are constituents of MCC – we see MCC as the extension of our local congregation that does the local and international relief and development work and MCC as an extension of the community and development work" (FG#2). As a SAH, MCC connects with local churches through its provincial offices and enables their direct engagement with refugee issues. In the context of refugee sponsorship, this commitment is a two-way street. As churches develop and embrace a culture of sponsorship, MCC buttresses their efforts with its reputation in refugee sponsorship and international aid and development, lending credibility to and supporting sustainability for church sponsorship efforts. With nearly forty years of experience supporting a wide range of congregations and non-church groups in refugee sponsorship, MCC has become well-known and widely respected in Canada and around the world.

Many sponsors attributed MCC's strong reputation to its long involvement with refugee assistance. MCC's involvement reassured CGs that they would be supported throughout the sponsorship process. One focus group member noted that even for sponsors who were not members of a church or religious group, MCC "represent[s] some trust, that this is going to be an alright organization to funnel money for sponsorship ... They do represent a vehicle that can be used" (FG#7). Other CGs also recognized MCC's reputation as vital, especially in terms of the financial aspect of sponsorship: "The partnership that we have with MCC also gives credibility to people ... The people in the congregation will feel, I guess, more comfortable about supporting the refugee program knowing that a respected organization like MCC is supporting us doing the work" (FG#6). Similarly, one respondent noted that respect for MCC reached beyond the Mennonite community: "There are people who aren't a part of a faith group who have contributed both financially and otherwise [to refugee sponsorship] because it involves MCC. The reputation of MCC as being a reputable group to give oversight to this sort of thing is huge" (FG#2).

Respondents described the importance of their trust in MCC – it gave them confidence to employ their own shared resources in sponsorship. This trust is also attributed to the practical support provided by MCC. Its capacity for sponsorship exceeds that of many other SAHs, especially those led primarily by volunteers with few paid staff or none at all.[26] Demonstrating the importance placed on refugee sponsorship, MCC's Ontario office has two full-time staff dedicated to the program who play a major role in motivating and supporting sponsors as well as shaping sponsorship relationships; they organize events and conferences to encourage and inform sponsors, while also appealing to churches to support specific cases requiring resettlement, and to support their sponsorship efforts in general. This level of engagement with local congregations is mirrored in other provincial MCC offices.

In addition to all this, long-standing congregational structures, practices, and relationships position affiliating churches to sponsor refugees. Congregations are established collectives whose members can provide financial and in-kind resources, form sponsorship groups, replace group members as necessary, generate additional supports and resources, and connect with community networks, besides offering ready access to physical spaces for holding events or meetings. Many churches have set aside funds for refugee support; this may involve a missions budget, a benevolence fund, or even a specific budget line item for refugee resettlement needs. Furthermore, a congregation can provide a financial and social safety net – that is, a pool of potential resources. Some groups have expanded the resources of their church by teaming up with other Mennonite congregations.

For some churches, refugee sponsorship is part of the culture of the congregation: sponsorship has become an obvious means to participate in the church's activities. As one focus group member put it, sponsorship is "what we do" (FG#5a). Many of the respondents who articulated this culture of sponsorship were members of a church with a sponsoring history that had begun with Indochinese refugees four decades ago. Several sponsors recalled their first involvement with refugee issues in the late 1970s and early 1980s; some personally participated in the church's sponsorship group at that time, while others remembered their parents' involvement with a refugee family.

Within the study sample, Ottawa Mennonite Church had sponsored the highest number of refugees – around 180 individuals since 1979[27]

– and its history is fused with the origins of the PSR program. Members of the church's long-standing Refugee Assistance Program have been engaged in sponsorship for between five to twenty years. One member noted that "it's just assumed that this is who we are and what we do," and that refugee sponsorship has become "a part of our identity as a church" (FG#6). Similarly, a sponsor from First Mennonite Church in Vineland reported that sponsorship is part of the culture or "rhythm" of the church, and described a system that had been developed to ensure that sponsorship is effective and efficient (FG#5a). Over the years, the rotation of individuals engaging in sponsorship or donating to the cause has increased awareness of refugee issues and of the resettlement program, further defining the church's identity and imparting a sense of duty among its members to participate in sponsorship.

GLOBAL SYNERGY: INTERPERSONAL AND INSTITUTIONAL CONNECTIONS ACROSS PLACE AND TIME

MCC's extensive international development work and the involvement of North American Mennonite churches were described as important factors for maintaining a vibrant refugee sponsorship program. MCC has programs in fifty-six countries and is involved in another ten, with 1,118 workers around the world,[28] and it depends on both local staff and a large contingent of North American Mennonite volunteers to implement its international programs. MCC has a unique capacity to provide popular international programs, and those programs have resulted a community of returned alumni – known as "MCCers" – who have developed interpersonal bonds in local congregations.

Church members who have worked overseas with MCC offer a global perspective that helps motivate the congregation to sponsor refugees. One respondent noted that working overseas "changes the whole trajectory of your life because ... It's like people who go to war together. So I think you can have that in a community organization, but I think that happens in a lot of Mennonite churches ... You have an already ready-made group of people that have those values" (FG#1).

MCC is able to use its connections to Mennonite churches and international MCC offices to inform, motivate, and engage former or prospective sponsorship groups. This enduring physical presence internationally, and long-term relationships with international partners in many parts of the world from which Canada has accepted refugees, have played out favourably in sponsorships. The high number of refugees sponsored from certain countries reflects the unique connections MCC has forged in specific regions of the world, while its ability to liaise with churches, governments, and refugee-serving agencies in Canada has allowed MCC to quickly mobilize sponsors. Within the time frame of our study (2007–15), for example, Colombians and Palestinians comprised a significant number of the total refugee newcomers sponsored by the Mennonite churches within the sample. In the case of Colombians, MCC had developed a unique relationship with the Teusaquillo Mennonite Church in Bogota, and in partnership with MCC Colombia, encouraged Mennonite churches in Canada to sponsor internally displaced Colombians (IDPs) under the "Source Country Class" program.[29] Seventy families were resettled between 2002 and 2015.[30] Of the thirty-four families to have been sponsored between 2007 and 2015 in the study's sample, twelve came from Colombia.

The second largest group of refugee newcomers within this sample consisted of six families from Palestine. In 2009, UNHCR and the Canadian government agreed that private sponsors could assist with resettling Palestinians displaced in the borderlands between Iraq and Syria.[31] MCC Ontario formed an ad hoc task force and facilitated the sponsorship of Palestinian refugees via nine CGs in Ontario; by 2011, more than 230 Palestinians had been resettled through private sponsorship, nearly half of whom were sponsored through MCC.[32]

While MCC Ontario staff worked to make the sponsorship of Palestinians possible, the experiences of individuals who had been in the Middle East as part of an MCC program and the connections this fostered encouraged local congregations to be receptive to the idea of sponsoring Palestinians. One focus group member described the multiple connections members of her congregation had to the Middle East that made the sponsorship a natural fit for her church:

> We've had a number of people in our congregation who have gone to the Middle East, we have young adults who have done Yella.[33] We've had adults who have gone for learning tours [to the Middle East]. So they come back and talk about their experience. So when the opportunity came to sponsor a Palestinian family, for example, that was kind of a no-brainer. The congregation was ready to do that. So there had been, I think, that work that makes people aware of the justice issue there. (FG#3b).

A SHARED REFUGEE HISTORY

Both Janzen and Epp-Tiessen identify the significance of an inherited refugee story, most specifically fleeing the Soviet Union, in motivating Mennonites to become involved in the sponsorship of Indochinese refugees. Epp-Tiessen explains: "They, their parents, or grandparents had been refugees, and they now wished to ease the suffering of others."[34]

Nearly half the respondents articulated a family refugee story. This sense of personal connection to "refugee-ness" was repeatedly identified as a motivating factor for sponsors: "I think one of the reasons that I feel strongly about this is that my parents were refugees after the Second World War. I lived with my parents – I was born in Canada – but we had that immigrant experience of how we were accepted" (FG#4).

Other respondents noted that their parents' stories of coming to Canada directly impacted how they positioned themselves and their ability to help: "I grew up knowing the refugee experience, I sat down with my father for a couple of weeks and got his story. It was a very moving, heart-warming story of coming to Canada from Russia and the difficulties they had, and so that refugee experience was always a part of that background, and I wanted to help" (FG#4).

One sponsor illustrated how the plight of refugees had been absorbed into his own identity as a Mennonite and how the story of "the refugee" had become his own story: "Many of us came from refugee families ourselves, as Russian Mennonites, and that story resonates especially strongly with me. My parents were both victims of violence and [witnesses to] murder in Russia and then came here as refugees, and their story became my story" (FG#5a).

Sponsors within Mennonite congregations who carried a refugee past not only turned to it as a motivation to sponsor but also acknowledged MCC's support for their own families in the early twentieth century, which had engendered loyalty to MCC. Some respondents felt a direct and intimate relationship with MCC, associating their current situation in Canada with the support and aid provided by MCC when they themselves, or their family, resettled in Canada as refugees. When asked why they chose to sponsor through MCC, an older couple noted: "When we talk about our family experience, it was MCC who was there, and they found sponsors for my parents and they found sponsors for [my wife] and family. The natural choice" (FG#2). Similarly, one respondent felt connected to the past work of MCC and believed he was continuing a tradition of helping others: "[MCC] is still there, and I can tell this Muslim family, 'The same organization that helped my ancestors come to Canada, now helps you, and it has been around a long time'" (FG#4). For these individuals, sponsorship offers a means to engage in the work of MCC and to give back to an organization from which they themselves, or their ancestors, had personally benefited.

MENNONITE IDENTITY FORMATION THROUGH SPONSORSHIP

For Mennonite sponsors who had a refugee past, sponsorship was clearly a means for them to strengthen their Mennonite identity by weaving their heritage into their current practice. Some also drew on classic formulations of Mennonite theology to explain their motivation to sponsor. One respondent specifically noted how Anabaptist principles remained the foundation of his church's approach: "Our congregation is very influenced by Anabaptist theology. Specifically, we recognize the call of the gospel to make a difference in the world and discipleship and service, so the thrust of our service is that we want to reach out to some of these people globally that are in stressed situations" (FG#5a). Discipleship, central to Mennonite theology and culture, emerged as an important element for some groups, who specifically described sponsorship through MCC as "an extension, a practical part of [Mennonite] faith" (FG#2) and of "loving mercy and acting justly" (FG#3a). One respondent from First Mennonite Church in Vineland, a congregation with a long history of sponsorship, noted that refugee sponsorship is a "Christian service" and there "seems to be this understanding that within the call to discipleship we should be *doing* something, and we do this" (FG#5a). Furthermore, some sponsors reflected on their appreciation of MCC's motto "in the name of Christ" and that sponsorship enabled them to "be as close as we can to a model of Christ" (FG#5a). For these sponsors, their role was informed and justified through their Mennonite faith and Anabaptist theology, and these were reflected in the values and heritage of MCC.

Not all North American Mennonites reference a family refugee past from the twentieth century; however, the Mennonite heritage and disposition is rooted in stories of the persecution of Anabaptists in the sixteenth century. This "posture" for the dispossessed and the marginalized has shaped the particular Anabaptist/Mennonite interpretation of biblical teaching as well as theological explanations for peace-building and service, which are reflected in MCC's vision and mission statement. As Brian Dyck notes, MCC has an understanding that it "isn't our role" to shape Mennonite theology; instead, MCC is to be "the service arm of the Mennonite church. So we are subordinate to the churches in that – our role isn't necessarily to develop their theology, although we have over the years because people do go back and forth, and it has had an impact on that" (Interview, July 2018). This emphasis on action allows for non-theological and non-religious identification. Indeed, not all sponsors grounded their engagement in religious duty. While some sponsors drew on the biblical teachings that define MCC, others emphasized the humanitarian values espoused in MCC's work of peacebuilding and global engagement, recognizing sponsorship as an act of "human dignity" and motivated by "being a good person" (FG#7). Although all respondents had some affiliation with a Mennonite church or heritage, a few explicitly articulated that their involvement in sponsorship was not tied to faith: "The fact that we can do it, is why we did it. Not out of any obligation, out of any faith, or anything else. It was just that we had the means, and therefore we could participate" (FG#5b). For these sponsors, MCC's "theological hands-off" stance made it possible to participate in "a hands-on, real thing – it's not just talking about it ... This is real. I can contribute to making a real difference, a meaningful difference" (FG#6). For Mennonites in Canada, whether they claim religious affiliation or not, sponsorship through MCC gives expression to a past refugee experience, a current privileged position, and a sustained collective identity as people of peace. A unique MCC sponsorship ethos is thereby reinforced.

AN INSTITUTIONAL SPONSORSHIP ETHOS: RELATIONSHIP-BUILDING AS PEACE-BUILDING

Despite a range of personal beliefs and contradictory expressions of proximity to or distance from religion and a Mennonite church, a common sponsorship ethos runs through official MCC discourse and all participant responses. This ethos, though articulated in various ways, is institutionalized in MCC and its constituent churches and is reinforced in the specific practices of synergy that are mutually constitutive and self-reinforcing for Mennonite organizations and churches, MCC programs, and participating individuals. Yet our research indicates that this steadfast institutional identification with the Anabaptist/Mennonite heritage, culture, and religion does not exclude sponsors or refugee newcomers based on religio-cultural affiliation. For example, one sponsor reflected: "I was brought up Catholic and I'm not a Mennonite ... but [my values] are exactly that – we're all a part of the same human family, and I strongly believe we have a moral duty to help each other, to live those values out loud, whether it's 'FAITH' in big capital letters, or a more humanistic perspective" (FG#6). Similarly, MCC's principle of "relationship-building as peace-building"[35] is put into practice in its commitment to sponsor refugees of all religions. One group reported that they had been asked, "Why is your church doing this for the Muslim people?" To which they responded, "Well it's MCC" (FG#4). Through its emphasis on relationships, this faith-based SAH demonstrates a willingness and capacity to partner with sponsoring and newcomer individuals and groups of diverse religions, beliefs, and cultures.[36]

CONCLUSION: A WAY FORWARD

Mennonite heritage is steeped in notions of "refugeeness." A specific Mennonite identity draws on the memory of family members fleeing the Soviet Union in the second and third decades of the twentieth century, as well as more distant roots among a people who were persecuted during the sixteenth-century Reformation. Traditional Mennonite theology is rooted in Anabaptist principles of community, sharing of material and social resources, a commitment to non-violent resistance, and the belief that faith must be expressed through action. This unique blend of heritage, collective identity, and theology has translated into long-held values that continue to define Mennonites' relationships with refugees. As the "active arm" of the church, MCC has institutionalized these values and further reinforced them as part of Mennonite identity. Shared principles such as relationship-building and practical engagement are given expression and reinforced through MCC's private sponsorship program.

The churches that have formed MCC's core constituency are those whose members have a personal or family connection to a refugee story. These groups engage in international work through MCC and are part of a larger Mennonite community that adheres to certain values and principles. As our research has shown, these features of Mennonite communities and their embodiment within the organizational structure of MCC have helped motivate and sustain refugee sponsorship since 1979. These relatively small churches, however, are declining in membership, and their long-time sponsors are growing older. It is the end of an era for private sponsorship in Canada, and the loss of these unique culminating factors raises questions about the future of Mennonite sponsorship. What can we learn from this significant period of refugee sponsorship and the specific makeup of MCC's constituent groups during this time?

First, we conclude that religion, or faith, is most accurately understood broadly, beyond common perceptions that limit religion to personal belief. Indeed, the Mennonite refugee sponsorship story reveals the complexity of the Mennonite religion as a close blend of belief, culture, practice, and ethnicity that operates at the individual, congregational, and institutional level to motivate and inform values, commitments, and world views.

Second, this unique religious heritage and culture is institutionalized in MCC and, in turn, is activated through its synergistic relationships with Canadian congregations and international partners, which continually ground and renew its refugee sponsorship program. Even more, MCC's engagement with national governments and humanitarian organizations all over the world reinforces a commitment to, and identification with, refugees that feeds back to the pews of Mennonite churches in Canada.

Third, this case study highlights the important role of the Sponsorship Agreement Holder. On an organizational level, creating a culture of sponsorship relies on the institutionalization and strengthening of these motivating values, as well as on direct support through a committed SAH. As the first Master Agreement Holder (now SAH) in Canada, MCC provides shared values, stability, credibility, and experience, all of which are vital to sustained and successful private sponsorships even beyond its own program. Indeed, MCC, in tandem with its provincial offices, sets out to educate sponsors and to influence how they come to view their own identity as Mennonites and their relationships with refugee newcomers. The MCC refugee program reveals the ways in which the public–private sponsorship agreement model can effectively function to directly engage, support, and sustain sponsorship groups.

NOTES

The authors would like to thank Kerry Fast, PhD, for her editing and consulting assistance. Her expertise in developmental editing and her past involvement in MCCC's refugee program helped shape this paper substantially. This research was supported by the Social Sciences and Humanities Research Council of Canada.

1. In October 1920, representatives from Mennonite churches in Manitoba, Saskatchewan, and Alberta met to organize a Canadian Central Committee similar to the Mennonite Central Committee just organized in the United States. The work of providing shelter and support for thousands of Mennonite refugees "until they were financially viable" prompted the formation of multiple Mennonite organizations, including the Canadian Mennonite Board of Colonization (CMBC) in 1922, the Mennonite Land Settlement Board in 1924, the Central Mennonite Immigration Committee (made up of Mennonite newcomers in Canada), and the Mennonite Central Relief Committee in Western Canada. Esther Epp-Tiessen notes that "by the end of 1963, a wide representation of Mennonite and brethren in Christ denominations had agreed to the transformation of their existing inter-Mennonite organizations into one new national entity known as Mennonite Central Committee Canada, with provincial counterparts." See Esther Epp-Tiessen, *Mennonite Central Committee in Canada: A History* (Winnipeg: CMU Press, 2013), 71; Frank H. Epp, *Mennonite Exodus; The Rescue and Resettlement of the Russian Mennonites Since the Communist Revolution* (Altona: Canadian Mennonite Relief and Immigration Council, 1962).
2. William Janzen, "The 1979 MCC Canada Master Agreement for the Sponsorship of Refugees in Historical Perspective," *Journal of Mennonite Studies* 24 (2011): 211–22.
3. Epp, *Mennonite Exodus;* Jacob Gerbrandt, "Canadian Mennonite Board of Colonization," *Global Anabaptist Mennonite Encyclopedia Online*, September 2011, accessed 4 March 2019, http://gameo.org/index.php?title=Canadian_Mennonite_Board_of_Colonization&oldid=132346.
4. Janzen, "The 1979 MCC Canada Master Agreement," 212.
5. See Stephanie Dyck, "Advancing Private Refugee Sponsorship: Engaging and Resourcing MCC Manitoba's Constituency" (MA thesis, University of Victoria, 2016). Dyck considers strategies for revitalizing MCC Manitoba's refugee sponsorship program.
6. For further investigation of what motivates sponsors, see Audrey Macklin, Kathryn Barber, Luin Goldring, Jennifer Hyndman, Anna Korteweg, Shauna Labman, and Jona Zyfi, "A Preliminary Investigation into Private Refugee Sponsors," *Canadian Ethnic Studies* 50, no. 2 (2018): 35–57.
7. One interview with a former refugee newcomer/family was conducted in each of the six main focus group regions. Individuals and families were chosen based on the overall diversity of the sample, considering factors

such as family make-up, country of origin, and time of arrival. Seven separate interviews were conducted, comprising a total of seventeen participants. Though these data were beneficial to the larger study, this chapter does not draw off any former refugee data.
8   For a list of MCCC's sponsoring denominations, see https://mcccanada.ca/learn/about/leadership.
9   For more on these discrete Mennonite migration histories and ancestries, see Luann Good Gingrich, *Out of Place: Social Exclusion and Mennonite Migrants in Canada* (Toronto: University of Toronto Press, 2016); Marlene Epp, *Mennonites in Ontario* (Mennonite Historical Society of Ontario, 2012).
10 Mennonite Central Committee, *Vision and Mission*, https://mcccanada.ca/learn/about/mission.
11 Epp-Tiessen, *Mennonite Central Committee*, 109.
12 Karen Treadway and Major Treadway, "MCC, Vietnam and Legacies of War," *Intersections: MCC, Vietnam, and Legacies of War* 5, no. 2 (2017): 1–2.
13 Royden Loewen, *Seeking Places of Peace: A Global Mennonite History* (Good Books, 2012), 186.
14 Ibid.
15 Janzen, "The 1979 MCC," 217.
16 Esther Epp-Tiessen, "Tensions in MCC Canada's Resettlement of Vietnamese Refugees," *Intersections: MCC, Vietnam, and Legacies of War* 5, no. 2 (2017): 11–13.
17 Treviranus and Casasola, "Canada's Private Sponsorship of Refugees Program," 184.
18 Janzen, "The 1979 MCC Canada Master Agreement," 212.
19 MCC, "2017/2018 Annual Report," https://mcccanada.ca/sites/mcccanada.ca/files/media/reports/canada/2018-11-05annualreport2018-web.pdf.; Jason Dueck, "Consider it (re)settled: MCC's 40 years of refugee resettlement in Canada," 28 February 2019, https://mcccanada.ca/stories/consider-it-resettled?utm_medium=email&fbclid=IwAR32wJ_8eZiBvsAApsw9EwH4dTAL9-KbldUhNy4nrdcIDjXTfZrDWP8pYLo.
20 Brian Dyck, personal communication, 20 February 2019; *Annual Reports to Parliament on Immigration*, http://publications.gc.ca/site/eng/359079/publication.html.
21 Brian Dyck (personal communication, 20 February 2019) reports that MCCC's refugee program coordinators have served on the national SAH Council for many years. Gloria Nafziger, the first MCC Canada refugee program coordinator, was involved in consultations regarding changes

to the program in the late 1980s to early 1990s. As the current National Migration and Resettlement Program Coordinator, Dyck wears a second hat as chair of the Canadian Refugee SAH Association.

22 For example, Brian Dyck (personal communication, 20 February 2019) notes that EU states and NGOs in Brussels invited him to speak from the SAH perspective about refugee sponsorship in June 2014 and March 2015. MCC staff have provided input for the Global Refugee Sponsorship Initiative (GRSI), particularly regarding collaboration with government and other partners in private sponsorship.
23 Treviranus and Casasola, "Canada's Private Sponsorship of Refugees Program," 195.
24 Rachel Bergen, "MCC Resettles One-Third of Canada's BVOR Refugees," https://mcccanada.ca/stories/mcc-resettles-one-third-canadas-bvor-refugees.
25 MCC, https://mcccanada.ca.
26 Treviranus and Casasola, "Canada's Private Sponsorship of Refugees Program," 195.
27 Ottawa Mennonite Church, *Serving with OMC*, https://ottawamennonitechurch.org/community.
28 MCC, *Where We Work*, https://mcccanada.ca/learn/where.
29 Nathan Toews, "Church Accompaniment with Colombian Displaced Families," *Intersections: Challenges and Opportunities in Refugee Resettlement* 5, no. 4 (2017). Further, it should be noted that the Source Country Class was repealed in 2011.
30 Ibid.
31 MCC, "Palestinian Resettlement Project Summary Sept 2012" (internal document).
32 Gladys Terichow, "Daring to Dream Big in a New Country," https://mcccanada.ca/stories/daring-dream-big-new-country.
33 Yella is a young-adult learning tour to the Middle East sponsored by MCC and Mennonite Church Eastern Canada, https://mcec.ca/story/yella-2018-young-adult-learning-trip.
34 Epp-Tiessen, *Mennonite Central Committee*, 150.
35 Ibid., 235.
36 Co-author Kaylee Perez (MCC Ontario Refugee Sponsorship and Settlement Associate), reported that at the end of 2018, MCC Ontario matched twenty new groups with BVOR cases. The majority were first-time sponsors to MCC. They included groups of friends, work colleagues, the missional arm of the Sikh faith called Sikhs Serving Canada, and members of the LGTBQ+ community. The majority do not identify as Christian.

6

Operation Ezra: A New Way Forward

Madison Pearlman

Whereas other groups have singled out a few individuals and/or families and fulfilled their responsibility toward those individuals, Operation Ezra ascended to a whole other level. Operation Ezra created a community. From the first family to arrive to the tenth family with the addition of forty federally sponsored families who aligned themselves with Operation Ezra based on need, Operation Ezra did not see them as singular entities but as a whole. They meet as a community, discuss issues as a community, socialize as a community, celebrate and cry together as a community. From many they have become as one.[1]

Some of the first Yazidi refugees came to Canada in the 1990s through private sponsorship.[2] Since then, the Yazidi population has primarily settled in Winnipeg, Manitoba, and London, Ontario. The Yazidi people are a Kurdish-speaking religious minority from Iraq who practise a monotheistic religion that reflects a spectrum of teachings and beliefs from various other religions including Gnostic Christianity, Judaism, Sufi Islam, and Zoroastrianism.[3] Yazidis have been labelled "devil worshipers," "infidels," and "non-believers," and this has alienated the Yazidis from other groups. This rhetoric has served as the basis for efforts to destroy Yazidi communities.[4] In the Yazidi collective memory, they have suffered and survived as many as seventy-four attempts at genocide.[5]

In 2014 the Islamic State of Iraq and the Levant (ISIS) attacked Yazidi villages in northern Iraq. More than 100,000 Yazidis tried desperately to escape to the top of Mount Sinjar and nearby towns, leaving many internally displaced and at risk of further attack. Many others ended up in nearby refugee camps.[6] Calls, emails, and text messages from family members, friends, and those with distant links to the Yazidi diaspora pleading for assistance and safety became constant for the Yazidi population in Winnipeg – a familiar experience known to many diaspora refugee communities around the world.

On 19 July 2016, Nadia Murad gave evidence to the Standing Committee on Citizenship and Immigration in the House of Commons about her personal experiences and the experiences of other Yazidi refugees at the hands of ISIS.[7] Murad is a Yazidi woman who was kidnapped by ISIS during the 2014 attacks and was forced into sex slavery by her captors. A 2016 UN report titled "They Came to Destroy: ISIS Crimes Against the Yazidis" found that ISIS had organized systematic gender-based violence against Yazidi women and girls that commenced immediately during the August 2014 attacks. Women and girls are considered the most vulnerable population of Yazidi refugees.[8]

In the aftermath of the mass displacement caused by the 2014 ISIS attacks, Operation Ezra was formed by a small number of individuals from Winnipeg's Jewish community and Nafiya Naso, a Yazidi resident of Winnipeg who has been a vocal advocate for her community. The group came together and decided to sponsor a Yazidi refugee family. Over the next four years, Operation Ezra evolved into a grassroots coalition of actors from a multitude of political, economic, social, and religious backgrounds. While Operation Ezra is a relatively new sponsorship initiative that focuses narrowly on a single refugee population, its influence and capacity underscore how private sponsorship can be a bottom-up, people-driven mechanism for refugee protection. Based on this chapter's case study, this approach can have both positive impacts and unintended consequences for refugee protection and for Canada's resettlement program as a whole.

The research in this chapter builds on a prior opinion piece written by the author in collaboration with members of Operation Ezra.[9] Three interviews were conducted – in May 2018, September 2018, and January 2019 – with two of Operation Ezra's founding members, Nafiya Naso and Anita Neville. An additional interview was conducted with a third founding member, Michel Aziza, in March 2019. These discussions provided first-hand accounts from a sponsor perspective of how Operation Ezra began and of its participants, programs, and partnerships. These interviews also delved into the members' motivations and expectations, as well as the project's successes, challenges, and collective vision. A separate interview with a member of Operation Ezra's Volunteer Committee was conducted in September 2018 so as to include an alternative perspective on how Operation Ezra works within the community.

ESTABLISHING OPERATION EZRA

In 2014, around 180 Yazidis were living in Winnipeg. Concerns and discussions about the plight of Yazidis and their protection needs were mostly limited to Yazidi households. However, in early 2015, a small ad hoc group formed that included Naso and eight or ten individuals with strong links to Winnipeg's Jewish community, business community, and local and national political circles. They set an initial goal of raising $35,000 to cover the cost of sponsoring one family of seven for one year.[10] Operation Ezra is the name that was collectively given to this coalition when it was formed with the Jewish community. "Ezra" is the Hebrew word for "help." Since Operation Ezra began in 2015, more than 3,600 families – in Canada and abroad – have reached out to the coalition for help coming to Canada or bringing more family members to Canada.[11]

Operation Ezra was organized as a direct, grassroots-led response to pleas for assistance made by members of the Yazidi community. It has a two-prong mandate: to privately sponsor and bring Yazidi refugees to Winnipeg, and to raise awareness about the treatment of the Yazidi people and their ongoing need for protection.[12] The creation of a robust private sponsorship framework was not part of the initial plans.

With its pre-existing institutional structure and capacity to provide settlement services, Jewish Child and Family Services (JCFS) became the "home base" for the coalition. Also, some members of Operation Ezra already had personal connections to the organization. In late 2015, JCFS became a constituent group (CG), which allowed it to submit sponsorship applications, and which also bound the other associated groups to the obligations of private sponsorship.[13] As a service provider, JCFS has access to different pools of funding that can be directed to support Operation Ezra's resettlement work. In 2016, as Operation Ezra continued its sponsorship efforts, Naso was hired as a resettlement coordinator for Yazidi refugees at JCFS. In this role, she works with JCFS to coordinate services and communicates directly with Yazidi families sponsored by the coalition, and with other members and partners of Operation Ezra. Clearly, Operation Ezra was already benefiting from a strong institutional framework.

Operation Ezra sponsored its first six families through an agreement with the Mennonite Central Committee of Canada. The group now has an agreement with another local SAH, Crossed Hands Refugee Committee, a joint committee of St. Matthew's and St. Paul's Anglican Churches, to bring more families to Winnipeg. The first two families arrived in July 2016, the next two in December 2016. By March 2018, 10 family units comprising 55 Yazidi refugees had arrived in Winnipeg. Many of these families had infants and school-age children.[14] As of February 2020, 11 family units – 73 individuals – have arrived, and a twelfth application has been submitted to IRCC.[15] In 2019, Operation Ezra also assisted with submitting nine Family Reunification applications for a total of 14 individuals.[16]

With its focus on one refugee population, Operation Ezra is gaining a better understanding of how to support and respond to the needs of Yazidis, especially many of the Yazidi women and girls who have particular vulnerabilities and needs. According to members, naming and reuniting families has been critical to understanding and addressing the psychosocial needs of Yazidis, many of whom suffer from severe PTSD and culture shock and who were separated from family members when ISIS attacked their villages.[17]

Operation Ezra also faces similar challenges to those of other sponsorship groups: application forms are long and complicated, and the bureaucracy is slow to process them; it is difficult and time-consuming to reach refugee families overseas; and on-the-ground conditions are unstable. All of this has an impact on expected arrival times. As with other refugee communities, the need for protection is much greater than the means available to offer it. As more families arrive, more families remaining in Iraq are identified as needing resettlement, and the list of names continues to grow.

From the beginning, Operation Ezra has been open about the fact that the first two sponsored families were related to one of its founding members, Nafiya Naso, given that she was the individual who raised concerns about her own family's safety in Iraq. Naso plays a critical role in the coalition by visiting with families and being a point of contact for Yazidi refugees in Winnipeg and abroad. However, Operation Ezra has been accused of nepotism and criticized for having exclusive selection criteria – that is prioritizing families who have connections to families already resettled.[18]

A new trend is emerging: already resettled families are identifying other family members to be resettled and contributing funds to sponsor them. This highlights Lenard's discussion in this volume about the often unacknowledged impact that sponsors have on admissions and on who will receive already scarce resettlement placements. Now that government-assisted Yazidis have been brought within the scope of the coalition's resettlement support, new naming opportunities may present themselves. It may also increase the burden experienced by sponsorship groups as more families ask for assistance, or it may cause resentment among government-assisted refugees who lack the administrative and financial resources to sponsor their own extended family members.

These realities demonstrate some of the tensions between naming as a fundamental component of Canada's private sponsorship scheme as a reflection of it being a society-led solution, and maintaining an international refugee protection system based on need. Sponsors face a difficult choice when deciding whom to sponsor: are named families taking spots away from other Yazidi refugees who have the same level of need for protection? Or does selection influenced by individual sponsors and families meet protection goals, in that it recognizes the importance of family and community in healing and integration, especially for high-needs populations?

Operation Ezra is the only coalition of its kind in Canada in terms of its organized effort to sponsor Yazidi refugees.[19] It has two formal committees – the executive, responsible for overall decision-making and selecting families, and a volunteer committee, responsible for program planning and the provision of resettlement support such as housing, clothing, and social/cultural events.[20] The three members I interviewed sit on both committees.[21] One member further explained that "outside of these two formal groups, we probably have another twenty-five volunteers actively engaged in the project, many of whom are Yazidi refugees who [are resettled] and are able to pay it forward."[22]

In its current form, the coalition has forty-two partners, which include local churches, synagogues, camps, schools, community organizations, the Salvation Army, local businesses, and corporations such as IKEA.[23] These groups as well as individual members have their own networks that support Operation Ezra's private sponsorship initiative through monetary and material donations and relationship-building. This speaks to the role that private sponsorship of refugees plays in promoting a sense of community and the growth of civil society. This is further discussed in this volume by McNally, as well as by Libal and Harding.

The coalition model makes Operation Ezra different from other sponsorship groups, such as groups of individuals or families who want to sponsor refugees. Noteworthy about Operation Ezra's structure is how it links individual members and community institutions. These links promote greater collaboration, communication, and access to resources. The resulting partnerships between actors have allowed Operation Ezra to undertake successive sponsorships and maintain and expand supports available to resettled refugees.

The personal identities and positions of influence of members of the executive and volunteer committees have been key to propelling the project and to the overall willingness to help Yazidi refugees come to Canada. Members include a former Canadian politician, leaders from the business and not-for-profit sectors, executives of local Jewish and multifaith organizations, and individuals with backgrounds in social work, education, and health care. The personal connections that members of Operation Ezra have to the Yazidi refugee population are another important factor in assessing the project's sustainability. Thus, it is not clear how and to what extent this type of sponsorship initiative would work in other communities.

REWARDS AND RISKS OF RETHINKING PRIVATE SPONSORSHIP

Cameron, in this volume, discusses how religious groups have historically played a vital role in privately sponsoring refugees and influencing policy. Religious communities, including Jewish communities and institutions, have been involved because they feel it is their duty to do so based on religious and cultural beliefs and teachings or on a shared identity or experience. This has positively influenced the development of private sponsorship in Canada and strengthened the international refugee protection regime.[24]

Operation Ezra's initial approach to sponsorship focused on crisis management and facilitating "protection spaces"[25] to meet the immediate needs of Yazidi refugees. As its network and visibility increased and families began settling into their new country and rebuilding their community in both a physical and a psychosocial sense, the group was forced to rethink how it was allocating "protection spaces" – that is, what protection actually meant and who it was protecting.

Members of Operation Ezra indicated that one of the coalition's ongoing challenges is how to respond to direct requests for help from government-assisted Yazidi families who have been arriving in Winnipeg since 2015. In November 2017, during a session of the Standing Committee on Citizenship and Immigration in the House of Commons, one of Operation Ezra's founders testified that "our future plans for 2018 are to continue to raise awareness, to continue to support the current Operation Ezra privately sponsored families, to continue to fundraise and privately sponsor Yazidi refugees, and to continue to provide support to government-sponsored families."[26] Operation Ezra desires to expand its mandate while continuing to meet the needs of the growing Yazidi refugee population in Winnipeg. As it rethinks its role, the risks and rewards of doing so will come to the fore.

Mobilizing and Building Communities

Operation Ezra was formed using the traditional private sponsorship naming process: partnering with an SAH, raising funds, committing to providing financial support for the first year after refugees have arrived, developing a settlement plan, and being a source of psychosocial and emotional support. Its work over the past three years demonstrates that the coalition has adopted a community-based understanding of private sponsorship beyond the humanitarian imperative of family reunification. In the context of Operation Ezra, private sponsorship is seen as a means both for providing refugee protection and for creating and strengthening community.

The resettlement work of Operation Ezra illustrates how private sponsorship can be a tool for social transformation. Often, through private sponsorship, knowledge exchanges increase tolerance and understanding between sponsors and refugee families. However, the two communities' shared experiences of genocide, refugeehood, and displacement have led to diverging narratives.

The coalition has become a symbol of multifaith solidarity and cooperation as well as a tool to combat anti-Semitism. At the local level, a challenge facing the group has been to overcome the fear of the "unknown other." Naso recounts being taught to hate Jews in the refugee camp in Syria, where she lived for several years.[27] At the same time, residents in the camp were taught to hate Yazidis, and this created barriers to building trust with other groups and integrating in a new country. Despite religious and cultural differences, common ground has been found through stories of a precarious existence and human rights violations.

The experiences shared by members in my interviews also reflect some of the practical challenges of private sponsorship. Over the past two years, there have been divisions and tensions within the broader Yazidi community. There have been accounts of individuals trying to isolate newly arrived refugees from Operation Ezra by perpetuating fears of conversion among the Yazidi refugee population as well as stereotypes of Jewish people as greedy and dishonest.[28] This illustrates that another dimension of private sponsorship, in the broader community sense, involves working with existing refugee diaspora communities and navigating a spectrum of interests.

As a private sponsorship initiative, Operation Ezra relies almost entirely on donations from private individuals and organizations. Locally sourced financial contributions are approximately two thirds from the Jewish community and one third from non-Jewish donors. Members of the executive describe receiving random one-time donations from individuals across Canada who hear about their efforts and the plight of the Yazidis and are motivated to donate. In its first year, the coalition received a significant donation from a man in Calgary, which was able to cover the costs of one family for an entire year. Now that some Yazidi families have been in Winnipeg for more than one year and have become self-sufficient, these families are contributing their time and money to assist in Operation Ezra's resettlement work. From this financial perspective, private sponsorship fosters a sense of community.

Although Operation Ezra has not faced specific dilemmas with regard to receiving donations, private sponsors must consider donor accountability and fatigue. When sponsors receive a large donation, decisions must be made on how to spend it and on whom. It is a challenge to balance donor expectations with the needs of resettled refugees. Donations and support are influenced by public opinion of refugees. The Yazidi genocide continues to have a prominent public profile and has garnered the attention and sympathy of many; even so, private sponsorship groups, including Operation Ezra, must be vigilant against donor disengagement when considering future sponsorship plans.

Members of Operation Ezra provide and coordinate material resources to meet the basic needs of newly arrived families, including housing, clothing, and food for the first year. Naso and members of her family have taken on community liaison and support roles for newly arrived families. The partnership between the Jewish and Yazidi communities helps manage refugees' expectations, bridge cultural differences, and reduce language barriers.[29]

The theme of "evolving organically" emerged in my interviews with members of Operation Ezra as well as in media coverage of the group's efforts. Operation Ezra's approach to resettlement has involved undertaking an inventory of its members and partners' skills and being open to reaching out to new individuals and organizations to meet the needs of families. Grassroots mobilization often has a domino effect. According to members of the coalition, there was no set formula for how relationships with many of their partners developed, beyond "it just happened" or "people said yes."[30] Often, one connection has led to another, expanding the network of support and the group's resource pool.

Operation Ezra has used a community engagement and multilevel partnerships approach to secure material resources to meet refugees' needs and provide educational, social, and emotional support.[31] This includes agreements with other faith-based institutions with long histories of fundraising and seeking donations from their congregations to support refugees. This partnership-based approach was also used by an ad hoc coalition in Windsor, Ontario, to resettle Indochinese refugees in the 1970s. In Windsor, the city's mayor facilitated the sponsorship group and brought together faith-based groups and other organizations to sponsor Indochinese refugee families.[32] Operation Ezra, with its roots in the community, is different in that it is a bottom-up model whereas Windsor's was top-down, led by a member of the state apparatus.[33]

Critically, this bottom-up model exists in Winnipeg because of the collaboration between an established community and a newer refugee community utilizing the pre-existing connections, skills, and resources those individuals and communities have. In contrast to the challenges in maintaining public interest and participation faced by sponsors in the BVOR program (discussed by McNally in this volume), Operation Ezra's partnerships are expanding, and there is evolving investment in the project.

Recognizing the Realities of Resettlement

Operation Ezra has established a range of community-based programs and supports. One such program is weekly English as an Additional

Language (EAL) classes; another is a home support program that provides private English lessons for parents whose kids are attending school. Temple Shalom, a local synagogue, provides space for the EAL classes, and Operation Ezra committee members use their connections to secure supplies as well as teachers willing to volunteer their time. Still another program is a food delivery program for government-assisted Yazidi refugees. Operation Ezra also coordinates monthly meetings about community matters, budgeting, social assistance, and driver's licences. These meetings, which are attended by privately sponsored and government-assisted refugees in the Yazidi community, address refugees' needs beyond what would otherwise be provided to newly sponsored refugees.

Various social and cultural events are helping bring the community together and foster a sense of inclusion. Since 2017, government-assisted Yazidi families have been invited to attend community feasts and celebrations. The earliest families to arrive have played an instrumental role in organizing and contributing to these events as a way of giving back and helping new families integrate.

Finally, Operation Ezra offers its sponsored families "institutional linkages." This involves volunteers helping sponsored families obtain necessary documents such as health cards, bank cards, and social insurance numbers. Volunteers also help these families access essential services such as medical and dental care, as well as schools for their children. New arrivals are connected with other settlement organizations and employment agencies with the help of previous arrivals who "know" life in Winnipeg. All of these efforts have resulted in a flourishing web of formal and informal connections and relationships.[34]

From the breadth of services offered through Operation Ezra, it is clear that private sponsorship is a readily adaptable approach – one that allows individual groups to interpret their year-long obligations in different ways. It also enables individual sponsors to tailor their supports based on a given family's unique needs. The work of Operation Ezra reflects the hard work and available skills and resources of a particular sponsor group. But can or should this be expected of all sponsors? Yazidi refugees are being provided with support that may be beyond the capacity of other sponsoring groups. Does this successful outcome skew the overall understanding of private sponsorship? Is it "fair" that sponsored refugees receive vastly different integration supports?

I am not arguing for Operation Ezra's independence to be curtailed or for stricter policies to be put in place to regulate the level and nature of services provided to privately sponsored refugees beyond minimum obligations. That said, while the breadth of support that sponsors are able and willing to provide needs to be acknowledged, it must also be recognized that refugee families have unique needs that cannot be met by a one-size-fits-all approach.

The breadth of programming that Operation Ezra provides reminds us of how much less government-assisted refugees often receive. This brings us to a common critique of the sponsorship model: that there are significant and long-standing disparities between privately sponsored and government-assisted refugees in terms of access to resources and consequent integration rates.[35]

In mid-2018, Operation Ezra received calls from thirty-six government-assisted Yazidi families who could not feed themselves, were struggling to meet other basic needs, and were experiencing cultural and social isolation. This raised questions about the adequacy of support and oversight provided by the federal government for refugees it had promised to assist.[36] It also highlighted the risk that people-driven solutions such as private sponsorship, in providing individualized supports and social capital for sponsored refugees, would result in ongoing protection gaps.

In response to the requests for assistance, Operation Ezra earmarked $20,000 it had previously raised to buy food for the thirty-six families and deliver it every two weeks. That money ran out in December 2018. For 2019, Operation Ezra partnered with a local church, which funded the food program while Operation Ezra volunteers, including privately sponsored families, continued to deliver the food.

Operation Ezra has shown it can mobilize resources and recruit new supporters in times of crisis. The coalition has taken pains to ensure that the collective best interests of the Yazidi community are respected. However, this has resulted in a reliance on private sponsors to step up and provide additional resettlement support and resources to other refugee groups, which contradicts what was meant to be the point of the multi-stream framework for refugee resettlement in Canada.[37] The result of this dynamic is generally referred to as the "privatization" of resettlement. The concern is that private sponsor contributions will end up taking the place of, rather than supplementing, government support for resettlement.

On 9 November 2017, Lorne Weiss, a member of Operation Ezra's executive committee, testified at a briefing in the House of Commons regarding Yazidi resettlement issues. In describing the coalition's work, he told the attendees that "we see ourselves as not being an alternative to IRCC but an enhancement to some of the programs they are providing. We're also stepping in to provide where there are voids for certain families."[38] His view of Operation Ezra's role in assisting government-assisted refugees reinforces the principle of additionality as the foundation of private sponsorship. His testimony also reflects how a willingness to strengthen protection efforts creates a grey zone of responsibility.

A related concern is that private sponsor initiatives that attempt to address deficiencies in resettlement services risk reducing government accountability to resettled refugees generally, and to government-assisted refugees in particular. It also risks exacerbating inequities in support for government-assisted refugees by providing a "top-up" to certain government-assisted groups and not others.[39] As the coalition enters its fourth year of operation, many of the concerns expressed in this section may be turning into a reality – at least temporarily. For 2020, Operation Ezra is shifting its focus toward its domestic resettlement supports for both groups and is putting a hold on new private sponsorship applications. This is due to the increasing needs of the government-assisted Yazidi families, funding uncertainties, and existing obligations to the families Operation Ezra has already sponsored.[40]

As a newcomer to the Canadian private sponsorship community, Operation Ezra has already undergone significant changes and expansions. This is especially true with regard to how its resettlement work is funded. In addition to donations, Operation Ezra secured more than $100,000 in federal government funding from IRCC for the 2018 fiscal year. The group applied through its constituent group, JCFS, who is already an IRCC beneficiary as a settlement services agency. This IRCC funding has been renewed until April 2020.[41] The funding covers the hiring of two settlement workers at JCFS, new programming spots for government-assisted refugees, and the cost of their transportation to and from the programs.

In the short term, this funding serves Operation Ezra as a cost-alleviating mechanism as the group takes on more resettlement responsibilities for government-assisted Yazidis. The funding allows Operation Ezra to address the resettlement needs of the broader refugee community it serves without taking away money from privately sponsored families. A potential drawback to this new partnership is the time required to meet reporting requirements and draft future proposals. It is too early to tell what impact this new relationship with the state will have on Operation Ezra's autonomy and ongoing sponsorship efforts.

That the government is funding a private sponsorship group highlights the problem of government overreliance on private sponsors to mitigate resettlement shortfalls. It also shifts expectations as well as accountability with regard to both the government and private sponsors. The government requires sponsors to show they have secured the necessary funds to resettle the refugees they name or have been matched with. At the same time, sponsors expect government funding of the settlement services sector to be sufficient to support government-assisted refugees. This new funding arrangement reflects how Operation Ezra is expanding protection spaces for resettled refugees in a local context and how its new initiatives continue to push the boundaries of private sponsorship and its commitment to refugee protection.

Further discussion and research into alternative funding agreements between government and private sponsorship groups responding to similar service shortfalls is required. It is important to examine the makeup of these groups to identify any limitations or opportunities this may be present in their ability to secure funding. For example, Operation Ezra can leverage its political and institutional connections to access resources to advance its work.

Advocacy and Expansion

Canada's private sponsorship program was established mainly in response to civil society advocacy. Since then, sponsors have sought to maintain private sponsorship as a means for individuals and groups to directly assist refugees and, in so doing, influence immigration policy. Operation Ezra's private sponsorship initiative has become a vehicle for persuading local and national governments to do more to protect and resettle Yazidi refugees. These efforts have been shaped largely by the political background and connections of some of the members of Operation Ezra's executive committee.

In 2016, the group aligned itself with Conservative immigration critic Michelle Rempel to lobby the federal government to increase its commitment to resettling Yazidi refugees, beyond what Operation Ezra was able to commit to. The group successfully advocated for 1,200 government-assisted Yazidi refugees, mainly women and girls, to be resettled in Canada. Coalition members are currently working with local Members of Parliament to expedite and expand the application process for private sponsorship and family reunification of Yazidis. Operation Ezra has also used its platform to draw the government's attention to the lack of support provided to government-assisted Yazidis as well as to the special needs of this refugee population.[42]

Clearly, the group has engaged in "overt political engagement"[43] by collaborating with and challenging government officials to act.[44] By politicizing resettlement, specifically in the Yazidi refugee context, Operation Ezra has helped to improve the quality of resettlement support for both groups of resettled Yazidis and to increase the number of protection spaces for government-assisted and privately sponsored Yazidis. The coalition has continued to use the partnership approach it employs in providing resettlement supports to build relationships and improve communication with politicians across jurisdictions and party lines.

Operation Ezra's advocacy work seeks to advance its own interests, the interests of the families it sponsors, and the interests of government-assisted Yazidis. During the interviews I conducted, it became clear that members were motivated to take up this advocacy work by their family/community ethos. They described feeling accountable to the Yazidi community as a whole when government-assisted and privately sponsored Yazidis required assistance.[45]

At the community level, this is working. At the systemic level, Operation Ezra's expanded provision of services and supports to government-assisted and privately sponsored Yazidis and its advocacy for an increase in the number of government-sponsored Yazidis has increased the burden on private sponsors and what is expected of them. This has further blurred the lines of responsibility for private sponsors and thereby jeopardizing the guiding principle of additionality. This raises the following question: should it be up to politically inclined, well-connected private sponsorship groups to advocate for the government to increase the level of its own commitments and to fill protection gaps?

TOWARD BECOMING A QUASI-GOVERNMENTAL ENTITY

On 20 July 2016, Weiss, on behalf of Operation Ezra, testified at the Standing Committee on Citizenship and Immigration that government intervention in the form of a large-scale government program is desperately needed to save the Yazidi people from extinction. The plight of the Yazidi people needs to be given priority in the face of this tragic genocide. We are proposing a hybrid program wherein the government brings in a large number of Yazidi families to Canada and the private sector becomes primarily involved with settlement integration of the refugees.[46]

This was the first time that Operation Ezra proposed a pathway to a public–private partnership. A year and a half later, the group reframed its proposal for a hybrid model that would address the unique resettlement needs of government-assisted Yazidis that the government was failing to meet. In light of concerns that it could not take funds away from its sponsorship efforts, but recognizing the "voids" that had to be filled, the group was asking the government to collaborate with it to fund the resettlement efforts it was undertaking on a voluntary basis.[47]

As Operation Ezra develops direct links to government in order to continue its resettlement efforts, the coalition is evolving into a quasi-governmental entity. Because of the various forms it can take, there is no consensus on the definition of a quasi-governmental entity.[48] In the context of Operation Ezra, the coalition can be described as a hybrid program "supported by the government but managed privately."[49] It also shares these key characteristics of quasi-governmental entities: it has a direct connection to the government, it has a public function, and it serves as a voluntary or charity-like organization.[50]

Private sponsorship, as a "complementary" resettlement program, is tied to the state legally, politically, and in practice.[51] Sponsors must contend with government-imposed caps on the number of refugees they can sponsor, as well as financial requirements and application procedures. As Operation Ezra continues to raise money to privately sponsor refugees and provide resettlement support to both its sponsored families and government-assisted refugees, it has developed new links to the state. These include Operation Ezra's new IRCC funding and its involvement with a new IRCC pilot project with other government-funded service providers. The pilot project reflects the government's effort to promote efficient and effective service delivery among local organizations. This latest attempt to eliminate duplication of services and to ensure that these GARs are receiving the supports they need will involve matching government-assisted

Yazidis with an existing local settlement agency in Winnipeg. Each family will receive an IRCC card and be assigned to a case manager and an organization. The goals are to improve access to service provision among government-assisted Yazidis, to engage other partners already responsible for assisting GARs, and to prevent individuals from "shopping around" for supports.[52] The coalition's involvement in this project suggests that IRCC views it as similar to formal resettlement organizations; this further distinguishes the group from other, smaller private sponsorship groups.

As it continues to fundraise, promote awareness, and form new partnerships, Operation Ezra maintains an important degree of autonomy and its civil society roots. The coalition has focused on doing what is "right" for resettled refugees, regardless of how they came to Winnipeg. This has culminated in Operation Ezra taking on the dual role of sponsorship group and one-stop-shop for resettlement support for more than three hundred Yazidi refugees, both privately sponsored and government-assisted, with local volunteers mainly undertaking these efforts.

Operation Ezra serves a public function by working to build a community and improving refugee integration rates; to those ends, it provides and coordinates supports and programs. A challenge associated with becoming a more visible private sponsorship initiative is navigating community dynamics and criticisms. In response to criticisms, the coalition appears to have established its own guidelines for selecting the families it will sponsor – guidelines that blend together various resettlement criteria. It now serves a gatekeeping function in selecting refugees to sponsor. Government officials generally hold this role. The group has set out that

> all of the families considered for potential sponsorship must have official UNHCR registration and ID documentation. Once that is established, the Operation Ezra working committee considers the geographic location of the family, the size of the family, the ages of the various family members, the employment potential of the adult family members, and the likelihood of the family adapting to a new culture and country.[53]

Yazidi refugees are generally viewed as high-needs refugees. Many female and child victims of gender-based sexual violence suffer from trauma-related mental health issues, and the uncertainty of the whereabouts of family members left behind in Iraq compounds the stresses that refugees face when they are resettled in a new country.[54]

A less well-known program, the Joint Assistance Sponsorship (JAS), follows a hybrid model similar to the one that Operation Ezra is developing. Private sponsors are matched with government-assisted families with high needs relating to trauma, medical disabilities, or the effects of systemic discrimination.[55] Given the anticipated resettlement challenges, the government provides financial support and sponsors provide psychosocial and emotional support for up to twenty-four months.[56]

The coalition has provided those it has sponsored with similar supports that JAS refugees would receive from sponsors and government – extended integration, as well as psychosocial and emotional support for longer than the one-year window – while also providing income support for the one year required of private sponsors.[57] It may be possible to assist other high-needs refugee populations with resources similar to those of the Jewish and Yazidi communities in Winnipeg. One important consideration is how these refugees will be identified for resettlement. Currently, Operation Ezra is naming Yazidi refugees, whereas refugees who arrive through the JAS program are included in GAR numbers and identified by an overseas Canadian visa office.

CONCLUSION

When Operation Ezra began in late 2015, it was an ad hoc initiative by members of two communities who knew little about each other or the sponsorship process. In three years, the coalition has served as a sponsorship group, an advocacy group, and a service provider. This presents a critical opportunity to consider questions about how private sponsors can meet the resettlement needs of refugees most effectively, and whose responsibility it is to ensure those needs are being met adequately and sustainably. This case study serves as a positive reminder that private sponsorship, as part of a larger refugee protection scheme, not only serves as a mechanism to resettle refugees in a safe third country, but also serves as a vehicle for mobilizing communities to support refugees in creative ways and build bridges between different groups and communities. At the same time, Operation Ezra's expansion as a formal sponsorship initiative points to chronic government shortfalls, as well as the underlying unfairness that the personal capacities and resources of individual sponsors influence resettlement opportunities. The overall aim of this chapter has been to discuss the risks and rewards that come with private sponsorship being primarily driven by individual and community interests. These collectively must be assessed when looking at a way forward for private sponsorship and refugee protection.

NOTES

The author would like to acknowledge and thank founding members of Operation Ezra, Nafiya Naso, Michel Aziza, and Anita Neville, for their significant contributions to this chapter.

1 Quotes from interviews have been used with permission. Volunteer interview, October 2018.
2 Flannery Dean, "Meet the 26 Year-Old Canadian Woman Fighting for Yazidi Refugees," *Flare*, 28 February 2017, https://www.flare.com/tv-movies/canada-yazidi-refugees.
3 Belle Jarniewski, "Interview with Nafiya Naso," UCObserver, July 2015, https://www.ucobserver.org/interviews/2015/07/interview_nafiya_naso.
4 House of Commons, Standing Committee on Citizenship and Immigration, "Evidence," 19 July 2016, https://www.ourcommons.ca/DocumentViewer/en/42-1/CIMM/meeting-24/evidence (evidence of Nadia Murad); Jarniewski, "Interview with Nafiya Naso."
5 Lyse Doucet, "Iraq Yazidis: 'The Forgotten' people of an Unforgettable Stort," BBC, 5 September 2018, https://www.bbc.com/news/world-middle-east-45406232. See also House of Commons, "Evidence."
6 International Federation for Human Rights, "Iraq: Sexual and Gender-Based Crimes against the Yazidi Community: The Role of ISIL Foreign Fighters," October 2018, https://www.fidh.org/IMG/pdf/irak723angweb.pdf.
7 House of Commons, Standing Committee on Citizenship and Immigration, "Evidence."
8 UN Independent International Commission of Inquiry on the Syrian Arab Republic, "They Came to Destroy: ISIS Crimes against the Yazidis," 15 June 2016, para. 77, presented at the UN Human Rights Council 32 Session.
9 See Madison Pearlman, "Ezra Project Brings Yazidis to Canada," *Winnipeg Free Press*, 11 July 2016, https://www.winnipegfreepress.com/opinion/analysis/ezra-project-brings-yazidis-to-canada-386239341.html.

10 A "family" is understood as a family name. For example, a "family" can refer to a family unit of one person.
11 Member interview, 16 May 2018.
12 Jewish Federation of Winnipeg, "Operation Ezra," https://www.jewish winnipeg.org/community-relations/operation-ezra.
13 Citizenship, Immigration and Refugees Canada, "Guide for Sponsorship Agreement Holders to Privately Sponsor Refugees (IMM 5413)," May 2018, https://www.canada.ca/en/immigration-refugees-citizenship/services/application/application-forms-guides/guide-sponsor-refugee-agreement-holder-constituent-group.html. See also Bernie Bellan, "Jewish Child and Family Service Organizing Aid Effort for Beleaguered Yazidi Community," *Jewish Post and News*, http://www.jewishpostandnews.ca/17-faqs/rokmicronews-fp-1/2056-jewish-child-and-family-service-organizing-aid-effort-for-beleaguered-yazidi-community.
14 Member interview, 16 May 2018. See also Jewish Federation of Winnipeg, "Operation Ezra."
15 Member interview, 12 March 2019, member communications, 9 February 2020
16 Member communications, 9 February 2020.
17 Member interview, 16 May 2018.
18 Carol Sanders, "Local Yazidi Refugees Ring in the New Year Apart," *Winnipeg Free Press*, 20 April 2017, https://www.winnipegfreepress.com/local/local-yazidi-refugees-ring-in-the-new-year-apart-419922363.html. See also: Jewish Federation of Winnipeg, "Operation Ezra."
19 Jewish Federation of Winnipeg, "Operation Ezra,"
20 There are eleven members on the Executive and nine members on the Volunteer Committee.
21 Member interview, 12 March 2019.
22 Member interview, 12 March 2019.
23 Operation Ezra has partnered with local Winnipeg businesses such as Crown Cap (for winter wear), Canadian Footwear (for shoes and boots), Sharp Professional Centre (for dental work) and Midwest Quilting (for blankets).
24 Many Jewish communities and institutions cite a "visceral" reaction to refugees in need of protection, recalling their history of being outsiders, "strangers wandering," and victims of genocide for getting involved in private sponsorship. See Mira Sucharov, "Sponsor a Refugee: For Canadian Jews 'It's the Human Thing to do,'" *Haaretz*, 12 December 2015, https://www.haaretz.com/opinion/.

premium-sponsor-a-refugee-for-canadian-jews-it-s-the-human-thing-to-do-1.5430236.
25 Protection spaces are the resettlement spaces allocated by the government. A protection space more broadly refers to the environment that refugees are resettled in. See: Jennifer Hyndman, "Private Sponsorship in Canada," *Forced Migration Review* 54 (2017), https://www.fmreview.org/resettlement/hyndman-payne-jimenez.
26 House of Commons, Standing Committee on Citizenship and Immigration, "Briefing on Resettlement Issues Related to Yezidi Women and Girls," 9 November 2017, https://openparliament.ca/committees/immigration/42-1/83/nafiya-naso-1 (Evidence from Nafiya Naso).
27 Jarniewski, "Interview with Nafiya Naso."
28 Member interview, 16 May 2018.
29 Michael Lanphier, "Sponsorship: Organizational, Sponsor, and Refugee Perspectives," *Journal of International Migration and Integration* 4, no. 2 (2003): 237.
30 Member interview, 16 May 2018; member interview, 18 September 2018; volunteer interview, October 2018.
31 Ottawa Centre Refugee Action (OCRA) is an example of a similar grassroots sponsorship initiative that has been successful in building partnerships and undertaking successive partnerships. See Ottawa Centre Refugee Action, "How We Work," http://refugeeaction.ca/how-we-work.
32 Giovana Roma, "The Indochinese Refugee Movement: An Exploratory Case Study of the Windsor Experience," *Refuge* 32, no. 2 (2016): 82.
33 Ibid.
34 See Navjot K. Lamba and Harvey Krahn, "Social Capital and Refugee Resettlement: The Social Networks of Refugees in Canada," *Journal of International Migration and Integration* 4, no. 3 (2003): 335.
35 Soojin Yu, Estelle Ouellet, and Angelyn Warmington, "Refugee Integration in Canada: A Survey of Empirical Evidence and Existing Services," *Refuge* 24, no. 2 (2007); Morton Beiser, "Sponsorship and Resettlement Success," *Journal of International Migration and Integration* 4, no. 2 (2003): 203.
36 Member interview, 12 September 2018.
37 See Shauna Labman, "Private Sponsorship: Complement or Conflicting Interests?," *Refuge* 32, no. 2 (2016); Teresa Wright, "Commons Committee Recommends Better Settlement Services for Vulnerable Refugees," *National Post*, 5 April 2018, https://nationalpost.com/pmn/news-pmn/canada-news-pmn/commons-committee-recommends-better-settlement-

services-for-vulnerable-refugees; Kathleen Harris, "Liberals Promise to Bring Yazidi Refugees to Canada within 4 Months," *CBC News*, 24 October 2016, https://www.cbc.ca/news/politics/yazidis-genocide-canada-conservatives-1.3818925.
38 House of Commons, Standing Committee on Citizenship and Immigration, "Briefing on Resettlement Issues Related to Yezidi Women and Girls."
39 In the case of Operation Ezra, the size of the Yazidi population and the coalition's direct links to community make it easier for the group to hear about and reach out to the government-assisted Yazidi population.
40 Member communications, 9 February 2020.
41 Member interview, 12 March 2018. This funding is expected to end 1 April 2020.
42 House of Commons, Standing Committee on Citizenship and Immigration, "Briefing on Resettlement Issues" (evidence of Lorne Weiss).
43 See Audrey Macklin, "Resettler Society: Making and Remaking Citizenship through Private Refugee Sponsorship," Pierre Elliott Trudeau Foundation Fellowship Project Description, http://www.fondationtrudeau.ca/sites/default/files/macklin-project-web-en.pdf.
44 Members of Operation Ezra have testified multiple times in front of the Standing Committee on Citizenship and Immigration. Throughout 2017 and 2018, the committee held seven meetings about the protection and resettlement needs of Yazidi refugees. See House of Commons, "Briefing on Resettlement Issues Related to Yezidi Women and Girls: Meetings."
45 As part of its advocacy mission, Operation Ezra successfully lobbied the federal government to resettle 1,200 survivors of ISIS – primarily Yazidi women and girls. Operation Ezra's has placed greater importance on the well-being of Yazidis as a collective, rather than the status of individuals and families.
46 House of Commons, Standing Committee on Citizenship and Immigration, 20 July 2016, https://openparliament.ca/committees/immigration/42-1/26/lorne-weiss-2.
47 House of Commons, Standing Committee on Citizenship and Immigration, "Briefing on Resettlement Issues," 1 (evidence of Lorne Weiss).
48 Joseph Mead and Katherine Warren, "Quasi-Governmental Organizations at the Local Level: Publicly Appointed Directors Leading Non-Profit Organizations," *Nonprofit Policy Forum* 7, no. 3 (2014): 290–1.
49 Merriam-Webster Dictionary, "quasi-governmental," https://www.merriam-webster.com/dictionary/quasi-governmental.

50 Sandra van Thiel, "Why Politicians Prefer Quasi-Autonomous Organizations," *Journal of Theoretical Politics* 16, no. 2 (2004): 176.
51 See, generally, Labman, "Private Sponsorship."
52 Volunteer interview, 16 September 2018.
53 "Operation Ezra," https://www.jewishwinnipeg.org/community-relations/operation-ezra.
54 See, generally, Lori Wilkinson, Pallabi Bhattacharyya, Annette Riziki, and Abdul-Bari Abdul-Karim, "Yazidi Resettlement in Canada – Final Report 2018," January 2019, https://mansomanitoba.ca/wp-content/uploads/2019/03/YAZIDI-FINAL-FEB14.pdf.
55 Refugee Sponsorship Training Program, "Chapter 9: Joint Assistance Program," https://www.rstp.ca/wp-content/uploads/2014/03/39chapter9.pdf.
56 Ibid., 2.
57 A limited number of families continue to receive financial assistance after the one year. See House of Commons, Standing Committee on Citizenship and Immigration, "Evidence," 30 November 2017, http://www.ourcommons.ca/DocumentViewer/en/42-1/CIMM/meeting-88/evidence#Int-9820056.

7

The Blended Visa Office-Referred Program: Perspectives and Experiences from Rural Nova Scotia

Rachel McNally

The UNHCR identified 1.4 million refugees in need of resettlement in 2019.[1] The Blended Visa Office-Referred (BVOR) program allows community groups to sponsor refugees identified by the UNHCR under a blended funding model. Canadian visa officers may choose to submit the profiles of UNHCR-referred refugees to the BVOR list to be matched with a sponsor, or send them to Canada as government-assisted refugees (GARs), although it is unclear what criteria officers use to select between the two programs. Sponsorship groups who have not identified a specific refugee to "name" for sponsorship may choose a preapproved refugee family or individual from the BVOR list.

A notable characteristic of engagement in BVOR is that many smaller communities that have not previously received refugees have participated. Between November 2015 and January 2017, more than 250 communities outside Quebec welcomed Syrian BVOR refugees, including more than two hundred small communities or suburbs that did not welcome any GARs.[2] One province that has seen significant rural engagement in BVOR is Nova Scotia, where 62 percent of BVORs (around 305 individuals of various nationalities) who arrived between 2015 and 2018 settled in smaller communities around the province instead of settling in Halifax, the province's only city.[3] This chapter draws on a case study of BVOR sponsorship in rural Nova Scotia, including twenty-two interviews I conducted in the summer of 2017 with sponsors, sponsorship agreement holder (SAH) staff, settlement workers, former refugees, and politicians, as well as personal experience as a BVOR sponsor starting in 2015 and as a summer student for a regional SAH in 2016.

This chapter begins with a brief history of BVOR, followed by a review of its benefits – especially in a rural context – and of the relationship of BVOR to other resettlement streams. The chapter argues that during the Syrian initiative, a time of high public interest in refugee sponsorship, the BVOR program was an effective tool for mobilizing sponsors, including new sponsors and groups in rural areas, and offered many benefits to participants and to the refugee system overall. However, during its routine operations both prior to the Syrian initiative and later on, the program struggled to remain sustainable.

BVOR HISTORY AND CONTEXT

The BVOR program began in 2013; however, there had been several pilot programs in previous decades that encompassed blended funding models for specific groups of refugees: Afghan Ismailis between 1994 and 1998, refugees from the former Yugoslavia, Sierra Leoneans in 2001, Iraqis in 2011, and LGBTQ+ refugees.[4] From the outset, the BVOR program faced numerous critiques from scholars, sponsors, and refugee advocates – it was argued, for example, that the government was privatizing its responsibility for refugee resettlement,[5] that it was asserting control by restricting sponsor choice in refugee selection,[6] and that resettlement spaces might go unused if sponsors did not match government targets.[7] Evidence for the claim that BVOR was driven by cost-saving imperatives flowed from the program's origins in a 2012 decision to change one thousand fully funded GAR spaces to partly sponsor-funded BVOR spaces.[8]

BVOR began as a small resettlement program: only 313 refugees were resettled in 2013 and 2014 – less than 1 percent of Canada's overall resettlement during this period.[9] The program swelled in response to the Syrian resettlement initiative, with 3,931 Syrian refugees arriving through the BVOR program between November 2015 and January 2017.[10] Between 2015 and 2018, 7,690 refugees of diverse nationalities arrived through BVOR (which, however, represented only 6.3 percent of all resettlement).[11] Note that there is considerable interprovincial variation in the importance of BVOR relative to the other resettlement streams: BVOR accounts for 3.6 percent of resettlement in Alberta, but 17.7 percent in Nova Scotia, where there is only one GAR-receiving community (Halifax), and where the Private Sponsorship of Refugees (PSR) program is smaller.[12]

The Canadian Council for Refugees maintains that the BVOR program serves several important purposes.[13] First, it can increase the overall number of resettled refugees, provided that it respects the principle of additionality (i.e., adds to the total number of refugee resettlement spaces).[14] However, as previously mentioned, the program began as a means to *replace* GAR spaces, not add to them.[15] During a period of high public interest such as the recent Syrian initiative, BVOR harnessed this interest to welcome a greater number of refugees. It also channelled some refugees toward sponsors instead of settlement agencies, which were overwhelmed with a large influx of GARs. From the perspective of SAHs, when there is high interest from their constituent groups, BVOR provides a way to dramatically increase the number of sponsorships. For example, the Canadian Baptists of Atlantic Canada, a regional SAH, typically sponsored one family each year prior to the Syrian initiative. In 2016, the organization applied to sponsor 303 people, primarily through the BVOR program. Named sponsorships face restrictive caps; by contrast, there are no constraints on the number of BVOR sponsorships a SAH can undertake, except for financial ones.

The BVOR program also increases the number of UNHCR-referred refugees resettled to Canada.[16] In this volume, Lenard makes the ethical argument that since resettlement spaces are a highly scarce resource, they should be reserved for the most vulnerable refugees, and UNHCR referral criteria adequately measure vulnerability. Elsewhere in this volume, Bradley and Duin explain that BVOR can help achieve broader strategic goals for resettlement and promote the UNHCR's priorities, which include protecting vulnerable refugees and contributing toward the resolution of protracted refugee situations. That is why UNHCR is actively promoting the BVOR model in Canada and beyond – for example, by sending the UNHCR representative in Canada to communities across the country to speak about the program.[17]

BVOR has the potential to encourage sponsors to choose refugees from a variety of countries of origin and refugee situations. Bradley and Duin note in this volume that the BVOR program mitigates the risk that refugees will be sponsored only if they come from high-profile situations or have personal connections to Canadians. In September and October 2018, the BVOR lists included refugees from more than fifteen countries, including Iraq, Somalia, Yemen, Eritrea, Pakistan, Afghanistan, South Sudan, Democratic Republic of the Congo, Myanmar, and Jamaica.[18] During the Syrian initiative, some groups in rural Nova Scotia initially planned to sponsor Syrians, but when there were no Syrian families on the BVOR list at the time, they decided to sponsor refugees from other countries, including from protracted refugee situations in Africa. Even so, nearly 4,000 Syrians arrived in Canada through BVOR between November 2015 and January 2017.[19] Sponsors continue to have a choice with the BVOR list, and while some sponsors took the opportunity to welcome refugees of diverse nationalities, other sponsors were adamant that they would wait for a Syrian family to become available, in large part because their group's mobilization had been a direct response to the Syrian situation. Overall, BVOR has only somewhat mitigated the risk of focusing on high-profile refugee situations, as it has acted largely as a framework for interested groups to sponsor Syrians.

BVOR AND RURAL RESETTLEMENT

BVOR can increase the number of resettled refugees and the level of public involvement by recruiting new sponsors who may not have a personal connection to refugees.[20] Many small communities may not be home to former refugees or to other residents with personal connections to overseas refugees who wish to be resettled. As the wide geographic distribution of BVOR shows, it has been successful at involving small communities across the country and at increasing the percentage of refugees who resettle outside of traditional refugee-receiving cities. However, it raises the question of secondary migration within Canada, a topic that requires further research.

While it is outside the scope of this chapter to explore in detail resettlement in rural areas, it is a mistake to assume that cities are the only good places for refugees to resettle. Small communities in Nova Scotia and beyond embraced refugee sponsorship as a community project. Many refugees who settled in rural Nova Scotia have stayed, found employment, and connected well to their new communities. In my interviews, many people, including former refugees, believed that rural areas are better than cities for resettlement, despite challenges such as limited transportation and the risk of ethnocultural isolation. One former refugee went so far as to say:

> I think it's the area that everyone should settle in instead of being in a city, because it's a smaller place that everyone can have the opportunity to grow and do so much, while in the city they will just be lost in the crowd. So I think settling in small villages and between supportive community is much [more] beneficial than being in a city.[21]

Another refugee family explained how they appreciated living in a rural area compared to the city where they used to live in Syria:

> The city of Aleppo is overly crowded. There [are so many] traffic jams, a lot of pollution. So when we came here, it was all gone and it's beautiful. Even when I was living in Aleppo I aspired to live in a house with greenery, with trees around, with a garden. So luckily this dream came true.[22]

For some refugees who prefer a rural lifestyle or whose skills match the employment opportunities available in rural areas, rural may be better.

From a sponsor perspective, the BVOR program has many benefits. Rural Nova Scotian sponsors explained that they appreciated the matching process, the lower amount of paperwork and funding required, and the shorter wait times to receive a family. One first-time sponsor commented: "I think that the program is amazing in terms of how it connects a sponsored family with a sponsor and the community. It's an easy entry into a refugee sponsorship opportunity because the government pays for half ... It makes the process as easy as possible."[23] Another sponsor commented: "For us the benefits were that everything was arranged ... We just picked a profile and the rest of it was done for us."[24] Another sponsor appreciated that "you don't have to go through a five-year selection process with your application ... We saw the lists and we chose somebody off the list. They're pre-vetted."[25] Sponsors also appreciated that six months of government income support gave time for additional fundraising after the family's arrival.[26]

As a classic example of Canadians welcoming strangers, similar to the Indochinese sponsorship initiative, BVOR can create strong relationships and a social support network. In their contribution to this volume, Macklin and colleagues explore family metaphors for the sponsorship relationship. Similar to what they found in their survey, which primarily included sponsors from urban Ontario, sponsors in rural Nova Scotia frequently referred to refugees as part of their extended family and used familial language to describe sponsorship: "We've sort of adopted them now, and they're ours, and in that sense we have that familial commitment."[27] Former refugees also used familial terms to describe their sponsors. One sponsor explained that the family called her "grandmother" in their language, so her role as a sponsor consisted of "whatever grandmas do."[28] One former refugee described the process of sponsorship as becoming family: "You feel homesick when you first arrive, but that is only before we were looked after by all of those Canadians. Then after a while, they became our family."[29] Sponsors, too, thought about the post-sponsorship relationship within a family framework:

> In your own family, do you always feel that you always have to stand on your own two feet? No, sometimes you rely on your brother, sometimes you rely on your mother, sometimes you rely on your children. So, you do have a reliance on other people. So, to make them stand on their own two feet, yes, but there's still ensuring to them that there is a family connection for support no matter what.[30]

While encouraging independence, rural sponsors whose families stayed in the community continued to give extensive support after the formal twelve-month sponsorship period had ended. When asked why families they had sponsored were staying in the community, sponsors often mentioned family-like relationships.

Although largely positive, sponsor–refugee relationships can include negative elements. As one SAH acknowledged:

> Relationships are the greatest thing for resettlement but they can also be the worst thing depending on the relationship. So by in large we have had most of our groups hit it out of the park and they were emotionally mature people who were able to really be good friends to these families. But we did have some less mature groups ... or maybe not as culturally competent people.[31]

Another interview participant cautioned that "you can get groups who are very, very overpowering or even the language when they talk about the refugees as through they're their children. But they're adults."[32] Others have criticized the market terminology in the BVOR program that presents refugees as if they were commodities available for purchase.[33] Scholars have argued that the sponsorship relationship "is essentially a mode of master-dependent relationship in which one party provides and the other party is provided for."[34] Although there can be "a positive affective bond reciprocated between the sponsor and the refugee," there are fundamental differences between sponsor and sponsored including "an economic and status difference, and a cognitive gap in terms of differences in perceiving and interpreting social realities, which the affective connection cannot bridge."[35] Similarly, Macklin and colleagues elsewhere in this volume problematize the power imbalance in the sponsorship relationship, the comparison of sponsorship with parenting, and the negotiation of autonomy and independence. In response to many of these concerns, training for sponsors through the Refugee Sponsorship Training Program emphasizes empowerment, independence, and self-sufficiency for refugees.[36]

In part because of how sponsorship is framed as family-like (in contrast to a more bureaucratic approach), sponsors in rural Nova Scotia expressed highly negative views about the GAR program. They often used strong language to describe that program, calling it "deplorable" and "almost inhumane."[37] It is important to note that in Nova Scotia, all GARs go to Halifax, so rural sponsors do not have direct interaction with GARs or with the settlement agency that supports them. They learned about the GAR program mainly through media reports about the Syrian initiative, which was a unique time in terms of the number and speed of arrivals and thus is not representative of the normal functioning of the GAR settlement program. In this context, sponsors may accept one-sided portrayals and misinformation. As one sponsor put it: "I don't know how government sponsorship works but I would presume they give them the money, they give them a place to stay, and then they go away."[38] In reality, GARs receive ongoing settlement support from a trained settlement worker along with services such as English classes. Sponsors' perceptions of the GAR program seem to be more negative than merited. That said, there are legitimate concerns about the support that GARs receive, especially in comparison to BVORs and PSRs. The government's Evaluation of the Syrian Refugee Initiative found that PSRs generally self-reported receiving more help than GARs, that PSRs were more likely to say the help they received addressed their needs, and that 63.6 percent of GARs compared to 74.9 percent of PSRs indicated that their immediate needs were mostly or completely met soon after arrival in Canada.[39]

It is apparent that rural Nova Scotia sponsors are deeply committed to the idea of sponsorship and see it as superior to government resettlement programs. Sponsors discussed sharp discrepancies in support between GARs and BVORs and expressed concerns over what would have happened to the families they sponsored if they had come as GARs. One sponsor said: "I dread to think what would have happened to our family, especially, if they were put in an apartment building and kind of left, nothing against social workers, but with a social worker that was able to give them three hours a week, just how they would have coped."[40] One Member of the Nova Scotia Legislative Assembly who was closely connected to a sponsorship group said that sponsorship

> [is] so, so superior to just the federal government sponsoring a family and sticking them in an urban centre and them having to fend on their own. When we saw the stories coming out of Halifax of folks that didn't have the community support, it really showed how strong it was to have a community come together and say "We're going to support this family." There's just so many more resources, certainly in the groups that I've seen, that have these supports of sixty people, it's just such a better way to help families integrate and make the adjustment to a new culture.[41]

Sponsors and local politicians highly value community sponsorship and see it as more supportive for refugees than government resettlement programs, drawing some motivation from the belief that sponsors can resettle refugees better than the government.

These concerns with the GAR program raise questions about additionality and responsibility. If, as these sponsors claim, community sponsorship is better for refugees, then should refugee advocates still be pushing for higher GAR numbers in relation to BVOR and PSR? Some BVOR sponsors explicitly supported privatization of refugee sponsorship: "If I were the government, I wouldn't spend another dime on the total government-sponsored [if] I've got a BVOR type group available to do a total job and not just the pay the money."[42] One sponsor, a member of the Nova Scotia Legislative Assembly, stated that welcoming refugees is a job for communities, not governments:

Government have a role with regards to regulation and making sure everyone passes security, that's very important ... But I believe that successful integration into our communities happens by the people of that community ... There's no government that could afford to pay for all of the volunteer work ... It's the community's decision to welcome and bring people that have lived through war like they have, it's a community that's going to bring them in and support them. So government have a role, but it's communities that will make it successful.[43]

Another sponsor suggested that only community sponsorship would work in a rural community: "I wouldn't want [refugees] to be dropped into a rural community as a pure government-backed one, I think that would be a disaster because we simply don't have the social services and resources and that kind of thing. If it's not done well in the cities it would be done even more poorly here."[44] From the perspective of these sponsors and politicians, community sponsorship was better for refugees and only resettlement models with a high degree of community involvement had the potential for success in rural communities.

IMPLICATIONS AND CONSEQUENCES

Despite the many potential benefits of the BVOR model, today it struggles to involve sponsors and remain sustainable. As Lehr and Dyck note elsewhere in this volume, the ability of sponsors to select or name refugees has been a core feature of Canada's private sponsorship program, and most sponsors are motivated by family links or personal connections to the refugees being sponsored, which means a program like BVOR that relies on the altruism of citizens to sponsor strangers may be hard to sustain. In Nova Scotia, some BVOR sponsors have become PSR sponsors after applying to sponsor relatives of an original sponsored family. Thus, as Labman and Pearlman predicted, "the BVOR program, while intended to diminish the family focus of named sponsorship, ultimately feeds back into the program."[45]

Several other factors reduce the likelihood of BVOR sponsors choosing to sponsor again through the program. First, declining public, government, and media interest makes it more difficult to motivate sponsors, to fundraise, and to rally community support. Second, many BVOR sponsors prioritize their commitments to existing relationships. BVOR sponsors who develop family-like relationships with the refugees they have sponsored often maintain strong connections far beyond one year, particularly in rural areas, where relationships with sponsors are even more important, given the limited opportunities for relationships with members of the same cultural group. In cases where refugee families are in greater need – perhaps they require long-term literacy programs – many sponsors have continued to provide extensive settlement support long after the end of the formal sponsorship period. When a community sponsors for a second time through BVOR, it is generally because the original sponsored family has moved away from the community, thus freeing up sponsors to welcome a new family.

Third, refugee sponsorship is time-consuming and emotionally draining for sponsors, especially in rural areas, where sponsors must fill in gaps in settlement services and provide frequent transportation due to limited public transit. Many sponsors reported needing a break after completing one year of sponsorship. In small communities, typically a core group of sponsors led the project and interacted directly with refugees, but the broader community became involved through financial and in-kind donations, as well as by volunteering to help with specific needs. It is a challenge to sustain a high level of community mobilization and financial support over the long term. Pursuing a second sponsorship may be prohibitively expensive. For all of these reasons, BVOR sponsors are unlikely to commit to a second sponsorship shortly after finishing the first.

For most of the existence of the BVOR program, there has been a mismatch between government targets and sponsor interest. In contrast to the PSR program, which as Cameron explains in this volume began as a response to advocacy on the part of religious groups, the government introduced BVOR without input from sponsorship groups. Given this, it is not surprising that the program had limited uptake in its first two years, with admissions well under government targets. In 2013, the government set a target of 200 BVOR refugees but only 153 were sponsored and admitted; in 2014, only 177 BVOR refugees were sponsored out of a target of 500.[46] In contrast, during the Syrian resettlement initiative, many sponsors in rural Nova Scotia and beyond who were prepared to immediately receive a BVOR family had to wait several months to be matched with a family, leading to frustration among prospective sponsors. Every time a BVOR list was posted, the families were matched with sponsors within forty-eight hours. One sponsor described it "like a bidding war trying to get people."[47] Meanwhile, the government was rapidly bringing hundreds of families to Canada as GARs, overwhelming settlement agencies. As one sponsor said: "We were ready to love a family and there were people being kept in hotels."[48] In times when interest in sponsorship is high, it is to the government's advantage to shift more refugees into BVOR sponsorship. As one sponsor argued: "The government should channel as many refugees as the BVOR groups can take, maybe with some more resources if necessary ... It's going to cost them less in the end ... and the results we're just absolutely sure will be better."[49]

After the Syrian initiative ended, participation in BVOR dropped and it became difficult to find enough sponsors to match families and meet government targets. By August 2018, more than 1,000 of the 1,500 spots allocated for BVOR refugees in 2018 were still unfilled.[50] On 22 August 2018, there were seventy-eight families or individuals on the BVOR list waiting for a sponsor match.[51] Refugee advocates have expressed the concern that if targets are not met, spaces may go unused, reducing the number of refugees who are able to resettle in Canada.[52] As a UNHCR fact sheet explained: "Every space counts when it comes to saving lives."[53] This concern is well-founded, given that the 2013 and 2014 numbers for BVOR resettlement fell far short of the program's targets. According to the Government of Canada's 2019–2021 Immigration Levels Plan, the 2019 target for BVOR admissions is 1,650 (with a range of 1,000 to 3,000); for 2020 and 2021, it is 1,000 (with a range of 500 to 2,500).[54] If current trends continue, it is unlikely that these targets will be reached, and many spaces may go unused. The government has recognized this challenge and has adjusted its planning, for example, by converting 700 resettlement spaces that were originally intended as BVOR spaces into GAR spaces for 2020 in order to preserve the same resettlement numbers.[55] Nevertheless, when the government sets targets, it becomes problematic if the targets do not match the capacity and willingness of sponsors, because more is expected from sponsors than they are willing to undertake, or because too few refugees are referred to the program, thus hindering the participation of interested sponsors.

The Canadian Council for Refugees notes that BVOR profiles can also hinder sponsor participation.[56] Many BVOR cases now have recommended destinations. Of the twenty-three BVOR cases posted on 4 September 2018, fourteen had a recommended destination in Ontario and only five cases had no recommended destination.[57] Recommended destinations are helpful when it comes to reunifying families, thus facilitating supportive connections to help in settlement.

However, they have the unintended consequence of reducing the number of possible sponsors, since only sponsors in one community can select the case. The trend toward suggesting destinations where BVOR refugees already have connections also raises the question of whether BVOR is becoming another family reunification program, which, as the chapter by Lehr and Dyck in this volume identifies, is a significant tension in the PSR program. In addition, since the UNHCR refers the most vulnerable refugees for resettlement, it can be a challenge to find profiles whose resettlement needs are not too complex for new sponsors or small communities.[58] Rural sponsors may find themselves restricted to refugees from a particular language group due to the limited availability of interpreters, or to refugees with low medical needs due to distance from medical services. If the government selects refugees that prospective sponsors are unable to support, owing to recommended destinations or particular settlement needs, it hinders successful matching and sponsor participation.

The Syrian initiative encouraged new sponsors to get involved through public and media campaigns as well as mobilization efforts by sponsoring organizations. Since then, however, it has been a challenge to maintain momentum for the program. A 2016 evaluation of the BVOR program recommended that IRCC "develop an engagement strategy for SAHs to increase uptake of the BVOR program."[59] At the time, IRCC responded that "activities to increase sponsorship uptake are not part of the strategy as they are not currently required."[60] Yet the context has changed since the Syrian initiative. The Canadian Council for Refugees maintains that it "is not realistic to rely on sponsor communities to promote the program," given that many sponsors are at their limit already, and given that, as largely volunteer organizations, SAHs have limited capacity to promote or supervise BVOR sponsorships.[61]

One promotion strategy that emerged in 2018 in response to concerns about unused resettlement spaces was a private funding initiative that reduced the financial burden on prospective sponsors. In August 2018, the University of Ottawa Refugee Hub, the Shapiro Foundation, the Giustra Foundation, and Jewish Family Services Ottawa established a fund to pay the sponsor portion of the cost of BVOR sponsorship to assist in the sponsorship of up to 1,000 refugees identified by the UNHCR; this made BVOR sponsorship free for those who applied before 17 September 2018.[62] Eight philanthropists donated $3.5 million toward the fund.[63] This facilitated the sponsorship of 685 refugees by more than 150 sponsoring groups in 49 communities.[64] Clearly, public–private partnerships and private donor contributions have the potential to "grow" refugee resettlement. However, that fund was a stopgap, limited-time solution for the immediate problem of unused resettlement spaces in 2018. Private funding is unlikely to provide a long-term solution to the sustainability issues the BVOR program faces. In May 2019, another BVOR fund was introduced to address the same problem: more than 1,000 unused resettlement spaces for the year.[65] This one included funding for SAHs to assist in supporting BVOR cases. By August 2019, although 99 groups had applied to sponsor more than 250 refugees, there were still 800 unused spaces for 2019, leading the Refugee Hub to extend the fund's deadline.[66] Another incentive, this one led by the government and extending from November 2018 to April 2019, involved granting SAHs one additional space for a named refugee for every BVOR refugee they committed to sponsoring.[67] This initiative had the effect of encouraging prospective sponsors to participate in BVOR in order to facilitate faster resettlement of their relatives or connections.

CONCLUSION

As a fresh approach to private sponsorship, the BVOR model has great potential, especially in the context of large-scale resettlement initiatives. It may mobilize small communities and new sponsors, increase the number of resettled refugees, promote the sponsorship of vulnerable UNHCR-referred refugees, diversify refugee demographics, simplify the sponsorship process, facilitate family-like relationships and support, and offer an alternative to the traditional GAR model in newer resettlement communities. Given that the program started in 2013, it is too early to draw definitive conclusions, yet in its short existence it has seen periods of high and low involvement. The current desperation to fill resettlement spaces bodes ill for the program's future. The pull of family reunification, declining public interest in resettlement since the Syrian initiative, the practical challenges and time commitments of sponsorship, ongoing commitments to original sponsored families, the chronic mismatch between government targets and sponsor interest and capacity, limited promotion, and controversy over the program's goals all threaten the sustainability of the program going forward. Moving into fall 2019, the program's future is uncertain because of ongoing challenges meeting targets. Looking beyond Canada, the BVOR model has potential in rural regions (like parts of

Nova Scotia) where a limited history of refugee settlement makes a structured matching process appealing, where limited settlement infrastructure requires community involvement, and where there is strong interest from new sponsors with significant community support. However, concerns about sustainability remain relevant. BVOR is being promoted abroad as a successful model of public–private partnership; even so, an accurate portrayal of the program should acknowledge its challenges as well as its successes.

NOTES

The author gratefully acknowledges the support of the R. Howard Webster Foundation for this research project, "Community Sponsorship and Integration in Rural Nova Scotia," which was conducted through the Politics Department of Acadia University in Wolfville, Nova Scotia under the supervision of Dr. Can Mutlu.

1 United Nations High Commissioner for Refugees, UNHCR *Projected Global Resettlement Needs 2019*, accessed 14 September 2018, http://www.unhcr.org/protection/resettlement/5b28a7df4/projected-global-resettlement-needs-2019.html.
2 Immigration, Refugees and Citizenship Canada, "Map of destination communities and service provider organizations," 29 January 2017, accessed 9 January 2019, https://www.canada.ca/en/immigration-refugees-citizenship/services/refugees/welcome-syrian-refugees/destination-communities-map.html.
3 Immigration, Refugees and Citizenship Canada "Canada – Admissions of Resettled Refugees by Province/Territory and Census Metropolitan Area (CMA) of Intended Destination and Immigration Category, January 2015 – December 2018" from *Resettled Refugees – Monthly IRCC Updates*, Open Government Portal, Government of Canada, accessed 6 March 2019, https://open.canada.ca/data/en/dataset/4a1b260a-7ac4-4985-80a0-603bfe4aec11.
4 Shauna Labman, "Private Sponsorship: Complementary or Conflicting Interests?," *Refuge* 32, no. 2 (2016): 69.
5 Labman, "Private Sponsorship," 72–3; Jennifer Hyndman, William Payne, and Shauna Jimenez, "The State of Private Refugee Sponsorship in Canada: Trends, Issues, and Impacts," 2 December 2016, accessed 10 January 2019, https://refugeeresearch.net//wp-content/uploads/2017/02/hyndman_feb'17.pdf.

6 Labman, "Private Sponsorship," 70.
7 Canadian Council for Refugees, "Blended Visa Office-Referred (BVOR) Program CCR Positions, February 2018," Canadian Council for Refugees, February 2018, accessed 7 September 2018, http://ccrweb.ca/sites/ccrweb.ca/files/bvor-feb-2018-positions.pdf; Labman, "Private Sponsorship," 68, 73.
8 Citizenship and Immigration Canada, *Departmental Performance Report For the period ending March 31, 2012* (Ottawa: Government of Canada 2012), 32, accessed 9 September 2018, https://www.canada.ca/content/dam/ircc/migration/ircc/english/pdf/pub/dpr-2012.pdf.
9 Immigration, Refugees and Citizenship Canada, *Evaluation of the Resettlement Programs (GAR, PSR, BVOR and RAP)* (Ottawa: Government of Canada 2016), 3.
10 Government of Canada, "#WelcomeRefugees: Key Figures," accessed 13 November 2017, http://www.cic.gc.ca/english/refugees/welcome/milestones.asp.
11 Immigration, Refugees and Citizenship Canada "Canada – Admissions of Resettled Refugees by Province/Territory and Census Metropolitan Area (CMA)."
12 Ibid.
13 Council for Refugees, "BVOR CCR Positions."
14 Ibid.
15 Citizenship and Immigration Canada, Departmental Performance Report For the period ending 31 March 2012.
16 Council for Refugees, "BVOR CCR Positions."
17 Refugee Sponsorship Training Program, "An Evening with Jean-Nicolas Beuze UNHCR Representative in Canada," August 2018, accessed 6 March 2019, http://www.rstp.ca/wp-content/uploads/2018/08/FINAL-UNHCR-Flyer-VAN.pdf.
18 Refugee Sponsorship Training Program, "The Blended Visa Office Referred (BVOR) Program," accessed 10 January 2019, http://www.rstp.ca/en/special-initiatives/how-can-i-sponsor-a-refugee-to-canada/.
19 Government of Canada, "#WelcomeRefugees: Key Figures."
20 Council for Refugees, "BVOR CCR Positions."
21 Refugee, interview by author, 19 August 2017.
22 Refugee family, interview by author, conducted in Arabic with interpretation, 19 August 2017.
23 Sponsor, interview by author, 17 August 2017.
24 Sponsor, interview by author, 31 July 2017.
25 Group of sponsors, interview by author, 3 August 2017.

26 Group of sponsors, interview by author, 26 June 2017.
27 Sponsor, interview by author, 3 August 2017.
28 Sponsor, interview by author, 4 August 2017.
29 Refugee family, interview by author, conducted in Arabic with interpretation, 19 August 2017.
30 Group of sponsors, interview by author, 4 August 2017.
31 Sponsorship Agreement Holder staff, interview by author, Saint John, New Brunswick, 26 June 2017.
32 Anonymous, interview by author, July 2017.
33 Shauna Labman and Madison Pearlman, "Blending, Bargaining, and Burden-Sharing: Canada's Resettlement Programs," *Journal of International Migration and Integration* 19, no.2 (May 2018): 445.
34 Kwok B. Chan and Lawrence Lam, "Resettlement of Vietnamese-Chinese Refugees in Montreal, Canada: Some Socio-Psychological Problems and Dilemmas," *Canadian Ethnic Studies* 15, no. 1 (January 1983): 5.
35 Chan and Lam, "Resettlement of Vietnamese-Chinese Refugees," 5.
36 Refugee Sponsorship Training Program, "The First Year and Beyond" in *Handbook for Sponsoring Groups* (Catholic Crosscultural Services and the Refugee Sponsorship Training Program, 2014), 84, accessed 5 March 2018, http://www.rstp.ca/wp-content/uploads/2014/03/Chapter-8-The-First-Year-and-Beyond-NOV-2017.pdf.
37 Group of sponsors, interview by author, August 4, 2017; Sponsor, interview by author, 3 August 2017.
38 Sponsor, interview by author, 20 June 2017.
39 IRCC Evaluation Division, "Rapid Impact Evaluation of the Syrian Refugee Initiative," December 2016, https://www.canada.ca/en/immigration-refugees-citizenship/corporate/reports-statistics/evaluations/rapid-impact-evaluation-syrian-refugee-initiative.html.
40 Two sponsors, interview by author, 29 June 2017.
41 Nova Scotia Member of the Legislative Assembly, interview by author, 9 August 2017.
42 Group of sponsors, interview by author, 4 August 2017.
43 Nova Scotia Member of the Legislative Assembly, interview by author, 29 August 2017.
44 Sponsor, interview by author, 3 August 2017.
45 Labman and Pearlman, "Blending, Bargaining, and Burden Sharing," 446.
46 Immigration Refugees, and Citizenship Canada, *Evaluation of the Resettlement Programs*, 14.
47 Group of sponsors, interview by author, 4 August 2017.
48 Ibid.

49 Ibid.

50 The Refugee Hub, "News Release: Hundreds of refugees to settle in Canada by year's end after receipt of $3.5 million in donations ensures community sponsorship spaces are filled," 14 November 2018, accessed 10 January 2019, https://refugeehub.ca/news-release-hundreds-of-refugees-to-settle-in-canada-by-years-end-after-receipt-of-3-5-million-in-donations-ensures-community-sponsorship-spaces-are-filled.

51 Refugee Sponsorship Training Program, "BVOR News," 1 no. 3, 22 August 2018, accessed 7 September 2018, http://www.rstp.ca/wp-content/uploads/2018/09/BVOR-News-3_fc.pdf.

52 Council for Refugees, "BVOR CCR Positions,"; Labman, "Private Sponsorship," 68, 73.

53 UNHCR Canada, "UNHCR BVOR Fact Sheet," August 2018, accessed 6 March 2019, https://www.unhcr.ca/wp-content/uploads/2019/01/UNHCR-BVOR-Fact-Sheet-FINAL.pdf.

54 Immigration, Refugees and Citizenship Canada, "Notice – Supplementary Information 2019–2021 Immigration Levels Plan," Government of Canada, 31 October 2018, accessed 6 March 2019, https://www.canada.ca/en/immigration-refugees-citizenship/news/notices/supplementary-immigration-levels-2019.html.

55 Ibid.

56 Council for Refugees, "BVOR CCR Positions."

57 Refugee Sponsorship Training Program, "Copy of BVOR Tracking - September 2018 (Week 1)," Refugee Sponsorship Training Program (RSTP), accessed 10 September 2018, http://www.rstp.ca/wp-content/uploads/2018/09/BVOR-Tracking-September-2018-Week-1.pdf.

58 Council for Refugees, "BVOR CCR Positions."

59 Immigration Refugees, and Citizenship Canada, *Evaluation of the Resettlement Programs*, v.

60 Ibid., viii.

61 Council for Refugees, "BVOR CCR Positions."

62 The Refugee Hub, "Hundreds of refugees to settle in Canada by year's end."

63 Ibid.

64 Ibid.

65 The Refugee Hub, "PRESS RELEASE: Funds Now Available for Canadians to Sponsor Hundreds of Refugees in 2019," 2 May 2019, accessed 15 August 2019, https://refugeehub.ca/press-release-funds-now-available-for-canadians-to-sponsor-hundreds-of-refugees-in-2019.

66 The Refugee Hub, "Announcement: BVOR Fund extended until September 9th!," 10 August 2019, accessed 15 August 2019, https://us17.campaign-archive.com/?u=af3cc2a54a495c5bd97f14ac7&id=0e0c4b04ce.
67 Refugee Sponsorship Training Program, "BVOR News," no.7, 25 January 2019, accessed 6 March 2019, http://www.rstp.ca/wp-content/uploads/2019/02/BVOR-news-January-2019-Fin_-Jan-25-2019.pdf.

8

Refugee Sponsorship in the Age of Social Media: Canada and the Syrian Refugee Program

Elizabeth Coffin-Karlin

For many Internet users in the global North, the 2015 photograph of toddler Alan Kurdi's corpse on a Turkish beach was their first exposure to the refugee experience and its inherent dangers. That image galvanized individuals to criticize the "dehumanizing" language used to refer to refugees and to demand that lawmakers do something in response to the crisis, and prompted citizens around the world to lobby their governments to address the crisis in Syria.[1] The photograph, which went viral on Twitter, launched an international engagement with the Syrian refugee crisis through social media and Internet-based, grassroots informational sources. In Canada, a public reckoning with the refugee crisis through social media aimed at an international and domestic audience continued through the first years of the "surge" of Syrian refugees into Canada, through Instagram posts, sponsorship blogs, Reddit and Quora forums, and other open source media.

Since that photograph went viral, the world has become used to watching various refugee crises play out in participatory social media, or what has been called "open source intelligence."[2] From Instagram videos and audiotapes of children taken from their parents' arms at the US/Mexico border in the summer of 2018,[3] to accusations of chemical weapons attacks on Damascus in April 2018,[4] to the January 2019 media storm around Saudi Arabian teenager Rahaf Mohammad's self-barricaded hotel room in Thailand in her effort to avoid repatriation (she was eventually resettled as a refugee in Canada after recommendations from UN officials),[5] social media users in the global North and around the world have responded repeatedly to disturbing images and stories that, for many, have defined their exposure to the refugee crisis. The image of Kurdi's corpse was among the first of these moments. At the time, many media outlets around the world engaged in intense debates over whether that image should even be published.[6]

Canada was among the earliest countries to respond to this first real "viral" moment in the global refugee crisis. This was for several reasons, including an approaching national election and the discovery that Kurdi had an aunt in Canada who had been trying to bring the family into the country.[7] As it turned out, the Canadian experience of taking in a large group of Syrian refugees, and how that experience was represented in social media, brought to the fore many ongoing issues and trends surrounding refugee reception and integration. This chapter will examine the Canadian engagement with the refugee crisis through both traditional and social media and grassroots participatory Internet forums during the Syrian "surge" and its aftermath. Part 1 reviews some of the problematic aspects of the practice of "visibilizing" the refugee crisis in Canada and internationally through the use of heart-rending images and blogs. Part 2 focuses on the Ripple Refugee Project, examining how that group's blog became a resource for new sponsors throughout Canada as well as a space for reflecting on the challenges of private sponsorship from both sponsors and refugees. Unintentionally, that blog highlighted many of the problems that arise when refugees are "othered" through social media. Part 3 concludes the chapter by exploring the grassroots debate around the private sponsorship program – a debate that has been conducted through social media, from Buzzfeed compilations of #welcomerefugees to anti-Muslim memetic trolling – and how that debate has intersected with the academic discourse on hate speech and Internet polarization.

PART 1: THE BENEFITS AND DRAWBACKS OF POSTING

By the time civil society around the world was galvanized by the photo of Syrian toddler Alan Kurdi dead on a beach in September 2015, the number of refugees welcomed to Canada through the Private Sponsorship of Refugees (PSR) program had fallen to historic lows, and Canada had pledged to take only 10,000 refugees for the year.[8] In its July 2015 report, Amnesty International wrote that until that point, "calls by the UN for the international community to resettle refugees from Syria [had] largely fallen on deaf ears," and only 23 percent of the UN humanitarian appeal for refugees had been funded.[9] In 2014 the UNHCR estimated there were 378,684 people in the main five host countries alone in need of resettlement (at the time of the report, according to AI, only 2.2 percent of Syrians registered with the UNHCR were likely to be offered resettlement by the international community).[10] Those resettlement numbers did not shift until after the world saw the image of Kurdi the following September – an image that caused a surge of attention to the Syrian crisis.

Francesco D'Orazio, a researcher with the Visual Social Media Lab, contends that the photograph of Kurdi substantively shifted the global conversation about the Syria crisis, changing the language the average searcher or poster on Twitter used from "migrant" to "refugee." This reflected a change in perspective regarding those who were attempting to leave Syria.[11] According to National Public Radio in the United States, average daily donations to the Swedish Red Cross campaign for Syrian refugees were fifty-five times greater in the week after the photo than they had been the previous week.[12] University of Oregon researchers studying the impact of tragic photographs such as Kurdi's on mass empathy wrote that "in this case, an iconic photo of a single child was worth more than hundreds of thousands of statistical lives" in terms of impact on people's decisions to care about the Syrian crisis. Their study demonstrated increases in short-term aid and refugee policies toward Syrians in several countries.[13]

While the specific content of Kurdi's story and the rapidity with which it spread was new to many, the "form" the moment took was familiar to academics who study how the public grapples with tragedy and crisis.[14] Brian Ott and Eric Aoki posit that for shared violent tragedies that grab a nation's attention, "the underlying form ... may have resonance with the news media's framing of other public traumas."[15] They suggest that after a public, brutal tragedy, media coverage and public reaction both tend to follow particular patterns.[16]

First, the event is "named" as a major news story. The authors argue that this is most likely to happen "based on its potential for drama,"[17] often found in the gruesomeness and incongruity of a visual scene.[18] Next, Ott and Aoki write, the victim must be turned into a "martyr" and/or a "political symbol" so as to create "wide-scale public guilt."[19] This publicly held guilt creates a motivation for change – for what the authors call "expunging the evil" – which involves lambasting those involved and crying out for justice.[20] Finally, the public processes its grief by "restoring the social order," which serves a "cathartic function."[21] The underlying social issues and crises that created the tragedy in the first place are left unaddressed by the surge in public anger around the issue. "The shortcoming of tragic framing," the authors write, "is that it brings about symbolic resolution without ... substantively alter[ing] its character as to insure that future instances are less likely."[22] In fact, they argue, this sequence "aggressively perpetuates the status quo."[23]

In Canada, Kurdi's death ignited the largest surge in public support for private sponsorship of refugees in Canada since the Indochinese surge of refugees of the 1970s. Of the more than 40,000 Syrian refugees resettled in Canada between 4 November 2015 and 29 January 2017, about 18,000 were wholly or partly funded through private sponsorship (of these, about 4,000 were Blended Visa Office-Referred [BVOR] refugees – typically refugees of heightened vulnerability – whose financial support was split between the government and private sponsors).[24] In an interview with CBC News a year after Kurdi's death, Brian Dyck, national migration and resettlement coordinator with the Mennonite Central Committee and chair of the Canadian Refugee Sponsorship Agreement Holder Association, noted a tenfold increase in inquiries into private sponsorship immediately after news spread about Kurdi's death: "We hadn't really seen a lot of interest [in private sponsorship] the last ten years or so ... but after that we began to get calls all the time."[25] After Kurdi's story became known, people were galvanized to do something: "They said, 'We can do more.'"[26] This push followed the steps described by Ott and Aoki: after being confronted by tragedy, the public requires a temporary push for change in order to "expunge the evil" of what has happened.

After the initial shock of Kurdi's death, a push for change, and the victory of Justin Trudeau's Liberal Party in a federal election, the Canadian #welcomerefugees movement went viral.[27] This was likely the stage Ott and Aoki would call "public guilt": evil was to be expunged[28] – here, by electing a new prime minister whose administration would not be associated with rejecting Kurdi's family application to Canada, and who promised newer, more open policies toward the Syrians."[29] This increase in interest in bringing the Syrians to Canada quickly led to globally popular photographs and videos of the dashing new prime minister hugging Syrian children and welcoming them "home."[30] These photos were downloaded around the world, and newspapers and cable news outlets worldwide published paeans to Canada's resettlement policy and to the open-heartedness of the Canadian people, who were scrambling to bring Syrians into their communities.[31] Al Jazeera reported that the top Google search in Canada in September 2015 – the same month as Kurdi's death and the subsequent revelation that he had an aunt living in Canada – was "how to sponsor a Syrian."[32] According to the *New York Times,* a picture of Prime Minister Trudeau with a young, recently arrived refugee had been shared 224,000 times on Twitter by late January 2017.[33]

Canada's welcome to these refugees painted the nation as a bastion of open-armed refugee policy – a public relations victory in the eyes of a world looking for a way to feel better about the tragedy.[34] While this was most notable in the early days of the refugee surge, there was significant ongoing media coverage of these "new Canadians" and their integration into their new home (see Part 2). For those who believe that increased resettlement is a universal "good," it is easy to think of these developments and this increased engagement with refugees as a uniform positive. Yet there is significant scholarship arguing that this type of engagement can be problematic in the long term even as it motivates action in the short term. First, as discussed by Ott and Aoki, the basic issues that created the tragedy in the first place often remain unchanged after the surge in attention. Paul Slovic and colleagues write that while a powerful image can generate short-term action, because there is no strong system of global governance around genocide and mass killings, true change is unlikely to result from surges of public interest and goodwill.[35]

Some also suggest that the opportunity to interact with a social media post – for example, by resharing, retweeting, or "liking" – can give users the false sense that they are helping solve a crisis, thus absolving them of feelings of guilt and helplessness, when in fact they are having little impact on the matter at hand.[36] This is referred to as "the strength of weak commitment" – that is, one's urge to help during a crisis is sublimated by the action of engaging on social media.[37] While donations to organizations such as the Swedish Red Cross surged in the month after Kurdi's death, they had largely flattened again by October of the same year.[38] This suggests that a large part of the public felt that they had "restored" the social sphere (to use Ott and Aoki's terminology) and could move on from the tragedy that had so affected them only a month earlier.[39] Similarly, in 2017, Canada's immigration office announced that it would "significantly reduce" its intake of private sponsorship applications for Syrian and Iraqi refugees.[40] While the numbers are slated to rise between 2019 and 2021,[41] it will be interesting to see whether those numbers will be adjusted if the court challenge from Canadian NGOs trying to end the Safe Third Country Agreement is successful.[42] While the programs are not formally tied, it is unclear how Canada's resettlement plans will be impacted if there are suddenly significantly higher numbers of eligible asylum-seekers applying at the nation's southern border, assuming the United States is no longer considered a "safe" country for refugees.

PART 2: THE RIPPLE REFUGEE BLOG: COMMUNITY-BUILDING THROUGH THE BLOGOSPHERE

In January 2016, private sponsorship groups in Canada were submitting about two hundred applications a week, and many of these applicants were first-time sponsors who had been inspired by the viral movement and who had no previous experience with the PSR program or ties to Syrians as an ethnic group.[43] While "direct participation by civil society in resettlement has been the hallmark of Canada's private sponsorship programme, and a major element in its success,"[44] over the past several decades, most of that work has been done by large Sponsorship Agreement Holder (SAH) groups that have systems in place to take on a few refugees a year, with the help of their (often religious) constituencies.[45] Yet given the rapid increase in the number of refugees admitted to the PSR program, those SAH groups with training and experience were stretched thin, and many groups of Canadians with no previous experience with refugee issues were banding together to take in Syrians. They were willing to help and full of an energy that had been lacking in the recent years of the PSR program, but by and large, they had no training in counselling victims of extreme trauma or bridging deep cross-cultural differences.[46] In addition, supplementary resources for the incoming refugees, including English classes and job training programs, were overwhelmed during those first months. Chris Friesen, president of the Canadian Immigrant Settlement Sector Alliance, said in an October 2015 interview with CBC News that "more consideration is needed post-arrival to actually figure out how to successfully integrate 25,000 Syrians over an eight-week period ... The challenges post-arrival are significant."[47]

For the first time in decades, many of these sponsorship groups were composed of young, secular urbanites. As other authors in this volume have noted, most SAHs in Canada are affiliated with religious groups,[48] and many new sponsor groups found themselves at political or philosophical odds with the organizations that under normal circumstances would have provided training and support. From the early days of the #welcomerefugees movement, the private citizens of the Ripple Refugee Project (RRP) set themselves up in the media and on their own blog as the archetype of this new form of private sponsorship group, both in their inexperience and in their new commitment to supporting a number of refugee families after being galvanized by Kurdi's photograph. The group was made up of a mix of doctors, nurses, and other Canadians with jobs entirely unrelated to refugee and health issues.[49] Early media coverage read:

> [The Ripple Refugee project] pledged to be [their sponsored refugees'] first friends, for life is more than basics. It is walks along the boardwalk and visits to the museum, and learning the difference between Vietnamese pho and Chinese ramen. Most of these people are average citizens, like you and me. They haven't done this before. They are learning, as they go. They are sure, only, that this is the right thing to do.[50]

The RRP soon launched a blog through the platform Blogger, which is owned by Google.[51] Members of the group wrote a series of posts that were a mix of fundraising, personal reflection, and networking with other sponsorship groups across Canada.[52] A photograph of their first sponsored family was used by the *Toronto Star*, Canada's largest daily newspaper, in its editorial welcoming the "newcomers from Syria" to Canada.[53] At its height, the RRP blog functioned simultaneously as an advertisement for the PSR program, a fundraising platform, a meeting place for media inquiries, and a self-reflective critical window onto the challenges of sponsoring refugees.

In one blogpost, titled "The Benefits of Private Refugee Sponsorship," the group wrote that for sponsors, "[sponsoring a refugee family] is a real participatory, community-building experience which helps foster neighborhood relationships, enable cross-cultural understanding, build grass-roots support for refugee issues ... and enhance citizens' awareness of the challenges faced by the lower-income segments in our society."[54] Yet the author almost immediately shifted to criticizing the

Canadian government's lack of support (financial and otherwise) for the PSR program.[55] Notably, this post cited the loneliness of "going it alone" as untrained refugee advocates responsible for the happiness and success of traumatized strangers.[56] Later, the page views and media attention lent the blog a more obviously instructional quality. For example, the post "A Few Things We Have Learned in the First Year" included RRP member Claudia Blume's ruminations on topics as serious as infantilization of the refugee family, the importance of managing one's expectations of the depth of the relationship one can build with the refugees, and the reality of the time commitment inherent in being a refugee sponsor.[57] Blume wrote: "All of a sudden we were responsible for eight complete strangers who did not speak a word of English, had never traveled anywhere besides Syria and Lebanon and did not know how things worked in Canada. It was very daunting – almost like adopting a child."[58]

The RRP blog's comments section came to serve as a fundraising tool for the group, which was supporting a three-generation family of eight, resulting in much higher expenses than originally anticipated (even with government support through the BVOR program).[59] It also occasionally served as a community tool, where members of the surrounding area cold introduce themselves, offer items such as free furniture, and (often) mention meeting members of the sponsored family around town. Some commenters posted their personal phone numbers.[60] Similar Facebook groups were operating in neighbourhoods throughout Canada during the same time period with the aim of helping with fundraising and supporting sponsors, but the RRP's reach was international in a way that other groups were not.[61] This decentralized approach was somewhat unlike that of countries such as Sweden, where groups like Al Tadamon ("solidarity" in Arabic) and Vi som tar emot flyktingar pa Stockholms central (We Who Welcome Refugees at Stockholm's Central Station) organized aid and support primarily through the Facebook platform and directly coordinated with the Swedish Migration Agency.[62]

The RRP blog was not especially groundbreaking in its content, and it did not coordinate directly with the Canadian government. Also, its banality is notable when considering the quantity of media attention and notice it received – as recently as November 2018, the RPP was featured in *Time Magazine* for a video it had tweeted of two sponsored Eritrean refugee children playing in the snow, which Prime Minister Trudeau had retweeted.[63] As Blume notes at the end of the first-year reflection post, "when we decided to sponsor refugees there were not many resources available."[64] In response, the group created both the blog and a publicly available database of resources, found in a Google Drive folder (link found in endnote), and became a frequently quoted "expert" source on private sponsorship.[65]

The long-lasting nature of blogs of this type raises issues of dehumanization and consent. Many academics "problematize the popular assumption that the humanitarian spectacle automatically mobilises viewers' response." Such spectacles create dynamics of the "other" that can negatively affect the long-term prospects for integration.[66] Even after refugees are resettled in their new homes, the sheer quantity of images posted online aimed at generating feelings of tragedy and vulnerability threaten to "massify" and dehumanize refugee bodies.[67] A group of Australian researchers analyzing images of refugees in the media and on social platforms noted that "the most striking result ... is the distinct lack of images depicting individual asylum-seekers with recognizable facial features"; furthermore, "the very absence of such images inevitably dehumanizes refugees."[68] Lilie Chouliaraki argues these "mass" images, in which refugees are depicted as a "multitude of indistinguishable individuals," deprives them of their "biographical specificity as human beings" and leaves them in the position of being defined in the minds of audiences as "sub-citizens" lacking personal legitimacy and/or the ability to self-advocate.[69] These critiques were aimed specifically at images of Middle Eastern refugees fleeing to Europe on rafts or walking up to land crossings; that said, images posted and archived in ongoing posts on blogs, on Facebook, and in the popular media tracking the newly resettled refugees in their new homes can serve a similar purpose, continuing the narrative of the "other" even as the former refugees are working to build new lives.

In particular, much of the language used by group members can be described as patronizing, for it emphasizes the helplessness and vulnerability of the new Canadians they are discussing in blogposts such as "A Few Things We Have Learned in the First Year," which talks about the enormous burden of caring for a family with few skills in such a way as to help them integrate more readily into Canadian society.[70] In describing the effort and time commitment involved in taking care of the family, the author of that post actually resorted to the metaphor of adopting a child.[71] "Infantilisation may ... aim at mobilizing empathy in the name of 'our' common humanity, yet, in portraying refugees as children in need, it ultimately deprives them of agency and voice," writes Chouliaraki.[72] Additionally, there is significant historical baggage in North America tied to the infantilization of non-white people, Indigenous people, and those from the global South, and this raises disturbing echoes of historically racist and antifeminist critiques that have been used repeatedly to justify a lack of voice for the infantilized and as a tool for private citizens and governments alike to disempower non-white ethnic groups.[73]

The frequent pictures posted of the resettled refugees on the blog, archived presumably for the foreseeable future, also raise issues of humanization, consent, and visibilization. These pictures, which depict several families from the moment of their arrival, during their first days as "new Canadians," range from photographs of full families arriving at the airport (presumably traumatized and exhausted) to the houses the sponsorship group has paid for.[74] "Photographs play a vital role in the revelation and reification of embodied vulnerability," and it is unclear what the terms of consent were for these photographs and whether the pictured families would wish some of their hardest moments to be archived on the Internet and easily searchable in perpetuity.[75]

Several of the pictures are of children, including the one recently retweeted by Prime Minister Trudeau of the two Eritrean children playing in the snow.[76] These children, who will presumably grow up as Canadians, will have their images forever online and retweeted potentially thousands of times, and in most countries they would not be viewed as capable of giving their informed consent. As Durham notes, "children's bodies ... have potent symbolic impact in terms of their vulnerability."[77] While the pictures of the children playing in the snow are not in the same league as those of "a starving Sudanese baby," it is worth considering the ethics of posting photographs of children as symbolic objects, either using their sadness and fear to show the depths of the refugee crisis or their joy as physical representations of Canadian generosity made flesh.[78] This dynamic continues to echo loud in the international discussion of what child refugees and asylums seekers "should" look like, and public judgments that many minor asylum-seekers do not "look like" children, as discussed by Carly McLaughlin in the UK context.[79] The idea of judging a child's facade to determine his or her eligibility for international protection is also a common issue in the Spanish context, with the government administering invasive, scientifically questionable age exams to asylum-seekers who do not "seem" young enough.[80]

These dynamics are not unique to the RRP blog; indeed, they have been present in much of the media coverage of the #welcomerefugees project. Tyyska and colleagues explore this dynamic more thoroughly in their critique of Canadian media content focused on resettlement of refugees in Canada from September 2015 – immediately after Kurdi's death – to April 2016.[81] Through an analysis of more than four hundred pieces of media in different modalities spread across several media groups, they explored coverage of the refugee crisis in which "the 'west' is contrasted to the 'rest,'" as well as the promotion of neoliberal ideology through the coverage of the private sponsorship of the resettled refugees.[82] They found that the media coverage included what many would consider the "positive" Canadian values of humanitarianism and generosity, but also included a systematic "representation of Syrian refugees as lacking agency, vulnerable, and needy amidst challenges"; it also promoted a "gendered representation" of male refugees as security threats.[83] The plethora of media coverage emphasizing the Canadians who were taking in the Syrian refugees as representatives of Canadian values perhaps unintentionally de-emphasized international treaties and obligations that could be viewed as requiring this type of hospitality in the long term. This allowed citizens to perceive refugee reception in times of crisis as a voluntary act made by kind Canadians, rather than an obligation the Canadian government was required to meet under international treaty law, and integrated into the domestic Canadian legal system.[84]

The authors further argue that "it is clear that the media engage in the process of 'othering' Syrian refugees. In all of the media sources we analyzed, Canadian citizens, politicians, and other public actors speak on behalf of refugees and exemplify a 'saviour complex' that marginalizes Syrian refugees while offering a narrative of humanitarian and generous Canadians." Also, that "feminist, orientalist, and neocolonial frameworks are evident in the media representation of Syrian refugees in Canada."[85] Finally, the authors found a distinct "lack of presence of Syrian refugees in their own stories."[86] While the RRP does post the occasional blog written by a formerly sponsored Syrian and calls out the importance of privileging refugee voices, most posts are from the perspective of the "old" Canadians doing the sponsoring.[87] This dynamic was also explored in a CBC radio article called "How Syrians Arriving in Canada Became 'Extras' in Their Own Stories," in which Kamal Al-Solaylee discussed his discomfort with "more and more news stories about sponsors hugging refugees in airports and Canadians knitting toques to keep refugees warm during their first Canadian winter," or what Al-Solaylee calls in the interview "the gaze turned inward instead of outward."[88]

PART 3: DYNAMICS OF POLARIZATION IN GRASSROOTS SOCIAL MEDIA USAGE AND #WELCOMEREFUGEES

In the very early days of the #welcomerefugees moment, the Internet was full of positive welcome for the "new Canadians."[89] While some of the newly activated sponsors were able to attend short webinars or trainings to prepare them for the arrival of the Syrians, the reality of being responsible for full families of traumatized, non–English-speaking people set in for many relatively quickly after arrival. Perhaps unique to the Internet Age is the manner in which open forum websites such as Quora and Reddit have hosted significant conversations on the success of the programs, both among sponsors and among those critical of the program. As Bozdag and Smets observe, "social media create diverse communication spaces in which users can debate social issues among 'networked audiences' ... Thus, social media ... [become] key sources for studying how various social issues are perceived."[90] Some threads on these platforms have hosted thorough, detailed discussions on the merits and faults of the integration of the Syrian immigrants coming through the PSR program (see examples in note 91), many of which sponsors or those with sponsors in their community participated in.[91] Yet as is common in this age, similar forums (as well as sites on the Dark Web that this piece will not discuss in detail) have hosted conversations about expelling refugees and have posted memetic content aimed at further "othering" refugees within Canada and aiming to exclude further ones from entering the country.

The screenshot below is from a conversation started on the forum Reddit by handler u/_coast_of_maine around 2018 (note: Reddit posts do not have exact dates). The question was: "[Serious] Those of you living in countries where Syrian refugees are resettling – how is the process really going? (serious replies only)." Of the forty-seven users who responded, many were truly thoughtful about the refugee crisis and the effect it was having on their communities.[92]

Not all the information in this thread and others like it is accurate or complete; that said, they represent citizens asking heartfelt questions

> [deleted] 41 points · 1 year ago
> Canada: 25,000 refugees. So-so. The problem is that many cannot find employment. Between language and skills gaps, it's a significant hurdle.
> Share Save
>
> > souIless 8 points · 1 year ago
> > The lacking skills and language is definitely a big issue. Without a job, it's hard to integrate, and a lot of refugees/immigrants are severely lacking in any useful skills.
> >
> > It's sad because I honestly believe that they'd love to contribute, but they just can't. And to think that a lot of children right now in Syria are prevented from receiving any kind of education due to the ongoing war makes the future look even bleaker.
> > Share Save
> >
> > > ioncloud9 0 points · 1 year ago
> > > Most legal immigrants aren't lacking in those things, just the illegal ones and the refugees.
> > > Share Save
>
> Professor226 2 points · 1 year ago
> We take in 250,000 refugees annually. The Syrians are a blip.
> Share Save

Figure 8.1 Reddit screenshot

about the refugee phenomenon in their country. In the subreddit r/CanadaPolitics (58,000 subscribers), ProBonoShill asked, "Why should we sponsor refugees not in immediate danger when we could support many more refugees abroad at the same cost?" The responses led to a back and forth discussing the ethics of international humanitarian aid, military intervention, and the economics of various international human rights policies.[93]

Yet both in Canadian threads and in others of similar types internationally, disruptive commenters ("trolls") repeatedly took over the discourse with accusations related to terrorism and the looming imposition of *sharia* law, as well as diatribes about wasting government money on refugees and the gutting of Canada's home-grown culture.[94] Some of these commenters have since been discredited as Russian Twitter agents intentionally sowing discord; others, though, were likely expressing their own actual racism.[95] Notably, the subreddit r/ImGoingToHellForThis has been tackled in academic literature as the pre-eminent example of fomented racist nationalism, much of which manifested itself in photoshopped memes of Alan Kurdi's dead body on the beach.[96] The site's racism functioned through "revers[ing] the terms of contemporary coded racism, converting subtle codes into blatantly racist statements excused as knowing jokes."[97] Reddit, Quora, and other sites – including Twitter – have struggled with how to balance protections for "self-expression" with the reality that "when sites are overrun by trolls, they drown out the voices of women, ethnic and religious minorities, gays – anyone who might feel vulnerable."[98]

In Canada, the death of thirteen-year-old Marisa Shen, which led to criminal charges against a Syrian refugee, has led to an upsurge in anti-refugee resentment among Canadians on the Internet, leading many news sites to close down their comments sections for articles surrounding the trial.[99] Media reports on her death include quotes that play to anti-Muslim stereotypes, specifically around violence against women, even though there is no indication the crime was religiously motivated or substantively differed from the everyday tragedy of a young woman dying at the hands of an older adult man.[100] CTV news quoted a "family friend" as saying, "We know what radicals in Syria do to women and children."[101] Relatedly, videos claiming that many Syrians are "fake" refugees who were not properly vetted by the Liberal government have attracted more than 12,000 views.[102]

As *Guardian* columnist Clare Allen has noted, "we seem to have a problem negotiating the different levels of reality the Internet offers."[103] This is especially true with regard to vulnerable people, who may both be mentally and emotionally affected by the content written about them online (and the implied rejection of their personhood),[104] or who may suffer hate crimes, discrimination, or attacks at the hands of those who believe the shared memetic content and act upon it.[105] In 2018, the incidence of hate crimes, especially against Muslims, rose significantly in Canada.[106] When asked about that rise in a media interview, Barbara Perry, the director of Ontario Tech University's Centre on Hate, Bias, and Extremism, said that the "very visibility and blatancy [of the organized far right movement] ... has contributed to that normalization of hate, that normalization of negative sentiment directed at targeted communities."

CONCLUSIONS

The Canadian #welcomerefugees movement exemplifies many of the challenges addressed by academic discourse regarding how the public understands and engages with crisis and tragedy through media. It is indisputable that however temporary the surge of interest in resettlement was, it resulted in thousands of refugees gaining the opportunity to leave dangerous and inhumane conditions for the safety of Canada. Yet a program's success should not immunize it from criticism when it has the potential for lasting, problematic results. The traditional and social media coverage of the initial surge of interest in the Syrian crisis upon the death of Alan Kurdi and the subsequent resettlement of many of those refugees in Canada through the #welcomerefugees program consistently "othered" the incoming refugees, frequently portraying them as vulnerable and childlike instead of seeing them as full, humanized individuals. While well-intentioned, blogs like the Ripple Refugee Project further privileged Canadian over Syrian voices in resettlement, using emotional photographs of "their" refugees, especially children, in ways considered problematic by those many academics who focus on childhood vulnerability and its intersection with critical race theory. Finally, conflicted narrations of the "other" through grassroots media outlets, including memes as well as public forums such as Reddit, are mimicked throughout much of the global North as pushback against refugees continues and hate crimes rise in number. While this chapter is by no means a comprehensive analysis of the dynamics of private refugee resettlement in Canada and media portrayal or grassroots participation in Internet-based informational sources, hopefully it can serve as a reminder in further coverage of refugees in Canada or when policies are being crafted to facilitate refugee integration that "victimhood and threat are by no means straightforward categories of visibility" and that "visualities of threat and hospitality, in a parallel move, both work on the assumption that refugee imagery is not only about who we care for but also who we denounce."[107]

NOTES

1 Adam Withnall, "If These Extraordinarily Powerful Images of a Dead Syrian Child Washed up on a Beach Don't Change Europe's Attitude to Refugees, What Will?," *The Independent*, accessed 26 February 2019, https://www.independent.co.uk/news/world/europe/if-these-extraordinarily-powerful-images-of-a-dead-syrian-child-washed-up-on-a-beach-don-t-change-10482757.html.
2 Michael Glassman and Min Ju Kang, "Intelligence in the Internet Age: The Emergence and Evolution of Open Source Intelligence (OSINT)," *Computers in Human Behavior* 28 (2012): 673–82.
3 "How Everyone Started Talking About Family Separations," *The Atlantic*, accessed 25 February 2019, https://www.theatlantic.com/technology/archive/2018/06/the-making-of-a-moral-problem/563114.

4 Colum Lynch and Elias Groll, "How Social Media Built the Case for Trump's Strike on Syria," *Foreign Policy*, accessed 25 February 2019, https://foreignpolicy.com/2018/04/17/how-social-media-built-the-case-for-trumps-strike-on-syria.

5 Mayuri Mei Lin and Heather Chen, "#SaveRahaf: How Twitter Saved a Saudi Woman," 10 January 2019, BBC, sec. Asia, https://www.bbc.com/news/world-asia-46819199; Harriet Alexander, "Canadian Prime Minister Confirms Saudi Teen Rahaf Al-Qunun to Be Granted Asylum," *Telegraph*, 11 January 2019, https://www.telegraph.co.uk/news/2019/01/11/saudi-woman-fled-family-granted-asylum-canada-thailand-airport.

6 Mette Mortensen, Stuart Allan, and Chris Peters, "The Iconic Image in a Digital Age: Editorial Mediations over the Alan Kurdi Photographs," *Nordicom Review* 28, no. 2 (2017): 78.

7 "'My Children Slipped Away from My Hands,' Drowned Syrian Boy's Father Says," CBC, 3 September 2015, https://www.cbc.ca/news/canada/british-columbia/syria-migrants-canada-drowned-migrants-1.3213772.

8 Martin Lukacs, "Harper's Canada Has More Than One Refugee Death on Its Hands," *Guardian*, accessed 21 September 2018, https://www.theguardian.com/environment/true-north/2015/sep/04/harpers-canada-has-more-than-one-refugee-death-on-its-hands.

9 Amnesty International, "The Global Refugee Crisis: A Conspiracy of Neglect" (2015), 10.

10 Ibid., 5.

11 Visual Social Media Lab, "The Iconic Image on Social Media," accessed 24 February 2019, http://visualsocialmedialab.org/projects/the-iconic-image-on-social-media.

12 "Study: What Was The Impact of the Iconic Photo of the Syrian Boy?," NPR.*Org*, accessed 24 February 2019, https://www.npr.org/sections/goatsandsoda/2017/01/13/509650251/study-what-was-the-impact-of-the-iconic-photo-of-the-syrian-boy.

13 Paul Slovic et al., "Iconic Photographs and the Ebb and Flow of Empathetic Response to Humanitarian Disasters," *Proceedings of the National Academy of Sciences* 114, no. 4 (January 2017): 640–4, https://www.pnas.org/content/114/4/640.full.

14 Brian Ott and Eric Aoki, "The Politics of Negotiating Public Tragedy: Media Framing of the Matthew Shepard Murder," *Rhetoric and Public Affairs* 5, no. 3 (Fall 2002): 485.

15 Ibid., 484.

16 Ibid., 485.

17 Ibid., 487.

18 Ibid.
19 Ibid., 489.
20 Ibid., 490.
21 Ibid., 494.
22 Ibid., 496.
23 Ibid.
24 "Canadians Desperate to Sponsor Refugees as Governments Dither," *CBC Radio*, 3 September 2015, https://www.cbc.ca/radio/thecurrent/the-current-for-september-03-2015-1.3213872/canadians-desperate-to-sponsor-refugees-as-governments-dither-1.3213897; Immigration, Refugees, and Citizenship Canada (hereafter IRCC), "#WelcomeRefugees: Key Figures," 2 December 2015, https://www.canada.ca/en/immigration-refugees-citizenship/services/refugees/welcome-syrian-refugees/key-figures.html.
25 "Image of Alan Kurdi's Body Led to Spike in Sponsorship of Syrian Refugees, Group Says," *CBC News*, accessed 21 September 2018, https://www.cbc.ca/news/canada/manitoba/image-of-alan-kurdi-s-body-led-to-spike-in-sponsorship-of-syrian-refugees-group-says-1.3746552.
26 Ibid.
27 Ibid.; IRCC, "#WelcomeRefugees."
28 Ott and Aoki, "The Politics," 476.
29 Lukacs, "Harper's Canada."
30 "Canada to Announce Plan to Resettle 25,000 Refugees Tuesday," *Business Insider*, accessed 21 September 2018, https://www.businessinsider.com/ap-canada-to-announce-plan-to-resettle-25000-refugees-tuesday-2015-11.
31 "Canada's New Prime Minister to Open Doors for Syrian Refugees," *TakePart*, accessed 21 September 2018, http://www.takepart.com/article/2015/10/20/trudeau-refugees.
32 Antonia Zerbisias, "Sponsor Syrian Refugee – Canada's Top Google Search," *Al Jazeera*, accessed 21 September 2018, https://www.aljazeera.com/indepth/opinion/2016/01/sponsor-syrian-refugee-canada-top-google-search-160118071153769.html.
33 Ian Austen, "In Canada, Justin Trudeau Says Refugees Are Welcome," *New York Times*, 28 January 2017, https://www.nytimes.com/2017/01/28/world/canada/justin-trudeau-trump-refugee-ban.html?_r=0&login=smartlock&auth=login-smartlock.
34 Craig Silverman and Ishmael N. Daro, "Canadians Are Tweeting the Most Beautiful Message to Newly-Arrived Refugees," *BuzzFeed*, accessed 21 September 2018, https://www.buzzfeed.com/craigsilverman/welcome-to-canada.

35 Slovic et al., "Iconic Photographs," 543.
36 Lin Proitz, "Visual Social Media and Affectivity: The Impact of the Image of Alan Kurdi and Young People's Response to the Refugee Crisis in Oslo and Sheffield," *Information, Communication, and Society* 21, no. 4 (24 February 2017): 556.
37 Ibid.
38 Slovic et al., "Iconic Photographs," fig. 3.
39 Ott and Aoki, "The Politics," 494.
40 Zi-Ann Lim, "Canada Limits New Private Sponsorships of Syrian Refugees," *Huffington Post*, 12 January 2017, https://www.huffingtonpost.ca/2017/01/12/canada-private-sponsorship-syrian-refugees_n_14136364.html.
41 IRCC, "Notice – Supplementary Information 2019–2021 Immigration Levels Plan," 31 October 2018, https://www.canada.ca/en/immigration-refugees-citizenship/news/notices/supplementary-immigration-levels-2019.html.
42 Canadian Council for Refugees, "Safe Third Country," accessed 11 March 2019, https://ccrweb.ca/en/safe-third-country.
43 Zerbisias, "Sponsor Syrian Refugee."
44 Jennifer Hyndman, William Payne, and Shauna Jimenez, "Private Refugee Sponsorship in Canada," *Forced Migration Review* 54 (February 2017): 58.
45 Barbara Treviranus and Michael Casasola, "Canada's Private Sponsorship of Refugees Program: A Practitioner's Perspective of Its Past and Future," *Journal of International Migration and Integration* 4, no. 2 (Spring 2003): 177–202.
46 Catherine Porter, "Citizens Step Up Where City Fails Refugees," *Toronto Star*, accessed 21 September 2018, https://www.thestar.com/news/canada/2015/09/23/citizens-step-up-where-city-fails-refugees-porter.html.
47 "Trudeau Urged to Reconsider 'Problematic' Goal of 25,000 Syrian Refugees by End of 2015," CBC *News*, 28 October 2015, https://www.cbc.ca/news/politics/trudeau-syria-refugees-settlement-groups-1.3291959.
48 IRCC, "Private Sponsorship of Refugees Program – Sponsorship Agreement Holders," 1 March 2019, https://www.canada.ca/en/immigration-refugees-citizenship/services/refugees/help-outside-canada/private-sponsorship-program/agreement-holders/holders-list.html.
49 Ripple Refugee Project, "A Healthy Beginning," 29 December 2015, http://ripplerefugee.blogspot.com/2015/12/a-healthy-beginning.html.
50 Porter, "Citizens Step Up Where City Fails Refugees."
51 "Canadians Desperate to Sponsor Refugees as Governments Dither."

52 Ripple Refugee Project, "The Benefits of Private Refugee Sponsorship," 9 September 2016, http://ripplerefugee.blogspot.com/2016/09/why-private-sponsorship-of-refugees-is.html.
53 Editorial, "To the Newcomers from Syria: Welcome to Canada," *Toronto Star*, accessed 14 March 2019, https://www.thestar.com/opinion/editorials/2015/12/10/to-the-newcomers-from-syria-welcome-to-canada-editorial.html.
54 Ripple Refugee Project, "The Benefits of Private Refugee Sponsorship."
55 Ibid.
56 Ibid.
57 Ripple Refugee Project, "A Few Things We Have Learned in the First Year," 13 November 2016, http://ripplerefugee.blogspot.com/2016_11_13_archive.html.
58 Ibid.
59 Ripple Refugee Project, "We Have Been Matched with a Syrian Refugee Family!," 22 September 2015, http://ripplerefugee.blogspot.com/2015/09/we-have-been-matched-with-syrian.html.
60 Ibid.
61 "(1) South Mountain Refugee Sponsorship Committee," accessed 11 March 2019, https://www.facebook.com/South-Mountain-Refugee-Sponsorship-Committee-1203369306408434; "TAC Welcomes Refugee Families," accessed 11 March 2019, https://www.facebook.com/pg/RefugeeSponsorship/community/?ref=page_internal.
62 Anne Kaun and Julie Uldam, "'Volunteering Is Like Any Other Business': Civic Participation and Social Media," *New Media and Society* 20, no. 6 (2018): 2195–6.
63 "Refugee Children Have a Ball Seeing Snow for the First Time," *Tine Magazine*, accessed 11 March 2019, http://time.com/5452136/refugee-kids-first-snow.
64 Ripple Refugee Project, "A Few Things."
65 "2 - Publicly Shared Resources - Google Drive," accessed 21 September 2018, https://drive.google.com/drive/folders/oB6tDTFPNX-b9WS1lWTV3Ry1US2c.
66 Lilie Chouliaraki, "Concluding Comment: Moral Responsibility and Civic Responsiveness: Spectacles of Suffering on Digital Media," *Javnost – The Public* 23, no. 4 (24 November 2016): 415.
67 Lilie Chouliaraki and Tijana Stolic, "Rethinking Media Responsibility in the Refugee 'Crisis': A Visual Typology of European News," *Media, Culture, and Society* 39, no. 8 (2017): 1164.

68 R. Bleiker, D. Campbell, and E. Hutchinson, "The Visual Dehumanisation of Refugees," *Australian Journal of Political Science* 48, no. 4 (11 December, 2013): 406.
69 Chouliaraki and Stolic, "Rethinking Media Responsibility," 1164.
70 Ripple Refugee Project, "A Few Things."
71 Ibid.
72 Chouliaraki and Stolic, "Rethinking Media Responsibility," 1168.
73 Susan Wendell, "Oppression and Victimization: Choice and Responsibility," *Hypatia* 5, no. 3 (1990): 15–46; Mahmood Mamdani, "Settler Colonialism: Then and Now," *Critical Inquiry* 41, no. 3 (Spring 2015); Dea H. Boster, *African American Slavery and Disability: Bodies, Property, and Power in the Antebellum South, 1800–1860* (New York: Routledge, 2013).
74 Ripple Refugee Project, "Please Help Us Bring an Eritrean Family of Five to Canada," 9 September 2018, http://ripplerefugee.blogspot.com/2018/09/please-help-us-bring-eritrean-single.html.
75 Meenakshi Gigi Durham, "Resignifying Alan Kurdi: News Photographs, Memes, and the Ethics of Embodied Vulnerability," *Critical Studies in Media Communication* 35, no. 3 (15 February 2018): 242.
76 "Refugee Children Have a Ball."
77 Durham, "Resignifying Alan Kurdi," 242.
78 Ibid., 242–3.
79 Carly McLaughlin, "'They Don't Look Like Children': Child Asylum-Seekers, the Dubs Amendment, and the Politics of Childhood," *Journal of Ethnic and Migration Studies* 44, no. 11 (29 December 2017): 1757–73.
80 Amaia Bravo and Iriana Santos-González, "Menores extranjeros no acompañados en España. Necesidades y modelos de intervención," *Psychosocial Intervention* 26, no. 1 (1 April 2017): 55–62.
81 Vappu Tyyska et al., "The Syrian Refugee Crisis in Canadian Media," *Ryerson Centre for Immigration and Settlement*, RCIS Working Papers, no. 2017/3 (n.d.).
82 Ibid., 2–3.
83 Ibid., 4–5.
84 "OHCHR Dashboard," accessed 11 April 2019, http://indicators.ohchr.org; Canadian Council for Refugees, "Brief History of Canada's Signing of the Refugee Convention," *40th Anniversary of Canada's Signing of the Refugee Convention through 2009*, http://ccrweb.ca/sites/ccrweb.ca/files/static-files/canadarefugeeshistory3.htm.
85 Tyyska et al., "The Syrian Refugee Crisis," 7, 14.

86 Ibid., 11.
87 Ripple Refugee Project, ": What It Means to Be a Permanent Resident in a Country for the First Time in My Life," 15 December 2016, http://ripplerefugee.blogspot.com/2016/12/what-is-means-to-be-permanent-resident.html.
88 "How Syrian Refugees Arriving in Canada Became 'extras' in Their Own Stories," CBC Radio, 21 February 2016, https://www.cbc.ca/radio/the180/refugee-arrival-stories-are-too-happy-the-harm-of-french-immersion-and-who-gets-to-decide-who-s-a-feminist-1.3452586/how-syrian-refugees-arriving-in-canada-became-extras-in-their-own-stories-1.3452625.
89 Silverman and Daro, "Canadians Are Tweeting."
90 Cigdem Bozdag and Kevin Smets, "Understanding the Images of Alan Kurdi with 'Small Data': A Qualitative, Comparative Analysis of Tweets about Refugees in Turkey and Flanders (Belgium)," *International Journal of Communication* 11 (2017): 4048.
91 "R/Vancouver – Got Some Perspective Today …," *Reddit*, accessed 24 September 2018, https://www.reddit.com/r/vancouver/comments/48q2ag/got_some_perspective_today/; "R/Canada – So … What Exactly Does 'Sponsoring a Refugee' Mean?," *Reddit*, accessed 24 September 2018, https://www.reddit.com/r/canada/comments/3udbqx/so_what_exactly_does_sponsoring_a_refugee_mean/; "Why Should We Not Bring Refugees in to Canada?," *Quora*, accessed 24 September 2018, https://www.quora.com/Why-should-we-not-bring-refugees-in-to-Canada; "How Do Fellow Canadians Feel about Trudeau's Decision to Allow Immigrants/Refugees into Canada?" *Quora*, accessed 24 September 2018, https://www.quora.com/How-do-fellow-Canadians-feel-about-Trudeau%E2%80%99s-decision-to-allow-immigrants-refugees-into-Canada.
92 "R/AskReddit – [Serious] Those of You Living in Countries Where Syrian Refugees Are Resettling – How Is the Process Really Going?," *Reddit*, accessed 24 September 2018, https://www.reddit.com/r/AskReddit/comments/57xjym/serious_those_of_you_living_in_countries_where.
93 "R/CanadaPolitics – Why Should We Sponsor Refugees Not in Immediate Danger When We Could Support Many More Refugees Abroad at the Same Cost?," *Reddit*, accessed 24 September 2018, https://www.reddit.com/r/CanadaPolitics/comments/4opeas/why_should_we_sponsor_refugees_not_in_immediate.
94 "FACT CHECK: Do 'Illegal' Refugees Receive $3,874 Per Month from the Government?," *Snopes.Com*, accessed 11 March 2019, https://www.snopes.com/fact-check/monthly-refugee-benefits.

95 "'They Find Hot-Button Issues': New Data Shows How Russian Twitter Trolls Targeted Canadians," *CBC News*, 3 August 2018, https://www.cbc.ca/news/canada/russian-twitter-trolls-canada-targeted-1.4772397.
96 Robert Topinka, "Politically Incorrect Participatory Media: Racist Nationalism on r/ImGoingToHellForThis," *New Media and Society* 20, no. 5 (2018): 2050–69.
97 Ibid., 2066.
98 Joel Stein, "How Trolls Are Ruining the Internet," *Time*, accessed 11 March 2019, http://time.com/4457110/internet-trolls.
99 "Marrisa Shen Homicide Update: Man Arrested, Charged with First-Degree Murder – BC," *Globalnews.ca*," 10 September 2018, https://globalnews.ca/news/4437619/marrisa-shen-homicide-update-death.
100 "Who Is Ibrahim Ali? New Details on Marrisa Shen's Accused Killer," *CTV News*, accessed 11 March 2019, https://bc.ctvnews.ca/who-is-ibrahim-ali-new-details-on-marrisa-shen-s-accused-killer-1.4091601.
101 Ibid.
102 Julie Mora, "Marrisa Shen Murder by Syrian Refugee and How a Muslim Told Us It Has Everything to Do with Islam," *YouTube*, accessed 24 September 2018, https://www.youtube.com/watch?v=Or1cUbIAZ74; Billy Joyce, #Trudeau #Giggles & Smirks RE: #1stDegMurder Suspect #Refugee – 13 Yr Old RIP!," *YouTube*, accessed 24 September 2018, https://www.youtube.com/watch?v=SJKn8zHIWZE; Zach Hing, "Marrisa Shen's Death by a Syrian 'Refugee,'" *YouTube*, accessed 24 September 2018, https://www.youtube.com/watch?v=GnTlTU-hQxA.
103 Clare Allan, "Internet Trolls Are a Very Real Threat to Vulnerable People," *Guardian*, 6 August 2013, https://www.theguardian.com/society/2013/aug/06/internet-trolls-real-threat-vulnerable-people.
104 Ciarán Patric Collins Galts, "Refugee Mental Health: How Canada Supports the World's Most Vulnerable in Their Transition to Becoming Canadian," *University of Ottawa Journal of Medicine* 6, no. 2 (2016): 30–2.
105 Carl Meyer, "Attacks against Canadian Muslims and Other Hate Crimes Are Surging," *National Observer*, 29 November 2018, https://www.nationalobserver.com/2018/11/29/news/attacks-against-canadian-muslims-and-other-hate-crimes-are-surging.
106 "Canada's 10 Worst Cities for Hate Crime," *Macleans.ca*, accessed 11 March 2019, https://www.macleans.ca/news/canada/top-10-cities-for-hate-crime.
107 Chouliaraki and Stolic, "Rethinking Media Responsibility," 1172.

PART THREE

Challenges

9

Kindred Spirits? Links between Refugee Sponsorship and Family Sponsorship

Audrey Macklin, Kathryn Barber, Luin Goldring, Jennifer Hyndman, Anna Korteweg, and Jona Zyfi

Private refugee sponsorship depends on establishing and maintaining personal relationships. The primary nexus is between sponsor and refugee, though relations among members of a sponsorship group are also critically important. Tacit assumptions about the nature, scope, dynamics, and effects of the sponsor–refugee relationship operate at governmental, civil society, and individual scales. They shape expectations of what private refugee sponsorship means and does for the participants. Yet the formal architecture of private sponsorship has no obvious contemporary referent and lacks historical antecedents. It has hardly changed since its design and launch in 1979. Little is known about how refugees and sponsors actually experience their relationships. This chapter draws from an ongoing research project that examines refugee sponsorship from the perspective of sponsors, particularly sponsors of Syrian refugees since 2015. The impetus for this chapter is the observation that several respondents to our online survey of sponsors spontaneously invoked a kinship analogy to describe their relationship to the refugees they sponsored. Because our research only engages sponsors, we cannot know whether or how the same analogy arises among privately sponsored refugees. We do note that kinship tropes have also caught the attention of scholars studying interactions between refugees/migrants and locals in European settings.[1] We do not, of course, take the analogy literally; we do not believe that relationships created through sponsorship correspond to actual familial relations. Rather, our interest lies in probing elements of commonality between private sponsorship and themes associated with the family as a social institution and web of social relations. We suggest that certain dynamics associated with kinship relations are embedded in the institutional structure and interstitial norms of private refugee sponsorship, and that these features surface tacitly and explicitly in sponsors' accounts of their relationships with sponsored refugees.

Our online national survey of sponsors who supported Syrians resettled in Canada after November 2015 furnishes one of the first datasets on sponsors and perhaps the largest to date. It is specific to sponsors involved in the Syrian Refugee Initiative promised by Prime Minister Justin Trudeau during the October 2015 federal election. A notable feature of the sample of more than 530 individuals is that 80 percent of them were new sponsors.[2] The high proportion of new sponsors among the research participants may have a bearing on the volume, content, and candour of the written comments, but we cannot specify its significance further than that. Their accounts are based on a single experience (although a few also participated in volunteer support for government-assisted refugees [GARs]), whereas veteran sponsors can place their most recent sponsorship in a comparative context.

The sponsors who responded to our survey were self-selected. We do not and cannot claim that the survey is representative of all sponsors in Canada; in the absence of data about private sponsors based on random sampling, no baseline for comparison exists. A disproportionate percentage of our respondents are from urban centres and from Ontario, with 37 percent from Toronto.[3] Particular demographic characteristics define survey respondents who are sponsors of the Syrian cohort. They are more likely to be women than men (74%), and older than fifty (74%, with 49% over sixty). Those surveyed are also highly educated; some 84 percent have at least one university degree, and more than half (53%) hold a graduate or professional degree. The self-selection of sponsors in the survey is a limitation in terms of representation, but it is also an opportunity, as their motivation to participate in and reflect on the sponsorship experience resulted in rich insights in the open-ended parts of the survey.

In addition to gathering quantitative data, the survey provided a venue for respondents to supplement their responses to various questions with written comments. One question was about the challenge(s) they encountered in their interactions with the sponsored family. We also posed the following open-ended question at the end: "If you would like to tell us more about your private sponsorship expectations or experiences, please use the following text box to discuss any experiences or ideas that you think are relevant and not otherwise captured in this survey."

Virtually all the material presented in this chapter is drawn from written comments to these two questions. We extracted all written comments from these sections and used open coding to identify emergent themes. Almost half the survey participants (256) took the opportunity to write a comment. Many contributions were detailed and introspective. They disclosed the types of insights we expected would be accessible only through in-person interviews. We interpret the enthusiastic take-up of our invitation as expressive of respondents' desire to offer nuanced accounts of their personal experience. We aim to include either frequently mentioned or markedly reflexive comments offered by a cross-section of more than 500 survey respondents, but we do not claim that these comments are representative of sponsors as such. Each quotation in this chapter comes from a different sponsor; all reside in an urban area,[4] and only one is male.

Our analysis sheds light on the way sponsors understood their role, how their relationships may have evolved, and how engaging in sponsorship transformed them in social terms. Recent research on sponsored refugees draws on psychological and sociological insights to explain their perspective, and in this volume and elsewhere Kyriakides and colleagues identify the recognition of refugees' "status eligibilities" as being at the heart of sponsor/sponsored relations.[5] Status eligibility here refers to the external affirmation of self-worth and "authority to act," which in turn is predicated significantly on pre-conflict social roles that precede the refugee experience.

We add to this scholarship with our work on sponsors. In asking how sponsors understand and assess their experience, we address wider questions about their role as sponsors and citizens and as private (non-government) social actors tasked with newcomer integration, a process that is otherwise mediated mainly by state actors. We attend to respondents' remarks as subjective accounts and make no claims about the veracity or accuracy of their depictions. Our research design does not enable us to compare sponsors' and newcomers' accounts of their relationship, and we do not purport to determine the "truth" of sponsor/sponsored relations. Rather, we seek to understand and theorize the motives and perceptions of sponsors and the impact of the experience on them.

The analysis of these write-in responses to our survey indicates that sponsors have varied and complex motivations and experiences. Respondents often point to the power imbalances built into the sponsor/sponsored relationship. Indeed, the label "sponsorship" already orients one to the asymmetry. Official and informal representations of the sponsors' role depict sponsors as guiding refugees through a transition from neediness and dependency to independence and self-sufficiency. This framing of the endeavour thus lends itself to articulation in the discourses of both family and citizenship, which in turn trades in a loose vocabulary and a set of tropes that can import parentalist expectations and practices.

During and after their twelve-month undertaking, sponsors reflect on the expectations they had for themselves and for those they sponsored; the evolution of their relationship with sponsored refugees along axes of trust, respect, and affect; and the impact of the experience of sponsorship on their own attitudes, feelings, and beliefs. Parentalist norms inflect sponsors' accounts of their relationships, but rather than being taken up uniformly, the accounts indicate that relationships with sponsored refugees are subtle and dynamic. Sponsors may variously reproduce and challenge the sponsor script. They may also generate their own narratives as they learn and muddle through a relationship that proceeds from a quasi-contractual undertaking but quickly layers in familial dimensions. These include entanglements of affect, performance of unpaid work, and tensions around autonomy, independence, and power inequalities.

EVALUATION OF THE SPONSORSHIP EXPERIENCE

The vast majority of survey participants evaluated the sponsorship experience very positively, notwithstanding the various challenges that many reported. On a 5-point scale where 1 represented a very negative experience and 5 represented a very positive one, respondents from the survey (432 of 530 people) overwhelmingly (86%) rated their experience highly (as either a 4 or 5). Furthermore, 64 percent of sponsors who responded said they would be involved in a private sponsorship again either as part of sponsorship group (45%) or in a more informal capacity (19%). Eighty-eight percent of all respondents stated that they would recommend private sponsorship to others, and 90.8 percent of all respondents agreed or strongly agreed that their efforts were valued by the Syrian family.

This strong positive bias is evident in respondents' written comments as well, which frequently recount how meaningful, rewarding, powerful and transformative the experience was for them. Several described it as one of the most worthwhile things they had done in their lives:

> I feel that this experience has changed me. It has grown my capacity to be empathetic. I can put myself in our family's shoes and see how difficult it would be to leave everything behind – including the simple idea of being able to communicate with everyone you meet.

Respondents frequently shared the personal and emotional satisfaction they derived from sponsorship, sometimes casting their feelings in terms of gratitude for the opportunity. One respondent effused, "When I'm driving home after a visit, I am smiling, with joy. That's how they make us feel – joyful." Equally significant is that many of these same respondents also reported challenges, demands, conflicts, disappointments, and unresolvable problems they confronted with the family, with other members of the sponsorship group, and with the government. Yet virtually all respondents remained resolutely positive about private sponsorship:

> Being involved in private sponsorship is the most positive and rewarding experience I have ever had. It has brought me great joy and feelings of accomplishment. I am incredibly grateful to have had the opportunity to be involved in this process, with an amazing group of people (co-sponsors) and a wonderful family from Syria.

Some respondents refracted the sponsorship experience through the lens of Canadian identity:

> Sponsoring has enriched my life, and my perspective on what it is to be a Canadian (and a human being).

> Our sponsored family is inspiring and I could not have imagined a more positive experience if I tried (despite the challenges). They are examples of resilience and optimism in the face of unimaginable difficulty, and they have been gracious and embraced

Canadian culture wholeheartedly. We love them and Canada is better off for having them here!

In what follows, we further unpack these quotes. While the remainder of this chapter highlights challenges and difficulties, it is important to situate them in relation to the overall favourable disposition of respondents. In addition, we are alert to the fact that our survey respondents were self-selected and that our sample may underrepresent sponsors whose overall experience was negative and/or who disengaged from sponsorship. Nor can we account for potential effects of the various cognitive biases or habits of self-presentation that shape human memory and reportage.

FAMILY RESEMBLANCE: SPONSORSHIP AND KINSHIP

The sponsorship program casts sponsors in the role of providing guidance and financial, social, and personal support to newcomers over the course of a year. The notional destination of this temporally compressed journey is independence, often distilled down to economic self-sufficiency. We contend that the concept of family is baked into the institution of refugee sponsorship. The delegation of resettlement support to private, volunteer actors makes the analogy between kinship and sponsorship both plausible and problematic. We view sponsorship as a structurally unequal relationship that can – not must – give rise to a dynamic of parentalism with overtones of orientalism.

The institutional structure of sponsorship mimics family class sponsorship, and not only in its material support obligations. The sponsorship regime apprehends a refugee family (or fragment thereof) as a social unit that not only socializes its own members but also itself must be "socialized" into Canadian society via a sponsor-led settlement and integration process.[6] Calling to the fore tensions between humanitarian impulses and professionalism articulated in the literature on aid work,[7] sponsorship does not rely solely on contractual obligation; it also depends on the formation of personal, affective bonds of partiality, commitment, and intimacy that are the ligature securing the formal relationship. Survey respondents report how they try to negotiate the tension between providing guidance and respecting the autonomy of refugees. They actively reflect on the complexities of providing support while encouraging self-sufficiency. Some sponsors critically engage the parentalist and orientalist foundations of sponsorship, and some act inconsistently with the presuppositions of the regime.

A. *Family as Metaphor*

Several written responses invoked kinship metaphors to describe the sponsor's relationship to the sponsored family. The version of the survey provided to sponsors after the twelve-month sponsorship period specifically asked whether the respondent regarded the sponsored family members as friends post-sponsorship, but neither version prompted respondents to consider an analogy between sponsorship and kinship.

The response of these four sponsors echoes the sentiments expressed by several others:

> You also asked if I considered them friends, but not sure how to answer that question. In a way, they are more like family.

> The family lived in our home for 10 days, and we became family. It was a much closer bond than we had expected. The relationship has continued with daily/weekly visits since February 2016 – more than we ever imagined.

> It has been a wonderful, eye-opening, enriching experience that has left me with 6 people who now feel like part of my extended family.

> It was such a wonderful experience. Our sponsored family quickly became part of our family. They refer to us as family.

Family as metaphor carries a lot of freight.[8] However broadly or narrowly defined, family matters deeply to people. Designating a relationship as familial denotes it as profound and enduring. Among actual families, mutual obligations and expectations of support (financial and emotional), socialization, labour, and sacrifice are mediated by affective economies of love, trust, gratitude, and intimacy. Decades of feminist and queer scholarship have revealed how the institution of the family is also replete with dynamics of hierarchy, power, dependence, inequality, and exploitation.[9] Discourses of privacy, nature, and sentiment often shield family from critical scrutiny and intervention.

We recognize that family is a complex, variable, and contested formation with multiple valences. Of course, we assume that when respondents speak of "family," they generally intend it in a positive sense. However, we do not presume that a preponderance of sponsors would consider the analogy to kinship a good fit for their own experience of sponsorship. We also note that the family metaphor is mobilized by sponsors and sponsored alike,[10] and observe that one respondent expressed unease with the implications of being regarded as "like a sister" by the sponsored family:

> Their housing situation could change because the house they rented is for sale; this will require a huge effort to help them find another place they can afford; and they do not understand mortgages or buying property in Canada. They keep saying that since I am like a sister to them, I should give them the money and they will pay me back. They do not understand why I am not willing to do this or why I am insisting they will have to take out a mortgage like others.

The personal relationship structured through the private sponsorship regime is novel, and 80 percent of survey respondents were newcomers to it. We query why familial tropes emerged as salient when one could as easily find similarities between the specific tasks that private sponsors perform and those of settlement workers employed by the various agencies and organizations that serve GARs. Yet no respondent likened him or herself to a settlement worker or cast their relationship in terms of service provider and client. Indeed, one respondent remarked that "some of us got the sense that the family thinks we are being paid for what we do" as a way of explaining group members' disappointment with the tenor of their interaction with the refugee family.

Apart from the fact that sponsors are unpaid, the comparison is not apt in another sense. Settlement workers are assigned to work with many GARs and must serve them equally and without preference. They are professionalized staff and, as public actors, are subject to public norms of neutrality. In contrast, private refugee sponsors are avowedly partial. They feel a commitment to advance the interests of the specific family they sponsor – or, as many sponsors say, "our" family. This partiality echoes the particularism of kinship relations. There is a certain paradox lurking here: some refugee sponsors may be animated to undertake sponsorship in the first instance by a cosmopolitan humanitarian ethos that regards all human beings as equal in their suffering and as equally entitled to aid in relief of suffering. These sponsors do not act *despite* the refugee being a stranger but (at least in part) *because* the refugee is a stranger. Yet refugee sponsorship trades on the formation of thick affective bonds that link specific sponsors to specific refugees, whatever the circumstances of the match that first brought them together. Sponsors are expected to care more about the individual or family they sponsor than about other refugees. Indeed, many respondents used "love" to describe their sentiment toward those they sponsored, and a similar level of emotional intensity is evident from the comments we have quoted so far.

For some, the depth of emotions they felt toward the family was also a source of worry and weariness, though not regret:

It has been vastly more time consuming and emotionally wrenching than I ever imagined. I do not regret sponsoring this family at all; in fact, it is one of the better things I have done in my life. However, it has definitely been good and bad for me personally.

We love this family but it has been extremely challenging and emotionally draining. We have been very involved with this family and we have now applied to sponsor several other members of their extended family. I am emotionally burnt out and sometimes feel as though I have "vicarious PTSD" from my involvement in their lives.

A few comments also conveyed a sense of deflation from the unrealized anticipation or the rupture of affective bonds. For example, where sponsors established a relationship via Skype or other social media prior to the refugee family's departure, bureaucratic obstacles that prevented the family's resettlement provoked a sense of loss. In other cases, families may initially reside near (or sometimes with) the sponsor, and then move far away, which reduces contact. Or the relationship may not develop the emotional richness that a sponsor had hoped for. Here are some illustrative quotes:

We were introduced to our first refugee family and made contact with them, collected birthday presents, sent emails, made phone calls, got library cards and rented accommodation. We then learned they would not receive travel clearance in the foreseeable future and had to opt for another refugee family. That was a wrenching experience.

Our team had a beautiful baby shower for [the mother] in our home, the first time I [had] really seen her laugh and have fun ... This would be our last family for it is very emotional to connect to a family like this then they leave.[11]

Although we have foregrounded the invocation of family, friendship also figured prominently in commentary. We incline toward interpreting references to friendship literally, not figuratively. In response to the question about whether the sponsor maintained a friendship with the family after the twelve-month period, one respondent replied:

I love the family and we have a lovely relationship, but because of language, it is hard to say we are friends. I care deeply for them – but are we friends – not sure.

In conversation, an Arabic-speaking sponsor explained that he also did not view the adult refugees as friends. He would not, as he put it, "call up [the father] to go out for a pint," although he devoted more time to sponsorship than others in the group and genuinely cared deeply for the family. He went on to explain that he regarded them more like extended family, people with whom you may not have much in common – the loud uncle you see at family events, or a distant aunt – but with whom you share a bond that transcends subjective affinity. In this version, friendship and kinship are not markers on a continuum of intensifying subjective affection (e.g., from indifferent, to like, to love), but are located differently in terms of the source and nature of the commitment. The cliché that "you choose your friends; you don't choose your family" captures some of this complexity and counts against ranking kinship more highly than friendship (or vice versa) as measures of the bond a sponsor feels toward sponsored refugees.

The specific form of kinship relations being invoked also matters to the analysis. We do not regard relations among parents and children, in-laws, cousins, grandparents, and so on as identical. But most notable to us was a subset of comments that analogized sponsorship to parenting:

The experience is life changing, for sure. It has been like raising a family, the toughest job you'll ever do (I thought it ended with raising my kids, but this is right up there), but the most rewarding thing you could ever do.[12]

Overall, this has been a powerful experience for me. From the onset, I knew this would be my primary focus for the year and that has been pretty accurate ... I did it for selfish reasons too ... It has given me a renewed sense of purpose since my own children have "launched" into their own adult lives.

Unpacking the comparison between the role of parent and that of sponsor requires little effort. Parents socialize their children into the norms, practices, and mores of the world around them. Through techniques of support, discipline, and authority, they guide children from the dependency of infancy to the independence and self-sufficiency of adulthood. For their part, refugee sponsors are expected to assist refugee newcomers in adapting and integrating into an unfamiliar society. Sponsors possess experience and knowledge of Canadian society that foreign newcomers typically lack. Sponsors aid in the transition from (putative) dependency on arrival to integration and, ideally, self-sufficiency. If the family is a vehicle of socialization, then sponsorship is a vehicle of integration. This is apparent in comments that blend the language of family with the language of citizenship or Canadian-ness. In either case, autonomy and self-sufficiency are functional attributes the promotion of which is ascribed both to parenting and to sponsorship. In the case of sponsorship, self-sufficiency is more explicitly tied to productive citizenship and contributing membership in Canadian society.

Critiquing this comparison between parenting and sponsorship is equally effortless. The obvious objection to the analogy (however well-meaning) is its parentalist and orientalist tone. In most cases, sponsored refugees arrive as a nuclear family with one or two parents, and sometimes adult children and/or grandparents. These newcomers are adults whose circumstances have, in Arendtian terms, stripped them of their place in the world and their capacity to flourish as they once could and did – as adults, as parents, as workers, and as agents directing their own lives.[13]

We do not contend that the private sponsorship model casts sponsors into the role of parents who socialize individual refugees as if they were children. Rather, we consider it more plausible to conceive of sponsorship as treating the family unit as an object of external socialization by a sponsorship group. But even this model carries obvious risks to the status of adults as autonomous agents who come with their own identity, biography, competencies, and "eligibility to exist."[14] In short, the parental comparison seems irremediably patronizing and, in relation to Syrian refugees, orientalist in its specific manifestation. However, as we elaborate below, the limited comparison we draw is primarily structural. It is not confined to those who subscribe to familial tropes, and it is avowedly not normative.

B. Institutional Structure of Sponsorship

In our view, the analogy between kinship and sponsorship does not originate solely in sponsors' imaginations. The relationships engendered by private sponsorship transpire within a policy framework that, in significant respects, mimics the more established family class sponsorship regime governing family reunification in Canadian immigration law.[15] When a Canadian or a permanent resident seeks reunification in Canada with a foreign national partner (spouse or common law), dependent child,[16] parent, or grandparent, s/he must apply to sponsor the family member. The close relatives scheme discussed by Cameron in this volume is tied to this family sponsorship. Like refugee sponsors, family class sponsors must submit a police clearance. They must also demonstrate an income above the low-income cut-off (LICO) minimum[17] or, when sponsoring a partner and/or children, must not be in receipt of income assistance. Likewise, refugee sponsors must prove they possess the total amount of funds necessary to support the sponsored family for one year as a prerequisite to sponsorship.

Family class sponsors accept financial responsibility for sponsored family members for at least three years and up to twenty, depending on the filial relationship.[18] The family class sponsorship undertaking with Immigration, Refugee and Citizenship Canada (IRCC) does not prohibit sponsored members of the family class from accessing income assistance during the period of the undertaking, but it does oblige the sponsor to fully reimburse the government for any amount of income assistance paid to the family member. Sponsored refugees cum permanent residents are barred from social assistance for the twelve-month duration of the sponsorship. The financial obligations of a family class sponsorship undertaking, and the concomitant enforcement power of the state against the sponsor, survive any ensuing relationship breakdown. When a refugee sponsorship breaks down,

Table 9.1
Comparison of the text of the family class sponsorship and the refugee sponsorship undertaking

Family class sponsor	Refugee sponsor
I undertake to provide for the basic requirements of the sponsored person and his or her family members who accompany him or her to Canada, if they are not self-supporting. I promise to provide food, clothing, shelter, fuel utilities, household supplies, personal requirements, and other goods and services, including dental care, eye care, and other health needs not provided by public health care ... I promise that the sponsored person and his or her family members will not need to apply for social assistance. I understand that the sponsored person and his or her family members will be admitted solely on the basis of their relationship to me (as sponsor) and that they do not need to have the financial means to become established in Canada ... I understand that the undertaking remains in effect no matter what may change in my life. For example, if I am divorced, change jobs, become unemployed ... I will still be responsible to the sponsored person ... I understand that all social assistance paid to the sponsored person ... becomes a debt owed by me to Her Majesty in right of Canada.	This undertaking specifies the obligations of the sponsoring group with respect to the principal applicant and all accompanying or non-accompanying family members: • Reception – Meet the refugee upon arrival in the community; • Lodging – Provide suitable accommodation, basic furniture and other household essentials; • Care – Food, clothing, local transportation and other basic necessities of life; • Settlement Assistance and Support – Assist the refugees to learn an official language, seek employment, encourage and assist them to adjust to life in Canada, as outlined in the Settlement Plan. I understand that, as a group member, I am jointly and severally or solidarity bound with the other group members to perform the obligations of the sponsorship undertaking and am liable with the sponsorship group for any breach of those obligations. The sponsoring group's obligations commence upon arrival of the sponsored persons in Canada. The refugees are supported for 12 months or until they become self-sufficient.

the sponsorship group is liable for default if it is found responsible for this; if not, it will be released from further obligations.[19]

The following excerpts from the texts of the family class[20] and refugee sponsorship[21] undertakings reveal the striking congruence between the two.

Family class and refugee sponsorship conjoin two facets of the "private" character of family and sponsor. First, they are private insofar as they operate in the realm of particularity, affect, and "thick" commitments that distinguish them from the universal, egalitarian, generic qualities identified with relations in the public sphere. Second, the undertakings represent a transfer of a public responsibility – income assistance and settlement support – to a private actor. Privatization typically refers to a delegation of responsibility and authority from the state to the (private) market, with its associated transactional norms. The privatization effectuated by family class and refugee sponsorship is slightly more complicated, insofar as family and charitable societies were, historically, the state's preferred locus for economic redistribution and social welfare. Contemporary family class and refugee sponsorship undertakings thus reinstate private actors – the family and groups of citizens respectively – as primary bearers of financial responsibility for certain newcomers.

The Syrian resettlement initiative also reinforced the family as an organizing principle in another way. In its roll-out of the program, the government indicated that it would not admit single, unaccompanied, heterosexual men and that it would prioritize fragmented or intact families. This was widely interpreted as a gambit to pre-empt the anticipated Islamophobic backlash that would have depicted young Muslim men as security risks. Only in the company of the paradigmatic refugee – woman and child – could men be figuratively disarmed and enrolled into the non-threatening category of harmless refugee victim.[22] The dominance of the family form among the population of resettled refugees may also have heightened the prominence of familial tropes and facilitated the discursive transition from "refugee family" to "our family" to "like family."

NAVIGATING THE PRIVATE SPONSOR/SPONSORED REFUGEE RELATIONSHIP

The formal obligations that structure sponsors' experiences of sponsorship build in a tension between providing guidance and support on one side and recognizing sponsored refugees' autonomy and promoting independence on the other. The refugee sponsorship regime has a temporal arc (one year) and a destination (self-sufficiency). It contemplates a twelve-month passage out of the alienation imposed by refugee status (with its connotations of passivity and dependency) and onto a path toward neoliberal citizenship. Perhaps inevitably, sponsors confront the discrepancy between the actual people they sponsor and these "before and after" caricatures of refugee victim and market citizen. As one respondent remarks:

Interesting personal experience from a sense of rescuing a family to understanding you can support and guide and must let them make their own decisions[23].

It is in this zone of quotidian interactions that the tensions described above are enacted, negotiated, and sometimes transformed.

The remainder of this chapter briefly explores how sponsors recognize, negotiate, and manage their roles as they confront a multitude of practical challenges relating to language barriers; expectations around availability and material support; medical, dental, and mental health problems; transportation; accommodation; bureaucratic hurdles; employment; gender dynamics; and childrearing. Rural sponsors also cope with longer distances and fewer support services. While each of these practical issues merits its own attention, we focus on the larger themes arising from the structural features of sponsorship that shape interpersonal relations: the asymmetrical power relations between sponsor and sponsored refugee; the tension between guidance and respect for autonomy; and independence as it relates to the capacity of refugee families to achieve sustainability in the management of their daily lives, including but not limited to economic self-sufficiency.

Power. A handful of respondents' comments reflected explicitly on the ineluctable power asymmetry between themselves and the refugees they sponsored. One respondent situated the inequality within a broader critique of the privatization of refugee integration and a propensity among some sponsors to enhance their own status by showing themselves to be the "better" sponsor or the sponsors of "better" refugees:

> The power imbalance between a sponsor and refugee family is immense ... Outside of my sponsorship group I have seen far too many examples of patronizing behaviour and "competition" (i.e., "Well I just bought 'my' family a car," "My family were very wealthy back in Syria") from other private sponsors.

Without belabouring the kinship/sponsorship analogy, the reported competitiveness among sponsors triggers a comparison to middle-class parents boasting about their children.

Apart from whether sponsors self-consciously advert to their structural power in relation to sponsored refugees, the practical issue is how they manage it in the daily, ordinary interactions that constitute their relationship.[24] As one respondent recounted, "I feel it is an uncomfortable power dynamic and it makes me shy away from spending social time with the sponsored family."

Autonomy. Sponsors clearly wrestled with how to provide guidance on matters where they believed they possessed superior knowledge and experience, while respecting the autonomy of the Syrian family to make their own decisions.

> It was a constant challenge and source of debate within our group determining the appropriate balance between assistance and promoting autonomy – this was perhaps the greatest of all challenges. We also constantly struggled with understanding how many of our own norms and expectations should be communicated to the newcomer family – particularly around self-care, gender roles, and childrearing and birth control.

Respondents repeatedly articulated their recognition of the sponsored Syrians' entitlement to make their own decisions, however much they disagreed with those decisions. The challenge was how to manage this friction while building or sustaining a level of trust that made it possible to maintain the relationship. Sometimes this meant "letting go" of certain issues – like ignoring smoking, or suppressing concerns about the expense of a car purchase. Admittedly, our respondent pool may underrepresent sponsors who withdrew from active participation in sponsorship out of dissatisfaction with how the tension between guidance and autonomy was negotiated.

Independence. The sponsorship undertaking explicitly states that the sponsored "refugees are supported for 12 months or until they become self-sufficient," effectively making one year the benchmark for self-sufficiency. Although sponsorship entails much more than financial support, economic independence plays a dominant role in defining "self-sufficiency," and the IRCC website makes refugees responsible for attaining it in the minimum amount of time.

Many sponsors extolled the initiative, resilience, and motivation of the people they sponsored. A few comments were notable for their alignment of hard work and self-sufficiency with the performance of Canadian citizenship:

> And the family, itself, is warm, loving, kind and very grateful for the small things we have been able to do for them. They are

committed to becoming good Canadian citizens, they are dedicated in their pursuit of English language training, and we are confident they will be amazing citizens and contributors.

As with autonomy, however, many sponsors were conscious of the tension between providing support and encouraging independence. Of those who addressed "providing support vs. encouraging independence" as a potential challenge, just over half reported it to be slightly or not challenging, one quarter reported it as moderately challenging, and the remaining 23 percent reported it as very or extremely challenging.

Many simply believed that "one year is very short time period to learn English, find a job, build a community of friends, make your way in a new city." Other sponsors were disappointed by what they perceived as a lack of adequate progress toward self-sufficiency by the family they had sponsored. Some attributed this to structural limitations in the job market, while others were more critical of the perceived efforts by family members, especially the husband/father, to find, undertake, or maintain paid employment.

CONCLUSION

Sponsors and newcomers inevitably contend with the fluidity and contingency of interpersonal relationships. We have traced one trope – kinship – as a thread that winds through different dimensions of sponsorship. Building on Hyndman,[25] Kyriakides and colleagues[26] provide an account of how sponsored refugees resist and subvert the refugee script of passivity and helplessness. We complement their analysis with evidence of how sponsors may perform, disrupt, or deviate from their assigned script. In particular, we note how sponsors manage the structural and affective analogies to kinship as both resource and constraint. Across the considerable range of written comments, we observed sponsors grappling, questioning, learning, reflecting, and simply muddling through. Of course, each sponsor's experience is unique, and this is true within and between sponsorship groups. We do not presume that any single sponsor's account is representative of sponsorship as such, or even of their own sponsorship group.

In terms of parentalism, and the inevitable conflicts around power, autonomy, and independence, we note that inequality of social, economic, legal, linguistic, and political status is not a contingent feature of sponsor/refugee relations; it is the very premise of the scheme.[27] As Fassin notes about compassion-induced action, the inequality between donor and beneficiary is sociological and political, not psychological[28]:

> It is not the condescension on the part of the person giving aid or the intention of their act of assistance that are at stake, but the very conditions of the social relation between the two parties, which whatever the goodwill of the agents, make compassion a moral sentiment with no possible reciprocity ... Thus, if there is domination in the upsurge of compassion, it is objective before it is subjective (and it may not even become subjective). The asymmetry is political rather than psychological; a critique of compassion is necessary ... because it always presupposes a relation of inequality.

Refugee sponsorship constitutes relationships between strangers, and between individual and state. Even as this chapter focuses on the perspective of sponsors toward the sponsored, it is vital to recall that as a matter of interpersonal relations, sponsors are equally strangers to refugees, and many sponsors commence as strangers to at least some members of their sponsorship group. But sponsored refugees are also strangers to Canada, and this fact decisively allocates power unequally between sponsors and sponsored. Our research and analysis suggest that the private sponsorship model is organized around what we provisionally call "structural parentalism." This structural parentalism consists of a repertoire of formal and tacit requirements that mobilize private actors to undertake roles of guidance and support, while simultaneously leveraging affective bonds associated with kinship to advance a public project of newcomer integration. This model creates the conditions of possibility for parentalism to inflect the performance of the sponsorship relationship, but it does not govern relationships in predictable, simplistic, or deterministic ways. Our agenda for future research will deepen our exploration of these relationship dynamics.

NOTES

This chapter comes from a larger collaboration with A. Macklin, K. Barber, L. Goldring, J. Hyndman, A. Korteweg, S. Labman, and J. Zyfi. The research was initiated through a SSHRC/IRCC Rapid Response Grant with A. Macklin as PI and expanded through the support of A. Macklin's

Pierre Elliott Trudeau Foundation project "Re-Settler Society: Making and Remaking Citizenship through Private Refugee Sponsorship."

1. Inka Stock, "Buddy Schemes between Refugees and Volunteers in Germany: Transformative Potential in an Unequal Relationship?," *Social Inclusion* 7, no. 2 (2019): 128–138; Ivi Daskalaki and Nadina Leivaditi, "Education and Hospitality in Liminal Locations for Unaccompanied Refugee Youths in Lesvos," *Migration and Society* 1 (2018): 51–65.
2. Our empirical research comprises two parts. The first is an online survey of more than 500 individual sponsors who chose to respond to a widely distributed invitation to participate. We developed one version for sponsors still in the twelve-month sponsorship period, and a modified version for those who had finished the formal sponsorship when they completed the survey. The survey was funded by Immigration, Refugees, and Citizenship Canada (IRCC). The second phase of the research consists of semi-structured interviews with individual sponsors in order to acquire a deeper understanding of their experience and perceptions.
3. Audrey Macklin, Kathryn Barber, Luin Golding, Jennifer Hyndman, Anna Korteweg, Shauna Labman, and Jona Zyfi, "A Preliminary Investigation into Private Refugee Sponsors," *Canadian Ethnic Studies* 50, no. 2 (2018): 35–57.
4. Designation of urban/rural status was made according to Canadian postal code definitions, where the second digit (numeric) indicates whether the address is urban (1–9) or rural (0).
5. Christopher Kyriakides, Arthur McLuhan, Karen Anderson, and Lubna Bajjalim ,"Status Eligibilities: The Eligibility to Exist and Authority to Act in Refugee-Host Relations," *Social Forces* 109 (2018): 1–23.
6. The vast majority of Syrian refugees resettled post-2015 arrived as families containing at least one parent and one child, so we generally refer to sponsored families rather than individuals. The main exceptions were LGBTQ men and women.
7. Liisa Malkki, "National Geographic: The Rooting of Peoples and the Territorialization of National Identity among Scholars and Refugees," *Cultural Anthropology* 7, no. 1 (2013): 24–44.
8. We recognize but do not pursue here the specific significance of familial metaphors in faith communities (where co-religionists may refer to one another as brothers and sister) or in Indigenous traditions, where the discourse of family ("all my relations") may embrace human and non-human creatures.
9. See, for example, Sylvia Walby, *Theorizing Patriarchy* (Oxford: Oxford University Press, 1990).

10 Kyriakides et al., "Status Eligibilities," 12.
11 Woman, urban New Brunswick.
12 Man, urban Ontario.
13 See also Christopher Kyriakides, Lubna Bajjali, Arthur McLuhan, and Karen Anderson, "Beyond Refuge: Contested Orientalism and Persons of Self-Rescue," *Canadian Ethic Studies* 50, no. 2 (2018): 59–78.
14 Ibid.
15 Geoffrey Cameron (this volume) draws out a historical linkage between family class sponsorship and refugee sponsorship in the form of the assisted relative program. Following the Second World War, the government created a "close relative scheme" that would enable people in Canada to sponsor close relatives (including refugees) from Europe. Churches were involved in the selection and transportation of close relatives and eventually parlayed their role in this scheme to widen the scope of the program to include refugees without close relatives.
16 A dependent child is defined as a biological or adopted unmarried child under the age of twenty-two, with age exceptions for children with disabilities.
17 Statistics Canada defines the LICO as the income threshold "below which families would likely have to spend a substantially larger share of their income than average on the necessities of food, shelter and clothing and thus would be living in a difficult economic circumstance." https://www150.statcan.gc.ca/n1/pub/75f0002m/75f0002m2016002-eng.htm.
18 The undertaking lasts three years for partners, three to ten years for dependent children (depending on age), and twenty years for parents. http://www.cic.gc.ca/english/helpcentre/answer.asp?qnum=1355&top=14.
19 IRCC, "Application to Sponsor and Undertaking," accessed 10 December 2018, https://www.canada.ca/content/dam/ircc/migration/ircc/english/pdf/kits/forms/imm1344e.pdf; IRCC, "Undertaking/Application to Sponsor Convention Refugees Abroad and Humanitarian-Protected Persons Abroad," accessed 4 January 2018, https://www.canada.ca/content/dam/ircc/migration/ircc/english/pdf/kits/forms/imm5373e.pdf.
20 IRCC, "Application to Sponsor and Undertaking," accessed 10 December 2018, https://www.canada.ca/content/dam/ircc/migration/ircc/english/pdf/kits/forms/imm1344e.pdf.
21 IRCC, "Undertaking/Application to Sponsor Convention Refugees Abroad and Humanitarian-Protected Persons Abroad," accessed 4 January 2018, https://www.canada.ca/content/dam/ircc/migration/ircc/english/pdf/kits/forms/imm5373e.pdf. Note that sponsors must also produce a settlement

plan that itemizes in detail how the obligations contained in the undertaking will be fulfilled.

22 Michel Agier, "Humanity as an Identity and its Political Effects (A Note on Camps and Humanitarian Government)," *International Journal of Human Rights, Humanitarianism, and Development* 1, no. 1 (2010): 29–45.

23 Woman, urban Alberta.

24 Financial control may seem like the most obvious way to exert power, but sponsors are obligated to provide monthly support to sponsored refugees. They are instructed that "refugees have the right to manage their own finances and should be encouraged to do so. Sponsoring groups cannot require the refugee(s) to submit their funds for management by others." Refugee Sponsorship Training Program (RSTP), "Private Sponsorship of Refugees (PSR) Program FAQs Post-Arrival Financial Support for PSRs," updated 20 August 2018, accessed 4 January 2019, http://www.rstp.ca/wp-content/uploads/2018/08/EN-FAQs_BVOR-parity-FINAL_AUG-20.docx.pdf.

25 Jennifer Hyndman, "Introduction: The Feminist Politics of Refugee Migration," *Gender, Place, and Culture* 17, no. 4 (2010): 453–9.

26 Kyriakides et al., "Status Eligibilities," 1–23.

27 As a practical matter, sponsors exercise power through persuasion and negotiation. Sponsors have no formal authority to compel or coerce, and they may not withhold financial support to extract compliance or otherwise direct expenditures: "Refugees have the right to manage their own finances and should be encouraged to do so. Sponsoring groups cannot require the refugee(s) to submit their funds for management by others" (RSTP, 2018).

28 Didier Fassin, *Humanitarian Reason: A Moral History of the Present* (Berkeley: University of California Press, 2012), 3–4.

10

Transactions of Worth in Refugee–Host Relations

*Christopher Kyriakides, Arthur McLuhan,
Karen Anderson, and Lubna Bajjali*

Between November 2015 and November 2016, 36,135 Syrian refugees were resettled in Canada, 17,055 of them with private sponsor involvement and support. In June 2016, the Social Science and Humanities Research Council of Canada and the federal Department of Immigration, Refugees, and Citizenship (IRCC) called for "Rapid Response Research on Syrian Refugee Arrival, Resettlement and Integration." Our study was one of twenty-seven funded.

We initially intended to focus our research on Syrian refugees' experiences of inclusion and exclusion in the *rural* resettlement context of Northumberland County, Ontario, but issues of sponsored/sponsor relations, expressed by our respondents, moved our research beyond issues of inclusion/exclusion toward more specific questions about status and the role played by status-confirming transactions of worth in refugee/host interactions. Status-confirming transactions of worth address interactional "need-states" such as verifying identities, accumulating resources, experiencing inclusion, establishing trust, and maintaining intersubjectivity.[1]

We developed this focus in a second study of sponsored resettlement in the urban context of Toronto in 2017–18. In our first study, we conducted 13 one-to-one interviews with public sector agencies (PSA); 13 focus group interviews with private sponsor groups (PSG) (47 individuals); and one-to-one interviews with 49 private sponsored Syrian refugees (PSR) during their first twelve months of resettlement in Northumberland County. Our follow-up urban comparative study included interviews with 95 participants from private sponsor groups and privately sponsored Syrian refugees in the Greater Toronto Area, some of whom had completed their twelve months of sponsored resettlement.

We orientated our approach around this question: "What constitutes the meaning of 'successful resettlement' from the perspective of sponsorship participants?" We began by probing through broad questions, such as "If you had the option to change anything about private sponsorship what would you change and why?"; "Would you recommend private sponsorship as a route to resettlement? Why/why not?"; and "Would you recommend [location of resettlement withheld] to others as a place of resettlement? Why/why not?" Group-specific questions were also included for the sponsors: "If you had the opportunity to sponsor again would you? If yes/no, why?" – and for the refugees: "Do you think you will remain in [location of resettlement withheld] after your twelve-month support ends? Why/not?"

A clear understanding of "the meaning of resettlement success" emerged from our interviews for both refugees and sponsors. Host/sponsored and host/community interactions that mobilized *transactions of worth*, confirming the *status eligibilities* of the sponsored, resulted in greater reports of resettlement success as well as consensus regarding that success. Refocusing our analytical attention on the relationship between status-confirming transactions of worth and resettlement "success" led to two related novel conceptual clusters in our research:

- Pre-arrival transactions of worth in the digital "third space" of refugee reception that recognized status eligibilities beyond the refugee role.
- Pre-arrival transactions of worth in the local reception context that allowed sponsors to actively defuse local discourses hostile to refugee resettlement and establish the worthiness of the yet-to-arrive refugees.

Elsewhere, we have published the empirical content from which these and other novel conceptual clusters were developed.[2] In this chapter we focus on the resettlement effects of pre-arrival transactions of worth taking place between (1) hosts and refugees in the digital "third space" of refugee resettlement and (2) sponsorship group members and other community members in the local resettlement context. We begin with a discussion of status.

TRANSACTIONS OF WORTH AND STATUS ELIGIBILITY

We were alerted to status as an important factor affecting the perception of resettlement success when the refugees we interviewed contrasted their roles during their flight from conflict with those they encountered in the Canadian resettlement context. Interviewees referenced significant events and situations they experienced during what they described as their "voyage of death/journey of self-rescue."[3] When referencing these events and situations, they described how they drew on their pre-conflict social roles as resources to contend with existential threats, pursue worth-affirming actions, and engage with others in resettlement communities prior to coming to Canada.[4] However, when they described their experiences following their arrival in Canada, they often emphasized their confrontation with role expectations that challenged their eligibility to make any status claims beyond those ascribed by the refugee role. Cecelia Ridgeway's 2013 ASA presidential address proved instructive in helping us understand why the "refugee" ascription was so vigorously resisted by interviewees. "When we think of inequality as merely a structural struggle for power and resources," argues Ridgeway, "we forget how much people care about their sense of being valued by others and the society to which they belong – how much they care about public acknowledgement of their worth ... This is status."[5]

The resistance to the "refugee role" that emerged in our interviewees' narratives required that we seek an explanatory framework beyond the structure/agency, acculturation, trauma, or labelling theories common to more traditional social scientific analyses.[6] The multidisciplinary context of Refugee Studies offered some insight but also presented issues. Refugee Studies grants status a privileged place through labelling theory, where the limited agentive capacity that comes with being labelled a "refugee" can be accepted, negotiated, or refused by those so designated.[7] However, our interviewees' narratives made it clear that accepting, negotiating, or refusing the refugee label was not the full status story for persons displaced by conflict, who had experienced (and successfully overcome) the threat of imminent social and possibly physical death.

If we take status eligibility to mean enjoying a publicly acknowledged worth expressed through esteem and respect, then the public acknowledgment of a person's worth actively constitutes their eligibility to claim a status.[8] Interviewees' "success" in drawing on their pre-conflict social roles (e.g., parent, provider, partner) to secure their safety was experienced as affirmation of their eligibility to claim status beyond refugeeness. "Successful" actions and strategies – undertaken in the capacity of a pre-conflict role, not in the role of refugee – constituted, for our interviewees, publicly acknowledged *transactions of worth* confirming their pre-conflict statuses as deliberative, competent agents.

This understanding provided us with an overarching framework through which we could analyze those instances, as presented in the narratives of the people we interviewed, where the self-ascribed status of persons, affirmed in their efforts to secure safety, was at odds with the diminished status afforded by the refugee role. We thus identified instances where transactions of worth between refugees and hosts confirmed pre-conflict status eligibilities, contributing to resettlement success. Relatedly, we also identified instances where transactions of worth between hosts and local community members countered negative discourses and opposition to refugee resettlement, establishing the worthiness of sponsored refugees prior to their arrival.

THE "DIGITAL THIRD SPACE" OF REFUGEE RECEPTION AND STATUS-VERIFYING TRANSACTIONS OF WORTH

Early on in our data collection and analysis, we learned that those private sponsors and privately sponsored Syrian refugees who had engaged in regular, pre-arrival contact – primarily through digital applications such as Facebook, Skype, and WhatsApp – tended to experience and report more "successful" resettlement outcomes than those who had limited or no contact.

Our research revealed four sources of information regarding the Canadian reception context that Syrian refugees could encounter independent of any pre-arrival contact with their sponsors: (1) media representations of resettlement, (2) online resettlement "facts," which sometimes overlapped with (3) diasporic resettlement rumour, and (4) Canadian government pre-arrival orientation sessions. When refugees did not have significant pre-arrival contact with their sponsors to mediate those sources of resettlement information, they often arrived with unrealistic resettlement expectations that could result in sponsor/sponsored mistrust and heightened uncertainty.

For the sociology of forced migration, the interactional dimensions of pre-arrival contact have important analytical implications beyond attending to the putative benefits of "information exchange." While research on forced migration has tended to focus on the physical contexts of displacement and resettlement, our research findings revealed that digitally mediated pre-arrival sponsor/sponsored interactions supported transactions of worth taking place in what we came to call a "third space" of refugee reception. Through the co-construction of, and participation in, this "digital third space" of refugee reception, sponsors and sponsored were able to engage in status-confirming transactions of worth and build mutual trust. With a foundation of mutual trust came the real potential for relational autonomy post-arrival, as the following example illustrates.

Prior to arrival, the five members of the Hamouda family and members of their sponsor group had interacted extensively via social media. Prior to any contact with the family they would sponsor, members of the sponsorship group had encountered news media reporting of people fleeing conflict in precarious "little boats without life jackets and drowning trying to get to safety." As John recounted, "it just broke your heart." These were people who were "running away from oppression, and they were landing on a beach with absolutely nothing." Frequent consumption of the same news coverage helped establish an image of refugees that was shared among most members of the sponsorship group.

Yet as we reported in another article, pre-arrival contact via social media between hosts and the families they sponsored "broke the mediatised signification of 'refugees' as socially unformed war-migrants, providing opportunities 'to develop the relationship, to start it now' and challenging understandings of 'the sponsored' as objects of rescue."[9] In the course of these contacts, hosts began to recognize and value family members as autonomous persons beyond the role of refugee. The effect of these transactions of worth is well illustrated by an incident that occurred shortly after they had arrived.

> John: Just after they arrived, the little girl was sick. Of course they had no idea where they should take her. So we went over and took them to emergency. This was over the Christmas holidays.

Jackie: And at this point they are brand new and want to stay as a core family. So with one little person sick, then maybe one parent goes? No, the whole family goes because they want to be together.

Pre-arrival contact had broken the mediatized signification of "refugees" as socially unformed war-migrants enough to allow members of the sponsorship group to share (not direct) the hospital experience with the Hamouda family post-arrival, a sharing premised on their recognition of, and willingness to support, the relational autonomy and deliberative actions of family members.

Relatedly, cases of pre-arrival contact in which communication was wholly procedural and impersonal, such as the exchange of basic information required for filing sponsorship applications and completing other sponsorship tasks, did not contribute to resettlement success. Contact of this type, even if consistent and appreciated, did not result in the development of status-confirming transactions of worth between hosts and refugees and did little to reduce resettlement uncertainty.[10]

The digital "third space" of pre-arrival contact is a neutral space in which sponsors and sponsored can develop familiarity and trust, preparing them for post-arrival relationships that merge pre-conflict histories with post-refuge aspirations and support agency and deliberative action throughout the resettlement process. Interactions in this third space of refugee reception constituted transactions of worth in which the refugees' eligibility to claim statuses associated with their pre-conflict social roles can be recognized and the potential for resettlement success enhanced.

TRANSACTIONS OF WORTH, RECEPTION DEFUSION, AND (RURAL VS URBAN) VISIBILITY

Pre-arrival transactions of worth, confirming statuses beyond the refugee role, were taking place not only between sponsors and sponsored but also between sponsors and those members of their communities – in both rural and urban contexts – who opposed refugee resettlement. As one sponsor, Allan, told us:

Allan: There was not by any means 100 percent support. I think it really reflected the national picture, at 50-50; 50 percent of Canadians in favour. We heard the comments in the stores. The guy who runs the café is from Lebanon ... [He] said he heard the customers talking about it and can't believe people can say that ... And somebody else said that they were in the pharmacy standing behind a woman who was going on about the refugees and "why would we ever bring them over?" So it wasn't all milk and honey by any means.

For the purposes of exploring this opposition, and how sponsors handled it, we first considered the possibility of a rural–urban continuum rather than a rural/urban divide. This proved useful because it not only attended to the changing scale of rural–urban interdependence and boundary crossing as dimensions of community life, but also permitted us to move our analytical lens beyond *urbanormative* stereotypes that either romanticize "the rural landscape" or represent rural populations as narrow-minded, parochial, and hostile toward outsiders.[11] While we recognized that distinctive attributes of rural culture and subjectivity exist, we wanted to avoid the analytical biases that urban/rural stereotypes can exert on refugee reception research.[12]

Through the PSR program, private sponsor groups voluntarily operationalize a federally mandated policy at the county level, which mediates a relationship between the rural–urban continuum and the international framework of refugee protection as mandated by the UNHCR. The policy provides a means through which subjective interpretations of "the refugee" operationalize the local, national, and global aspects of a particular reception context. How the reception of refugees plays out in a specific reception context is the outcome of the complex interplay of the subjective states and social interactions of various actors. As our research confirmed, these states and interactions cannot be attributed solely to geographical, cultural, or political designations of "rurality" or "urbanity." However, some noteworthy differences between "rural" and "urban" contexts did emerge.

Findings from our research conducted in rural settings during 2016–17 indicate that when members of private sponsor groups were confronted by oppositional discourses prior to the arrival of sponsored refugees, they actively defused those voices so as to create a public space more hospitable to resettlement. Our follow-up urban comparative study in late 2017 and early 2018 found that while anti-refugee discourses are also salient in the urban context, the key urban/rural differential turned out to be "visibility" and "anonymity." Sponsors and those who opposed them were more "visible" to each other in the rural context. This visibility provided sponsors with conditions conducive to defusing negative discourses and replacing them with discourses that better established the worthiness of the yet-to-arrive refugees.

Three main oppositional discourses emerged in both urban and rural reception contexts: terrorism, Islam, and relative deservingness.[13] Sponsors countered with arguments that effectively separated the fact of the presence of refugees in the community (the emotional trigger of negative responses) from the rationalizations that underlay those negative responses, thus establishing new discourses in support of the worthiness of the newcomers. For example, Angela told us she deflected, and redirected concerns for the well-being of Canadians in need, expressed by a sixth grader who asked why her sponsorship group was "bringing new problems into Canada and then having to support them."

> Angela: [W]hen somebody brought that up, I said, "You know what, it doesn't matter what you choose [to support]. Choose what you are passionate about. There are so many issues in Canada that you can believe in. And a little boy said, "Oh, that makes me feel so much better because that's the question my parents have been asking – why am I supporting these people over there when we've got so many of our own issues?"

Sponsor groups in both rural and urban contexts relied on financial donations and voluntary contributions of time and assistance, but sponsors in small-town rural contexts depended to a greater extent on support from the immediate, local community. This immediacy raised the visibility of sponsorship in the dual sense of building public momentum around community buy-in *and* of raising the possibility of confrontation with oppositional voices.

In rural reception contexts, the absence of anonymity presented private sponsors with opportunities to defuse voices of opposition in ways not readily available to sponsors in urban reception contexts. Sponsors in rural contexts used specific types of transactions of worth – what we came to identify as interactions involving submerging, redirecting, deflecting, and absorbing oppositional voices – in order to establish the trust- and status-worthiness of yet-to-arrive refugee families.[14] While refugee sponsors' visibility in rural contexts resulted in both positive and negative reception reactions, most sponsors in rural contexts attempted to leverage their visibility to gain wider community support and challenge reception resistance. Visibility – the opposite of anonymity – allowed pro-refugee voices to be heard and to defuse opposition in what became pro-refugee public spaces, including chance encounters in coffee shops, hardware and grocery stores, hockey arenas, and other public places. For example:

> Liz: You know the way we combated the negativity that we knew was just below the surface in many areas was to take every opportunity to talk about it. So we were always at our local coffee shops. If the people that we were with didn't bring it up, we would bring it up ... So the conversation went like this: they had the impression that these guys were coming over and that the government was giving them thousands of dollars a month, you know, they are living better than we are. All of that, we would discuss it, we would dispel that. Usually ... we could change their minds and they would pop up with donations or if we had a little fundraiser somewhere, they would be there to support it.

These and other encounters constituted, in effect, pre-arrival transactions of worth in that they confirmed the value of sponsorship and the worthiness of refugees prior to their arrival, defusing the potential impact of negative statuses ascribed to refugees – as terrorists, Islamists, and undeserving.

We recorded many similar countering responses made by private sponsors to the dynamic anti-refugee voices they encountered in their rural communities, demonstrating how the context of local reception shaped and was shaped by status eligibility both before and after the refugees arrived. Rurality is not homogenous; rather, it comprises a domain of contested publics that, taken together, create the (always emergent) meaning of refugee reception. On this contested terrain, opposition to refugee resettlement was countered by progressive status evaluations, providing evidence of how community activism was able to defuse contentious situations and stake a transformational claim over rural resettlement contexts. Although defusion did not necessarily transform all oppositional status scripts, it did rob many of them of their public force.

Moreover, refugees did not experience the absence of anonymity in rural reception contexts as wholly negative. Our research revealed that same-ethnic or religious community presence and visibility was not crucial to determining the commitment to stay in a particular reception context. Instead, transactions of worth, establishing a status eligibility beyond that of refugee, played a more significant role.[15]

Private sponsorship in rural reception contexts entails that sponsors engage in highly visible community fundraising and preparation prior to the arrival of the refugees being sponsored. They are more immediately recognized and known in the wider community than is possible in urban contexts. Their rural community profile provides social and cultural capital from which both sponsors and refugees can benefit during resettlement. We developed the concept of reception defusion in order to capture pre-arrival transactions of worth underpinning rural visibility. The absorption of opposition by progressive reception practices provides evidence of how community activism can stake a transformational claim on the resettlement terrain. Submersion, deflection, and redirection, by contrast, do not necessarily transform opposition; rather, they vitiate its public force. Opposition is not obliterated, and may lie dormant, but it is not strong enough to negatively affect the resettlement commitments of sponsored refugees. For refugees, the dynamic of visibility is not defined by anti-refugee sentiment.

While the pursuit of "community buy-in" raises the pre-arrival public visibility of refugees, with advantageous resettlement effects, it is not sufficient to ensure long-term resettlement in the rural context. Rural visibility can merge with structural factors to affect refugees' commitments to long-term resettlement. Employment precarity reinforces negative public exposure, inhibiting status attainment in keeping with the attainment of a desired life beyond refuge, turning rural contexts into feeder zones for the "multicultural" metropoles. But where structural opportunities, positive sponsor/sponsored interactions, and proactive community involvement merge through transactions of worth, exposure to oppositional discourses is muted and rural visibility is experienced as beneficial, with concomitant resettlement effects.

CONCLUSION

In 2015, Prime Minister Justin Trudeau pledged to markedly increase Syrian refugee resettlement through the PSR program. One year later, public receptiveness to refugee reception was affirmed with the establishment of thousands of private sponsor groups across Canada, and with the Liberal government promoting PSR as a "successful resettlement" policy for other nations to adopt. However, what constitutes "successful" resettlement is open to interpretation, and where three sets of actors are involved – refugees, sponsors, and government – the definition of "success" may not be shared by each party. While a further six countries have since established their own private sponsorship schemes, there is little systematic evidence that demonstrates what successful resettlement might actually mean to refugees. Moreover, given that PSR formalizes a state-sanctioned "private" relationship between "sponsors" and "sponsored," who interact on a regular basis during the first twelve months of resettlement, and given that sponsor group "hosts" are expected to help sponsored "refugees" attain self-sufficiency, the interactive sponsor/sponsored relationship offers a much neglected micro-level lens through which we can understand "resettlement success" from the perspective of those who play a key role in making it happen.

In attending to "sponsor/sponsored" interaction, the research findings reported on here allow us to offer a novel analytical framework through which to understand the unique dynamic between refugees and hosts, and between hosts and oppositional voices in their communities, which emerged as a consequence of the PSR program. In turn, we are able to identify the definition of "success" according to the principle actors and the fundamental relationship in which privately sponsored resettlement is enacted.

"Sponsor/sponsored" interactions are transactions of worth, and they commence prior to arrival. For refugees, transactions of worth have an existential function in that the eligibility to draw on pre-conflict social status afforded by pre-conflict roles – father, mother, spouse, breadwinner – is affirmed. It is these roles, and the statuses they entail, that the refugees we interviewed aimed to sustain after refuge. Sponsor/sponsored transactions of worth, confirming pre-conflict status eligibilities, provided the means through which the potential structural violence of refugee role confinement after resettlement was countered. Pre-conflict socio-cultural histories are not erased by the deindividuating and homogenizing refugee role. The members of private sponsor groups and the refugees who engaged in pre-arrival contact in the digital third space were able to co-create mutual recognition of trust, needs, and expectations congruent with pre-conflict identities and the unknown demands of resettlement. In this way, resettlement uncertainty was reduced, and the esteem congruent with pre-conflict social roles and identities was made visible.

For sponsors, particularly in rural reception contexts, implementing PSR meant potential for conflict in the localized communities in which they were engaged. Sponsors were able to defuse opposition by engaging in pre-arrival transactions that established the worthiness of those they sponsored. Reception defusion prepared a terrain of reception in which rural visibility was not one-dimensionally experienced as negative.

As a final note, it is clear that, while we have focused on resettlement success, not all privately sponsored refugees are received through transactions of worth that facilitate the attainment of a life beyond refuge. And it remains to be seen whether such positive indicators of success can be sustained in the years following the end of sponsorship.

NOTES

1 Jonathan H. Turner, "Extending the Symbolic Interactionist Theory of Interaction Processes: A Conceptual Outline," *Symbolic Interaction* 34, no. 3 (2011): 330–9.
2 Christopher Kyriakides, Karen Anderson, Lubna Bajjali, and Arthur McLuhan, "Splits in the Neighbourhood?: Negotiating Visibility in a Rural Reception Context," in *A National Project: Canada's Syrian Refugee Resettlement Experience*, ed. L. Hamilton, L. Veronis, and M. Walton-Roberts (Montreal and Kingston: McGill-Queen's University Press, forthcoming 2020); Christopher Kyriakides, Arthur McLuhan, Lubna Bajjali, Karen Anderson, and Noheir Elgendy, "(Mis)Trusted Contact: Resettlement Knowledge Assets and the Third Space of Refugee Reception," *Refuge* 35, no. 2 (2019): 24–35; Christopher Kyriakides, Arthur McLuhan, Karen Anderson, and Lubna Bajjali, "Status Eligibilities: The Eligibility to Exist and Authority to Act in Refugee–Host Relations," *Social Forces* 98, no. 1 (2019): 279–302; Christopher Kyriakides, Lubna Bajjali, Arthur McLuhan, and Karen Anderson, "Beyond Refuge: Contested Orientalism and Persons of Self-Rescue," *Canadian Ethnic Studies* 50, no. 2 (2018): 59–78.
3 Kyriakides, Bajjali, McLuhan, and Anderson, "Beyond Refuge."
4 Peter L. Callero, "From Role-Playing to Role-Using: Understanding Role as Resource," *Social Psychology Quarterly* 57, no. 3 (1994): 228–43.
5 Cecilia L. Ridgeway, "Why Status Matters for Inequality," *American Sociological Review* 79, no. 1 (2014): 1–16.

6 Oliver Bakewell, "Some Reflections on Structure and Agency in Migration Theory," *Journal of Ethnic and Migration Studies* 36, no. 10 (2010): 1689–708; Ruth L. Healey, "Asylum-Seekers and Refugees: A Structuration Theory Analysis of their Experiences in the UK," *Population, Space, and Place* 12, no. 4 (2006): 257–71; Anthony H. Richmond, "Sociological Theories of International Migration: The Case of Refugees," *Current Sociology* 36, no. 2 (1988): 7–25; Vicki Squire, "Unauthorised Migration beyond Structure/Agency? Acts, Interventions, Effects," *Politics* 37, no. 3 (2017): 254–72.

7 Bhupinder S. Chimni, "The Birth of a 'Discipline': From Refugee to Forced Migration Studies," *Journal of Refugee Studies* 22, no. 1 (2009): 11–29; Martha Kuwee Kumsa, "'No! I'm Not a Refugee!' The Poetics of Be-longing among Young Oromos in Toronto," *Journal of Refugee Studies* 19, no. 2 (2006): 230–55; Christopher Kyriakides, "Words Don't Come Easy: Al Jazeera's Migrant–Refugee Distinction and the European Culture of (Mis)Trust," *Current Sociology* 65, no. 7 (2017): 933–52; Bernadette Ludwig, "'Wiping the Refugee Dust from My Feet': Advantages and Burdens of Refugee Status and the Refugee Label," *International Migration* 54, no. 1 (2016): 5–18; Giulia Scalettaris, "Refugee Studies and the International Refugee Regime: A Reflection on a Desirable Separation," *Refugee Survey Quarterly* 26, no. 3 (2007): 36–50; Nando Sigona, "'How Can a Nomad be a Refugee?' Kosovo Roma and Labelling Policy in Italy," *Sociology* 37, no. 1 (2003): 69–79; Dallal Stevens, "Legal Status, Labelling, and Protection: The Case of Iraqi 'Refugees' in Jordan," *International Journal of Refugee Law* 25, no. 1 (2013): 1–38; Roger Zetter, "More Labels, Fewer Refugees: Remaking the Refugee Label in an Era of Globalization," *Journal of Refugee Studies* 20, no. 2 (2007): 172–92.

8 Turner, "Extending."

9 Kyriakides, Bajjali, McLuhan, and Anderson, "Beyond Refuge," 73.

10 Kyriakides, McLuhan, Bajjali, Anderson, and Elgendy, "(Mis)Trusted Contact."

11 Gregory M. Fulkerson and Alexander R. Thomas, eds., *Reimagining Rural: Urbanormative Portrayals of Rural Life* (London: Lexington, 2016); Daniel T. Lichter and James P. Ziliak, "The Rural–Urban Interface: New Patterns of Spatial Interdependence and Inequality in America," *The Annals of the American Academy of Political and Social Science* 672, no. 1 (2017): 6–25; Hugh Massey, "UNHCR and De Facto Statelessness: Legal and Protection Policy Research Series" (Geneva: UNHCR, 2010).

12 Mirek Dymitrow and Marie Stenseke, "Rural–Urban Blurring and the Subjectivity Within," *Rural Landscapes: Society, Environment, History* 3, no. 1 (2016): 1–13, 4.
13 Kyriakides, Bajjali, McLuhan, and Anderson, "Beyond Refuge."
14 Ibid.
15 Ibid.

11

Mobilization of the Legal Community to Support PSR Applications through the Refugee Sponsorship Support Program

Kelsey Lange

This chapter discusses the recent history of the private sponsorship of refugees (PSR) application process and its implications for sponsors and refugee applicants alike. It then discusses the steps and measures put in place by the Canadian government to address challenges with the application process, including the creation of the Refugee Sponsorship Training Program (RSTP). The chapter focuses on the Refugee Sponsorship Support Program (SSP), which was created to provide access to justice for sponsors and refugee applicants seeking to submit PSR applications. Finally, it discusses the broader question of whether there is a need for programs such as the RSTP and SSP, and if so, why, and what implications this has for private sponsorship more generally.

APPLICATIONS AS A BARRIER TO SPONSORSHIP

Since 2012, the complexity of the administrative requirements for undertaking a private sponsorship has gradually increased. This has turned PSR applications into a barrier for those who would participate in the program. As the application process has become more cumbersome, the demand for capacity-building programs has increased. In an unintentional reflection of Canada's resettlement program itself, these programs have been provided by both the government and the private sector.

Until 2015, private sponsorship in Canada was undertaken mainly by a small number of organizations and ad hoc groups that sponsored refugees on a repeated and regular basis – in particular, Sponsorship Agreement Holders (SAHs). Settlement workers equally engaged in the process, given their contacts with many immigrants seeking to bring their family members to Canada. As a result, programmatic expertise in this sector has been concentrated in a handful of organizations, which are often volunteer-based. Outreach initiatives for new sponsors have been internalized, as has the passing down of knowledge of the application process. Over time, changes in legislation and government policies have resulted in ongoing changes to PSR application forms and processes. In 1978, the *Immigration Act* came into force;[1] this was the first piece of federal legislation to mention private refugee sponsorship, thus marking the program's formal inception. From this point on, there have been ongoing changes to the program's legislative framework, most notably the coming into force of the *Immigration and Refugee Protection Act* (IRPA) in 2002[2] and regulatory changes in 2012 that added new application requirements.[3]

The Government of Canada introduced regulatory amendments to the IRPA in 2012 in order to address some of the processing challenges identified by the government at the time. According to the government, these challenges were: "Low approval rates, large inventories and long processing times."[4] At the time, the PSR process had two parts. First, the sponsor submitted an application to an immigration office in Canada, where it was determined whether the sponsor met the requirements for sponsorship. Second, the applicant overseas submitted an application to a visa office abroad; that application was assessed where it was submitted. The PSR application, however, was not processed until the officer in Canada had both parts of the application, and as a result, processing times took up to thirty-four months.[5]

According to the government, two key factors contributed to delays in the processing of these applications and the resulting backlogs. First, there were delays between the submission of both sides of the applications, and second, the applications themselves lacked basic and essential information. Therefore, considerable time was spent following up with the sponsors for this information.[6] The low approval rates were mainly due to a finding of ineligibility for the applicants, whereas government-assisted refugee (GAR) applicants, having previously been determined to be refugees by the UNHCR, had approval rates of around 90 percent.[7] This is confirmed by the fact that the PSR approval rates from 2006 to 2010 were on average 57 percent, while for G5s from 2008 to 2010, they averaged 64 percent.[8]

With the goal of reducing backlogs and delays and increasing approval rates, the 2012 regulatory changes created new requirements for application details and submissions, including that sponsor- and refugee-side applications be submitted together. They also gave officers the authority to return applications deemed incomplete.[9] Furthermore, to assist with approval rates, the government introduced a requirement for a refugee status determination (RSD) document for Group of 5 (G5) and Community Group (CG) applications to be eligible for sponsorship, although as discussed below, this requirement was lifted for Syrian and Iraqi refugees between September 2015 and January 2017.[10] In 2012, the government also added an administrative measure to cap the number of applications that SAHs can submit each year.[11] Then, in 2017, the government centralized operations for resettlement processing in the Resettlement Operations Centre in Ottawa.[12]

The amendments over the years have attempted to address the issue of backlogs but have not addressed another problem: sponsors and applicants struggle to provide basic and essential information in these applications. Furthermore, all of these policy and legislative amendments have caused difficulty and confusion both for sponsors and for applicants when they prepare their applications.

Recognizing the need for capacity-building with regard to sponsorship applications, the Canadian government established the RSTP in 1998 with the aim of supporting SAHs, G5s, and CSs that lacked expertise.[13] As is stated on the RSTP website, the RSTP's objective is to address "[sponsor's] information and on-going training needs as well as the initial information needs of sponsored refugees."[14] The RSTP has been able to provide public education to sponsors and has hired trainers in cities across the country; however, due to their limited mandate and capacity, those trainers are still unable to provide direct application support for each individual sponsor requesting assistance.[15]

The 2015–16 Syrian refugee program also created new demands for assistance with sponsorship applications. After the Liberal Party won a majority government in 2015, Prime Minister Trudeau announced that the government would resettle 25,000 Syrian refugees by the end of February 2016. This goal was to be achieved through a combination of government-assisted refugee (GAR) and PSR arrivals.[16] This was a significant increase from recent levels, as 10,466 refugees had been resettled in total in 2014–15.[17] The campaign promise created momentum and capacity for Canadians, who mobilized to sponsor refugees.[18] Furthermore, weeks before the election, a new public policy temporarily exempted Syrian and Iraqi refugees from the requirement to provide formal refugee status determination documents (RSDS) with their applications. This meant that a large number of previously ineligible applicants who were located in places where RSDS were not issued could now be sponsored by Canadians.[19] This was a temporary policy, one that created a limited time frame in which these applications could be submitted, which added to the sense of urgency to finalize and submit these cases as soon as possible.

During this increase in interest in sponsorship, many inexperienced and first-time sponsor groups sought out support and guidance with preparing their applications. Most of the people who had previously provided support with these applications, such as settlement workers and SAHS, were experienced but too under-resourced and overwhelmed to deal with these demands.[20] In particular, settlement workers funded by government programs are not legally able to represent or advise on applications under Section 91 of the IRPA, and this limited their ability to assist.[21] Also, the RSTP was receiving a growing number of requests for support from sponsors.[22] Due to capacity constraints, the RSTP was unable – and still is not able – to meet the demand for one-on-one assistance when it came to filling out all the required forms to initiate private refugee sponsorship.[23]

A handful of immigration and refugee lawyers were by then assisting with sponsorship applications, which was generally not considered a legal service. Typically, lawyers only assisted sponsors with completing forms for complex cases and refusals; in such cases, they submitted applications for leave and judicial review to the Federal Court of Canada, almost always for a significant fee. Legal aid (provincially funded legal services) was also not available for these applications, because the clients (refugee applicants) were located overseas and not in the regional catchment area required for legal aid coverage. Thus, free legal services were not available to sponsors.

THE REFUGEE SPONSORSHIP SUPPORT PROGRAM (SSP)

The Refugee Sponsorship Support Program (SSP) was developed in response to this problem. In the fall of 2015, a small group of refugee lawyers in Ottawa and Toronto imagined ways they could provide targeted legal assistance in support of Syrian refugees. They began soliciting refugee law practitioners across the country who might be willing to offer pro bono assistance. This was facilitated by early partnerships with the Canadian Association of Refugee Lawyers (CARL) and the Canadian Bar Association (CBA). Very quickly, more than one hundred refugee lawyers from across Canada agreed to join the lawyer list. More than fifty University of Ottawa law students applied for a course that was created to focus on sponsorship support, and more than eighty Ottawa lawyers registered to be trained to provide pro bono services in Ottawa.[24] On 1 October 2015, more than 450 individuals were served at the SSP's initial sponsorship clinic in Ottawa (held in conjunction with a public education event hosted by Ottawa Mayor Jim Watson); this marked the birth of the SSP.[25] Around half the SSP's clients were Syrian Canadians, who required careful, one-to-one support to understand how private sponsorship could help their family members.

The SSP soon began receiving calls from sponsor groups across Canada seeking support, and lawyers in other Canadian cities continued to express interest in providing support. To meet the growing need, the SSP partnered with the RSTP, which was already established in the sponsorship community, to create a customized training program for SSP lawyers and law students. Following the national engagement and training of lawyers and law students, the SSP on-boarded coordinators on a volunteer basis in certain communities to organize legal clinics and match lawyers and sponsors in cities across Canada.[26]

Then, in January 2017, the government concluded the temporary public policy and reinstated the requirements for RSDs for Iraqi and Syrian refugees, which once more blocked many potential sponsors and refugees from eligibility for the program.[27] While some Syrian and Iraqi refugees are no longer eligible to be sponsored due to this change, service providers such as the SSP and RSTP have continued to receive requests from sponsors in need of individual application support for eligible refugees from a variety of countries.

To this day, the SSP continues to serve the refugee sponsorship community; with the RSTP, it has trained more than 1,400 lawyers and law students in eleven centres across Canada.[28] The SSP continues to provide programming through (1) a capacity building program, which trains lawyers and law students to support sponsorship applications and includes expert assistance; (2) a matching program, which connects sponsor groups, including SAHs, with direct support from pro bono lawyers and law students; and (3) a public information program, which provides public information regarding the refugee sponsorship process. In all, the program has supported almost 3,000 refugees from a variety of countries, and it continues to provide individualized support to sponsors and refugees preparing PSR applications.[29]

ACCESS TO JUSTICE

The SSP was created to provide access to justice to sponsors in Canada and refugee applicants overseas through the volunteer efforts of lawyers and law students. While application support could be provided by anyone interested in volunteering, the SSP was able to capitalize on a profession that promotes access to justice and pro bono services and that also has specific legal skills in research and analysis to support applications.

Access to justice is defined generally as the ability for all populations to access the legal system.[30] The key factors that have been found to lead to the inability to access the legal system are finances, class, vulnerability, and inequality; this last factor encompasses language, culture, education, poverty, sexual orientation, and mental illness.[31] According to the Canadian Bar Association, the primary barrier for accessing justice is a lack of financial resources; as a person's marginalization increases, their ability to access legal rights decreases.[32]

The legal profession as a whole has been and continues to be encouraging of access to justice initiatives, which includes pro bono work such as the SSP. The term "pro bono" has been defined as legal work done without compensation for the public good.[33] Historically, when the legal field was comprised of only the upper class of society, it urged those in privileged positions to assist those less fortunate.[34] Now, as the pool of lawyers is expanding, and people's reasons for entering the legal profession are becoming more diverse, so too are the factors driving participation in pro bono work. These factors include enhancing one's reputation and marketing, as well as gaining experience, emotional intelligence, and a sense of fulfilment.[35] And, since at least 1970, pro bono work has become relevant where legal aid coverage is unavailable.[36] The two concepts co-exist, with legal aid driven by the demand for legal support through legal aid certificates, and pro bono work driven by the support of volunteer lawyers, as was the case for refugee sponsorship applications, which could not receive legal aid assistance.[37] Pro bono organizations in particular provide administrative support to lawyers, who volunteer their time to assist clients with unmet legal needs. This typically includes file work, in which the client is treated like any other paying client.[38]

As a pro bono organization, the SSP places significant emphasis on training and supporting volunteer lawyers and law students. This has been made possible through partnerships, in particular with the RSTP, which provides custom training on private sponsorship to SSP volunteer lawyers, available both online and in person. The training focuses on form completion as well as on what to address in the detailed refugee forms. In addition to training, SSP provides ongoing support through various online resources and sample documents. Moreover, the SSP has volunteer expert lawyers, who are experienced immigration and refugee lawyers available to assist volunteer lawyers with their applications throughout the process. While lawyers gain additional training in the subject matter when they join the SSP, they also apply the broader professional skills they possess in analytical thinking, legal research, organization, attention to detail, logical reasoning, and persuasiveness. In this regard, SSP lawyers are able to more easily contribute as they are working within their professional realm, which is the crux of skills-based volunteering.

REFLECTIONS ON SSP SUPPORT

Through surveys conducted by the SSP, sponsors confirmed that they were in need of assistance and that they benefited from SSP lawyers applying their legal skills and knowledge to their sponsorship applications. Two sets of surveys were administered in 2018, one to sponsors who had accessed SSP services (specifically, through attendance at a legal clinic or a remote match to a lawyer), and one to SSP lawyers (to those who were recorded as having attended a training session). Both surveys were administered from January to March 2018. For the sponsor survey, 62 responses were received from sponsors in the Greater Toronto Area, Ottawa, and Vancouver. For the lawyer survey, 105 responses were received from lawyers and students in the GTA and Ottawa.[39]

For 66 percent of the sponsor respondents, it was their first time sponsoring; 27 percent of the respondents had sponsored between two and five times.[40] As new sponsors lack knowledge of and experience with the application process, they stand to greatly benefit from additional support with their applications.

Respondents shared that "[the lawyer] took initiative and managed the documents, reviewing and editing them until we completed them."[41] Another sponsor stated that "being matched to a SSP lawyer was most useful for the close scrutiny of our application and helpful comments that greatly strengthened it."[42] Some of the sponsors also spoke to other positive impacts the assistance had on their sponsorship experience:

> Invaluable expert diligent pro bono assistance from [lawyer] at UofO to prepare our sponsorship application.[43]

> The workshop was very well structured and informative. It also allowed us the chance to meet with other people involved in sponsoring refugees.[44]

> The legal clinic was a great start, the ongoing contact and review with the lawyer is immensely helpful.[45]

As Suneet Kharay from the RSTP notes,

> SSP has the capacity to provide this one-on-one support with completing the application forms through its network of lawyers across the country. RSTP regularly refers sponsors that need support with completing the forms to SSP ... [T]he support that SSP and the lawyers affiliated with the program provide is invaluable as there would be a service gap if the program did not exist.[46]

Some sponsors did provide suggestions for program improvement, which included being matched to a volunteer lawyer more quickly or being able to meet with the lawyer in person more often. Others were less clear on the mandate of the SSP, saying that they would like follow-up once the application is submitted,[47] or to be able to request lawyers to file an application for judicial review with the Federal Court of Canada.[48] These suggestions would require further resources and staff for the SSP to have the capacity to provide further one-on-one support and information to sponsors.

It is not surprising that as a volunteer-based program with limited long-term funding, the SSP has a restricted capacity to mobilize volunteers or part-time staff on the ground in various communities. Also, the program relies on volunteers, whose time, interest, and energy can fluctuate drastically. In addition to volunteer lawyers and law students, the program depends on volunteer interpreters and support staff, in particular during clinics. As most volunteers are not immigration or refugee lawyers, there is a need for training on an ongoing basis, and this is equally labour-intensive. To sustain the program, the SSP staff work to provide regular training and engagement opportunities, to allow the community to gather together. Other opportunities are offered to lawyers and law students depending on their capacity to contribute, such as providing case research or resource support to the SSP. However, the SSP volunteers are not able to support every sponsorship application being prepared for submission to IRCC.

Furthermore, even with the existence of the SSP, there continue to be gaps in services for sponsors and refugees completing PSR applications. Where the applications involve complex admissibility issues, excluded family members, post-submission visa office communication, and refusals, the SSP does not currently have the resources or breadth to assist with all requests. So there continue to be sponsors and refugee applicants who are unable to receive assistance in preparing their PSR applications.

CONCLUSION

This final section considers the enduring challenges posed by the application process in the PSR program. The SSP's existence highlights a number of concerns regarding the viability of the PSR program, related to whether the PSR application process is one in which sponsors need, or should have, additional support in order to provide a complete application, as well as to what impact legal support may have on the PSR program overall.

If the application process is complex to the point of limiting the success of applications submitted, one must ask: who are the successful applicants, and which applications are accepted and acceptable? Given that many sponsors are applicants sponsoring their family members overseas, and that many are newcomers themselves, their lack of experience in Canada, their potential limited language abilities, and their weak connections to settlement and other support networks pose significant barriers to preparing and submitting clear and complete applications. The best-placed sponsor to ensure a successfully prepared application would therefore be one with experience in and knowledge about refugee sponsorship, or one with resources in their networks who can assist, and one with strong English or French communication skills so as to both understand the requirements and correctly write down the particulars in each and every required government form. In practice, many sponsors lack the ability to prepare a compelling application and lack the resources to hire and pay an experienced and fully trained refugee or immigration lawyer. This is demonstrated in the higher need for support for G5s and CSs over SAHs, as noted in the 2016 IRCC evaluation of the PSR program.[49] The SSP in this regard could level the playing field by removing the barriers faced by sponsors and applicants in preparing an application and by providing free one-on-one application support.

With legal or other application support, the forms will be fully completed and may also contain stronger arguments related to the refugee claim itself, as well as clear and concise explanations related to any inconsistent or missing information. While the support of a lawyer cannot remedy gaps in basic requirements for eligibility, it can greatly strengthen a case through the application of the legal skills of critical analysis, research, and writing. It would benefit both sponsors and refugee applicants to submit a complete and clearly presented application; IRCC would gain as well, for its staff would spend less time on reviews, returns, and requests for post-submission follow-up information. Because of its limited capacity as a small-scale not-for-profit, volunteer-based program, the SPP is unable to provide support to all sponsors across Canada preparing applications for the PSR program.

Sponsors, refugee applicants, and IRCC all benefit from having legal support with PSR applications, especially if that assistance is pro bono. This, however, is not to suggest that legal support is necessary for a successful application. Any type of application assistance is better than none, especially for first-time sponsors or for more complex cases. Prior to the SSP, sponsors received support mainly through settlement and community workers and a small number of organizations, SAHs, and ad hoc groups that sponsored refugees on a repeated and regular basis. But as noted earlier, these had insufficient resources relative to the demand for them.

With this in mind, one must ask whether providing pro bono support for PSR applications has a broader impact on the application process as a whole. What are the long-term consequences of offering support as applications become more complicated? Is the bar now being raised for sponsors and refugee applicants in their applications? Does that assistance allow or even encourage the government to create a still more complex application process that focuses on other priorities over accessibility to clients?

The PSR program ultimately has to balance being a humanitarian program with being an immigration stream for permanent residents, and this is reflected in the application process. Under the IRPA, the PSR program does at times pay heed to its humanitarian nature: it requires no application fee and provides exemptions to recognize the particular circumstances of refugees, such as the exemptions of inadmissibility for misrepresentation,[50] and of medical inadmissibilities other than those likely to be a danger to public health.[51] But there are limits to the exceptions that can be made, since the program has to ensure that it meets the broader requirements for eligibility and admissibility and that the integrity of the program is maintained. However, on top of the requirements to submit a compelling application demonstrating that the sponsor and refugee meet the basic requirements, the often changing, complex, and numerous forms, which are required to be typed and submitted in certain formats, continue to pose challenges for sponsors and refugee applicants alike.

Although each case is assessed on its own merits against the requirements, the question remains whether legal support is setting a precedent regarding the expectations IRCC may place on applicants. If programs such as the SSP result in a higher standard of applications, could this lead to more complex requirements from IRCC in the future, making it even harder for applicants to apply on their own, and consequently creating a cycle of demand and supply? In this scenario, IRCC's expectations could increase so greatly that no sponsor would be able to prepare and submit an application on their own; this would force them to seek support for their application, which is not currently possible for all sponsors due to limited volunteer resources, capacity, and accessible legal services.

The SSP has worked on about 4,000 applications since its beginnings in 2015; it is not close to matching the much higher number of PSR applications that IRCC processes per year. The impact of applications completed with legal support on the PSR program is therefore more likely to be individual than systematic. However, with increased admission targets in 2018–20 set by the government, the SSP may see a continued need for support from sponsors – indeed, a growing need. The expectations remain that the PSR program will continue to evolve, and resettlement has remained a hotly debated topic in politics and media. Access to justice, on the other hand, is a growing concern in the legal profession, and pro bono work continues to be a priority. What is lacking are the resources to capitalize on this interest through outreach, training, and engagement of volunteers.

A major consideration in this equation relates to IRCC's own efforts to continue its humanitarian efforts to resettle, and to have this reflected in their application forms. For example, in 2018, IRCC released a new set of application forms that included more user-friendly "dynamic" forms and that removed duplication in questions and added more specific questions; it also extended sponsorship obligations for biological children born after the application had been received at IRCC (to quicken processing).[52] As well, regular conversations between sponsors, in particular the SAHs through the SAH Association Council and IRCC, highlight the collaborative efforts by the community as well as IRCC to work toward improving application processing.[53] However, IRCC continues to require that, for example, the applicants submit typed forms, which as mentioned above poses a barrier to refugee applicants in remote areas or with limited resources.

It might be useful for future research to examine the outcomes of assistance in PSR applications, from RSTP, settlement workers, lawyers, volunteers, and so on. By understanding the outcomes of various forms of support, we could better understand which support tools are the most accessible and efficient and would best support an application's approval by IRCC.

The PSR program has evolved and progressed over the decades. We can expect that it will continue to do so in terms of political priorities, policies, and regulations. This is why support is expected to continue to be beneficial for preparing a PSR application. In recent years, pro bono legal support has permeated the sponsorship community to the point that one-on-one legal support is available for the application process. The SSP continues to meet a need, but as a small-scale program, it also faces challenges in providing access to sponsors.[54] While legal support has been presented as beneficial, it is not an obligation or a requirement. It is important to remember that the members of the sponsorship community are the experts and key players in the process. Each group has a role to play in that process, and all parties stand to gain from shorter and more efficient application processing. However, IRCC must continue to strive to place the client at the centre of that process.

NOTES

1. *Immigration Act, 1976–77*, c 52, s 1.
2. *Immigration and Refugee Protection Act*, SC 2001, c 27.
3. Government of Canada, "Evaluation of the Resettlement Programs (GAR, PSR, BVOR and RAP)," 7 July 2016, https://www.canada.ca/en/immigration-refugees-citizenship/corporate/reports-statistics/evaluations/resettlement-programs.html.
4. Government of Canada, "Regulations Amending the Immigration and Refugee Protection Regulations," 9 June 2012, http://www.gazette.gc.ca/rp-pr/p1/2012/2012-06-09/html/reg1-eng.html.
5. Ibid.
6. Ibid.
7. Ibid.
8. Ibid.
9. Ibid.
10. Government of Canada, "Evaluation of the Resettlement Programs."
11. Government of Canada, "Regulations Amending the Immigration and Refugee Protection Regulations."
12. Refugee Sponsorship Training Program, "Message to External Stakeholders on the Implementation of the Resettlement Operations Centre – Ottawa," 14 March 2017, http://www.rstp.ca/en/refugee-sponsorship/latest-policy-program-update/message-to-external-stakeholders-on-the-implementation-of-the-resettlement-operations-centre-ottawa.
13. Canadian Refugee Sponsorship Agreement Holders Association "History of the Association," http://www.sahassociation.com/about/history.
14. Refugee Sponsorship Training Program "About the RSTP," http://www.rstp.ca/en/about-the-rstp.
15. Suneet Kharay, RSTP, interview, August 2018.
16. Ibid.; "Justin Trudeau's Promise to Take 25,000 Syrian Refugees This Year 'Problematic,'" *CBC News*, 28 October 2015, https://www.cbc.ca/news/politics/trudeau-syria-refugees-settlement-groups-1.3291959; Michelle Zilio, "Liberals' Revised Goal Met as 25,000th Syrian Refugee Arrives in Canada," *Globe and Mail*, 28 February 2016, https://www.theglobeandmail.com/news/national/liberals-revised-goal-met-as-25000th-syrian-refugee-arrives-in-canada/article28944527.
17. Jennifer Hyndman, William Payne, and Shauna Jimenez, "The State of Private Refugee Sponsorship in Canada: Trends, Issues, and Impacts," 2 December 2016, https://refugeeresearch.net//wp-content/uploads/2017/02/hyndman_feb%E2%80%9917.pdf.

18 Government of Canada, "ARCHIVED – Temporary public policy to facilitate the sponsorship of Syrian and Iraqi refugees by Groups of Five and Community Sponsors – 2015," 19 September 2015, https://www.canada.ca/en/immigration-refugees-citizenship/corporate/mandate/policies-operational-instructions-agreements/sponsorship-syrian-iraqi-refugees-groups-five-community-sponsors-2015.html.
19 Ibid.
20 Naomi Alboim, "Lessons Learned from the Indochinese and Syrian Refugee Movements," *Policy Options*, 18 May 2016, http://policyoptions.irpp.org/fr/magazines/mai-2016/lessons-learned-from-the-indochinese-and-syrian-refugee-movements.
21 *Immigration and Refugee Protection Act*, SC 2001, c 27, s 91.
22 Refugee Sponsorship Training Program, "About the RSTP."
23 Suneet Kharay, RSTP, interview, August 2018.
24 Refugee Sponsorship Support Program, "Refugee Sponsorship Support Program Project Proposal Submitted to the Law Foundation of Ontario Access to Justice Fund," 3–4.
25 Ibid., 4.
26 Ania Kwadrans, The Refugee Hub, interview, February 2019.
27 Nicholas Keung, "Cap on Refugee Sponsorships Means Syrians in Canada Remain Separated from Family Members" *Toronto Star*, 25 September 2017, https://www.thestar.com/news/immigration/2017/09/25/cap-on-refugee-sponsorships-means-syrians-in-canada-remain-separated-from-family-members.html.
28 Refugee Sponsorship Support Program, "Refugee Sponsorship Support Program Final Report to the Law Foundation of Ontario," 10, 29.
29 Ibid., 28.
30 Trevor C.W. Farrow, "What Is Access to Justice?" *Osgoode Hall Law Journal* 51, no. 3 (2014): 957–87, 968–74.
31 Farrow, "What Is Access to Justice?," 972.
32 Canadian Bar Association Access to Justice Committee, "Reaching Equal Justice Report: An Invitation to Envision and Act" (November 2013), 17.
33 Lorne Sossin, "The Public Interest, Professionalism, and Pro Bono Publico," *Osgoode Hall Law Journal* 46, no. 1 (2008), 131–58, 132.
34 Ramanujam, "The Shifting Frontiers of Law: Access to Justice and Underemployment in the Legal Professions," *Osgoode Hall Law Journal* 54, no. 4 (2017): 1091–116 at 1102–3.
35 Sossin, "The Public Interest," 133; Ramanujam, "The Shifting Frontiers of Law," 1112–4.
36 Government funded legal representation and assistance.

37 Sossin, "The Public Interest," 135, 149.
38 Canadian Bar Association Access to Justice Committee, "Reaching Equal Justice Report: An Invitation to Envision and Act," 42.
39 Refugee Sponsorship Support Program, "Refugee Sponsorship Support Program Sponsor Survey Report: Comments, Feedback and Suggestions"; Refugee Sponsorship Support Program, "Refugee Sponsorship Support Program Lawyer Survey Report: Comments, Feedback and Suggestions."
40 Refugee Sponsorship Support Program, "Refugee Sponsorship Support Program Sponsor Survey Report."
41 Ibid., respondent 22.
42 Ibid., respondent 14.
43 Ibid., respondent 21.
44 Ibid., respondent 33.
45 Ibid., respondent 63.
46 Suneet Kharay, RSTP, interview, August 2018.
47 Refugee Sponsorship Support Program, "Refugee Sponsorship Support Program Sponsor Survey Report," Respondent 50.
48 Ibid., respondent 20.
49 Government of Canada, "Evaluation of the Resettlement Programs."
50 *Immigration and Refugee Protection Regulations*, SOR 2002–227, s 22.
51 *Immigration and Refugee Protection Act*, SC 2001, c 27, s A38 (2)(b).
52 Government of Canada, "Changes to PSR Forms," July 2018, http://www.rstp.ca/wp-content/uploads/2018/07/Changes-to-PSR-Forms-2018-conference.pdf.
53 "Canadian Refugee Sponsorship Agreement Holders Association FAQs," http://www.sahassociation.com/faqs.
54 In April 2020, the SSP moved out of the University of Ottawa's Refugee Hub and began to be administered by Catholic Crosscultural Services (CCS) under the expert guidance of the RSTP.

12

Judicial Review in Canada's Refugee Resettlement Program

Pierre-André Thériault

In Canada, much of the research on the private sponsorship of refugees (PSR) program, and on refugee resettlement more generally, has tended to frame refugee resettlement as a voluntary act on the part of the state and has focused primarily on evolving policies and integration issues. Few studies, until recent years, have examined refugee resettlement as a *legal* process. Looking at refugee resettlement from a legal perspective allows us to recognize refugee resettlement applicants as bearers of rights and to assess to what extent national and international legal processes respect those rights.[1]

This chapter is concerned with the legal infrastructure of private sponsorship and refugee resettlement more broadly. While Lange's chapter in this volume examines the legal and administrative needs of private sponsors, and community responses to those needs, this chapter examines the legal process farther down the road. What happens to refugee resettlement applicants, in both the PSR and government-assisted refugee (GAR) streams, who receive a negative decision following their interview with a visa officer? A case rejection is a defining moment for private sponsors, who often lack information as to why the case was rejected and what steps can be taken to challenge the refusal. More importantly, a negative decision is a devastating outcome for refugee applicants abroad, who typically have been waiting for years for a decision in a precarious situation. Also, persistent shortcomings in the quality of decision-making and lack of review opportunities can potentially undermine broader program objectives and sponsor support in the long run.

What follows is an empirical investigation of the operation of judicial review in Canada's refugee resettlement program. Judicial review is a legal process that allows individuals to challenge the decisions of government decision-makers. Judicial review is especially important in the refugee context, where a "false negative" decision can lead to persecution or death.[2] Judicial review plays many fundamental roles in legal systems. Chief among them are correcting individual injustices and providing an ongoing check on government decision-making practices.[3] Relying on quantitative data on judicial reviews of rejected resettlement applications submitted between 2011 and 2015, this chapter examines whether judicial review achieves these two purposes in the resettlement system. Throughout the analysis, the role of various actors in the judicial review process, including refugee applicants, private sponsors, and lawyers, as well as practical and legal obstacles to review, will be investigated.

I make the argument that judicial review plays a limited role in the refugee resettlement system, at both the individual and structural levels. From the perspective of individual justice, the limited role of judicial review stems from the fact that relatively few rejected applicants in the PSR stream, and virtually no rejected applicants in the GAR stream, have the financial or informational means to pursue judicial review. It is clear from the data that private sponsors play a major role in supporting judicial review proceedings. Refugee applicants who manage to initiate judicial review face the additional hurdle of the "leave requirement." This requirement contributes to a significant access to justice deficit for overseas refugee applicants. From a structural perspective, the limited role of judicial review can be explained to a large extent by doctrinal factors and the low numbers of resettlement cases heard by the Federal Court. A surprising finding is that a large proportion of cases that are granted leave are ultimately settled out of court between the parties, further limiting judicial scrutiny. In conclusion, I maintain that quality decision-making and effective review mechanisms are essential features of a successful refugee system. A few practical suggestions that would strengthen Canada's overseas program are offered.

DECISION-MAKING AND JUDICIAL REVIEW

Decision-Making Procedure

The administrative apparatus set up to process resettlement applications bears very little resemblance to Canada's *inland* refugee system. Inland refugee claims are determined by an independent administrative tribunal – the Immigration and Refugee Board (IRB). Members of the IRB receive substantial training in refugee and immigration law.[4] As a quasi-judicial tribunal, the IRB affords refugee claimants an array of procedural rights. Refugee claimants are generally eligible for legal aid,[5] and most are represented by counsel.[6] Since 2012, most refugee claimants who receive a negative determination at the Refugee Protection Division of the IRB have had access to an appeal to the Refugee Appeal Division (RAD).[7] Over the past thirty years, the IRB has undergone significant scrutiny by legal scholars and refugee organizations.

In contrast, decision-making in Canada's refugee resettlement system is administered directly by Immigration, Refugees and Citizenship Canada (IRCC) and has received relatively little outside scrutiny until recently. Visa officers processing refugee applications often work on various types of immigration matters and are expected to process a large number of cases.[8] Their training in refugee law is reported to be insufficient and inconsistent.[9] Under these conditions, shortcomings in decision-making can easily appear and persist, with devastating consequences for those affected and for the program as a whole.

The eligibility determination process is essentially the same for refugee applicants in both the GAR and PSR streams. The most significant difference is that GAR applicants are generally referred by the UNHCR, whereas PSR applicants are generally referred by their sponsor in Canada. In all cases, the principal applicant and family members are called for an interview with a Canadian visa officer in their current country of residence, which typically lasts between forty and sixty minutes. An interpreter is provided by the Canadian government if one is needed. At the interview, the onus is on the applicant to satisfy the visa officer that he or she meets all of the criteria for resettlement (see Cameron and Labman's introductory chapter). Even those refugee applicants who have previously received an individual refugee determination from the UNHCR or a foreign state must satisfy the visa officer that they qualify as refugees, and the visa officer is not bound by the previous decision.[10] Refugee applicants are not eligible for state-funded legal aid, and very few can afford or coordinate legal representation at this stage.

Rejection Rates and Shortcomings in Quality of Decision-Making

Between 2011 and 2014, the average approval rate for PSR applicants sat just below 70 percent. In 2015, 2016, and 2017, approval rates

Table 12.1
Resettlement applications approval rates (2011–2018)*

	PSR approval rate (principal applicants)	GAR+BVOR approval rate (principal applicants)
2011	68.78% (2,577/3,747)	88.91% (2,758/3,102)
2012	67.12% (2,378/3,543)	87.78% (2,183/2,487)
2013	68.54% (2,958/4,316)	68.94% (2,572/3,731)
2014	67.38% (2,018/2,995)	93.11% (7,876/8,459)
2015	84.74% (5,146/6,073)	93.86% (12,436/13,249)
2016	89.94% (7,723/8,587)	94.30% (6,930/7,349)
2017	88.23% (7,251/8,218)	86.30% (3,375/3,911)
2018	70.23% (8,841/12,589)	86.93% (3,272/3,764)

* Data obtained from customized statistical reports produced by IRCC and on file with author.

increased to the 85 to 90 percent range, mainly because of the large number of Syrian refugees being assessed on a *prima facie* basis.[11] It appears that PSR approval rates have since then decreased to pre-2015 levels. Approval rates in the GAR program have traditionally been higher than in the PSR program, averaging between 88 and 93 percent in 2011–14, with the exception of 2013.[12] The GAR program also saw an increase in approval rates during the Syrian refugee movement, albeit a much smaller one. In the GAR program as well, approval rates have since decreased to pre-2015 levels.

It is not my contention that approval rates are necessarily lower than they should be. I also recognize that refugee status determination is an extremely difficult task, fraught with pitfalls.[13] That being said, the quality of decision-making in the resettlement program has been a concern of refugee organizations for some time. In 2010, the Canadian Council for Refugees published a report outlining widespread failures in decision-making at the Canadian visa office in Cairo, including lack of knowledge of country conditions, lack of understanding of the refugee definition, faulty credibility assessments, bias against members of the Pentecostal faith, failures to take into account documentary evidence, poor interview techniques, and poor note-taking.[14] In 2011, a group of around forty failed refugee applicants assessed through the Cairo visa office successfully challenged their refusals at the Federal Court.[15] IRCC's own 2011 quality assurance evaluation identified a number of shortcomings in decision-making in the refugee resettlement program, including failures to confront applicants with credibility concerns and the scant use of objective country documentation.[16] These concerns over the quality of decision-making highlight the need for adequate review mechanisms.

Avenues for Review

Failed refugee resettlement applicants have access to few recourses to challenge a negative decision. Unlike most inland refugee claimants, rejected resettlement applicants do not have access to an appeal on the merits. They can make a request for reconsideration directly to the visa office, but reconsideration is highly discretionary and unreliable. The only formal recourse available is judicial review before the Federal Court in Canada.

In all immigration matters, judicial review applicants must obtain "leave," or permission, from a Federal Court judge before proceeding to a hearing on the merits of their case.[17] Leave determinations are not appealable, and no reasons are given by the leave judge.[18] Although the leave test is in theory a very permissive one (whether the application discloses a "fairly arguable case" or a "serious question to be tried"), empirical research in the context of inland refugee claims has shown that it poses a significant obstacle to applicants.[19] Moreover, when leave is granted, applications are not reassessed on a *de novo* basis by a Federal Court judge. In most cases, courts apply the very deferential "reasonableness" standard of review.[20] A judicial review decision on the merits can only be appealed to the Federal Court of Appeal if the judge at the Federal Court level certifies a "question of general importance for the legal system as a whole," which, as will be shown below, rarely happens in the refugee resettlement context.[21] Most importantly, a positive judicial review does not result in the original administrative decision being overturned, but results in the case being quashed and sent back for redetermination by a different visa officer.[22] Unlike inland refugee claimants, failed resettlement applicants are not eligible for legal aid at the judicial review stage.

Methodology

The data reviewed in this study includes all judicial review applications of negative refugee resettlement decisions filed in the Federal Court between 2011 and 2015 inclusively (403 cases). The cases were identified through access to information requests (283 cases) and by manually reviewing the Federal Court's caseload (120 cases). Information about the judicial review process for each case (application date, number of principal applicants, lawyer name, leave judge name, hearing judge name, leave outcome, hearing outcome, whether the case was opposed, etc.) was gathered manually from the online Federal Court docket search tool. The paper file in each case was reviewed to determine the type of application (GAR or PSR) and whether the judicial review application was settled by the government. Information on the basis of claim and reason for refusal was also collected and analyzed in each case. A separate forthcoming study will focus on the quality of visa officer decision-making.

Judicial Review Statistics

From 2011 to 2015, 403 judicial review applications of overseas refugee decisions were filed in the Federal Court. Many applications involved multiple "principal applicants" (492 principal applicants in total). The 403 cases include 4 *mandamus* applications, that is, applications for an order compelling the government to make a decision in a particular case. In all, 393 applications were identified as PSR applications (475 principal applicants). One of these applications was a *mandamus* application. In total, 8.47 percent of the 5,597 PSR principal applicants rejected during that period sought judicial review. During the same period, 10 judicial review applications (17 principal applicants) in the GAR stream were initiated. Two of those cases were *mandamus* applications (9 principal applicants). Overall, 0.25 percent of the 3,203 rejected GAR applicants sought judicial review.

Table 12.3 provides a breakdown of the outcome of the 403 applications in the dataset. The analysis shows that 76 applications were either discontinued by the applicant before being perfected or were not perfected and were denied leave for that reason.[23] The relatively high number of "not perfected" and "discontinued" cases (18.86%) is likely a result of the rules of disclosure in immigration matters. Full reasons are not disclosed to applicants as a matter of course and can only be obtained through a formal access to information request or by launching a judicial review application. Delays in obtaining a reply to an access to information request can bring applicants outside the judicial review time limit, which is sixty days in the case of refugee resettlement applicants.[24] As a result, it is common practice for lawyers to file an application as soon as judicial review is contemplated and assess whether continuing with the application is warranted later when

Table 12.2
Overview of judicial review applications (2011–2015)

	PSR				GAR			
JR applications	Principal applicants	*Mandamus* applications†	Rate of seeking JR*		JR applications	Principal applicants	*Mandamus* applications†	Rate of seeking JR*
393	475	1	8.47% (474/5,597)		10	17	9	0.25% (8/3,203)

† Principal applicants equivalent
* Excluding mandamus applications

reasons are disclosed through the judicial process. A further 7 cases were granted on consent or settled before having been perfected. The remaining 320 cases were perfected. Seven perfected cases were granted on consent before leave was decided, and 45 cases were discontinued after being perfected (13 of which included evidence of a settlement, and a further 11 cases were discontinued after a declaration by the government that it was not opposing leave). Two hundred sixty-eight perfected cases proceeded to a leave determination.

Leave was opposed by the government in 245 of the 268 perfected cases that proceeded to a leave determination. Leave was granted in 150 of those 245 cases, for a leave grant rate of 61.22 percent for "opposed and perfected" cases. Leave was also granted in all but one of the 23 unopposed leave applications. Thirty-eight cases were discontinued after receiving a positive leave determination, 14 with evidence of a settlement in the court record. It is likely, however, that many more, if not all, were in fact settled, as not all lawyers follow the practice of placing settlement letters in the court record. Of the 134 remaining cases, 22 were granted with the consent of the government, 56 were granted on their merits after a hearing, and 56 were dismissed after a hearing. The success rate for opposed cases at the hearing stage was exactly 50 percent (56/112).

Overall, as many as 154 cases (38.21% of all cases) had a positive outcome, taking into account explicitly settled cases, cases granted on consent, perfected cases discontinued following a notice that leave was not opposed, cases discontinued following a positive leave determination, and cases granted on their merits. The success rate at the leave stage in this group of cases is much higher than reported leave grant rates in cases stemming from Canada's inland refugee system.

Table 12.3
Summary of judicial review outcomes (2011–2015)

Pre-leave stage (403 cases)

- 76 cases not perfected or discontinued before being perfected
- 7 cases granted on consent or settled before being perfected
- 320 perfected cases, including:
    - 7 cases granted on consent before leave was decided
    - 45 discontinued cases (13 with evidence of settlement, 11 where leave was not opposed)
    - 268 cases that proceeded to a leave determination

Leave stage (268 cases)

- 172 leave granted (22 leave not opposed; 150 leave opposed)
- 96 leave denied (1 leave not opposed; 95 leave opposed)

Post-leave stage (172 cases)

- 38 cases discontinued after leave granted (14 with evidence of settlement)
- 134 cases proceeded to a hearing, including:
    - 78 JR granted (56 on their merits, 22 on consent)
    - 56 JR dismissed

A study by Sean Rehaag reported an overall leave grant rate of 22.16 percent for perfected and opposed cases originating from the inland refugee system between 2013 and 2016, compared to 61.22 percent in this study's dataset.[25] It is also noteworthy that a surprisingly large proportion of cases were settled by the government: 63 cases were granted on consent or explicitly settled at various stages of the process, 24 cases were discontinued after a positive leave determination, and 11 cases were discontinued after a notice that leave was not opposed by the government. In total, as many as 98 cases (24.32%) have likely been settled.

A "serious question of general importance," which opens the door for an appeal to the Federal Court of Appeal, was submitted for certification in 36 cases by the applicant and in 1 case by the government. All but one of the questions for certification submitted by the applicant were refused, while the sole question submitted by the government was accepted for certification. Neither case actually proceeded to an appeal. In the 112 cases that were decided on the merits, judges issued published reasons in 82 cases (73.21%), and unpublished orders in 30 cases (26.79%), in a fairly equal proportion between positive and negative cases. Finally, it is interesting to note that applicants were represented by counsel in all but 8 cases (98.01%). All eight cases without counsel were denied leave, three for not having been perfected.

Judicial Review as Individual Redress

The data presented in the previous section constitutes strong evidence that judicial review is not an effective legal recourse for failed resettlement applicants. As mentioned above, leave grant rates are significantly higher for refugee resettlement applicants as compared to inland refugee claimants. The fact remains, however, that the leave requirement bars access to the courts to a significant number of applicants. More than one third of perfected and opposed cases that proceeded to a leave determination were denied leave (96 cases). It is also worth noting that studies of the inland system have shown wide variations in leave grant rates between individual Federal Court judges, which calls into question the reliability of the leave process.[26] The relatively small number of applications decided by individual Federal Court judges in this study's dataset is too small to draw reliable statistical inferences on that issue. The negative impact of the leave requirement on refugee applicants should not be minimized. That being said, the most significant obstacle to redress through judicial review for rejected resettlement applicants appears to be a more practical one: conducting litigation in Canadian courts is simply unachievable for the vast majority of displaced persons abroad. Overall, only 5.48 percent of the 8,800 failed PSR and GAR applicants combined sought judicial review between 2011 and 2015. As a comparator, the proportion of failed inland refugee claimants seeking judicial review before the RAD was implemented was more than four times higher.[27]

It can be hypothesized with confidence that resettlement applicants lack not only the financial but also the informational resources necessary to pursue a judicial review application. In the case of PSRS, it is certain that private sponsors play a major role in funding and coordinating judicial review proceedings. Privately sponsored applicants also often have family or other personal contacts in Canada who can assist in the judicial review process. It is clear, however, that for private sponsors, especially Groups of Five and Community Sponsors, navigating the Canadian judicial system can be costly and intimidating. As Lange's chapter in this volume shows, the legal process of private sponsorship is complex and daunting for private sponsors. The Refugee Sponsorship Support Program (RSSP) now provides *pro bono* legal support to private sponsors, but only at the initial stage of completing the immigration application. The important role played by private sponsors and Canadian contacts in challenging visa officer decisions is evident when we consider that between 2011 and 2015, GAR applicants sought judicial review in only ten cases, despite there being more than 3,000 GAR refusals. Generally speaking, GARs have fewer support networks in Canada and tend to be in more vulnerable situations than PSRs.[28] The data shows that for them, hiring a lawyer and initiating litigation in Canada is virtually impossible. This view is reinforced by looking into the nine GAR cases in the dataset where the background of the applicant was discussed. Those included four cases with immediate family in Canada, one case of a former UNHCR lawyer, one case of an applicant who had previously lived in Canada, and one case of a fairly well-off businessman. In only two cases did the applicant appear to have no connections to Canada, to have minimal knowledge of the Canadian legal system, and to be of modest means. One of these cases involved a self-represented applicant who was denied leave. In that case, the applicant requested an extension of time on the basis of "Difficulty of getting who to represent me in Canada due to lack of financial support [sic]" and "late reception of how and where to follow up information [sic]". One wonders who would have appeared in court on behalf of this applicant had leave been granted.

The Structural Role of Judicial Review

Before addressing the structural role of judicial review in the resettlement system, it is worth noting that Canadian courts have had a major influence on the evolution of the inland refugee system, at both the procedural and substantive levels. The IRB was created in the aftermath of the Supreme Court's decision in *Singh*,[29] where it was recognized that inland refugee claimants are protected by the *Canadian Charter of Rights and Freedoms*[30] and have the right to an oral hearing where credibility is at issue. There is a vast body of Federal Court case law dealing with both procedural and substantive issues in the inland refugee system. In fact, in the years preceding the implementation of the RAD at the IRB in 2012, judicial review of inland refugee matters made up around half of the Federal Court's caseload.[31] The IRB maintains an online legal resource with extensive references to Federal Court case law.[32] This is not the case with the overseas refugee system. While the case law pertaining to the interpretation of the Convention refugee definition developed in the inland context equally applies in the overseas context, the usefulness of inland refugee case law ends there. Even the *Immigration and Refugee Protection Act* reference material published by major Canadian legal editors contains only scant references to refugee resettlement cases.[33] That is because very little case law exists on key substantive legal issues specific to the overseas refugee system, such as the Country of Asylum class, the concept of durable solutions, and the successful establishment criteria. The same can be said about the procedural aspects of refugee resettlement decision-making. The case law is thin and has had little impact on the development of decision-making procedures.

The limited role of the Federal Court at the structural level can be explained by process-oriented and doctrinal factors. At the process level, three issues are worth noting. First, a remarkably low number of resettlement cases are judicially reviewed. On average, 22 PSR cases were reviewed each year on their merits by the Federal Court between 2011 and 2015. During the same period, only two GAR cases were reviewed on their merits. It is somewhat troubling that a surprisingly high proportion of cases were settled or granted on consent. This raises concerns around IRCC's potential use of case settlement as a strategy for insulating objectionable practices from judicial and public scrutiny, and for avoiding restrictive precedents. Further qualitative analysis should be pursued to identify trends in case settlement and determine whether this practice leads to the repetition of failures in decision-making. Second, a significant portion of Federal Court decisions are unpublished. As mentioned above, 26.79 percent of Federal Court decisions on the merits were decided with the issuance of an unpublished order. These orders are, however, compiled by the Department of Justice, which is thus able to build a significant body of case law that is unavailable to refugee applicants. Third, the restriction on appeals to the Federal Court of Appeal, much like the leave requirement, limit the development of a comprehensive body of case law. As mentioned in the previous section, a "question of general importance for the legal system as a whole" was certified on only two occasions, despite such questions having being submitted in thirty-seven cases. It appears that the last refugee resettlement case decided by the Federal Court of Appeal dates back to 2004.[34] No refugee resettlement case has ever been heard by the Supreme Court of Canada.

At the doctrinal level, it is noteworthy that the Federal Court has adopted a very deferential approach in overseas refugee matters. The court has taken the position that overseas refugee decisions, contrary to inland refugee determinations, are "purely administrative" and that visa officers deciding overseas refugee cases enjoy "extensive discretion."[35] In *Oraha*, the Federal Court stated that the duty of fairness is "somewhat limited by comparison to that owed Convention refugee claimants applying from within Canada."[36] In *Qarizada*, the Federal Court stated that case law developed in the context of inland refugee claims is of little assistance in the administrative context of overseas refugee matters.[37]

The root of this approach to overseas refugee decisions lies, for the most part, in Canadian courts' view on the extraterritorial application of the *Charter*. In the precedent-setting *Singh* decision, where the Supreme Court decided that the *Charter* applied to inland refugee claimants, Justice Wilson reasoned that the term "person" in section 7 of the *Charter* "includes every human being who is physically present in Canada and by virtue of such presence amenable to Canadian law."[38] This interpretation did not preclude, however, the application of the *Charter* to someone outside Canada but still "amenable to Canadian law."[39] In *Khadr*[40] and *Hape*[41], the Supreme Court determined that the *Charter* can also apply to a Canadian citizen outside Canada. The issue of whether the *Charter* can apply to a non-citizen outside Canada but who is also "amenable to Canadian law," and in particular to refugee applicants, has yet to be determined by the Supreme Court. In *Slahi*, the Federal Court of Appeal concluded that the *Charter* did not apply in circumstances similar to those in *Kadr*, but where the applicant was a non-citizen.[42] In *Crease*, however, the Federal Court found that the *Charter* did apply to a non-citizen outside Canada who sought a declaration that he was eligible for Canadian citizenship.[43] The *Crease* decision appears to have had little impact on Federal Court jurisprudence. In the cases of *Jallow* and *Oraha*, cited above, refugee resettlement applicants sought to have the decision rejecting their application quashed on the grounds that the decision-making process failed to follow the directions set out in *Singh*. In both cases, the Federal Court determined that the *Singh* decision did not apply to refugee claimants outside Canada.

Getting a fuller picture of the role of courts in overseas refugee matters would require a deeper investigation into how legal developments find their way to decision-makers on the ground, and a qualitative analysis of visa officer decisions. What is clear, however, is that the factors reviewed above contribute to minimizing judicial impact on refugee decision-making. It is noteworthy that out of the hundreds of visa officer decisions reviewed, only 6 cited case law.

CONCLUSION: STRENGTHENING OVERSEAS REFUGEE DECISION-MAKING

Effective judicial review is essential for upholding the rights of refugees and, more generally, for upholding the rule of law. Legal barriers to judicial review, such as the leave requirement in immigration and refugee matters, are difficult to reconcile with the principle of the rule of law. Audrey Macklin, writing on the inland refugee system, offers the following:

> One of the foundational tenets of the rule of law is the guarantee of access to an independent and impartial court [...] to challenge the legality of a decision affecting fundamental rights [...]. The use of a leave requirement to constrict that access, however compelling the administrative exigencies animating it, directly and incontrovertibly breaches that fundamental principle. [...]
> The leave requirement has never been justified on a principled basis. More specifically, it would be untenable to contend that the rule of law does not apply to asylum seekers, or that anything about the current system provides a satisfactory alternative to, or substitute for, judicial review for those who do not obtain leave[44].

Macklin's statements certainly apply in the case of overseas refugees, especially considering existing concerns over the quality of visa officer decision-making, training, and caseloads. I would like to caution against the view that a weak rule of law is an inherent and necessary feature of immigration and refugee law.[45] Significant improvements to the inland refugee determination process have been made in the past thirty years. The overseas refugee resettlement system is lagging behind, in my assessment, in large part because it is allowed to unfold away from public and judicial scrutiny. With that in mind, I propose a few concrete and rather modest policy changes that would strengthen the resettlement program by facilitating access to review and ensuring accurate decision-making by visa officers.

There is little doubt that abolishing or reforming the leave requirement would lead to better access to justice for both overseas and inland refugee claimants. This recommendation has been voiced by others and would require very few changes at the Federal Court beyond an increase in judicial appointments.[46] In the case of resettlement applicants, however, it is clear that measures must be adopted to support and guide applicants throughout the process. I make three recommendations in this respect. First, additional efforts should be made to inform applicants of the eligibility and admissibility requirements of resettlement to Canada. Easy-to-understand instructions in plain language could be proactively offered well before the interview. Under the current practice, it is common for visa officers to simply read the Convention refugee definition and the Country of Asylum class verbatim at the start of the interview, add that the applicant must establish that they are not inadmissible to Canada, and ask the applicants if they understand. Eligibility and inadmissibility requirements are highly complex. Refugee applicants are typically unfamiliar with Canadian law, and many are illiterate. The standard *pro forma* interview script is clearly not serving its purpose. In the hundreds of case notes reviewed, there was not a single mention of an applicant asking follow-up questions to the visa officer. More active steps must be undertaken to explain resettlement requirements in plain language and in a less intimidating and stressful context. In the case of PSRs, the government should not overly rely on private sponsors to prepare applicants for their interview, as the level of involvement of sponsors in the application process varies widely.

Second, visa officers should be required to better explain their reasoning in their decision letters. The issue of boilerplate decision letters was mentioned in CIC's 2012 quality assurance evaluation.[47] Far too many applicants still receive rejection letters with insufficient details.

In the dataset, 12.62 percent of decision letters issued in 2013 or after contained no information specific to the applicant's case. A further 14.65 percent of decision letters contained only between one and five lines of text specific to the applicant. Requiring that visa officers provide more fulsome decision letters would procure many benefits.[48] It would have a disciplining effect in terms of improving decision-making and provide more opportunity for oversight. More fulsome reasons are also required so that applicants can make informed decisions about whether to seek judicial review. Under the current system, applicants must make a formal access to information request to obtain the full notes of the visa officer. It is likely that this added step dissuades applicants from pursuing judicial review.

This brings me to my third and last recommendation. Policies should be adopted to ensure that rejected applicants understand how to challenge a negative decision. It is clear that many rejected applicants are unaware that they can seek judicial review. Judicial review is not mentioned during the interview and is not mentioned in refusal letters. At the minimum, policy-makers could consider offering easy-to-understand guides on how to retain counsel and initiate judicial review. In the case of GARs, it is clear that such support is critically needed.

NOTES

1 See Suzan Kneebone, "The Rule of Law and the Role of Law: Refugees and Asylum Seekers," in *Refugees, Asylum Seekers and the Rule of Law: Comparative Perspectives*, ed. Susan Kneebone (Cambridge: Cambridge University Press, 2009), 32–77.
2 For a detailed analysis of how common refugee adjudication approaches can lead to wrong decisions, see Hilary Evans Cameron, *Refugee Law's Fact-Finding Crisis: Truth, Risk, and the Wrong Mistake* (Cambridge: Cambridge University Press, 2018).
3 See Peter Cane, "Understanding Judicial Review and its Impact," in *Judicial Review and Bureaucratic Impact: International and Interdisciplinary Perspectives*, ed. Marc Herthog and Simon Halliday (Cambridge: Cambridge University Press, 2004), 15–42.
4 House of Commons, Standing Committee on Citizenship and Immigration, "Responding to Public Complaints: A Review of the Appointment, Training and Complaint Processes of the Immigration and Refugee Board," 2018.

5 It should be noted, however, that access to legal aid for inland asylum-seekers varies from province to province and is not recognized as a constitutional right by Canadian courts. Legal aid for asylum-seekers is vulnerable to budgetary cuts, as evidenced by the Ontario government's 2019 decision to cut all legal aid funding for asylum-seekers. See Sharry Aiken and Sean Rehaag, "Ontario's Cuts to Legal Aid for Refugees: Racist, Xenophobic and Possibly Unconstitutional," *The Conversation*, 16 April 2019. See also Emily Bates, Jennifer Bond, and David Wiseman, "Troubling Signs: Mapping Access to Justice in Canada's Refugee System Reform," *Ottawa Law Review* 47, no. 1 (2016): 1–72.
6 Sean Rehaag, "The Role of Counsel in Canada's Refugee Determination System: An Empirical Assessment," *Osgoode Hall Law Journal* no. 49 (2011): 71–116.
7 See Angus Grant and Sean Rehaag, "Unappealing: An Assessment of the Limits on Appeal Rights in Canada's New Refugee Determination System," *UBC Law Review* 49, no. 1 (2016): 203–74.
8 See Vic Satzewich, *Points of Entry: How Canada's Immigration Officers Decide Who Gets In* (Vancouver: UBC Press, 2015), 57.
9 IRCC, "Evaluation of the Resettlement Programs (GAR, PSR, BVOR and RAP)," 2016, 5.2.3.
10 See *Ghirmatsion v Canada (MCI)*, 2011 FC 519.
11 During the Syrian refugee movement, visa officers were directed to consider that all Syrian nationals outside Syria met the refugee definitions and to focus their assessment on security screening. See IRCC, "Syrian Refugee Resettlement Initiative – Looking to the Future," https://www.canada.ca/en/immigration-refugees-citizenship/services/refugees/welcome-syrian-refugees/looking-future.html.
12 In 2013, approval rates in the GAR program were exceptionally low in a handful of visa offices that had accepted applications under the Source Country Class, repealed in 2011.
13 See Grant and Rehaag, "Unappealing: An Assessment of the Limits on Appeal Rights in Canada's New Refugee Determination System," 203–6; Cécile Rousseau, François Crépeau, Patricia Foxen, and France Houle, "The Complexity of Determining Refugeehood: A Multidisciplinary Analysis of the Decision-Making Process of the Canadian Immigration and Refugee Board," *Journal of Refugee Studies* 15, no. 1 (2002): 43–4.
14 Canadian Council for Refugees, "Concerns with Refugee Decision-Making at Cairo," 2010, https://ccrweb.ca/en/concerns-refugee-decision-making-cairo. See also Canadian Council for Refugees, "The Private Sponsorship

of Refugees Program: Current Challenges and Opportunities," 2006, https://ccrweb.ca/sites/ccrweb.ca/files/static-files/PSRPBriefing.pdf.
15 See *Ghirmatsion v Canada*.
16 CIC, "The PSR Quality Assurance Project: Managing Quality Counts," 2011.
17 *Immigration and Refugee Protection Act*, SC 2001, c 27, s 72(1).
18 *Immigration and Refugee Protection Act*, s 72(2).
19 See Sean Rehaag, "Judicial Review of Refugee Determinations: The Luck of the Draw?," *Queen's Law Journal* 38, no. 1 (2012): 1–58; Sean Rehaag, "Judicial Review of Refugee Determinations (II): Revisiting the Luck of the Draw," *Queen's Law Journal* (forthcoming), available at SSRN: https://ssrn.com/abstract=3249723.
20 See *Canada (MCI) v Vavilov*, 2019 SCC 65.
21 *Immigration and Refugee Protection Act*, s 74(d).
22 *Federal Courts Act*, RSC 1985, c F-7, s 18.1(3).
23 A "perfected" application is one in which all the required documents have been filed.
24 *Immigration and Refugee Protection Act*, s 72(2)(b).
25 Rehaag, "Judicial Review of Refugee Determinations (II)." See also Rehaag, "Judicial Review of Refugee Determinations."
26 Ibid.
27 The proportion of failed inland refugee claimants who sought judicial review in 2010–11 and 2011–12 was 30.01 percent. This data point was created relying on online Federal Court statistics and IRB Departmental Performance Reports for the relevant years. See also Department of Justice, *Immigration and Refugee Legal Aid Cost Drivers* (2002), https://www.justice.gc.ca/eng/rp-pr/other-autre/ir/rr03_la17-rr03_aj17/toc-tdm.html.
28 See IRCC, "Rapid Evaluation Impact of the Syrian Refugee Initiative," 2016, 1.3.
29 *Singh v Canada (MEI)*, [1985] 1 SCR 177 [*Singh*].
30 *Canadian Charter of Rights and Freedoms*, Part I of the *Constitution Act, 1982*, being Schedule B to the *Canada Act 1982* (UK), 1982 c 11 [*Charter*].
31 See Federal Court, "Statistics," https://www.fct-cf.gc.ca/en/pages/about-the-court/reports-and-statistics/statistics.
32 Immigration and Refugee Board, "Legal Resources," https://irb-cisr.gc.ca/en/legal-policy/legal-concepts/Pages/index.aspx#LC-RC.
33 See Henry M. Goslett and Barbara Jo Caruso, *The 2020 Annotated Immigration and Refugee Protection Act of Canada* (Toronto: Carswell,

2019); Lorne Waldman, *Canadian Immigration and Refugee Law Practice, 2020* ed. (Markham: Lexisnexis, 2019).

34 *Ha v Canada (MCI)*, 2004 FCA 49. However, in a more recent case, the Federal Court of Appeal considered whether the cessation clause in section 108(1)(a) of the *Immigration and Refugee Protection Act* applied to a permanent resident who had come to Canada as a resettled refugee: *Siddiqui v Canada (MCI)*, 2016 FCA 134, reconsidered in 2016 FCA 237.

35 *Jallow v Canada (MCI)* (1996), 122 FTR 40 at 18.

36 *Oraha v Canada (MCI)* (1997), 39 Imm LR (2d) 39 at 9. The Federal Court has held that the level of procedural fairness owed to overseas refugee applicants is, however, higher than in non-refugee cases. See *Krikor v Canada (MCI)*, 2016 FC 458 at 12–13.

37 *Qarizada v Canada (MCI)*, 2008 FC 1310 at 27.

38 *Singh* at 35.

39 See Jamie Chai Yun Liew and Donald Galloway, *Immigration Law*, 2nd ed. (Toronto: Irwin Law, 2015), 636–43.

40 *Canada (Prime Minister) v Kadr*, 2010 SCC 3.

41 *R v Hape*, 2007 SCC 26.

42 *Slahi v Canada (Minister of Justice)*, 2009 FCA 259.

43 *Crease v Canada*, [1994] 3 FC 380 (TD).

44 Audrey Macklin, "Asylum and the Rule of Law in Canada: Hearing the Other (Side)," in *Refugees, Asylum Seekers and the Rule of Law*, ed. Susan Kneebone (Cambridge: Cambridge University Press, 2009), 104–5.

45 See Catherine Dauvergne, *Making People Illegal: What Globalization Means for Migration and Law* (Cambridge: Cambridge University Press, 2008).

46 See Sean Rehaag, "Judicial Review of Refugee Determinations," 34–9.

47 CIC, "The PSR Quality Assurance Project: Managing Quality Counts," 53–4.

48 See Mary Liston, "'Alert, Alive and Sensitive': Baker, the Duty to Give Reasons, and the Ethos of Justification in Canadian Public Law," in *The Unity of Public Law*, ed. David Dyzenhaus (Oxford: Hart Publishing, 2004), 113–41.

PART FOUR

Comparison

13

"Doing Something to Fight Injustice": Voluntarism and Refugee Resettlement as Political Engagement in the United States

Scott Harding and Kathryn Libal

While the protection of refugees is fundamental to international human rights law, rising xenophobia in Europe and the United States has undermined long-standing commitments to forced migrants and immigrants. The US government has historically touted its generosity and support for refugees, claiming that the program reflects "the United States' highest values and aspirations to compassion, generosity and leadership."[1] This humanitarian framing is in sharp contrast to the today's nativist rhetoric from President Trump and US policies that seek to sharply curtail refugee admissions.[2] In two executive orders issued in early 2017, Trump "proclaim[ed] that the entry of more than 50,000 refugees in fiscal 2017 would be detrimental to the interests of the United States."[3] The Presidential Determination for refugee admissions in fiscal year 2018 set the maximum level of refugees at 45,000, with fewer than 20,000 refugees likely to be resettled.[4] The threshold for the fiscal year 2019 was set at 30,000 refugees.[5]

In addition to the sharp cut in refugee admissions, Trump has called for "special measures" that would be adopted for "certain categories of refugees whose entry continues to pose potential threats to the security and welfare of the United States."[6] In June 2018, the Supreme Court ruled that the president could lawfully exclude from admission to the United States refugees and other visitors from particular – mostly Muslim majority – countries. The ruling maintained, however, that refugees with a "credible claim of a bona fide relationship" with "a person or entity in the United States" from any given "ban list" should still be granted access to visas following security clearances.[7] The Trump White House has been largely unresponsive to political pressure and calls by voluntary agencies to maintain US global leadership in refugee resettlement, and only a small number of refugees from Muslim majority states have been granted admission since 2017.

In the context of these radical policy shifts, voluntarism has taken on new meanings. Community mobilization in support of refugees has recently become more visible, representing one manifestation of citizen action to counter what many Americans see as unjust policies. Based on qualitative interviews and field observation in Connecticut and New York, this chapter underscores how involvement in community "co-sponsorship" of refugees has led to new forms of political engagement and lateral organizing among local residents and between communities.[8]

What we call "co-sponsorship" of refugees in the United States is different from private sponsorship in Canada, the United Kingdom, or Australia.[9] In the United States, selection of refugees for resettlement is carried out by the federal government in cooperation with UNHCR and the International Organization for Migration in the same manner as the Canadian government resettlement program. These refugees are assigned to one of nine voluntary agencies, which work with a network of affiliate organizations at the local level to carry out the practical work of resettlement.[10] These agencies, in turn, cooperate with local affiliate groups, which carry out "co-sponsorship" by supporting refugees, with funding from the US government, supplemented by private fundraising.

A key difference from Canada is that even if voluntary groups have the capacity to resettle more refugees than the president has determined, there is no established procedure for increasing admissions based on additional private support. Thus, the US case does not adhere to the principle of additionality, whereby individuals engaged in private sponsorship "add to the government's existing commitments" and increase the numbers of refugees resettled in a given time period.[11] It also does not allow "naming," in the same sense that this principle applies in Canada, even though voluntary groups have some discretion when agreeing to resettle individuals and families assigned to them by the State Department.

Despite recent gains in community co-sponsorship and other voluntarist approaches to refugee resettlement in the United States, private and community sponsorship has been contentious among some refugee advocates. First, it devolves resettlement work to the local level and reduces the federal government's responsibility for providing resources and services to refugees. Also, some fear that such efforts may affect the quality of services to refugees during their initial resettlement. Moreover, volunteerism may undermine the legitimacy of resettlement agencies and their partners, inadvertently giving policymakers a reason to privatize the refugee resettlement system more fully. As one resettlement agency provider noted, "we always have to say ... in the same breath that we talk about the great advantages of community-based resettlement, we have to immediately add the only way it will work is if there is a refugee resettlement agency involved. Vetting the groups, training the groups, overseeing the groups, and picking up the case if the group collapses and can't do it."[12] Despite these concerns, engaging community supporters as volunteers and advocates has become part of a broader movement to challenge US policies that restrict access to those seeking asylum and permanent resettlement as refugees. While citizen/refugee solidarity in the United States remains nascent, our research reveals how supporting refugees is understood by community members as both "humanitarian" and an act of political resistance.

HISTORICAL INVOLVEMENT IN PERMANENT RESETTLEMENT OF REFUGEES

Since the Second World War, the United States has been a prominent global actor in the permanent resettlement of refugees; until recently, in raw numbers, it resettled the most refugees on an annual basis. Since 1975 the United States has offered permanent resettlement to more than three million refugees.[13] Despite this leadership, however, this same period has seen severe restriction on immigration and admissions of refugees. The 1948 *Displaced Persons Act* was the first piece of US legislation to provide a humanitarian response to the effects of war; that act was intended to allow certain categories of displaced Europeans to resettle in the United States through community and private sponsorship.[14] Cold War politics strongly shaped refugee resettlement well after the passage of the 1980 *Resettlement Act*. As Haines notes, "[a]nticommunism has been crucial to virtually all refugee admissions up until the 1990s."[15] At the height of the Cold War, and especially in the 1970s, the United States accepted hundreds of thousands of Cuban and Southeast Asian refugees through the US Attorney General's "parole" authority.[16] Under this mechanism, refugees gained temporary residence status and many eventually became permanent US residents or citizens.

The 1980 *Refugee Act* passed by the US Congress sought to "provide uniform procedure for refugee admissions," to eliminate political considerations in choosing who to admit, and to authorize federal funding to resettle refugees throughout the country.[17] Thresholds for admissions and actual admissions have fluctuated considerably with the historical context and from one administration to the next. Except for the years following the 11 September terrorist attacks, annual refugee admissions to the United States have regularly exceeded 50,000 and have averaged between 70,000 and 80,000.[18] Thus, the Trump Administration's proposals to severely restrict refugee admissions, in terms of which nationalities and religious groups would be prioritized or excluded and how many refugees would be admitted, is a radical departure from nearly forty years of US refugee policy.

Anti-immigration policies contributed to Trump's election in 2016 and have been key to his administration's political agenda. As Greenhill argues, Trump resorts to psychological manipulation to "fan fears that have little or no basis in objective reality but ring viscerally true to target audiences" to build support for his actions.[19] Despite widespread support in parts of the United States, and within the Obama administration, for increased resettlement of Syrian refugees between 2014 and 2016, opposition to Syrian and other Muslim refugees has intensified. After the Paris attacks of November 2015, a majority of US state governors asserted that they would not permit Syrian refugee families to be resettled in their states.[20] Prominent among them was then Governor Mike Pence, who became Trump's vice-president.[21]

Once in the White House, Trump began fulfilling his campaign promises by naming anti-immigration activist Stephen Miller as a key domestic policy adviser. In concert with other anti-immigration advocates, the Trump administration crafted immigration policy changes that limited access to all types of visas, enhanced border security, lengthened the refugee vetting process, expanded the criminalization of asylum-seekers and undocumented migrants who resided in the United States or attempted to cross borders to claim asylum, attempted to end the Deferred Action for Childhood Admission Program (DACA), and instituted a radical "deterrent" policy of family separation for those without legal authorization to be in the United States. Deportation without due process has accelerated, and the administration has often ignored court orders to modify or halt its policies. In short, President Trump has enacted a range of policies that severely limit immigration.

PRIVATE AND COMMUNITY SPONSORSHIP IN HISTORICAL CONTEXT

Private sponsorship of refugees in the United States predates the development of an international definition of refugee as well as international humanitarian law. In the early twentieth century, US citizens often sponsored family members displaced by conflict abroad. As Bier and La Corte note, "[R]eligious and ethnic groups provided resources and sponsors to refugees without families in the United States."[22] As was also the case in Canada, Jewish and Christian communities and institutions were particularly active in refugee sponsorship prior to the 1970s. For example, for more than a century the Hebrew Immigrant Aid Society (HIAS) has resettled Jewish immigrants and refugees in the United States.[23] In the 1960s and '70s, the Catholic Church and Cuban-American organizations mobilized to sponsor more than 700,000 Cuban asylum-seekers and refugees.[24] Voluntary organizations, most of them tied to religious institutions such as HIAS, the US Conference of Catholic Bishops, Church World Service, and the US Committee for Refugees and Immigrants, also played a vital role in developing refugee policy. In the 1970s, following the US accession to the 1967 Optional Protocol to the UN Refugee Convention, these organizations began lobbying for more systematic and comprehensive refugee policy reform. Their advocacy for stronger federal involvement followed on the heels of the first wave of Cuban resettlement and the provision of parole status to several hundred thousand Vietnamese, Cambodian, and Laotian refugees after the Vietnam War.[25]

Until the mid-1970s, the costs of refugee sponsorship were generally borne by the sponsoring family or organization in a manner similar to the private sponsorship program that evolved in Canada. The 1980 *Refugee Act* formalized the US government's role in setting annual admissions levels. The same Act required that federal guidelines be established and enforced for refugee resettlement services provided at state and local levels. It created a coordination mechanism between the Office of Refugee Resettlement and officially recognized voluntary agencies (Volags). While the government moved to monitor and regulate refugee resettlement practices, non-governmental organizations and volunteers were vital to the implementation of the US refugee resettlement program. Eby, Iverson, Smyers, and Kekic argue that the United States has been a global leader in resettlement "because of the long-standing active engagement and support of communities of faith."[26] They highlight the important contributions of non-state actors, particularly the "role of churches, synagogues, mosques, and other faith groups at the local level, whose congregations play an important role as volunteers welcoming refugees to their communities."[27] Between 1986 and 1995, the Reagan and Clinton administrations experimented with private sponsorship in a "private sector initiative" intended to increase opportunities for resettlement of refugees based on the ability of private actors to raise funds. Around 16,000 Jews from the former Soviet Union, as well as Cubans, Vietnamese, and Iranians, were resettled through this initiative.[28] But after the mid-1990s, the experiment with private sponsorship was not renewed, and community sponsorship efforts remain a small part of the US refugee resettlement program.

In 2014, in response to record numbers of refugees, the UNHCR called for greater support for refugees from the private sector and from communities in Europe, North America, and elsewhere with significant refugee resettlement programs.[29] By 2015, voluntary agencies and organizations in Connecticut and other states were beginning to explore or implement community sponsorship programs, an idea that was gaining public support. In 2016, the Urban Justice Center, the International Refugee Assistance Project, and Human Rights First jointly authored a report establishing guidelines for private sponsorship of refugees in the United States.[30] The Cato Institute, a libertarian think tank, also argued for private sponsorship, noting the president's responsibility to consider private sources of funding when setting admissions ceilings.[31] And in 2016, the Niskanen Center, another think tank based in Washington, D.C., renewed its call for private and community sponsorship.[32] One month later, after Trump was elected president, the effort was largely tabled, though some continued to advocate in the press for private or community-based resettlement.[33]

REVIVAL OF "COMMUNITY CO-SPONSORSHIP": COMMUNITIES DEMAND A ROLE

In Connecticut, one of the smallest states by area in the United States, Integrated Refugee and Immigrant Services (IRIS) is one of two non-governmental organizations participating in refugee resettlement. While the organization previously worked with several community co-sponsorship groups, the backlash to President Trump's proposed travel ban and dramatic reduction of refugee admissions opened up new possibilities for such efforts. A groundswell of public support for refugees across the United States in the wake of the Syrian migration crisis coincided with Trump's explicit anti-immigrant/anti-Muslim rhetoric and xenophobic policies. In Connecticut, thousands of people spontaneously protested and staged rallies across the state in opposition to these policies, calling for the government to welcome Syrians fleeing war and persecution. IRIS, whose executive director, Chris George, had publicly stated a willingness to resettle Syrian refugees, was inundated with interest in sponsoring refugee families from dozens of local communities and Christian, Jewish, and Muslim faith-based institutions. "This is really the year ... of the volunteers," said George. "It's really taken off here, and we'd like to see it replicated across the country. It's better for the refugee family to have a community group working with them that knows the schools and knows where to shop and knows where the jobs are."[34]

Community co-sponsorship groups must work directly with an official resettlement organization, such as IRIS, and take responsibility for the costs associated with resettling refugees for at least one year. IRIS required interested groups, many of which formed specifically for this purpose, to formally apply and indicate their capacity to resettle a refugee family in their community. Volunteer groups must link refugees to services, help families secure housing and employment, and provide connections to schools, English-language courses for adults, and transportation to help facilitate refugee "self-sufficiency." Interviews with volunteers from several community groups and IRIS staff highlight both manifest and latent goals of the community co-sponsorship model. For IRIS, the program enhances its capacity and lets the organization resettle more people throughout Connecticut. This allows IRIS to maximize its resources, providing more refugees with more services than would otherwise occur. Community co-sponsorship is also well suited to promote "self-sufficiency" – a key premise of US refugee policy – by strengthening refugees' ties to community institutions and residents with deep knowledge of a local community.

Implicitly, co-sponsorship serves the needs of resettlement agencies like IRIS, as well as the local community. Notably, the co-sponsorship model establishes a bridge between refugees and the community. Volunteers, many of whom are respected and/or well connected, promote interaction between refugees and the local community as they link refugees to local institutions and services. This increases the likelihood that refugees will have more points of community contact than if they interacted mainly with resettlement agency staff (under the traditional resettlement model). With their many connections in the community, volunteers can also help address real or potential problems facing refugees and advocate on behalf of refugee families.[35] By developing diffuse nodes of community support, local volunteers promote community integration and self-sufficiency among refugees, helping them generate social capital in their new environment. In this sense, the social networks that refugees typically form in host countries – networks that are essential to their ability to thrive – depend more heavily on the support of co-sponsorship volunteers than typically occurs in resettlement. Community co-sponsorship also encourages local residents to "invest" in welcoming refugees; and it helps build understanding of the program as a means to address stereotypes and any opposition toward newly relocated refugee families. This is significant in Connecticut; under the co-sponsorship model, many refugee families there have been placed in small communities with limited ethnic, racial, and religious diversity and that have no history of refugee resettlement.

Setting aside its limited scope within one state, in some key aspects co-sponsorship has been notably successful in Connecticut. Within a two-and-a-half year period, that state saw a dramatic increase in co-sponsorship efforts: forty-five (mostly new) groups worked with IRIS to resettle fifty-seven refugee families (nearly three hundred individuals) in more than thirty communities.[36] As a result of grassroots mobilization, hundreds of people without prior experience became involved in refugee resettlement. While many of these individuals are linked to faith-based groups, the participants represent a diversity of backgrounds – they come from education, the business sector, local governments, and ethnic associations, for example. Interviews with these volunteers make clear that community co-sponsorship provided increased visibility and support for refugee resettlement across Connecticut.

At its peak, in 2016, IRIS more than doubled the number of refugees resettled in the state, and nearly 40 percent of this increase was a result of co-sponsorship. More significant, according to IRIS staff, co-sponsorship has produced positive results for refugees. Those resettled by community groups in Connecticut were able to find employment, learn English, and integrate more quickly than those resettled by IRIS.

VOLUNTARISM AS (LOCAL) POLITICAL WORK – RESISTANCE THROUGH COMMUNITY-BUILDING

For many volunteers interviewed for this study, widespread media coverage of the Syrian refugee "crisis" demanded a moral response. This sense of obligation intensified in the wake of press coverage of the death of Alan Kurdi, the Syrian toddler who drowned near Turkey in September 2015.[37] In the words of one volunteer, "Well, I just think that *we all can do something*. It may not be a big thing, but if we can do something to fight injustice, then we should do it. And if *we can help one family at a time*, that's one family that has the benefit."[38]

Many volunteers suggested that after the 2016 election of President Donald Trump, sponsoring a refugee family represented a public rebuke of a growing politics of fear and anti-refugee sentiment. "Before Trump was elected [we were] trying to fly under the radar screen because we didn't want all that pushback and controversy," said one New York volunteer. "When Trump was elected, the whole situation changed, and we realized that staying off the radar screen wasn't going to do anybody any good."[39] The same volunteer asserted: "We want the message to get to Washington that there is an enormous amount of support for refugee resettlement in [X] county, so that at least whatever pressure we can apply to change policies, either in the White House or Congress, that we are applying that pressure."[40]

In the interviews analyzed for this chapter, this was one of the few overt expressions of interest in changing national policies and discourse on refugees. To date, few community groups have engaged in sustained efforts to combat anti-immigrant and anti-refugee policies at the national level. Thus, while most volunteers expressed a desire to "make a difference" or "do something" to fight injustice, most have only been involved in sporadic political action to oppose Trump's restrictionist policies. This is not surprising, given the long-standing reluctance of voluntary agencies to publicly critique presidential actions regarding resettlement. Indeed, some resettlement staff leaders have been told by Office of Refugee Resettlement officials that they should not engage in advocacy; their work should focus on education and awareness raising.

While some volunteers (such as the interviewees above) see their work as a form of resistance to Trump's xenophobic policies, more often their ideas and actions represent "political" engagement and community-building at the local level. As one volunteer shared:

> I have an activist heart, so this gives me an outlet for my frustration and anger with what's going on in Washington right now. And a lot of people I work with say the same thing. The head of one of the co-chairs of our committee at one of our meetings ... said, this feels so good; I'm so tired of making phone calls to my legislators and feeling like my voice is just lost. But this really feels like I'm doing something and it's going to matter and it's going to matter for a long time.[41]

Supporting refugees in their local communities could help combat a sense of powerlessness over decisions being made by the Trump administration. The same volunteer added:

> Our country is, like, so divided along political lines. And I'm so tired of the anti-immigrant, anti-refugee this ... It's really racist – I'm so tired of it. And it's just ... my frustration. I'm doing something about it. *It just feels really good to do something about it.*[42]

Resettlement staff emphasized the need to "outlast" the Trump administration. One staff member said that after Trump's election they "knew things were going to go down. Not a week after the inauguration – the first Executive Order [came] – the slashing of the number [of refugees]. So we still want to persist, right? We're not going to just roll over."[43] This staff member expressed a common theme among resettlement agency workers: "We're all just trying to hope for the best, keep praying, *keep outlasting*, keep struggling and we'll have to kind of pick up the pieces when this is all over and see what kind of serious lasting damage has been done." In this context, fostering co-sponsorship capacity increases support for beleaguered resettlement organizations. Thus, resettlement agencies continue to train and support community groups to host refugee families in the future.

Community-building to support refugees, then, is not just a form of humanitarian work. Expressing solidarity with refugees and immigrants not only creates stronger ties with newcomer individuals and families, our interviews suggest, but also strengthens and expands relationships between long-time community members. These ties may be between faiths, as one volunteer from New York described: "Like *it binds you together*; you know, the emotional reward is you're making new friends, you share a common goal, we're members of a faith community, we're holding hands and working together. *It builds solidarity.*"[44]

Other volunteers highlighted the intrinsic value of promoting social inclusion by resettling refugees as a way to strengthen and renew communities that were relatively homogenous:

> [X] is a very white, middle-class community. Just to have families from different backgrounds as part of the community, their kids going to the schools ... It's a learning experience for everybody. And, I think that's part of why I'm committed to it ... I think you get to know these people. They go to the supermarket wearing headscarves. They're normal, they love their kids – yeah, I think it's good for the whole community."[45]

Many interviewees discussed the importance of renewed or emerging understandings of community created by the co-sponsorship process. The case of Connecticut and New York reveals an additional dimension to such community-building. Throughout 2015 and 2016, organizing across geographic locales began to occur organically between community groups. As New York residents along the border watched Connecticut communities mobilize to sponsor refugees, they began to pressure New York–based voluntary agencies to help them do the same. After initial relationships were established with voluntary agencies in their respective states, these horizontal connections between co-sponsorship groups expanded largely outside formal supports and oversight of voluntary agencies. Those connections, importantly, helped build local capacity for resettlement and deepened community links. One volunteer in New York identified how high levels of community interest along the New York–Connecticut border enabled co-sponsorship groups across communities to share information and resources. Thus, a "grassroots coalition" coalesced to facilitate community co-sponsorship. This group acted as "a clearinghouse," connecting volunteer team leaders to other communities who had developed innovative approaches to resettlement.[46]

This lateral organizing crossed boundaries of faith groups, including churches, synagogues, and mosques. It also encompassed other ethnic and cultural associations made up of immigrants from the Middle East and individuals from local businesses, schools, and government agencies. Such efforts linked constituencies with little prior relationship, strengthening ties within groups in specific communities as well as between those from different geographic regions. As one Connecticut-based resettlement staff member emphasized, co-sponsorship also increased the opportunity for refugee families to create ties to the community:

> This is precisely how you build community, that's how you connect people to others. And I think it means very quickly that the refugee family feels they have a fabric of connections in their community. And when you have a group of ten people, usually from a congregation, which means there are another fifty to one hundred people who are tangentially involved, that is incredible to have that number of people focused on a family of four or five or six.[47]

Co-sponsorship has also provided an opportunity to build local support for resettlement in the face of anti-refugee sentiment. As the Connecticut resettlement staff member noted, co-sponsorship builds community because it "connects people to a different part of the world, and different cultures, who might not otherwise have connected. And it opens up forums for debate and discussion."[48] He also noted that once residents realize that resettlement can revitalize local institutions, the value of co-sponsorship becomes more evident. "In Connecticut, and I know other parts of the country, some congregations are losing members, losing funding, and this kind of activity gives them purpose, direction and often builds their own community, bringing in new members."[49]

CONCLUSION

Scholarship on private and community sponsorship models of refugee resettlement in Canada (and other countries) has necessarily focused on key outcomes related to securing refugee well-being and longer-term integration.[50] In the United States, at the time such an approach was poised to take off, a new presidential administration radically remade refugee resettlement and placed the entire program at risk of closure. At the same time, communities in the US Northeast have demanded a more central role in supporting refugees and promoted a new form of citizen–refugee solidarity. And while activism aimed at US refugee policy remains limited, our research reveals how refugee resettlement is understood by community members as both "humanitarian" in nature and as an act of political resistance. Fundamentally, resettlement staff and volunteers seek to survive the Trump administration, and meanwhile, some community groups are shifting to support other populations, such as asylum-seekers and undocumented migrants.

Despite its limited scale, we suggest that the US approach to community co-sponsorship has potential advantages over other models. The ability to link to a professional resettlement organization for training, for case management in a complex social welfare system, and for resources if a co-sponsorship relationship faces challenges, is a strength of this system. Moreover, as we demonstrate, the way in which co-sponsorship has created community-level and cross-community relationships constitutes a significant innovation. Yet resettlement organizations and other community stakeholders continue to debate the wisdom of promoting a co-sponsorship model in light of attacks by the Trump administration on the refugee resettlement program; some are concerned that the expansion of community co-sponsorship is creating a rationale for the eventual privatization of resettlement in the United States. Opponents of a prominent federal role in refugee resettlement may thus seize on the success of co-sponsorship as a pretext for further limiting the resettlement program. For example, they could argue that community groups are more efficient and effective in resettling refugees at the local level than the existing traditional public–private resettlement model. This implies a need for those involved in community co-sponsorship to play a prominent role in advocating for refugees. Such increased political engagement can both address feelings of powerlessness and channel resistance toward developing more just US refugee policies.

NOTES

1 US State Department, "Refugee Admissions," accessed 10 September 2018, https://www.state.gov/j/prm/ra.
2 International Crisis Group, "How to Save the US Refugee Admissions Program," 12 September 2018, https://www.crisisgroup.org/united-states/002-how-save-us-refugee-admissions-program.

3 Executive Order 13769 of January 27, 2017 and Executive Order 13780 of March 6, 2017; 82 *Federal Register* 13209, March 9, 2017.
4 Executive Office of the President. "Presidential Determination on Refugee Admissions for Fiscal Year 2018." *Federal Register*, 82, no. 203 (23 October 2017), 1–2, https://www.federalregister.gov/documents/2017/10/23/2017-23140/presidential-determination-on-refugee-admissions-for-fiscal-year-2018. The ceiling for Near/Far East Asia was set at 17,500. With only one month left in FY 2018, only 3,683 refugees had arrived from the region; Refugee Processing Center, Arrivals by Region as of August 31, 2018, http://www.wrapsnet.org/admissions-and-arrivals/
5 Executive Office of the President, "Presidential Determination on Refugee Admissions for Fiscal Year 2019," Federal Register, 83, no. 212 (1 November 2018), 1–2, https://www.govinfo.gov/content/pkg/FR-2018-11-01/pdf/2018-24135.pdf.
6 Presidential Executive Order on Resuming the United States Refugee Admissions Program with Enhanced Vetting Capabilities, 13815 (24 October 2017), https://www.whitehouse.gov/presidential-actions/presidential-executive-order-resuming-united-states-refugee-admissions-program-enhanced-vetting-capabilities/.
7 US Supreme Court of the United States, (October Term 2017), https://www.supremecourt.gov/opinions/17pdf/17-965_h315.pdf.
8 This chapter is based on data from a qualitative research study on voluntarism and resettlement in the United States. For this chapter we analyze interviews with six staff members from refugee resettlement agencies and 11 volunteers in Connecticut and New York. The larger study also includes respondents from Kentucky and Utah. Interviews were transcribed verbatim and uploaded into NVivo 11.0. Analysis of the interviews yielded a number of themes; for this chapter we focus primarily on political and values-based motivations of volunteers supporting refugee resettlement.
9 Shauna Labman and Madison Pearlman, "Blending, Bargaining, and Burden-Sharing: Canada's Resettlement Programs," *Journal of International Migration and Integration* 19, no. 2 (2018): 439–49.
10 Jessica H. Darrow, "Getting Refugees to Work: A Street-level Perspective on Refugee Resettlement Policy," *Refugee Survey Quarterly* 34 (2015): 78–106.
11 Refugee Council of Australia and Settlement Services International, *Canada's Private Sponsorship of Refugees Program: Potential Lessons for Australia* (Melbourne, Australia: Refugee Council of Australia), https://www.refugeecouncil.org.au/publications/reports/canada-private-sponsorship/.

12. Interview with Connecticut resettlement agency staff member (P-14), 22 November 2017.
13. US Bureau of Population, Migration, and Refugees, "History of US Refugee Resettlement," https://2009-2017.state.gov/documents/organization/244270.pdf.
14. David W. Haines, *Safe Haven? A History of Refugees in America* (Boulder, CO: Kumarian Press, 2010).
15. Haines, *Safe Haven?*, 4.
16. US Congressional Research Service, *Review of the US Refugee Resettlement Programs and Policies: A Report Prepared at the Request of Senator Edward M. Kennedy, Chairman, of the Senate Judiciary Committee* (Washington, DC: US Government Accounting Office, 1980), 3–18.
17. Keith Welch, *A Pivotal Moment for the US Refugee Resettlement Program* (Berkeley, CA: Haas Institute for a Fair and Inclusive Society, 2017), 8.
18. Phillip Conor and Jens Manuel Krogstad, "For the First Time, US Resettles Fewer Refugees than the Rest of the World," *Pew Research Center*, 5 July 2018.
19. Kelly M. Greenhill, "How Trump Manipulates the Migration Debate: The Use and Abuse of Extra-Factual Information," *Foreign Affairs*, 25 July 2018, https://www.foreignaffairs.com/articles/united-states/2018-07-05/how-trump-manipulates-migration-debate.
20. Welch, *A Pivotal Moment*.
21. Michael R. Pence, Letter to the Indiana Congressional Delegation, 2 December 2015, https://assets.documentcloud.org/documents/2636574/Governor-Pence-Letter-to-Congressional.pdf.
22. David Bier and Matthew La Corte, *Private Refugee Resettlement in US History* (Washington, DC: Niskanen Center, 2016), 1.
23. Gideon Aronoff and Mark Hetfield, "New York City, the Jewish Community, and Refugee Resettlement in the 21st Century," *Journal of Jewish Communal Service* 85 (2010): 264–71.
24. Between 1962 and 1979, nearly 700,000 Cubans entered the United States under the Attorney General's parole authority. In light of the large scale resettlement efforts, faith and ethnic community support for paroled Cubans was supplemented for the first time by the federal Department of Health, Education and Welfare offered grants to aid organizations in Cuban resettlement, US Congressional Research Service, *Review of the US Refugee Resettlement Programs and Policies,* 13.
25. Haines, *Safe Haven?*

26 Jessica Eby, Erika Iverson, Jenifer Smyers, and Erol Kekic, "The Faith Community's Role in Refugee Resettlement in the United States," *Journal of Refugee Studies* 24, no. 3 (2011): 587.
27 Eby et al., "Faith Community's Role in Refugee Resettlement in the United States," 587.
28 Bier and La Corte, *Private Refugee Resettlement in US History*, 9–11.
29 Judith Kumin, *Welcoming Engagement: How Private Sponsorship Can Strengthen Refugee Resettlement in the European Union* (Washington, DC: Migration Policy Institute, 2016).
30 Vasudha Tahla, "Private Sponsorship of Refugee Resettlement in the United States: Guiding Principles and Recommendations," http://www.humanrightsfirst.org/sites/default/files/Private_Sponsorship_of_Refugees_in_the_United_States_White_Paper.pdf.
31 David Bier, "Statement on the 'Refugee Program Integrity Restoration Act of 2017 – H.R. 2829," 14 June 2017, https://www.cato.org/publications/public-comments/statement-refugee-program-integrity-restoration-act-2017-hr-2826.
32 Bier and LaCorte, *Private Refugee Resettlement*; David Bier and Matthew La Corte, *Privately Funded Refugee Resettlement: How to Leverage American Charity to Resettle Refugees* (Washington, DC: Niskanen Center, 2016).
33 Reihan Salam, "A Better Way to Absorb Refugees: Affluent City Dwellers Are Some of the Most Vocal Champions of Refugee Admission – And They are in a Position to Assist," *The Atlantic*, 6 September 2018, https://www.theatlantic.com/ideas/archive/2018/09/the-future-of-the-refugee-act/569359/.
34 Ed Stannard, "Register Person of the Year: Chris George, Leader in Refugee Resettlement," *New Haven Register*, 24 December 2017, https://www.nhregister.com/news/article/Register-Person-of-the-Year-Chris-George-leader-12453322.php.
35 Eby, "Faith Community's Role in Refugee Resettlement in the United States," 597–602.
36 Integrated Refugee and Immigrant Services, "Community Co-Sponsorship: An Essential Complementary Model for Refugee Resettlement Agencies," July 2018, Unpublished report.
37 Robert Mackey, "Brutal Images of Syrian Boy Drowned Off Turkey Must Be Seen, Activists Say," *New York Times*, 2 September 2015, https://www.nytimes.com/2015/09/03/world/middleeast/brutal-images-of-syrian-boy-drowned-off-turkey-must-be-seen-activists-say.html.
38 Interview with Connecticut volunteer (P-2), 22 August 2017.

39 Interview with New York volunteer (P-9), 31 October 2017.
40 Interview with P-9, 31 October 2017.
41 Ibid.
42 Ibid.
43 New York resettlement staff member (P-24), 16 March 2018.
44 Interview with P-9, 31 October 2017.
45 Interview with volunteer from Connecticut (P-6), 5 October 2017.
46 Interview with P-9, 31 October 2017.
47 Interview with Connecticut resettlement agency staff member (P-27), 29 August 2018.
48 Interview with P-27, 29 August 2018.
49 Ibid.
50 Shauna Labman, "Private Sponsorship: Complementary or Conflicting Interests?" *Refuge* 32, no. 2 (2016): 67–80; Adele Garnier, Liliana Lira Jubilut, Kristin Bergtor Sandvik, *Refugee Resettlement: Power, Politics, and Humanitarian Governance* (Oxford, UK: Berghahn Books, 2018).

14

Private Humanitarian Sponsorship: Searching for the Community in Australia's Community Refugee Sponsorship Program

Anthea Vogl, Khanh Hoang, and Asher Hirsch

In 2013 the Australian government announced its first program for the full private sponsorship of humanitarian entrants by individuals, businesses, or community organisations, the Community Pilot Program (CPP). The pilot program ran for four years, from 2013–17. The permanent program, the Community Support Program (CSP), was introduced in mid-2017 and began operating on a permanent, national basis in 2018. When announcing the program in 2013, then Labor government minister Brendan O'Connor stated: "We are now acting on the calls of community groups to give organisations an opportunity to nominate people at risk overseas to be reunited with family or friends here in Australia. Under the pilot, communities in Australia may be able to financially contribute to bring those individuals or families to live permanently in Australia."[1] The minister went on to emphasise that the pilot would "encourage stronger partnerships between community organisations and the government in the resettlement of people" and that it would "build on the goodwill that we know exists in our communities."[2]

In the announcement of the program and in the above statements, the strengthening of government–community partnerships was presented as a core objective of Australia's sponsorship program. Participation in the program was presented as an opportunity for and of benefit to "communities" in Australia. The name of the pilot program made no reference to refugees or sponsorship but did refer to "community." The role of communities and community partnerships was also prominent in the promotion of the subsequent CSP.[3] The persistent emphasis on community participation, particularly on "business community" participation, raises the following questions: To what extent does the Australian sponsorship program meet the objectives of *involving* and *benefiting* communities? And who constitutes these communities?

In this chapter, we lay out the design and details of Australia's new humanitarian sponsorship program as well as a number of critiques of it, with a focus on the promise and potential of community involvement. In so doing, we address both the contemporary sponsorship program in Australia and the lesser-known Community Refugee Settlement Scheme (CRSS), which preceded the CSP and ran from 1979 to 1997. Although the CRSS focused on community *settlement* rather than the full sponsorship of humanitarian entrants, it facilitated significant community involvement in Australia's resettlement policies in the 1980s and early 1990s and helped successfully settle more than 30,000 refugees.[4]

The concepts "private humanitarian sponsorship" and "community humanitarian sponsorship" are at times used interchangeably. In the Australian context, however, it is important to interrogate and distinguish these terms. The CSP holds significant potential for expanding Australia's resettlement commitments and improving its humanitarian program. However, the CSP in its current form falls short of these objectives and hinders broader community participation in humanitarian sponsorship. We focus on three main issues regarding the current CSP – the absence of the principle of additionality;[5] the high upfront costs of sponsorship and visa application fees; and the over-reliance on individual family sponsors. As such, we argue that due to both the design of the program and the lack of community engagement in its implementation, the CSP is a private refugee sponsorship program rather than a truly community-oriented one.

Where sponsorship programs are promoted as an opportunity for national citizens and community members to participate in and benefit from humanitarian resettlement, at a minimum they should not "privatize" existing resettlement places, nor should they be characterised as a government "revenue-raising" mechanism, as has been the case in relation to the CSP in Australia.[6] In contrast to Canada's private sponsorship program, the Australian one does not uphold the idea of additionality either in principle or in practice and the cost of sponsorship is not limited to the forecasted cost of resettlement but includes sizable outright fees paid to the Australian government. Although individuals and community groups have shown significant interest in participating in private sponsorship,[7] Australia's current program presents barriers to such involvement and challenges assumptions that private sponsorship necessarily enhances national humanitarian and resettlement commitments.

We explore these issues by examining the CRSS, CPP, and CSP, with a particular focus on the notion of "community" in each of these schemes. Our analysis suggests that Australia has yet to implement a truly "community-led" sponsorship program. As highlighted in Bradley and Duins's chapter in this volume, the notion of community and the extent of community involvement are important factors that shape sponsorship programs and their interaction with the broader resettlement practices of states in both positive and negative ways.

THE COMMUNITY REFUGEE SETTLEMENT SCHEME

After the fall of Saigon in April 1975, Indochinese asylum-seekers began to flee the communist regime, seeking asylum in neighbouring Southeast Asian countries. Australia's immediate response in the following months was to provide financial aid – in total, AU$4.75 million – to international agencies working in Indochina.[8] On 22 April 1975, the left-leaning Labor government, led by Prime Minister Gough Whitlam, announced that Vietnamese who had spouses and children in Australia or those with long and close association to Australia were eligible for temporary entry.[9] Because these criteria were so narrowly drawn, by 10 July 1975 some 5,269 persons had been nominated for entry into Australia by family members but only 542 had been approved for entry: 355 for permanent residence and 187 for temporary residence.[10] The Whitlam government had also resettled a small number of refugees following referrals from UNHCR in 1975–76 – around 1,800 individuals in all.[11]

The conservative Liberal Country Party led by Malcolm Fraser, then in opposition, criticized the Whitlam government's response to the Indochinese refugees as "politically motivated procrastination" that had cost lives.[12] In June 1975, the Whitlam government asked the Senate Standing Committee on Foreign Affairs and Defence to report on Australia's response to Indochinese refugees and how Australia might render "appropriate and effective assistance." In 1976, the committee published its report, *Australia and the Refugee Problem*, in which it recommended, among other things, the urgent "formulation of a comprehensive set of policy guidelines and the establishment of appropriate machinery"[13] to address sudden and often unforeseen refugee flows.

When Fraser came into office in November 1975, he set out to implement many of the committee's recommendations. This launched the development of formal refugee law and policy in Australia, which hitherto had been a matter of ad hoc implementation.[14] These policy changes facilitated the resettlement of more than 54,000 planned refugees by air and the admission of nearly 2,000 spontaneous arrivals by boat between 1977 and 1982.[15]

This significant increase in arrivals from Vietnam posed a challenge to the government's settlement policies, as refugees were accommodated and processed in government-run hostels and migrant centres prior to being dispersed into the wider community. The migrant centres had been set up to provide refugees with initial access to government services – such as health care, employment services, and orientation – but it soon became clear that government officials were ill-equipped to deal with Indochinese refugees.[16] Because the needs of refugees were different from those of other migrants, migrant centres relied on input and support from "local settlement committees" comprised of volunteer and community organizations that had greater experience in dealing with settlement. The Senate Standing Committee's 1976 report thus observed: "It is apparent to the Committee that 'resettlement' is a complex process which requires co-operative and well-coordinated action by government agencies, voluntary agencies and individuals ... The Committee believes that a community response is an essential ingredient to the effective promotion of resettlement ... In one way or another, active participation of all sections of the community is called for".[17]

As migrant centres and hostels struggled to keep pace with the increased numbers of arrivals, immigration minister Michael MacKellar observed there was a "need to cope with the transition from hostels to the community."[18] Cabinet documents in 1980 demonstrated that there were fourteen migrant centres in Australia with a combined capacity of 10,300 beds and effective occupational capacity of 9,800 compared to the estimated need to accommodate about 30,000 refugees and migrants in 1980–81.[19]

A FORMAL ROLE FOR COMMUNITY SPONSORSHIP

The CRSS was introduced on 30 October 1979 by the immigration minister, MacKellar, following a recommendation from the Australian Refugee Advisory Council.[20] It followed Canada's PSR program, established one year earlier, as discussed in other chapters of this volume. The CRSS was meant to allow refugees to bypass migrant centres and hostels and go directly into the Australian community and the care of those who had undertaken to provide assistance.[21] Another stated objective of the CRSS was to allow the "community to become directly involved in the settlement of refugees and contribute to their successful integration."[22]

Under the CRSS, sponsors had to register with the Department of Immigration and Ethnic Affairs. The CRSS was open to participation by established voluntary agencies (including religious organizations), groups of individuals, and employers. It was envisaged that most offers would come from voluntary agencies; however, offers from individuals who could demonstrate a capacity to fulfill sponsorship obligations would also be considered.[23] Individuals were required to have "back-up" support from an established group or organization in the event that they could not fulfill their responsibilities.[24] In practice, the majority of support groups under the CRSS were "church-based or part of an organization with specific refugee interests."[25] Few sponsors were individuals, and even fewer (if any) were identified as employers or businesses.

Applications to be registered as a CRSS group or individual were vetted by the Community Refugee Resettlement Committee (located in each state and territory) and then submitted to the minister's office for approval.[26] The committee had to be satisfied as to the eligibility of the persons or group to participate in the CRSS as well as to the viability of the support offer. Whether a person or group was *eligible* to participate depended on a number of factors, including the standing of the group or organization, the level of financial resources, and their demonstrated capacity to assist refugees, including previous experience with refugee settlement and community welfare.[27]

Sponsorship groups were also eligible for government grants to assist with the cost of second and subsequent refugee families. These grants were introduced in 1981 and by 1985 had grown to AU$350 for a single refugee, AU$520 for four persons, plus AU$80 for each additional person. These grants were not payable directly to the refugees, and sponsors had to provide evidence to the department that the monies had been spent on supporting the integration of refugees.

THE PARTICULAR PROBLEM OF "NAMED" CASES AND FAMILY REUNIFICATION

For most of its lifespan, the CRSS was available to two different categories of resettled refugees and humanitarian entrants to Australia: "open/unnamed" cases and "named/nominated" cases.

"Open" or "unnamed" cases were selected from a "pool" of refugees that had passed the "normal refugee selection criteria" by overseas post.[28] Having found the person/s suitable for resettlement and entry into Australia, case officers then decided whether the case would benefit from CRSS support. If the case was determined to require CRSS support, then the officer referred the case back to Australia to a CRSS coordinator. The coordinator then attempted to match the refugee to a registered sponsor who had agreed to support refugees in their area. Sponsor groups or individuals could nominate a preference for entrants with a specific ethnic origin or religion, particular language skills, family size, and composition, or specific employment skills.[29] If a match was made, refugees would be resettled to Australia and given CRSS support upon arrival, bypassing the migrant centres. Initially, sponsors were discouraged from nominating specific persons for the CRSS as "it was argued that this would result in the displacement of refugees with strong claims for selection."[30]

Over time, as more resettled Indochinese and others sought to reunite with families, the government allowed sponsorship groups to identify and alert the Immigration Department of individuals who might benefit from the CRSS. This was seen as a means of "encouraging family reunion and to expand the CRSS."[31] These named cases involved the nomination of a person in need of resettlement at the same time as a nomination from a sponsoring group offering CRSS support upon arrival (in effect a form of co-sponsorship).[32] With the introduction of the Special Humanitarian Program (SHP) in 1981 – a program that allowed individuals to nominate family members for resettlement to Australia – individuals and community organizations began to lodge a significant number of named cases under both refugee and SHP streams.[33]

This issue of named cases gave rise to considerable debate within the Department of Immigration and Ethnic Affairs as to the purpose of the CRSS and the role of the community. From the government's perspective, the CRSS was never intended to allow the community to *sponsor individuals for entry* into Australia. Its role was limited to providing post-settlement assistance once the Australian government had decided to resettle a refugee. However, because family members could nominate persons *for entry* under the CRSS policy, where that application was also co-sponsored by a community group with a nomination under the CRSS, it was perceived that the CRSS had some effect on the decision as to whether a refugee was entitled to resettlement. Such perceptions were compounded by the fact that under the refugee resettlement policy, CRSS nominations were a factor considered in the prioritization of cases for entry into Australia, again diverting the program from its original intention.[34]

Indeed, community groups and individuals perceived the CRSS differently. As early as 1983, a governmental memo identified that "there is a comment by some States that family reunion will be a feature of CRSS in the future. Named (nominated) cases now constitute a significant number of CRSS placements (approximately 60%). This feature of the CRSS is seen as continuing commitment by CRSS sponsors to this form of settlement."[35]

There was concern within government that the availability of named cases had given rise to "the perception that CRSS … [was] an alternative form of sponsorship and in some way expedite[d] the selection of people for resettlement." There was also concern that certain groups were seen as "having considerable power" in determining the outcomes of applications, thus leading to abuses.[36] Such examples included instances where CRSS groups lodged large numbers of applications for named individuals but with little evidence that such individuals were personally known by these groups.[37] The Immigration Department was aware that lists of potential support groups "circulate[d] in refugee camps" and were being used to elicit offers of support.[38] That such nominations – made on the basis of having close ties with Australia – were given priority was seen as "queue-jumping" or as a "de facto sponsorship" mechanism that circumvented uniform management of the humanitarian program.[39]

Recommendations were made to government by departmental officers to ensure that "control of CRSS sponsorship remains with the government."[40] One proposal was to cease named sponsorships under the CRSS while simultaneously seeking to expand open cases.[41] An expansion of open cases was considered necessary since named cases constituted a significant proportion of the CRSS and prohibiting them would cause a drastic reduction in program numbers.[42] The recommendation to cease named nominations by CRSS groups was put forward for consideration before the National Population Committee (NPC) in July 1986, but a decision was made to defer consideration of the problem partly because of the risk of "adverse community reaction" if the issue were to be tackled head on.[43] Instead, the NPC supported proposals to ensure that the CRSS was "post-driven" (i.e., more resettlement decisions made from overseas posts, identifying entrants requiring CRSS support), with greater emphasis on unnamed humanitarian applicants being considered.[44]

The Immigration Department acted on the recommendations advanced by the NPC. A memo from Acting Assistant Secretary of the Settlement Branch, Dario Castello, was sent on 13 December 1986 to migration officers and all overseas posts informing them of the NPC's recommendations and asking them for cooperation on the new policy. The memo stated that the present "drastic shortage of open case referrals impinges upon CRSS credibility."[45] Posts and other migration officers were urged to "give greater consideration" to the benefits of the CRSS in assessing all funded humanitarian entrants. In public documents, the department reiterated that priority under the CRSS included those who had no family or links in Australia; who had experienced torture and trauma; and who fell under the "woman-at-risk category."[46]

The place and role of named cases and family reunification are questions common to the design of sponsorship programs generally. Indeed, this issue is also debated in the Canadian context, as Lehr and Dyck's chapter in this volume discusses. As we show in the following section, these questions have persisted in Australia's contemporary program. However, in the case of the CRSS these questions were central to how, and on whose terms, community members engaged in humanitarian resettlement. We argue that one lesson from the CRSS is that in designing community sponsorship schemes, governments must be attentive not only to the potential role that the "community" – however defined – can play in enhancing resettlement opportunities, but also to the needs of the particular community or communities involved.

A failure to consider and mediate the demands of community participants risks derailing public confidence in the idea of community sponsorship. In the case of the CRSS, the government sought to tightly control how communities involved themselves in resettlement efforts even while relying on community resources and support. The following section addresses the new barriers to community participation under the current program. We argue that despite the availability of named sponsorees *and* government focus on community in promoting the program, the CSP's primary objective appears to be the privatization of the costs and labour of humanitarian resettlement.

AUSTRALIA'S CONTEMPORARY PRIVATE SPONSORSHIP PROGRAMS

When the CPP was formally announced in mid-2013, it constituted Australia's first program for the full private sponsorship of humanitarian entrants by individuals, businesses, or community organizations.[47] For the purposes of the CPP and the subsequent CSP, humanitarian entrants are defined as refugees or persons outside of their home country who are subject to gross violations of their human rights. The pilot was to provide for up to five hundred places per annum *within* the offshore component of Australia's humanitarian program, rather than in addition to existing humanitarian commitments.[48] Sponsors could only participate in the program via non-government organizations selected and approved by the Department of Immigration, known as approved proposing organisations (APOs). APOs were to be responsible for assessing sponsor applications and supporting the sponsors with paperwork and other requirements. This meant that an APO's role was to manage the sponsorship application and ensure that sponsors were able to meet the costs of sponsorship and resettlement. While APOs were somewhat similar to sponsorship agreement holders in Canada, they were also markedly different in this way: they charged applicants fees for their services instead of raising those fees through donations. Under the pilot, there were five recognised APOs, four of which were based in two Australian states (New South Wales and Victoria).[49] The costs of sponsorship, which we discuss further below, included a significant fee paid to APOs for their services in managing and filing the sponsorship application with the department in addition to the visa fees paid directly to the government.

Prior to the introduction of the pilot program, the Commonwealth government had expressed interest in a community sponsorship program in its 2012 budget and released a discussion paper examining the "feasibility of a pilot which would enable organisations to propose a person, in a humanitarian situation, for entry to Australia under the Humanitarian Program."[50] More than sixty submissions were received in response to the paper from humanitarian organizations, faith-based groups, community organizations, settlement service providers, and state and local governments.[51] The government did not make any of the outcomes or recommendations of this six-month consultation period publicly available. Notably, submissions to the 2012 discussion paper were not published, despite publication being the usual practice.

The first CPP applications were lodged in October 2013, soon after the program was announced, and the first visas were granted in February 2014.[52] Over the course of the 2013–14 financial year, 154 applications were received under the CPP, representing 570 individuals. Over the same period, 245 visas were granted under the CPP.[53] Between the lodgement of the first applications under the CPP in October 2013 and the review of the program on 29 March 2015, 305 applications had been received under the pilot, representing more than 1,100 individuals. Over this period, 667 visas were granted. The highest number of applications and grants were made in relation to sponsorees from Syria, followed by Iraq. Other visa grants were made to individuals from Afghanistan, Eritrea, and Somalia.[54]

In 2015, the Liberal Coalition government sought public submissions to a review of the CPP. Once again, the submissions in response to a formal discussion paper were not made public, and neither was the government's view of those submissions. However, in data released to the authors under freedom-of-information laws, the government's own summary of public submissions notes that thirteen of the seventeen respondents recommended that the CPP operate *in addition to* the existing humanitarian program. Furthermore, it was noted that "stakeholders" supported the standard humanitarian eligibility criteria being retained (rather than the addition of new criteria such as capacity to work) and that "most organisations" submitted that visa application charges should be lowered.[55]

Yet when the CSP was announced in 2017, the legal frameworks that governed it more or less exactly mirrored those of the CPP, albeit with further selection criteria and higher fees. The most significant change to the policy was an increase in the number of available places to 1,000 per annum (from the previous 500). Once again, CSP places were to come from *within* Australia's overall offshore humanitarian and refugee quota, rather than being additional to them. Another marked difference was that new criteria for sponsorees were introduced (see below).

The formal announcement of the CSP in Australia coincided with a meeting of UN General Assembly states in September 2016. That meeting resulted in the New York Declaration for Refugees and Migrants, under which the member states agreed to embark on negotiations toward a Global Compact on Refugees in order to strengthen the international refugee regime's response to large refugee movements. That compact, and the resulting final draft of the Global Compact on Refugees, calls upon states "to establish private or community sponsorship programs that are additional to regular resettlement" in order to provide timely access to durable solutions for refugees.[56] In the lead-up to the New York Declaration, just as the sponsorship pilot was drawing to an end, then Australian prime minister Malcolm Turnbull announced that "in addition to our existing programs, Australia will ... create new pathways for refugees to resettle in Australia through the establishment of 1,000 places under a Community Support Programme, where communities and businesses can sponsor applications and support new arrivals."[57]

However, rather than being "in addition," the CSP takes places from within Australia's existing refugee and humanitarian resettlement quota. Furthermore, while we do not focus on this important aspect of the program in this chapter, the overall profile of an eligible applicant confirms that the CSP is not designed, as a matter of priority, to resettle the most vulnerable or at-risk refugees and humanitarian applicants.[58] Under the CSP, applicants must be deemed to be what the Australian government describes as "job-ready," which includes being between the ages of eighteen and fifty and having "functional English" and "a job offer or skills to enable you to get a job quickly."[59] The government has also confirmed that "priority [will be] given to applicants who have an employment offer" and also to "applicants willing to live and work in regional Australia."[60] Unlike the Canadian program, which considers ability to speak or *learn* French or English as well as potential for employment, the Australian criteria require primary applicants to already speak functional English, and be employed or employable, at the time of the application.[61] Finally, a further exceptional aspect of the Australian criteria is that even though sponsors bear the costs of supporting the settlement of the sponsored refugees, priority is given to CSP applicants from countries the government deems to be "resettlement priorities." The precise details of these priorities are unclear; however, the government has confirmed that priority is given to refugees from select countries.[62]

The elderly, those without "relevant qualifications," and those without English language skills are unlikely to be viable candidates for sponsorship under the program. The criteria are also likely to compound women's uneven access to education and work in some countries of origin and exclude those whose significant care responsibilities have prevented them from securing relevant qualifications or paid employment. The program clearly prioritizes those who have the capacity to integrate as quickly and as independently as possible.

PRIVATE VERSUS COMMUNITY SPONSORSHIP: CRITIQUES OF THE COMMUNITY SUPPORT PROGRAM

A marked difference between the CRSS and the CSP is the lack of engagement of the wider community in the sponsorship and settlement process. As we have argued elsewhere,[63] the new CSP amounts to an outsourcing and privatization of humanitarian principles rather than an inclusive program that harnesses the wider community. The absence of broader community participation also distinguishes the current CSP from the Canadian program, which historically and in its present design has been taken up by community organizations and groups, as well as by individuals coming together to form sponsorship groups of five.

This privatization can be seen, first, in the lack of additionality. Unlike in the Canadian program, the CSP quota of 1,000 places is not additional to the government's Refugee and Humanitarian Program (RHP). This means that each sponsored refugee takes a place away from the government's own resettlement commitment. In 2014, the Australian government announced that it would increase the RHP quota from 13,750 to 18,750 by 2018–19, including 2,750 places reserved for in-country asylum applicants.[64] However, with the introduction of the CSP, it became clear that this increase would be offset by 1,000 places set aside for private sponsors. As such, the CSP can be seen as a way to outsource the government's existing commitments, exploiting the community's goodwill or, as is more often the case, a family's desperation. As one community member noted during Refugee Council of Australia consultations, "it's a way that the government has been able to save money on a program that it already promised to pay for and hasn't actually added any numbers to the overall size of the humanitarian program."[65]

Second, the high cost of sponsorship creates further barriers and disincentives for wider community participation. Indeed, the Australian government has promoted the CSP as a means to create "a sustainable model of private sponsorship for refugees that *minimises costs to governments.*"[66] According to government estimates, the program "will provide a revenue gain to the budget of $26.9 million" over the first four years.[67] This revenue gain comes from the high costs of the visa fees, including a AU$2,740 non-refundable application fee, a second instalment fee of AU$16,444 for the main applicant, and AU$2,680 for each secondary applicant (family member).[68] In addition to visa fees, sponsors are required to pay fees to the APO. These fees are not fixed or regulated by the Australian government and are as high as approximately AU$20,000 per application.[69] Sponsors are also required to cover the costs of airfares and medical checks prior to arrival. Most notably, the visa application charges do not directly cover or fund the cost of the applicant's resettlement. That is, they are simply transaction fees paid to the Australian government that are not attached to any clear service provided by the government to the humanitarian entrant or sponsor.[70] Once the sponsored refugee has arrived, sponsors are required to cover all living costs and settlement support for the first year, or otherwise repay the government for any use of social security benefits through an assurance-of-support arrangement.[71] All together, these fees and payments can total more than AU$100,000 for a refugee family of five.

Finally, due to the desperation of refugees to reunite with loved ones and bring their families to safety, the CSP, like the CPP before it, risks becoming a de facto family reunion program. As the CSP does not require a core group of sponsors, or that sponsors be drawn from the wider Australian community, the program allows families that can afford the high visa fees to be sponsors. Family reunion through other pathways can take several years and faces a significant backlog,[72] whereas the CSP is prioritized, allowing sponsors to fast-track their family members.

As discussed earlier, refugee family reunion in Australia takes place primarily through the SHP, a subset of the RHP. However, the program faces a backlog of at least 7:1, meaning that many applicants can wait years to reunite with loved ones.[73] In addition, refugees who arrived in Australia by boat after August 2012 have no access to any form of family sponsorship. Furthermore, in 2016, it was directed that applications made by those who arrived by boat before this date be given the lowest processing priority. These policies, directed toward "irregular" arrivals, reinforce concerns (discussed below) that private sponsorship in Australia is an expensive proxy form of family reunion that exploits the undersupply or absence of other family reunion pathways. Moreover, it is well recognised that other existing migration pathways for family reunion such as partner, child, and parent visas are out of reach for many refugees due to high application costs and stringent eligibility criteria, or simply because some visas are subject to extremely prolonged waiting periods. As long as the lack of family reunion pathways in Australia persists,[74] the current CSP risks becoming a privatized and extortionately expensive family reunion program rather than a model that draws upon the support of the wider Australian community. Indeed, over 90 percent of the current applications have been from family members of the sponsored refugee.[75]

CONCLUSION: SEARCHING FOR THE COMMUNITY

A key question raised by the history of the CRSS and the CSP is, what constitutes the "community" and what constitutes community involvement in humanitarian sponsorship? The term community may be read narrowly, to refer only to Australian citizens, or as an otherwise exclusionary conception of what constitutes an "Australian community member." However, a truly community-led sponsorship program should seek to utilize and rely upon a much broader definition of community, one that includes former refugees or those who are not yet Australian citizens. Indeed, former refugees have much to offer new arrivals, for they have first-hand experience of the settlement process. Likewise, it is to be expected that former refugees will use community sponsorship as a way to reunite with family, especially in light of the lack of family reunion places under Australia's current refugee program.

However, the flaws of the current program mean that difficult questions about who constitutes the community, and on what terms the community is to be involved, have been neither raised nor addressed. Instead, the program is marked by direct barriers to any form of community participation. The neoliberal, market-driven nature of the program raises the already significant costs of sponsorship beyond the reach of many "community" groups or members and exploits the absence of family reunion pathways for refugee families already living in Australia. In a market-driven system in which family reunion places are limited, the Australian government has elected to charge extraordinary amounts to private individuals and to promote the program as a revenue-raising mechanism. Acknowledging that the CSP is in its early stages, we contend that the program's high costs and the absence of the principle of additionality will prevent many community members from participating in it, especially given that community members see it as subsidizing the government's existing resettlement commitment rather than improving and expanding resettlement opportunities.

A final tension that is present in both the CRSS and the CSP relates to named versus unnamed or UNHCR-referred refugees. As Lenard's chapter in this volume highlights, the practice of named sponsorships raises a number of normative considerations for the design, function, and considered success of the Canadian program. A program that allows named refugees is more likely to become a de facto family reunion program and is unlikely to prioritize vulnerable entrants. This is the current experience of the CSP. However, the ability to name certain refugees for resettlement is popular with the wider community and can further enhance the community aspect of sponsorship. The ability to name refugees may also allow for sponsorship of vulnerable refugees who may not have access to resettlement, such as Rohingya currently in Bangladesh. When designing a community sponsorship program, these tensions cannot be sidestepped, and a likely way forward is to allow for both named and UNHCR-referred refugees, as was introduced under the CRSS and as exists in Canada, primarily through the Blended Visa Office-Referred program.

Despite the two community consultations on the CPP and the CSP, and Australia's previous history with refugee sponsorship, the Australian government does not seem to have considered any of the recommendations from the community when designing the CSP. As such, from the outset, the program did not grapple with broad community participation, in both its design and implementation. As the CSP develops into the future, at a bare minimum, further and wider engagement with the community will be necessary.

NOTES

1 Brendan O'Connor, Minister for Immigration and Citizenship, "Community Refugee Sponsorship Trial Begins" (media release, 3 June 2013).
2 Brendan O'Connor, Minister for Immigration and Citizenship.

3 Alex Hawke, Assistant Minister for Home Affairs, "Turnbull Government Announces Community Support Programme," 6 May 2017, http://minister.homeaffairs.gov.au/alexhawke/2017/Pages/community-support-programme.aspx.
4 Department of Immigration, Local Government, and Ethnic Affairs, *Our Good Friends: Australians Helping Refugees to a New Life* (Canberra: Australian Government, 1991), 62.
5 The "principle of additionality ensures that private efforts expand refugee protection spaces by complementing government commitments to resettlement": Jennifer Hyndman, William Payne, and Shauna Jimenez, "Private Refugee Sponsorship in Canada," *Forced Migration Review* 54 (2017): 56, 59. On the "interpretive malleability" of the concept, see also Shauna Labman, "Private Sponsorship: Complementary or Conflicting Interests?" *Refuge: Canada's Journal on Refugees* 32, no. 2 (2 September 2016): 67–80.
6 Janet Phillips and Harriet Spinks, "Immigration and Border Protection Overview," Parliamentary Library, Parliament of Australia, accessed 29 July 2018, https://www.aph.gov.au/About_Parliament/Parliamentary_Departments/Parliamentary_Library/pubs/rp/BudgetReview201718/Immigration#_ftn9.
7 Applications under the CPP exceeded available places, and initial responses to the program from potential sponsors and community organizations were enthusiastic: Asher Hirsch, Audrey Macklin, and Susan Kneebone, "Private Resettlement Models Offer a Way for Australia to Lift Its Refugee Intake," *The Conversation*, accessed 9 February 2018, http://theconversation.com/private-resettlement-models-offer-a-way-for-australia-to-lift-its-refugee-intake-65030.
8 Senate Standing Committee on Foreign Affairs and Defence, "Australia and the Refugee Problem," Parliamentary Paper 329/1976, 1976, 5.
9 Ibid., 12.
10 Ibid., 24.
11 Ibid., 8.
12 Katrina Stats, "Welcome to Australia? A Reappraisal of the Fraser Government's Approach to Refugees, 1975–83," *Australian Journal of International Affairs* 69, no. 1 (2 January 2015): 69–87 at 73.
13 Senate Standing Committee on Foreign Affairs and Defence, "Australia and the Refugee Problem," 89.
14 These policies included the establishment of a Refugee and Special Programs Branch within the Immigration Department, as well as the establishment of a Standing Interdepartmental Committee on Refugees

to advise the Minister for Immigration and Ethnic Affairs. The interdepartmental Determination of Refugee Status Committee was established in March 1978 to help assess refugee claims in a fair and consistent manner.
15 For an overview of the policy during this period, see Claire Higgins, *Asylum by Boat: Origins of Australia's Refugee Policy* (Sydney: NewSouth, 2017).
16 Senate Standing Committee on Foreign Affairs and Defence, "Australia and the Refugee Problem," 59–68.
17 Ibid., 80.
18 Michael MacKellar, Minister for Immigration and Ethnic Affairs, "Immigrants or Refugees," 19 August 1978, 16.
19 Cabinet Minute Decision No. 16299, Memorandum 1581 – The Effect of the Community Refugee Settlement Scheme on Migrant Centre Accommodation, 16 July 1981, NAA A12930 1581.
20 Michael MacKellar, Minister for Immigration and Ethnic Affairs, "Refugee Council Calls for Community Understanding and Support," media release, 157/79, 30 October 1979. The Australian Refugee Advisory Council was established to provide advice to the minister on aspects of movement to and settlement in Australia of refugees from all sources. At its first meeting, this committee "recommended the adoption of a comprehensive program to assist refugees from wherever they may come to settle in Australia."
21 Barry York, "Australia and Refugees, 1901–2002: An Annotated Chronology Based on Official Sources," Chronology Online, Australian Parliamentary Library, https://www.aph.gov.au/About_Parliament/Parliamentary_Departments/Parliamentary_Library/Publications_Archive/online/Refugeess3. York notes that one of the aims of the CRSS was to "limit residential concentrations of particular groups."
22 Other goals of the CRSS were to: provide an alternative means of resettlement for refugees who have a capacity to integrate quickly into the Australian community; encourage greater awareness of the Government's refugee settlement program; and achieve a more widespread settlement of refugees through the Australian community. MSJ Keys Young Planners, *An Evaluation of the Community Refugee Settlement Scheme* (Canberra: Department of Immigration and Ethnic Affairs, 1981), 3.
23 Department of Immigration and Ethnic Affairs, "Community Hosting and Friendship Scheme and Community Refugee Settlement Scheme: Information for Individuals, Groups and Organisations Wishing to Assist in the Settlement of Refugees in the Community."

24 Department of Immigration and Ethnic Affairs, *A Handbook for Support Groups Participating in the Community Refugee Settlement Scheme*, 2nd ed. (Canberra: Australian Government Publishing Service, 1983), 1.

25 Sue Ingram Submission to the Minister, "Community Refugee Settlement Scheme," 20 December 1985, *Settlement Branch – CRSS [Community Refugee Settlement Scheme] – Program Management*, NAA A446 1986/75554.

26 In 1980, this committee comprised of representatives from the following organizations: Migrant Settlement Council of NSW, the Local Government Shires Association, Australian Jaycees, the Uniting Church of Australia, St Vincent de Paul, Department of Immigration and Ethnic Affairs, Lao Community, Indochinese Refugee Association Inc., Care Force, and NSW Adult Migrant Education Service.

27 The decision-making process of the committee has not been subject to any academic scrutiny.

28 Department of Immigration and Ethnic Affairs, *A Handbook for Support Groups Participating in the Community Refugee Settlement Scheme*, 5.

29 Ibid., 5.

30 John Moorhouse (CRSS Unit), CRSS Policy — The Expanding Frequency of Named Cases, Draft Discussion Paper to Ms Glen and Mr Hoffman, "Community Refugee Settlement Scheme Policy and Plan," 17 October 1983, NAA A446 1983/76959.

31 Ibid., 3.

32 Ibid., 2. Moorhouse also indicated that in 1980 the Assistant Secretary of the Settlement Branch was of the view that the Department had initially missed the opportunity to "give the scheme a significant boost" by allowing potential sponsors to bring to the Department's attention refugees who had good settlement prospects.

33 At the time, three categories of sponsorships under the SHP were available: applications by those who have close relatives in Australia, down to first cousins; applications by those who have close ties with Australia (through being nominated by distant relatives and friends and/or a CRSS group); and applications by those who have good settlement prospects, including CRSS nomination.

34 Note for file of meeting between Mr. Ratnam, Dr. Edwards and Richard Derewlany, 21 April 1987. The parties agreed that Policy Circular 61 should be amended to remove any confusion as to the role of the CRSS as a settlement scheme, *Settlement Branch – CRSS [Community Refugee Settlement Scheme] – Program Management*, NAA A446 1986/75554.

35 Memo from Sue Ingram (A/g Assistant Secretary Settlement Branch) to Mr. D Wheen, Regional Director North Asia, Hong Kong, 15 March 1983, "Community Refugee Settlement Scheme Policy and Plan," 3.
36 Memo from G. Kane (CRSS Coordinator) to Assistant Director Settlement Branch, 27 November 1986, *Settlement Branch – CRSS [Community Refugee Settlement Scheme] – Program Management*, NAA A446 1986/75554.
37 Ibid.
38 Minute from Harley Baulch (CRSS Unit) to Mr. R. Toohey, Director of the Settlement Services Section, "Named CRSS Indochinese Cases," 27 September 1985, *Community Refugee Settlement Scheme Policy and Plan*, NAA A446 1983/76959. Other ways in which CRSS groups came to know of refugees included instances where a former refugee approached a community group to sponsor a "friend" whom they knew in the camps or where voluntary workers in a camp took particular interest in a refugee and wrote back to their groups requesting support.
39 Minute from Dario Castello to all Migration Officers and Overseas Post, Community Refugee Settlement Scheme (CRSS), 13 December 1986, *Settlement Branch – CRSS [Community Refugee Settlement Scheme] – Program Management*, NAA A446 1986/75554, 5.
40 Memo from G. Kane (CRSS Coordinator) to Assistant Director Settlement Branch, 27 November 1986, *Settlement Branch – CRSS [Community Refugee Settlement Scheme] – Program Management*, NAA A446 1986/75554, 3.
41 Memo from G. Kane (CRSS Coordinator) to Assistant Director Settlement Branch, 27 November 1986, 3; Memo from R.B. Penkethman (Refugee and Humanitarian Branch) to Mr. Richardson, 29 July 1996; Dario Castello, Memo to all Regional Directors, Discussion Paper on "Community Refugee Settlement Scheme," 4 June 1986, *Settlement Branch – CRSS [Community Refugee Settlement Scheme] – Program Management*, NAA A446 1986/75554.
42 Dario Castello, Memo to All Regional Directors, Discussion Paper on "Community Refugee Settlement Scheme," 4 June 1986, *Settlement Branch – CRSS [Community Refugee Settlement Scheme] – Program Management*, NAA A446 1986/75554.
43 Minute from G. Ratnam to the Minister for Immigration and Ethic Affairs, Community Refugee Sponsorship Scheme, 16 December 1986, *Settlement Branch – CRSS [Community Refugee Settlement Scheme] – Program Management*, NAA A446 1986/75554.
44 Ibid., 3.

45 Minute from Dario Castello to all Migration Officers and Overseas Post, Community Refugee Settlement Scheme (CRSS), 13 December 1986, *Settlement Branch – CRSS [Community Refugee Settlement Scheme] – Program Management*, NAA A446 1986/75554.
46 Department of Immigration and Ethnic Affairs, *Community Refugee Settlement Scheme: Information for Organisations, Groups, and Individuals Who Wish to Help Refugees Settle in the Community*, 2nd ed. (Canberra: Australian Government Publishing Service, 1983).
47 Brendan O'Connor, Minister for Immigration and Citizenship, "Community Refugee Sponsorship Trial Begins."
48 Department of Immigration and Border Protection, "Australia's Humanitarian Programme Information Paper" (Australian Government, December 2013), 8, https://www.homeaffairs.gov.au/Refugeeand humanitarian/Documents/humanitarian-program-information-paper-14-15.pdf#search=%22community%20proposal%20pilot%22.
49 Department of Immigration and Border Protection, 8.
50 Minister for Immigration and Citizenship, "Explanatory Statement: Migration Amendment Regulation 2013 (No 2) (Select Legislative Instrument 2013 No 75)," Parliament of Australia, 1 June 2013, 2. As early as 2009, the Refugee Council of Australia was asked to advise the government on '"What role should the community, business and local governments have in resettling refugees under the offshore Humanitarian Program? What role might private sponsorship play?" (Correspondence on file with authors).
51 Minister for Immigration and Citizenship, 2.
52 Department of Immigration and Border Protection, "Community Support Programme Discussion Paper," June 2015, 13.
53 Ibid.
54 Ibid.
55 Department of Home Affairs, Freedom of Information Section, Request FA18/05/00515 (3 December 2018, on file with authors).
56 Global Compact on Refugees, Final Draft, accessed 6 May 2018, http://www.unhcr.org/en-au/events/conferences/5b3295167/official-version-final-draft-global-compact-refugees.html.
57 Malcolm Turnbull, Prime Minister of Australia, "Media Release: Leaders' Summit on Refugees," 21 September 2016, https://www.pm.gov.au/media/leaders%E2%80%99-summit-refugees.
58 On this point, see Refugee Council of Australia, "Submission: Community Support Program Consultation," July 2015, https://www.refugeecouncil.org.au/wp-content/uploads/2015/07/1507-CSP.pdf.

59 Department of Home Affairs, "The Community Support Program," accessed 29 July 2018, https://www.homeaffairs.gov.au/trav/refu/offs/community-support-program. In reporting to the Parliament on the early stages of the CSP, a Departmental spokesperson stated that most of those "primary applicants had a direct job offer," which, he noted, "is exactly the intent of the program." Commonwealth, *Legal and Constitutional Affairs Legislation Committee*, Senate, 22 May 2018, 117 (Mansfield).

60 Department of Home Affairs, "Community Support Program – Frequently Asked Questions," 1 July 2018, https://www.homeaffairs.gov.au/Refugee andhumanitarian/Documents/csp-faq.pdf.

61 Under Australia's offshore refugee and humanitarian visas, a primary applicant who meets the criteria for the grant of a visa can also bring members of their family unit with them. Family members are referred to as "secondary applicants."

62 Parliament of Australia, "Legal and Constitutional Affairs Legislation Committee, Estimates, Department of Home Affairs," 22 May 2018, http://parlinfo.aph.gov.au/parlInfo/search/display/display.w3p;query=Id%3A%22committees%2Festimate%2F75507344-48f1-4665-8f23-623c6eb5c20d%2F0002%22. These countries include Democratic Republic of Congo, Afghanistan, Eritrea, Ethiopia, Myanmar, Bhutan, Syria, and Iraq.

63 Asher Hirsch, Khanh Hoang, and Anthea Vogl, "Australia's Private Refugee Sponsorship Program: Creating Complementary Pathways or Privatising Humanitarianism?," *Refuge: Canada's Journal on Refugees* 35, no. 2 (2019): 109–22.

64 Lyndal Curtis, "Government Moves to Increase Refugee Intake by 7,500 Places," *ABC News*, 3 December 2014, http://www.abc.net.au/news/2014-12-03/refugee-intake-to-rise-by-7,500-places-over-four-years/5936614.

65 Refugee Council of Australia, "The Community Support Program: Providing Complementary Pathways to Protection or Privatising the Humanitarian Program?," 4 July 2017, https://www.refugeecouncil.org.au/ourwork/16445/.

66 Hawke, "Turnbull Government Announces Community Support Programme."

67 Phillips and Spinks, "Immigration and Border Protection Overview."

68 Department of Home Affairs, "Fees and Charges for Visas," accessed 29 July 2018, https://www.homeaffairs.gov.au/trav/visa/fees#tab-content-4.

69 AMES Australia, "Community Support Program for VIC," accessed 29 July 2018, https://www.ames.net.au:443/csp/victoria.

70 The Government has described the VAC as offsetting the costs to the government for support services available to humanitarian entrants after arrival in Australia such as Medicare and some employment services: Commonwealth, *Legal and Constitutional Affairs Legislation Committee*, Senate, 23 May 2017, 119–23 (Wilden).
71 Department of Social Services, "Assurance of Support," 14 June 2018, https://www.dss.gov.au/about-the-department/international/policy/assurance-of-support.
72 Sahar Okhovat et al., "Rethinking Resettlement and Family Reunion in Australia," *Alternative Law Journal* 42, no. 4 (1 December 2017): 273–8.
73 Refugee Council of Australia, "Addressing the Pain of Separation for Refugee Families," 3 November 2016, https://www.refugeecouncil.org.au/publications/reports/family-separation/#read-report.
74 Okhovat et al., "Rethinking Resettlement and Family Reunion in Australia."
75 Communication from an APO, on file with the authors.

15

A Model for the World?
Policy Transfer Theory and the Challenges to "Exporting" Private Sponsorship to Europe

Craig Damian Smith

Justin Trudeau's Liberal Party won Canada's 2015 federal election partly on a promise to increase the pace and scope of resettling Syrian refugees. While responding to genuine demand, the policy was also a tactic to defeat the incumbent Conservative Party and to mobilize domestic pro-refugee sentiment as a vehicle for regaining international prestige. It is in this context that the Trudeau government threw its weight behind the 2016 New York Declaration for Refugees and Migrants, announcing an early and tangible contribution through the Global Refugee Sponsorship Initiative (GRSI).

The GRSI began as a bottom-up initiative led by senior bureaucrats and academics in Ottawa and was supported by the Open Society Initiative and UNHCR. Its stated goal was to export Canada's private sponsorship scheme, primarily to Europe but also to South America.[1] It was launched with a good deal of fanfare as well as optimism that private sponsorship could provide a "model for the world," particularly by expanding burden-sharing through increased commitments to international resettlement. Those lofty goals met a mixed reception from civil society organizations (CSOs), policy-makers, and politicians in Europe. As of early 2019 it has yet to result in any additional third-country resettlement. GRSI has scaled back its goals from fully "exporting" the Canadian model to providing training, technical support, and capacity-building for community-based support programs – the majority of which existed independently of Canadian intervention.

The export project was based on the doubtful premise that the Canadian model was readily transferable to other legal and political contexts. As the other chapters in this volume illustrate quite comprehensively, Canada's unique geographical position far from regions of origin means it can largely manage international resettlement. The history of private resettlement has generated a unique and mutually reinforcing set of institutional, legal, and social dynamics, in which the nature and content of the "private sponsorship model" is malleable, as are government commitments to its scope in a wider immigration regime.[2] To put the matter simply, the Canadian model works because of Canada's history and geography, and it continues to evolve. The widely different institutional contexts across Europe militate against a "one size fits all" model. While not impossible, each Canadian mission would have to tailor its support to a local context, resulting in high transaction costs for a small team of civil servants, academics, and lawyers.

Nonetheless, some optimism was warranted, particularly given that as of 2016 Canada had so far resisted the growing nativist, anti-refugee and anti-immigrant hysteria that was infecting liberal democracies. John McCallum, the Trudeau government's first immigration minister, liked to declare that he was the world's only immigration minister criticized for admitting too few refugees. His successor, Ahmed Hussen, claimed that European states "love" the Canadian model and were seeking guidance on private sponsorship mechanisms. But these observations were only surprising from a uniquely sheltered Canadian perspective and reflected an undue amount of optimism about the appetite for additional resettlement to Europe.

Indeed, GRSI was launched in the immediate aftermath of Europe's refugee crisis, the final months of which saw cascading border closures, recriminations, and burden-shifting between EU Member States, along with a failed relocation scheme and a rightward shift in asylum policies, all of which threatened the stability of the European project.[3] The EU's response was to double down on external control policies to keep asylum-seekers at bay; this included striking deals with the Turkish government and Libyan militias and warehousing migrants in squalid Greek camps. Hardly an auspicious time for exporting Canada's good news story.

The remainder of this chapter uses *policy transfer* theories from political science to argue that the barriers faced by GRSI can be explained by low incentives from Canada, high domestic adoption costs for additional resettlement to Europe, and lack of fit with disparate political and institutional contexts. In short, the export project was a supply-side attempt at policy transfer in the face of weak demand. This explains why GRSI narrowed its objectives from exporting the Canadian model to low-stakes capacity-building. The analysis reveals potential consequences for Canada's contribution to global migration governance and international burden-sharing. Most significantly, Canada pushed for GRSI to be included in the Global Compact on Refugees (GCR), adopted by the UN in December 2018. Waning political will for resettlement in the global North could render the GRSI dead on arrival. On a positive note, understanding the barriers to policy transfer offers a chance for GRSI to support community sponsorship in Europe, while shifting the bulk of Canada's financial and political capital toward supporting global South host states, with more immediate and tangible impacts for international responsibility-sharing.

PRIVATE SPONSORSHIP AND THE CRISIS OF INTERNATIONAL BURDEN-SHARING

As noted throughout the volume, the photograph of Alan Kurdi's lifeless body on a Turkish beach fixed Canadians' attention on Syrian refugees. Beyond its emotive impact, the image offered a window onto shortfalls in global humanitarian funding and burden-sharing that have helped drive refugees toward irregular migration routes. The global distribution of refugees imposes unequal and different types of burdens between donor and host states. Over 85 percent of refugees are hosted in the global South, half of them in states with a GDP per capita of $5,000 or less. Millions are in protracted situations, with no prospect of return to their countries of origin. Solidarity from donor states is comprised largely of short-term humanitarian funding, with third-country resettlement accounting for a tiny fraction of support.

The 2016 New York Declaration, and subsequent GCR, were framed around ameliorating this unequal and untenable distribution by creating new responsibility-sharing mechanisms for large-scale refugee crises. While officially based on consensus-oriented consultations, the representatives of the Canadian federal government, UNHCR, and civil society organizations interviewed for this chapter reported significant contention and hard bargaining around the meaning of responsibility-sharing. A marked North/South division in negotiations reflected the uneven burdens between donor and host states.

The GCR frames new modes of responsibility-sharing, primarily through the Comprehensive Refugee Response Framework and program of action. It calls for new and additional development mechanisms for host states, with the goal of moving beyond typical "care and maintenance" humanitarian approaches toward durable inclusion for refugees, involving, *inter alia*, access to health care, education, and jobs and livelihood opportunities, as well as incorporation into host-state social services.[4] The Global Refugee Forums, to take place in 2019 and 2021 and every four years thereafter, will provide a venue for donor and host states to make voluntary, non-binding commitments. The focus on development is an admission that existing durable solutions (i.e., third-country resettlement, host-state nationalization, and return to countries of origin) have failed to address protracted displacement crises.[5] Traditional durable solutions take a back seat to host-state capacity-building.

The final draft of the GCR reads: "resettlement is *also* a tangible mechanism for burden- and responsibility-sharing and a demonstration of solidarity, allowing states to help share each other's burdens and reduce the impact of large refugee situations on host countries" (emphasis added).[6] As Labman and Pearlman note, the practice of international resettlement has proliferated in recent years, with the number of states growing from twenty-two in 2011 to thirty in 2015.[7] However, the diffusion of the practice has plateaued, and the total number of resettlement spots has dropped precipitously given the Trump administration's slashing of resettlement quotas and de facto bans on Muslim refugees. In 2018 the international community resettled fewer than 92,000 of the 1.2 million refugees in urgent need, meaning that only 0.3 percent were offered this durable solution.[8] In short, while invaluable to those who are selected, resettlement plays a very small role in international burden-sharing.

The GCR's "Complementary Pathways for Admission to Third Countries" specifically calls for contributions "to facilitate effective procedures and clear referral pathways for family reunification, or to establish private or community-based programmes promoted through the Global Refugee Sponsorship Initiative (GRSI)."[9] GRSI avoided neatly delineated policies and sought instead to lobby states to increase resettlement through private sponsorship schemes, based on Canada's experience.[10] Indeed, much of the criticism around the GCR argues it was a missed opportunity to establish binding, objective criteria for burden-sharing.[11] The GRSI reflects this missed opportunity in that it makes private sponsorship entirely voluntary and ad hoc, as well as dependent on the domestic politics of potential resettlement countries. Thus, a project that was conceived while the Liberal government was riding high on its international reputation for resettlement was enshrined in the GCR at a time when the international community had shifted focus to host-state development.

EXTERNAL INCENTIVE MODELS AND POLICY TRANSFER

The basic assumption underlying policy transfer and diffusion theory is that policy choices in one place or time can be actively transferred or influence policy selection in other jurisdictions or organizations.[12] Diffusion and transfer occur at all levels of analysis – that is, among institutions, municipalities, states, and international organizations. Causal mechanisms for transfer or diffusion include: imposition through coercion or conditionality (e.g., withholding preferential trade access, imposing sanctions, or controlling terms of negotiations; or through incremental incentives for meeting benchmarks for policy adoption); competition (e.g., creating attractive regulatory environments for corporations); learning and emulation (e.g., when evidence changes ideas about how to approach an issue); leadership (e.g., providing evidence of dividends from either innovative or well-tested models); and a range of more ideational mechanisms.[13]

Causal mechanisms are not mutually exclusive, and transfer does not necessarily rely on an exact transposition of a set of laws and policies. For example, states looking to reform immigration systems in order to attract high-skilled talent might look to successful models of labour market integration, and take on different aspects of welfare policy, points-based criteria, or recognition of foreign credentials. In this case, transfer and diffusion might occur through mechanisms of competition and learning.[14] Whereas policy *diffusion* is more systemic – relating, for example, to the globalization of sovereign states, waves of democratization, and the spread of market capitalism – policy *transfer* is more purposeful and agent-based.[15] Transfer relies on direct knowledge of administrative arrangements, policies, or programs.[16]

For example, OECD countries align all manner of policies through active learning from colleagues in parallel ministries.

Taken together, we can say that exporting Canada's private sponsorship model through the GRSI is a case of attempted transfer through a mixture of learning, emulation, and leadership. The success or failure of policy transfer depends on supply/demand balance, incentives from suppliers and costs to adopters, and goodness of fit for a new context. In policy learning and emulation, demand comes from policy-makers or policy entrepreneurs such as civil society organizations (CSOs) seeking to solve a specific problem. These actors may then ally themselves with like-minded policy-makers or CSOs from successful contexts, or borrow from best practices and expertise to make the case for policy change at home.

The fact that GRSI hosted several dozen delegations from EU Member States to Canada from 2016 to 2018 provides some evidence for demand.[17] A typical delegation involved a well-curated set of visits with Sponsorship Agreement Holders, settlement sector organizations, training initiatives like the Refugee Support Training Program, academics, sponsorship groups, employers, and faith groups, as well as with politicians and bureaucrats from municipalities, provincial ministries, and federal departments. The general tone was a good news story about the PSR experience and its impacts on refugee integration. In addition, GRSI, in cooperation with Canadian foreign missions, held round tables, public events, and private sessions with CSOs and governments across Europe.

Interest from Europe implied a desire to learn about Canada's integration successes, settlement sector, governance, and legislation, as well as the scope of public/private partnerships, in order to help address policy problems associated with the arrival of more than a million new refugees. European interest in Canada, however, did not imply desire to adopt the PSR model. Interviews with policy-makers from Germany, the Netherlands, and Belgium, scholars with international think tanks, UNHCR personnel, and European CSOs found that a central lesson from delegations and round tables was that Canada's success was a function of its unique history and geography. Transferring the model to Europe would involve high political costs and significant changes in immigration regimes – a point I address in detail below. The narrative that Canada could act as a "model for the world" was driven by supply-side attempts at policy leadership rather than demand for transfer.

Supply-side policy transfer faces an uphill battle and must offer either significant positive incentives or negative costs in order to overcome adoption costs or non-compliance. For example, IMF structural adjustment programs mean that debtor states take on a set of policies related to privatization, selling public assets, cutting subsidies, and lowering barriers to trade despite the damage to domestic markets. States comply because the alternatives are disastrous. Of course, GRSI was not a coercive exercise, and instead depended on selling the Canadian model as an adaptable policy model for additional resettlement to Europe.

Perhaps the most successful and well-studied cases of supply-side policy transfer based on positive incentives come from the period of post–Cold War EU enlargement to Central and Eastern Europe. While the long accession process meant high adoption costs in terms of creating new bureaucracies, reforming laws, and adopting liberal market economies, that process was helped along by massive funding mechanisms, infrastructure projects, capacity-building, and bureaucratic twinning arrangements. It mattered a great deal that post-Communist states had massive lacunae in their institutions, laws, and bureaucracies.

While EU enlargement was by no means an apolitical process, and varied significantly in terms of pace, breadth, and depth of change across states and issues, policy transfer proceeded at a relatively steady pace because positive incentives were offered for staged compliance targets.[18] The golden carrot of access to the EU's common market and free mobility regime far outweighed adoption costs. Moreover, public sentiment was overwhelmingly in favour of "returning to Europe" at this unique historical moment.[19]

Lessons from the EU's successful supply-side policy transfer offer insights into the conditions for the successful export of Canada's PSR model to Europe. Transfer of the model, as envisaged by GRSI, would require strong demand for additional resettlement. However, Europe's pressing policy problem is how to integrate already arrived refugees, manage irregular migration, and overcome intra-European burden-shifting. These challenges are set against a wider political backdrop of anti-refugee sentiment and electoral gains for xenophobic political parties.[20]

POLITICAL CONTEXT AND ADOPTION COSTS IN EUROPE

GRSI faced not only an uphill battle between costs and incentives but also a mismatch between the Canadian model and European policy concerns. Any reasonable attempt to export policy must understand the institutional, social, and political contexts in target jurisdictions, and overcoming the imbalance will mean tailoring the model and offering incentives for its transfer. Convincing European states to increase resettlement is like planting seeds in rather rocky soil. In the aftermath of the 2015–16 European migration crisis, EU institutions were buffeted by anti-Brussels sentiment, and public opinion was strongly against immigration in general. Voters rewarded parties with anti-migrant, xenophobic, and Eurosceptic political platforms. As Geoffrey Cameron shows in this volume, the origins of private sponsorship and its periods of renewal in Canada were consistently driven by domestic demand for resettlement – precisely the opposite situation as contemporary Europe.

GRSI's export experiment is about pushing a model for global burden-sharing at a time when most European states are locked in a cycle of burden-shifting with their closest allies. States view hosting refugees as a zero-sum proposition, and burden-shifting means offsetting social welfare costs.[21] During the 2015 refugee crisis, EU Member States allowed asylum-seekers to move through their territory, in some cases actively transporting them from one border to another, in contravention of EU law. The EU suspended its Dublin regulations rather than face the legal ramifications of addressing these actions. Member States showed a strong preference for free-riding on one another's commitments to hosting asylum-seekers.[22] Brussels-led burden-sharing mechanisms, such as the binding redistribution quota system to disperse refugees from front-line reception states, were a non-starter in many countries as well as an easy foil for populists. Hard-line policies against asylum-seekers paid off for electoral gain, regardless of the actual number of asylum-seekers present in a country.[23] States from Sweden, to Austria, to Denmark, to Italy curtailed social services for asylum-seekers to make for less attractive destinations.

From a certain perspective, GRSI might be seen as an attempt to ameliorate this situation by fostering public support for refugees. Indeed, the rightward electoral shift and more restrictive welfare policies were mirrored by a groundswell of support from NGOs, CSOs, and volunteers. Support from EU citizens remains the underrepresented story in Europe's response to the migration crisis, and many grassroots initiatives have coalesced into full-time campaigns and organizations that now facilitate integration. But the political timing for GRSI could perhaps not have been worse, given the ascendance of populist parties.

European states were promising to curtail arrivals by any means necessary at the same time as Justin Trudeau's Liberals won an election based partly on the promise to resettle an additional 20,000 Syrians. Europe saw a 123 percent increase in the number of asylum-seekers, from 562,000 in 2014 to 1,255,640 in 2015. Driven by the need to stop burden-shifting, and indeed to save the European project, Europe "ended" the refugee crisis through a deal that offered €6 billion to Turkey to stop the flow of migrants.[24] Since then, the EU and Member States have signed new deals with transit states in Africa and the Middle East to contain irregular migrants, curtailed maritime rescue operations, and criminalized rescue-focused NGOs.

Put simply, Europe already had more refugees than domestic political sentiment would bear, and adopting private sponsorship as a form of international burden-sharing would increase their numbers on European soil. Policy-makers were also concerned about the impending family reunifications from recognized refugees and acted to curtail these. Committing to additionality through GRSI could spell electoral suicide for incumbents or challengers in many European states. To wit, an EU-wide resettlement scheme for the most vulnerable refugees – for example, victims of torture in Libyan detention camps – pledged only to resettle 20,000 people to twenty-eight member states (with a total population of 512 million) from 2015 to 2017, and an additional 50,000 over the subsequent three years. The safer bet is for political parties to promise fewer refugees.

All of which is not to say that there is no appetite for Canadian expertise. But the demand for private sponsorship based on additionality comes primarily from civil society, and this has little influence on policy-making. Civil society is stymied by the fact that European states lack a Canadian-type "settlement sector" and do not share Canada's unique history of complementarity among CSOs, newcomer communities, and governments that allow such a sector to exist.[25] Indeed, the concept of "settlement sector" and its influence on policy often have to be explained to European delegations to Canada. Likewise, most European states have eschewed the concept of multiculturalism, which has become part of the bedrock of support for private sponsorship. Most European states employ a thin concept of integration, limited to labour market performance and language acquisition. Cultural integration generally means assimilationist policies rather than the dynamic adaptation implied by Canadian multiculturalism.

All of this nonetheless leaves room to draw lessons from Canada's success in refugee integration, particularly given the focus on privately sponsored refugees' success relative to that of other refugees. At the time of writing, small-scale pilot projects were under way for community sponsorships in Ireland, Portugal, Germany, and the UK, and for humanitarian corridors in Belgium, Italy, and France. Many of these pilots have engaged with Canadian civil servants and experts affiliated with or engaged by GRSI. However, most of these projects existed before GRSI and apply to asylum-seekers already residing in Europe, and those that work with newly resettled refugees identify them from existing quotas rather than through additional resettlement spots.

In Portugal, for example, private sponsorship is limited to the EU's relocation directive as it relates to Italy and Greece. Pilot community resettlement programs in the UK and Ireland operate within the governments' established resettlement quotas and do not entail increased resettlement numbers. Instead, "additionality" is construed as additional "support" from CSOs and private citizens rather than additional international resettlement.[26] In Eastern Europe and Italy, community-based settlement schemes privilege Christian refugees. While not abrogating the norms of international protection per se, resettlement in the Czech Republic, Poland, and Slovakia has been politicized in the context of a general anti-Muslim bias and supported a Christian civilizational discourse.

Political contexts, adoption costs, and differences between European and Canadian integration models all feed the rationale for, and pose the most significant challenges to, exporting the Canadian model. In short, while GRSI has had some success in supporting small-scale pilots, it has yet to achieve any meaningful policy transfer. Success therefore relies on substantially increasing incentives or changing the policies on offer.

MATCHING INCENTIVES WITH CONTEXT

Export entrepreneurs must offer sufficient incentives if policy transfer is to succeed in the face of high compliance costs and political barriers. In the current context, the Canadian government, UNHCR, and GRSI simply do not enjoy sufficient leverage to export the PSR model. But lesson-learning and incentives for adoption are not limited to wholesale policy transfer. We can identify at least three basic incentives for lesson-learning and emulation, with varying barriers to adoption.

First, additional resettlement options could help meet the burden-sharing commitments included in the Global Compact on Refugees. Unfortunately, the EU and Member States are far less committed to resettlement. Unlike Canada, the EU has committed significant resources to funding mechanisms such as Trust Funds for Africa, Compacts in Jordan, Lebanon, and Turkey, and development schemes in sending and transit states throughout Africa and the Middle East. Ethical concerns and political motivations aside, development aid to host regions represents Europe's preferred choice for international burden-sharing.

Second, private sponsorship might help alleviate irregular migration pressure on Europe, since offering safe and legal channels can alter decision-making logics for refugees entertaining the option of irregular migration. However, European resettlement schemes focus on the most vulnerable cases, which are some of the least likely to undertake irregular journeys. Quotas are paltry on a per capita basis and would have to be scaled at orders of magnitude in order to offset the demand for irregular migration. European policies to deter irregular migration instead rely on bolstering border controls, curtailing search and rescue, signing third-country readmission agreements and migration control deals with autocratic and authoritarian governments. In such a climate, the Canadian model therefore has very little to offer, given Europe's long and evolving history with externalized migration controls.[27]

Third, and most promising, aspects of the Canadian model can meet the demand to improve integration for refugees who are already in Europe, as well as offset costs to private citizens and CSOs. While this aspect of the Canadian model can help meet the demand to spend less on integration, it means abandoning the GRSI's stated goals of promoting additional pathways for resettlement. This is not entirely a negative prospect, as has been born out in the response from Europe. This limited range for transfer largely explains why GRSI has narrowed its goals to more mundane (and more realistic) capacity-building. In conversations about why GRSI had little uptake in terms of its original goals, the answer from the delegations from Austria, Belgium, Germany, the Netherlands, Italy, and Sweden was much the same: the Canadian story is inspiring, but the European context is radically different.

As the contributions to this volume aptly demonstrate, the origins of private sponsorship in Canada are complex.[28] Its success has depended on contingent historical moments, the unique influence of different actors, and Canada's capacity to dictate broad immigration policies. Public support is based on more than seventy years of experience in normalizing the process.[29] The situation in Europe is likewise dictated by historical and social contingencies, but these have resulted in an altogether different set of policies. In the absence of a major shift in incentives, success in exporting the Canadian model will thus be measured incrementally, rather than in terms of a grand ambition of providing a model for the world.

CONCLUSION: WHAT ROLE FOR CANADIAN EXPERIENCE?

History and public sentiment cannot be exported, and Europe is an altogether more cynical policy environment when it comes to immigration. Likewise, the good news story of Canada's private sponsorship model masks some pervasive shortcomings and knowledge gaps around whether and to what degree it influences refugee integration. Policy entrepreneurs will have to admit the shortcomings in order to offer lessons to Europe. Taken together, these considerations point to a set of alternative ways of framing incentives and adoption costs.

First, some politicians like the fact that the Canadian model can shift costs onto private citizens. This incentive is ethically ambiguous, and it remains questionable whether privatizing international protection is a trend that Canada ought to promote. Private sponsorship models risk displacing state-based international responsibility as envisaged in the 1951 Convention.[30] However, policy transfer to Europe will have to directly address the financial costs of policy adoption. GRSI has underemphasized the tertiary costs to states. As Hyndman and colleagues argue, "an unspoken but major reason that private refugee resettlement happens in Canada is because various levels of government are willing to pay for education, health, and social services on par with those of citizens."[31] Civil servants and NGO personnel I interviewed in Belgium, Italy, and the Netherlands relayed anecdotes that politicians were quick to point out these types of costs. Framing policy transfer as a way to lower costs means not letting the good aspects of the Canadian model become a victim of the perfect.

Second, it remains unclear how, precisely, private sponsorship improves integration outcomes – a crucial point when dealing with European policy-makers. In public forums and private discussions throughout Europe, policy-makers, CSOs, and private donors routinely noted that evidence of integration outcomes is anecdotal.[32] The lack of robust empirical evidence and reliance on positive narratives are serious impediments, since the EU and member states are committed to evidence-based integration programming with clear monitoring and evaluation frameworks. Indeed, evidence-based programming is key in order for pilot schemes to be eligible for the EU's main refugee funding envelopes.[33] A Migration Policy Institute study on the feasibility of private sponsorship models in Europe (funded by the European Commission) focused explicitly on this hurdle.[34]

At the risk of putting too fine a point on the matter, telling a good news story about Canada comes off as rather quaint to European policy audiences. Canadians would do well to admit that their experience has never been as harmonious as the one they present to international delegations. The Canadian model can result in conflicts between the sponsorship community and government, as well as breakdowns in sponsorships.[35] A model that relies on interpersonal relationships offers uplifting stories but also inevitable conflict.

Nonetheless, the Canadian experience shows that community-based sponsorships are important for building social networks. Indeed, part of the success of private sponsorship lies in the fact that beneficiaries can be named, and the family reunification aspect of sponsorship means that people arrive to ready-made social networks and the social capital they provide. This comports well with theories about the effect of social networks on integration.[36] However, causal evidence for the relationship is lacking, and Canada's system does not lend itself to measuring the effects, given the absence of benchmarking and randomized interventions.[37] The Canadian export experiment must raise its own bar when providing evidence.

Finally, Canada should recognize that private sponsorship is not comparable to systematic burden-sharing through funding of host-state development initiatives. While resettlement is a durable solution to displacement, Europe's rather small quotas will have little measurable impact on the global refugee crisis. Likewise, as Bradley and Duin argue in their contribution to this volume, exporting private sponsorship risks enabling states to avoid responsibilities to other forced migrants and misallocating support for the neediest populations. The official narrative around Canada's private sponsorship model tends to focus on high-profile emergencies mobilized for political gain, rather than protracted refugee situations.

Taken together, these realities mean that in addition to devoting more financial and political capital toward burden-sharing in host states, Canada can ensure that GRSI does not become a dead letter of the Global Compact on Refugees by supporting community sponsorship models for refugees who are already in Europe. While the export experiment did not result in the easy soft-power win Canada had hoped for, small-scale community support pilots can help foster positive public attitudes toward refugees. Indeed, if the Canadian model offers any generalizable lesson, it is that a history of public support may be a necessary condition for Canada's status as a global leader in integration. Canada can serve as an exemplar provided that it keeps its hubris in check and policy entrepreneurs proceed with a respect for Europe's more complicated and cynical political context.

NOTES

The author has been invited by Global Affairs Canada to speak on community support for refugee newcomers throughout Europe, some as part of Global Refugee Support Initiative roundtables. Global Affairs paid his travel expenses. He is the principal investigator and academic lead on a project with a civil society implementing partner in The Netherlands to match volunteers with newcomers, which is based on lessons from private sponsorship models. He earns consulting fees from these projects. From 2015 to 2017 he was the Research Director and co-founder of an NGO in Ontario which matched volunteers with Government-Assisted Refugee newcomers, through which he interacted with European delegations hosted by GRSI.

1 Kristen Shane, "Exporting a Canadian Success Story," *Hill Times*, 8 February 2017, https://www.hilltimes.com/2017/02/08/exporting-canadian-success-story/94736; "Canada to Join with UN, George Soros to Export Private Refugee Sponsorship," *CBC News*, 19 September 2016, https://www.cbc.ca/news/politics/private-refugee-sponsorship-soros-un-1.3769639.
2 See Cameron's chapter in this volume.
3 Kelly M. Greenhill, "Open Arms Behind Barred Doors: Fear, Hypocrisy and Policy Schizophrenia in the European Migration Crisis," *European Law Journal* 22, no.3 (2016): 317–32.
4 Volker Türk and Madeline Garlick, "From Burdens and Responsibilities to Opportunities: The Comprehensive Refugee Response Framework and a Global Compact on Refugees," *International Journal of Refugee Law* 28, no.4 (2016): 656–78.

5 Guy S. Goodwin-Gill, "International Refugee Law – Yesterday, Today, but Tomorrow?" *Refugee Law Initiative Working Paper Series*, https://rli.sas.ac.uk/sites/default/files/files/RLI_final.pdf.
6 UNHCR, The Global Compact on Refugees: Final Draft, UN Refugee Agency, 26 June 2018.
7 Shauna Labman and Madison Pearlman, "Blending, Bargaining, and Burden-Sharing: Canada's Resettlement Programs," *International Migration and Integration* 19 (2018): 439–49.
8 Randall Hansen, "The Comprehensive Refugee Response Framework: A Commentary," *Journal of Refugee Studies* 31, no.2 (2018): 131–51.
9 UNHCR, The Global Compact on Refugees.
10 See Lehr and Dyck in this volume.
11 James C. Hathaway, "A Global Solution to a Global Refugee Crisis," *Open Democracy*, 29 February 2016, https://www.openglobalrights.org/global-solution-to-global-refugee-crisis; Refugees International, *Issue Brief on the Global Compact on Refugees: Establishing Effective Mechanisms for Responsibility-Sharing*, https://static1.squarespace.com/static/506c8ea1e4b01d9450dd53f5/t/5ad12b0b758d46ce63e5592e/1523657483923/GCR_April2018_Final_Final.pdf.
12 Fabrizio Gilardi, "Who Learns What in Policy Diffusion Processes?," *American Journal of Political Science* 54, no.2 (2010): 650–66.
13 Erin Graham, Charles R. Volden, and Craig Shipan, "The Diffusion of Policy Diffusion Research," *British Journal of Political Science* 43, no. 3 (2013): 673–701; Frank Dobbin, Beth Simmons, and G. Garrett, "The Global Diffusion of Public Policies: Social Construction, Coercion, Competition, or Learning," *Annual Review of Sociology* 33 (2007): 449–72.
14 Hugh Ward and Peter John, "Competitive Learning in Yardstick Competition: Testing Models of Policy Diffusion with Performance Data," *Political Science Research and Methods* 1, no. 1 (2013): 3–25.
15 David Marsh and J.C. Sharmin, "Policy Diffusion and Policy Transfer," *Policy Studies* 30, no. 3 (2009): 269–88.
16 D.P. Dolowitz and David Marsh, "Learning from Abroad: The Role of Policy Transfer in Contemporary Policy-Making," *Governance* 13 (January 2000): 5–24.
17 See "GRSI Newsletters," http://refugeesponsorship.org/news.
18 Heather Grabbe, "Europeanization Goes East: Power and Uncertainty in the EU Accession Process," in *The Politics of Europeanization*, ed. Kevin Featherstone and Claudio M. Radaelli (Oxford: Oxford University Press,

2003), 303–28; Frank Schimmelfennig and Ulrich Sedelmeier, eds, *The Europeanization of Central and Eastern Europe* (Ithaca: Cornell University Press, 2005).

19 Heather Grabbe, "Six Lessons of Enlargement Ten Years On: The EU's Transformative Power in Retrospect and Prospect," *Journal of Common Market Studies* 52 (2014): 40–56.

20 James Dennison and Andrew Geddes, "A Rising Tide? The Salience of Immigration and the Rise of Anti-Immigration Political Parties in Western Europe," *Political Quarterly* 90, no.1 (27 November 2018): 107–16.

21 Maurizio Ambrosini, "Irregular Migration and the Welfare State," in *The Routledge Handbook of Immigration and Refugee Studies*, ed. Anna Triandafyllidou (London and New York: Routledge, 2016).

22 Eiko Thielmann, "Why Refugee Burden-Sharing Initiatives Fail: Public Goods, Free-Riding, and Symbolic Solidarity in the EU," *Journal of Common Market Studies* 56, no. 1 (2018): 63–82.

23 Gallya Lahav, "Threat and Immigration Attitudes in Liberal Democracies: The Role of Framing in Structuring Public Opinion," in *Immigration and Public Opinion in Liberal Democracies*, ed. Gary P. Freeman, Randall Hansen, and David L. Leal (New York: Routledge, 2013); Daniel Stockemer, "Structural Data on Immigration or Immigration Perceptions: What Accounts for the Electoral Success of the Radical Right in Europe?," *Journal of Common Market Studies* 54, no. 4 (2016): 999–1016.

24 Kelly M. Greenhill, "Open Arms behind Barred Doors: Fear, Hypocrisy, and Policy Schizophrenia in the European Migration Crisis," *European Law Journal* 22, no. 3 (2016): 317–32.

25 Daniel Hiebert, *What's So Special about Canada? Understanding the Resilience of Immigration and Multiculturalism* (Washington, DC: Migration Policy Institute, 2016), https://www.migrationpolicy.org/research/whats-so-special-about-canada-understanding-resilience-immigration-and-multiculturalism.

26 European Commission, "Study on the Feasibility and Added Value of Sponsorship Schemes as a Possible Pathway to Safe Channels for Admission to the EU, Including Resettlement: Final Report," *DG Migration and Home Affairs, European Commission* (Luxembourg: Publications Office of the European Union, 2018), 40–1.

27 Ruben Zaiotti, "Mapping Remote Control," in Externalizing Migration Management: Europe, North America and the Spread of "Remote Control" Practices, ed. Ruben Zaiotti (New York: Routledge, 2016).

28 See Cameron's chapter and Lehr and Dyck's chapter in this volume.

29 Michael Adams, "Canada in 2018 Is a Country of Global Citizens," *Globe and Mail*, 15 April 2018, https://www.theglobeandmail.com/opinion/article-canada-in-2018-is-a-country-of-global-citizens.
30 James C. Hathaway, "Selective Concern: An Overview of Refugee Law in Canada," *McGill Law Journal* 33, no. 4 (1988): 677–9.
31 James C. Hathaway, "A Global Solution to a Global Refugee Crisis," 29 February 2016, https://www.openglobalrights.org/global-solution-to-global-refugee-crisis.
32 Jennifer Hyndman, *Research Summary on Resettled Refugee Integration in Canada* (Geneva: UNHCR, 2011), https://www.unhcr.org/4e4123d19.html; Jennifer Hyndman, William Payne, and Shauna Jimenez, *The State of Private Refugee Sponsorship in Canada: Trends, Issues, and Impacts* (Refugee Research Network / Centre for Refugee Studies Policy Brief, 2017).
33 See European Commission, DG Home and Migration, "Asylum, Migration and Integration Fund (AMIF)," https://ec.europa.eu/home-affairs/financing/fundings/migration-asylum-borders/asylum-migration-integration-fund_en.
34 European Commission, "Study on the Feasibility and Added Value of Sponsorship Schemes as a Possible Pathway to Safe Channels for Admission to the EU, Including Resettlement: Final Report," *DG Migration and Home Affairs, European Commission* (Luxembourg: Publications Office of the European Union, 2018).
35 Shauna Labman, "Private Sponsorship: Complementary or Conflicting Interests?" *Refuge* 32, no. 2 (2016): 67–80; Craig Damian Smith, Lina Alipour, and Tea Hadziristic, "Private Sponsorship Is Not Panacea for Refugee Integration," *Refugee Deeply*, 4 April 2017, https://www.newsdeeply.com/refugees/community/2017/04/04/private-sponsorship-not-panacea-for-refugee-integration-researchers.
36 Alison Strang and Alastair Strang, "Refugee Integration: Emerging Trends and Remaining Agendas," *Journal of Refugee Studies* 23, no. 4 (2010): 589–607; Dina Gericke, Anne Burmeister, Jil Löwe, Jürgen Deller, and Leena Pundt, "How Do Refugees Use their Social Capital for Successful Labour Market Integration? An Exploratory Analysis in Germany," *Journal of Vocational Behaviour* 105 (2018): 46–61.
37 Louise Ryan and Alessio D'Angelo, "Changing Times: Migrants' Social Network Analysis and the Challenges of Longitudinal Research," *Social Networks* 53 (2018): 148–58.

Conclusion:
Sponsorship's Success and Sustainability?

Shauna Labman

The popular image of private refugee sponsorship is the celebratory airport greeting. Anxious sponsors waiting with flags, coats, and signs of welcome. Hesitant, exhausted, excited refugees searching for familiar or welcoming eyes. When the first planeload of Syrian refugees arrived in December 2015 as part of the Canadian government's commitment to resettle 25,000 Syrians through the government-assisted refugee program, the prime minister's presence at the airport turned this government action into one of belonging and connection. As prime minister Justin Trudeau addressed staff and volunteers at Toronto's Pearson International Airport before welcoming the arrivals, he noted: "This is a wonderful night, where we get to show not just a planeload of new Canadians what Canada is all about, we get to show the world how to open our hearts and welcome in people who are fleeing extraordinarily difficult situations."[1]

Yet even while Canada moved forward on its resettlement commitments, it was the parallel program of private refugee sponsorship that drew the attention of the Canadian government and the world. Filipo Grandi, UN High Commissioner for Refugees at the time, declared that "Canada has taken the mantle of humanitarian leadership in the world," while talk grew of sponsorship as a means to "take some of the pressure off European states teeming with asylum-seekers."[2] As discussed in the introduction and explored in Smith's chapter, the Global Refugee Sponsorship Initiative set out to promote Canada's sponsorship program in other states. Within Canada, the government has conveyed its support for and confidence in Canadian private sponsors by reversing traditional resettlement allocations and setting private sponsorship targets at double the government targets. Government resettlement numbers were in the 7,000 range throughout the first decade of the 2000s, with private sponsorship numbers at less than half of that, reaching a high of 42 percent of resettlement in 2011.[3] The projected Immigration Levels Plan for 2019–2021 calls for government resettlement levels between 9,500 and 11,000, and for private sponsorship levels between 17,000 and 23,000.[4] Sponsorship numbers are rising significantly. In Trudeau's words, the Syrian arrival showed both what Canada is about and how Canadians open their hearts. With this volume, our goal has been to understand what this phrasing means as it applies to private refugee sponsorship. Where did the program come from, what is it about, how does it look in practice, and what does it show the world? Is it successful? Is it sustainable? Rather than a single answer, the contributors have provided a broad spectrum of responses and considerations that must be understood together.

Canada's sponsorship model, in operation now for more than forty years, has historically garnered little international attention.[5] This changed quickly as the migration crisis in Europe escalated. In 2017 the Migration Policy Institute released a policy brief titled "Engaging Communities in Refugee Protection: The Potential of Private Sponsorship in Europe." The report noted:

> Since the onset of the migration crisis in 2015, the settlement of refugees through community-based or private sponsorship schemes has attracted increasing attention from governments and civil-society groups across Europe. In addition to helping meet the rising need for resettlement places, such programmes may also mitigate the scepticism about immigration and refugee flows that has emerged in many societies. By involving community members directly in the process of welcoming refugees, sponsorship has the potential to build stronger relationships between refugees and receiving communities and to improve refugee integration outcomes. Sponsorship may also grant communities a sense of ownership over the immigration and humanitarian channels that are shaping their societies. Finally, where sponsored refugees are admitted over and above government resettlement quotas, such schemes can provide an additional pathway to safety for refugees who would otherwise have been excluded from traditional resettlement.[6]

The sponsorship pitch seems golden. Private refugee sponsorship undoubtedly builds community connections between citizens and refugees, engages citizens in refugee advocacy, and creates an atmosphere of welcome for newcomers. Chapters in this volume highlight the energy, commitment, and relationship-building nature of sponsorship, all of which lead to both individual integration success and broader support for refugee protection. However, these relationships are not without frustrations and challenges for both refugees and sponsors, which many of the contributors to this volume are working to outline and understand or remedy. Finally, others in the volume have challenged the framework of private sponsorship itself. What is integral to the program's success? How is success defined? Is it really about refugee protection?

In this final chapter I want to bring these observations together in their connected themes. As I see it, private sponsorship can be understood along four intersecting axes: history and expansion; privatization and peripheral support; relationship-building and integration; and selection and protection. The points of intersection highlight the complicated considerations related to refugee protection. Assessing the expansion of the private sponsorship program both in Canada and beyond requires careful attention to how and why it developed and the points of tension that emerged as it progressed. Intersecting here are questions about the extent to which the program is private, the scope of this privatization beyond the direct act of resettlement, and the peripheral supports from both the government and the wider community that enable the program to succeed and grow. Program success is often tied to the relationship-building between citizens and refugees inherent in the sponsorship design – that is, the human dimension of the social capital and social networks that ease integration; but the reality is that these relationships are sometimes fraught. The final intersecting question asks, who is being selected and protected through the program? At various moments the program has operated as both a protection mechanism in times of crisis and a means to reunify extended families. The program structure allows for this accordion reach, but what is the right balance? Depending on the points of interest, differing understandings of sponsorship result, but policy-makers and academics alike need to be clear on their position and understanding of each axis.

HISTORY AND EXPANSION

Too often, refugee protection is crisis-focused. Claudena Skran has noted that "the notion that the contemporary refugee crisis is unique lacks a historical perspective."[7] The UN High Commissioner for Refugees (UNHCR) has been challenged for "lack[ing] institutional memory."[8] We are in a similar moment in Canada. The selective focus on Syrian resettlement in Canada, which was expanded and celebrated by an incoming government, has had consequences for our understanding of the resulting program. In partnership with Immigration, Refugees, and Citizenship Canada (IRCC), the Social Sciences and Humanities Research Council established a targeted research grant on Syrian Refugee Arrival, Resettlement, and Integration.[9] The chapters by Macklin and colleagues and Kyriakides and colleagues partly grew out of that grant and provide useful insight into the relationships between sponsors and refugees in this particular moment. Similarly, *Refuge: Canada's Refugee Journal* published a special issue on private refugee sponsorship following the Syrian arrivals.[10] In responding to media challenges that comprehensive data on Syrian arrivals are lacking, IRCC's assistant deputy manager for settlement and integration, David Manicom, responded: "We know far, far more about this cohort than any arrival cohort in Canadian history."[11]

To properly understand the Syrian resettlement and the future of Canada's and other states' sponsorship programs, it is important to know the historical origins of Canada's private sponsorship program. In this volume, Cameron traces Canada's program back to negotiations between religious groups and immigration officials after the Second World War as well as the slow policy evolution into law by the late 1970s. As I have argued elsewhere, this development occurred in ways that reflected the geographic reality that Canada did not regard itself as a country of first asylum well into the 1980s[12] – a reality tied to Canada's "cold ocean geography."[13] In *Running on Empty*, a volume resulting from the efforts of the Canadian Immigration Historical Society, Molloy and colleagues note that with the Indochinese, "Canadians took up the challenge and opportunity afforded by the as-yet-untried private sponsorship program."[14] The Indochinese crisis did not launch Canada's sponsorship program; rather, it reconfigured a model born from a different reality. Cameron's chapter outlines the Mennonite Central Committee of Canada's (MCCC) role in both negotiating the regulatory provision and transforming the program through a master agreement. Enns, Gingrich, and Perez carry the MCCC's influence forward in their chapter, exploring how religious heritage was institutionalized in such a way that a synergistic renewal of private sponsorship support was created. Within this development, Lehr and Dyck's chapter sets out the inner challenges faced by private refugee sponsorship as it grew beyond the Indochinese effort. Both the government and sponsors have navigated issues of naming, additionality, family reunification, and refugee protection from the program's beginnings to its current moment. The presumed static structure of the program until the introduction of the Blended Visa Office-Referred (BVOR) program in 2013 belies much movement beneath the surface.[15]

Smith, in his chapter, has outlined some of the challenges facing Canada's export or policy transfer of the sponsorship model from the perspective of Europe, where the reception issues it awakens include the structure of such immigration regimes, political pressure, and public responses to asylum flows. Beyond this I would argue that Canada has lacked a historical understanding of its own program's religious ties and internal debates. Even the formal export announcement was met with skepticism owing to the lack of prior consultation with private sponsors. Citizens for Public Justice (CPJ), a Christian advocacy group, has noted that "Canada's interest in sharing best practices with other countries will be worthwhile only when the resettlement process at home is overhauled to reflect more equity and efficiency."[16] For CPJ, two major concerns were the narrow focus of the Syrian resettlement and the burden of transportation loans, which had been lifted for some Syrian refugees but not for other resettlement refugees. None of the authors in this volume have touched directly on the transportation loans, but it is important to note that resettlement refugees are responsible for repaying the costs of their medical exams prior to departure as well as airfare.[17] In recognition of the immensity of this burden, the loans were relieved for Syrian refugees arriving between 4 November 2015 and 29 February 2016. This was a governmental act of differential treatment that, while welcome, made little sense. Refugee advocates continue to push for the elimination of the loans entirely, but the government position has shifted only incrementally.[18]

While sponsors may be called upon to assist with these additional transportation costs and other expenses (as outlined by Pearlman in her chapter), other scholars have noted the "in-kind government contributions to education, health care, and social assistance during and after year one of the sponsorship"[19] that operate to make private sponsorship so feasible for Canadians. As Cameron's chapter noted, private sponsorship has long been a "reluctant partnership" characterized by negotiation between sponsors and the government over the distribution of financial responsibility for settlement costs. This raises the issues of privatization and peripheral support, which are examined from other perspectives in this volume. Significantly, while much of the concern here relates to the argument that Syrian sponsorship is not representative of *all* sponsorship, it was during the Syrian resettlement that some of the challenges posed by the private model became most apparent.

PRIVATIZATION AND PERIPHERAL SUPPORT

The origins of the sponsorship program and the sheer numbers of refugees it involves show Canada as a leader in refugee resettlement, with individual Canadians contributing much in both funds and energy to complement government resettlement efforts. The original negotiation of private refugee sponsorship was a simple offer to the government – essentially, "let us bring the people we choose to Canada, who we know need protection, and we will pay the costs." As Catherine Dauvergne has noted: "Private sponsorship both allows the government an easy response to domestic pressure to act more humanely and allows it to withdraw from direct responsibility for admission totals."[20] Yet the contributors to this volume point to the demands of private sponsorship beyond direct financial support. Pearlman's chapter shows the wide-reaching potential of the private model to evolve into a "quasi-governmental" structure. Much of this entails an ad hoc privatization of settlement services, which play a gap-filling role.[21] Coffin-Karlin's chapter raises real questions about the need to train and support sponsors, particularly in the context of a new cohort of inexperienced sponsors, as played out with the Syrian sponsorship surge. These new efforts build on more formalized responses to sponsors' needs over two decades. The Refugee Sponsorship Training Program (RSTP) was created in 1998, establishing a support framework for sponsorship, and permanent government funding for it was secured in 2003.[22] Sponsorship groups have formalized their structure over the years; they incorporated into a Sponsorship Agreement Holder (SAH) Association in 2007 with a mandate to promote awareness, develop training, monitor government practices, work with government, and support members.[23] The chapter by Enns, Gingrich, and Perez notes how the Mennonite Central Committee has taken a leadership role with the SAH Council and also works with the UN and with various governments. Pearlman's chapter shows a similar trajectory with Operation Ezra, a newly formed constituency group. The introduction of the BVOR program, as detailed in McNally's chapter, resulted in a matching of support between government and sponsors. The dynamic relationship between private sponsors and government reaches far beyond, and requires much more than, the simple ask to bring more named refugees to Canada.

And that ask is not always successful. The legal chapters by Lange and by Thériault outline the challenges of submitting sponsorship applications and the limited legal options for applicants who are rejected. The extent of privatization is further limited by the fact that the government is the ultimate decision-maker.[24] And even while showing the positive pro bono energy of the Sponsorship Support Program, the undercurrent of the chapter by Lange is that the "legalizing" of applications is done in ways that complicate the program beyond pure volunteerism. Compare this to the simple forms that accompanied the early Indochinese sponsorships.[25] Lange writes that the need for legal support is clear from the very fact of the Refugee Sponsorship Training Program's existence, although Coffin-Karlin's chapter highlights the other, and additional, online mechanisms sponsors use for guidance. Lange's chapter points to further questions: Does legal support encourage the further complicating of forms? Does pro bono assistance draw the lawyers into further refugee-related volunteerism, advocacy, or even their own sponsorships? Conversely, does the need for professional volunteerism by lawyers pull these individuals away from other citizen-directed support or their own sponsorship of refugees? Lange's chapter does not speak directly to Thériault's to address whether the Sponsorship Support Program is reducing rejection rates of sponsorship applications or the need to pursue judicial review. When thinking along the further axis of selection and protection, does this legal framework of access to assistance for some refugees make sense while the majority of refugees wait with no access to resettlement, as Lenard notes, or no access to broader protection as explored in the chapter by by Bradley and Duin?

Overall, privatization of resettlement through private sponsorship fails to encompass the broad reach of peripheral program supports by both government and other organizations; it also fails to acknowledge the wider community reach of many sponsorships. In many respects, private sponsorship is not private at all. It is a responsibility-sharing arrangement between institutions, groups of citizens, and the state.

RELATIONSHIP-BUILDING AND INTEGRATION

Perhaps the concept of community- and relationship-building captures Canadian sponsorship more than the notion of a privatized program. This is reflected in the use of the term "community sponsorship of refugees" by the Global Refugee Sponsorship Initiative.[26] In their chapter, Lehr and Dyck align private sponsorship with models of community sponsorship that are developing in other states. Vogl, Hoang, and Hirsch take a critical look at the newly permanent Community Support Program in Australia and find that it lacks actual community engagement.

Cameron's chapter emphasizes the formative role played by groups institutionally affiliated with religious communities, underscoring that since its inception the sponsorship program has relied upon the mobilization and support of groups with broad bases of community support. The chapters by both McNally and by Pearlman point to energized community efforts that are attentive to integration success, although the success of this integration requires further research. And Kyrakides and colleagues note that refugees, sponsors, and government all have different interpretations of success. In both the chapter by McNally and the one by Macklin and colleagues, the language of family flows into the sponsor-sponsored relationships, with attendant positive and negative associations. Lehr and Dyck discuss how the principle of naming blurs refugee sponsorship into a program of extended family reunification, one of the challenges the BVOR program was intended to address. Vogl and colleagues similarly speak about family tension in Australian resettlement policy.

The attention paid to the Syrian resettlement in Canada is interesting for how it so little resembles the typical sponsorship experience in Canada. This reflects the large number of first-time sponsors and the absence of pre-existing familial, language, and cultural connections that often accompany sponsorship. Macklin and colleagues note that a striking 80 percent of their large survey sample identified as first-time sponsors. Coffin-Karlin's chapter and the one by Lange likewise point to the new cohort of Syrian sponsors.

Personal relationships are at the core of refugee sponsorship. This is evident whether the relationships are pre-existing or newly created. As Pearlman and I have argued elsewhere, in Canada this has led to an echo effect, one that reaches out from all asylum and resettlement routes, including the BVOR program, back to named private sponsorships connected to family reunification.[27] Countering this to some extent, McNally demonstrates the BVOR program's success in rural communities that lack rooted refugees. Her chapter further explores the integration benefit of rural settlement, an observation supported by Kyriakides and colleagues' study of urban/rural differentials, where it was found that rural visibility encouraged efforts to address and diffuse challenging beliefs. From a wider lens, even Bradley and Duin, while questioning the role of sponsorship in the global context of refugee protection, acknowledge that sponsorship plays a significant role in "fostering relatively supportive sentiments towards refugees" and influencing government refugee policy.

The challenges of sponsorship remain, and the centrality of relationships can both foster and endanger sponsorship success. Kyriakides and colleagues point to the risks of unrealistic expectations, mistrust, and uncertainty when there is inadequate pre-arrival contact or a failure to establish "transactions of worth." With regard to the religious connection to sponsorship in the chapters by Enns and colleagues and by Pearlman, it is clear that refugee histories garner sponsorship support; however, Pearlman also acknowledges issues with antisemitism that have caused some refugees to distance themselves from their sponsors. The chapters in this volume also raise real concerns about sponsors' perceptions of the government resettlement program. McNally points to the multiple understandings of the various resettlement programs that result in some sponsors viewing government resettlement as "deplorable and inhumane." Pearlman's chapter similarly examines how Operation Ezra is reaching beyond its own sponsorships to support the wider community of Yazidi GAR arrivals. And as McNally notes, the government's evaluation of the Syrian resettlement in 2016 did conclude that privately sponsored refugees were more likely than GARs to respond that their needs were being met.[28] Tied to the concern noted earlier about increased dependence on private organizations offering gap-filling services, as well as to the sense that sponsorship fosters support for refugees, there is a risk of creating differential public support and treatment between GARs and PSRs. Tied to concerns with selection and protection, too much focus on and support of the PSR program risks diluting the government's prioritization of protection if the family reunification direction of private sponsorship holds strong. With PSR numbers now doubling GAR numbers for the first time, this points to significant change in the overall direction of Canadian resettlement.

The tension between government and private programs may require that the integration benefits of sponsorship be seen through a different lens. As the space for refugee protection and resettlement diminishes in the United States, Harding and Libal show an alternative means of relationship-building: community co-sponsorship of arriving refugees through government programs. In looking at the viability of sponsorship programs in Europe, Smith suggests abandoning the goals of promoting additional pathways for resettlement and shifting the focus onto host integration of arrived refugees. McNally notes the creation of a fund in August 2018 by several philanthropists that rendered BVOR sponsorships free for willing sponsors. The fund was again offered in 2019, highlighting both a different means of program privatization and the unlikelihood of the stand-alone success of the BVOR program.[29] Canadian settlement organizations also operate programs that connect Canadians and newcomers.[30] Returning to the need for historical understanding, during the Indochinese resettlement of the 1970s, hosting of government-assisted refugees was promoted as a "training ground for private sponsorship."[31] These are important reminders that the integration and relationship-building aspects of refugee sponsorship have little connection to the selection and financial support aspects of refugee sponsorship and can be achieved through other programs.

SELECTION AND PROTECTION

Neither the broader offering of resettlement nor private sponsorship will ever be the primary means of refugee protection. The numbers are small and less than 1 percent of refugees benefit from resettlement as a durable solution. The chapters by Lenard, and by Bradley and Duin, raise serious questions about who is included (or excluded) in selection processes. Lenard asks whether it is fair that those with a connection to Canada have greater access to the scarce resource of resettlement spaces through naming by private sponsors. But here we must take into account the perspective of those in Canada, be they citizens or permanent residents, who are seeking both protection and reunification with their families, something Lehr and Dyck point out is an objective of the *Immigration and Refugee Protection Act*.[32] Named refugees may integrate more easily because pre-existing relationships await them in Canada. In the absence of naming, there is the need for new supports, as outlined in the chapters by both Coffin-Karlin and Lange.

Lenard contends that the most vulnerable should be selected, given the limited resettlement places; whereas Bradley and Duin worry that the focus on resettlement neglects other forced migrants, including asylum-seekers, refugees, and internally displaced persons living in the global South. For Lenard, the solution is to restrict naming to within the parameters of UNHCR's resettlement priorities. But such a move would mark a significant diminishment of the scope of Canadian resettlement and might not be viable. The BVOR program seeks to respond to some of the tensions in naming and family reunification and to focus on the selection of UNHCR-referred refugees, but McNally's chapter and the need for the BVOR fund raise concerns about the sustainability of the model.

Lenard further suggests that beyond prioritized need, there should be a system to admit family members of Canadian citizens and permanent residents. Family reunification is permitted as an admission class in Canadian immigration,[33] at levels almost double those of humanitarian and refugee admissions.[34] As Macklin and colleagues outline, the structure of refugee sponsorship parallels that of family class sponsorship. Resettled refugees, both government and privately sponsored, also have access to a "One-Year Window" process for bringing over non-accompanying family members.[35] The definition of family in these processes is narrow. Broader family reunification was previously permitted under the "Assisted Relative Class," which extended reunification to other relatives. The program ended in 2002,[36] and by 2004 the Canadian Council for Refugees had issued a resolution noting that "Cancellation of the Assisted Relative category has greatly increased the pressure on the Private Sponsorship program."[37] One of the current challenges is that private sponsorship is used a tool for family reunification without being set out as such. As I have noted elsewhere, Canada would do well to set out a separate category of extended family class reunification for those in need of protection,[38] but it should also clarify allocations for pure protection cases.

CONCLUSION

Canada's private refuge sponsorship program can be viewed as at an inflection point, although its direction remains somewhat unclear. It has grown into a protection process that is both successful and challenging and that is not always focused on protection. It is now accompanied by many supports it lacked at the outset that may arguably enable, uplift, or hinder. It has shaken things up at home in Canada with increased numbers, increased publicity, a swell of new sponsors, and the introduction of the BVOR stream. And it is trying to situate itself moving forward both at home and abroad with a role in global protection. In 2018, Canada was the leading resettlement country in the world, admitting a total of 28,100 resettled refugees.[39] Unfortunately, this accomplishment speaks more to the diminishment of resettlement places elsewhere than to increases in Canada.[40] And, approximately 2/3 of this resettlement was through private sponsorship.[41]

As Canadian sponsorship numbers soar above those for government resettlement, it is important to pay attention to how much the Canadian program is, in fact, responding to the *need* for protection. This may require more clearly identifying extended family reunification through naming outside of UNHCR referrals. This may require aiming Canadian volunteerism more toward community hosting and supporting successful refugee claimants and government-assisted refugees. Could such efforts garner the same relationship-building benefits that extend to support for refugee policy? Would BVOR and named private sponsorship from within UNHCR's prioritized referrals be a sustainable means of balancing interests? How different would the needs for peripheral supports look with these changes in place? Where are more supports needed to ensure that this one-to-one sponsor/sponsored personal relationship is indeed successful? What sort of greater oversight might be required? Is the gap-filling by strong sponsorship groups hindering the proper acknowledgment of necessary integration support? Much effort has been made to share the Canadian sponsorship model. Rather than replicating, it may be time to reflect and reorient. How can the program sustainably achieve both protection and integration?

NOTES

1 CBC News, "Full Text of Justin Trudeau's Remarks ahead of Refugees' Arrival," *CBC News*, 11 December 2015, https://www.cbc.ca/news/canada/toronto/syrian-refugees-justin-trudeau-remarks-1.3360401.
2 CBC News, "Canada Has Taken the Mantle of Humanitarian Leadership in the World," *CBC News*, 21 March 2016, https://www.cbc.ca/player/play/2685680470.
3 Shauna Labman, "Private Sponsorship: Complementary or Conflicting Interests?," *Refuge: Canada's Journal on Refugees* 32 no. 2 (2016): 71.

Conclusion

4 Immigration, Refugees and Citizenship Canada, "Notice – Supplementary Information 2019–2021 Immigration Levels Plan," 31 October 2018, https://www.canada.ca/en/immigration-refugees-citizenship/news/notices/supplementary-immigration-levels-2019.html.

5 But see Refugee Council of Australia, "Australia's Refugee and Humanitarian Program: Community Views on Current Challenges and Future Directions" (2010), 2010 Intake Submission at 3.

6 Susan Fratzke, *Engaging Communities in Refugee Protection: The Potential of Private Sponsorship in Europe* (Brussels: Migration Policy Institute Europe, 2017).

7 Claudena M. Skran, *Refugees in Inter-War Europe: The Emergence of a Regime* (Oxford: Clarendon Press, 1995), 4.

8 Gil Loescher, *The UNHCR and World Politics: A Perilous Path* (Oxford: Oxford University Press, 2001), 4.

9 Social Sciences and Humanities Research Council (Government of Canada), "Targeted Research: Syrian Refugee Arrival, Resettlement and Integration," 9 October 2018, http://www.sshrc-crsh.gc.ca/funding-financement/programs-programmes/syrian_refugee-refugie_syrien-eng.aspx.

10 "Refugee Sponsorship: Lessons Learned, Ways Forward," *Refuge: Canada's Journal on Refugees* 35, no. 2 (2019).

11 Nadine Yousif, "Settled in a Strange Land: What Life Is Like in Canada for Syrian Refugees," *The Star*, 8 February 2019, https://www.thestar.com/news/canada/2019/02/08/settled-in-a-strange-land-what-life-is-like-in-canada-for-syrian-refugees.html.

12 Shauna Labman, *Crossing Law's Border* (Vancouver: UBC Press, 2019), 39–41.

13 Jennifer Hyndman, William Payne, and Shauna Jimenez, "The State of Private Refugee Sponsorship in Canada: Trends, Issues, and Impacts," *Refugee Research Network* and *Centre for Refugee Studies,* 2 December 2016, https://refugeeresearch.net//wp-content/uploads/2017/02/hyndman_feb%E2%80%9917.pdf.

14 Michael Molloy et al., *Running on Empty: Canada and the Indochinese Refugees, 1975–1980* (Montreal and Kingston: McGill-Queen's University Press, 2017), 13.

15 Labman, "Private Sponsorship."

16 Bolu Coker, "Canada's Refugee Policy Must Be Improved before Export," *Citizens for Public Justice*, 28 September 2016, https://www.cpj.ca/canada-s-refugee-policy-must-be-improved-export.

17 Immigration, Refugees, and Citizenship Canada, "Loans: Procedures – Transportation Loans," 31 March 2016, https://www.canada.ca/en/

immigration-refugees-citizenship/corporate/publications-manuals/operational-bulletins-manuals/service-delivery/immigration-loans-program/procedures-transportation.html.

18 See, for example, Stephanie Levitz, "Loan Program Blamed for Leaving Refugees in Financial Rrouble To Be Reworked," *CTV News*, 2 October 2017, https://www.ctvnews.ca/canada/loan-program-blamed-for-leaving-refugees-in-financial-trouble-to-be-reworked-1.3615275. See also Immigration, Refugees, and Citizenship Canada, "Evaluation of the Immigration Loan Program," September 2015, https://www.canada.ca/en/immigration-refugees-citizenship/corporate/reports-statistics/evaluations/immigration-loan-program.html; Immigration, Refugees, and Citizenship Canada, "Notice – Helping Refugees Succeed – Changes to the Immigration Loans Program Come into Effect," 21 February 2018, https://www.canada.ca/en/immigration-refugees-citizenship/news/notices/changes-immigration-loans-program.html.

19 Hyndman et al., "The State of Private Refugee Sponsorship in Canada."

20 Catherine Dauvergne, Humanitarianism, Identity, and Nation: Migration Laws of Australia and Canada (Vancouver: UBC Press, 2005), 93.

21 Standing Committee on Citizenship and Immigration (House of Commons of Canada), "Road to Recovery: Resettlement Issues of Yazidi Women and Children in Canada" (March 2018), 16, http://www.ourcommons.ca/Content/Committee/421/CIMM/Reports/RP9715738/cimmrp18/cimmrp18-e.pdf.

22 Citizenship and Immigration Canada, "Departmental Performance Report for the Period Ending March 31, 2003" (Ottawa: Minister of Public Works and Government Services, 2003).

23 Canadian Refugee Sponsorship Agreement Holders Association, "History of the Association", n.d., http://www.sahassociation.com/about/history.

24 See also Labman, *Crossing Law's Border*, 60.

25 Molloy et al., *Running on Empty*, 124.

26 Global Refugee Sponsorship Initiative, http://refugeesponsorship.org.

27 Shauna Labman and Madison Pearlman, "Blending, Bargaining, and Burden-Sharing: Canada's Resettlement Programs," *International Migration and Integration* 19 (2018): 446.

28 Immigration, Refugees, and Citizenship Canada, "Rapid Impact Evaluation of the Syrian Refugee Initiative," 21 December 2016, https://www.canada.ca/en/immigration-refugees-citizenship/corporate/reports-statistics/evaluations/rapid-impact-evaluation-syrian-refugee-initiative.html.

29 The Refugee Hub, *BVOR Fund 2019*, refugeehub.ca/program/bvor.

30 See, for example, the Immigrant and Refugee Community Organization of Manitoba's Family-to-Family Program: "Family-to-Family," Immigrant and Refugee Community Organization of Manitoba, n.d., http://www.ircom.ca/programs/volunteer-program/volunteer-opportunities-family-to-family.
31 Deborah Ashford in Molloy et al., *Running on Empty*, 420.
32 *Immigration and Refugee Protection Act*, SC 2001, c 2, s 3(2)(f) [IRPA] ("The objectives of this Act with respect to refugees are [...] to support the self-sufficiency and the social and economic well-being of refugees by facilitating reunification with their family members in Canada").
33 Ibid., s.12(1).
34 Immigration, Refugees, and Citizenship Canada, "2018 Annual Report to Parliament on Immigration," 26 February 2019, https://www.canada.ca/en/immigration-refugees-citizenship/corporate/publications-manuals/annual-report-parliament-immigration-2018/report.html#plan.
35 Canada, SOR/2002–227, s 141–142.
36 The cancellation of the Assisted Relative category occurred through the repeal of the *Immigration Regulations, 1978*, SOR/78-172, by the *Immigration and Refugee Protection Regulations*, SOR/2002–227, s 364(a), which accompanied the introduction of the new *Immigration and Refugee Protection Act*, *supra* note 32.
37 "Assisted Relatives" (Resolution), *Canadian Council for Refugees*, November 2004, https://ccrweb.ca/en/res/assisted-relatives.
38 Labman, Crossing Law's Border, 165–6.
39 UNHCR, *Global Trends: Forced Displacement in 2018*, (19 June 2019), 32, https://www.unhcr.org/statistics/unhcrstats/5do8d7ee7/unhcr-global-trends-2018.html.
40 Jynnah Radford and Phillip Connon, "Canada Now Leads the World in Refugee Resettlement, Surpassing the U.S." Pew Research Centre (19 June 2019).
41 Immigration, Refugees, and Citizenship Canada, "Notice – Supplementary Information 2018-2020 Immigration Levels Plans," 1 November 2017, https://www.canada.ca/en/immigration-refugees-citizenship/news/notices/supplementary-immigration-levels-2018.html.

Contributors

KAREN ANDERSON is associate professor of sociology, Department of Sociology, York University. Anderson is author of *Thinking about Sociology* (OUP, 2016).

LUBNA BAJJALI is a research fellow with the Department of Sociology, York University. Bajjali has over twenty years of experience as a practitioner and researcher in human rights and conflict in the Middle East, Europe, and North America and is currently training in social work in Toronto.

KATHRYN BARBER is a PhD candidate (ABD) at the sociology department of York University and managing editor of *Refuge: Canada's Journal on Refugees*. Her recent publications have appeared in the *Journal of Urban Technology* and *Canadian Ethnic Studies*.

MEGAN BRADLEY is associate professor of political science and international development studies at McGill University. She is the author of *Refugee Repatriation: Justice, Responsibility and Redress* (Cambridge University Press), editor of *Forced Migration, Reconciliation and Justice* (McGill-Queen's University Press), and co-editor of *Refugees' Roles in Resolving Displacement and Building Peace: Beyond Beneficiaries* (Georgetown University Press).

GEOFFREY CAMERON is a research associate with the Global Migration Lab, Munk School of Global Affairs and Public Policy, University of Toronto. He teaches at McMaster University. His forthcoming monograph is *Send Them Here: Religion, Politics, and Refugee Resettlement* (McGill-Queen's University Press).

ELIZABETH COFFIN-KARLIN is a JD/master in public policy candidate at Harvard Law School and the Harvard Kennedy School of Government. Elizabeth focuses her research on comparative cross-border migration structures and practices, human rights, and practical solutions for complex international problems. She was an Open Society Foundation fellow in Rights and Governance, a Cravath International Fellow and has worked with the Harvard Immigration and Refugee Clinic.

CATE DUIN graduated with a master's degree in political science from McGill University. Her research focuses on refugee resettlement and local responses to it. Prior to beginning her degree at McGill, Cate worked as the community engagement lead for the Minnesota affiliate of Lutheran Immigration and Refugee Service (LIRS).

BRIAN DYCK is the National Migration and Resettlement Program Coordinator for Mennonite Central Committee.

THEA ENNS works in the area of refugee resettlement in Canada. She holds an MSc in migration studies from the University of Oxford and has worked on various research papers focusing on the private sponsorship of refugees program.

LUIN GOLDRING is professor of sociology at York University. Her current research examines non-citizenship, precarious legal status pathways, and precarious work. She is co-editor (with Patricia Landolt) of *Producing and Negotiating Non-citizenship: Precarious Legal Status in Canada*.

LUANN GOOD GINGRICH is director of the Global Labour Research Centre and associate professor in the School of Social Work at York University. She is the author of *Out of Place: Social Exclusion and Mennonite Migrants in Canada* (2016), and co-editor (with Stefan Köngeter) of *Transnational Social Policy: Social Welfare in a World on the Move* (2017), as well as numerous journal articles and book chapters on social exclusion/inclusion, migration, and border studies.

Contributors

SCOTT HARDING is associate professor of social work and director of the Doctoral Program at the University of Connecticut. He has co-authored *Counter Recruitment and the Campaign to Demilitarize Schools* (Palgrave) and *Human Rights-Based Community Practice in the United States* (Springer).

ASHER HIRSCH is a senior policy officer with the Refugee Council of Australia and a PhD candidate at Monash University in refugee and human rights law.

KHANH HOANG is a PhD candidate and affiliate of the Andrew and Renata Kaldor Centre for International Refugee Law at the University of New South Wales. His research focuses on community sponsorship and Australian migration law and policy in Australia.

JENNIFER HYNDMAN is professor and resident scholar at the Centre for Refugee Studies at York University in Toronto. Her research focuses on the geopolitics of forced migration, the biopolitics of humanitarian responses to displacement, and refugee resettlement in North America. Her most recent book is *Refugees in Extended Exile: Living on the Edge*, with Wenona Giles (Routledge, 2017).

ANNA KORTEWEG is professor and chair of sociology at the University of Toronto Mississauga. She has published *The Headscarf Debates: Conflicts of National Belonging* (Stanford University Press, 2014, with Gökçe Yurdakul) and *Debating Sharia: Islam, Gender Politics, and Family Law Arbitration* (edited with Jennifer Selby, University of Toronto Press, 2012), as well as numerous articles in a wide range of journals.

CHRISTOPHER KYRIAKIDES holds the Canada Research Chair in Citizenship, Social Justice and Ethno-racialization with the Department of Sociology at York University.

SHAUNA LABMAN is associate professor of human rights at the Global College, University of Winnipeg. She writes extensively on the relationship between resettlement and asylum and is the author of *Crossing Law's Border: Canada's Refugee Resettlement Program* (UBC Press, 2019).

KELSEY LANGE worked as the senior legal officer for the Refugee Sponsorship Support Program, a program of the University of Ottawa's Refugee Hub, from 2017 to 2019. Prior to this, Kelsey worked as an immigration and refugee lawyer at Mamann, Sandaluk & Kingwell LLP in Toronto, Ontario.

SABINE LEHR is Private Sponsorship of Refugees Manager at the Inter-Cultural Association of Greater Victoria and associate faculty at Royal Roads University, Victoria, where she teaches in the Global Leadership Program. She has published in *Refugee Review* and *Canadian Ethnic Studies*.

PATTI TAMARA LENARD is associate professor of ethics in the Graduate School of Public and International Affairs, University of Ottawa. She is the author of *Trust, Democracy and Multicultural Challenges* (Penn State, 2012) and *How Should Democracies Fight Terrorism?* (forthcoming with Polity Press in 2020).

KATHRYN LIBAL is associate professor of social work and human rights and director of the Human Rights Institute at the University of Connecticut. Her publications include co-edited volumes *Human Rights in the United States: Beyond Exceptionalism* (Cambridge) and *Refugees and Asylum Seekers: Interdisciplinary and Comparative Perspectives* (ABC-Clio). She co-authored *Human Rights-Based Community Practice in the United States* (Springer).

AUDREY MACKLIN is professor of law, chair in human rights, and director of the Centre for Criminology and Sociolegal Studies. She teaches and researches in the field of migration, refugee, and citizenship law. She is a CIFAR Fellow and a Trudeau Fellow, and thanks the Trudeau Foundation for supporting this research.

ARTHUR MCLUHAN is a research fellow in the Department of Sociology at York University. His articles on forced migration may be found in *Canadian Ethnic Studies, Refuge,* and *Social Forces*.

RACHEL MCNALLY is studying toward her master's in political science at Carleton University. She researches refugee resettlement policy in Canada.

MADISON PEARLMAN is a lawyer in Ontario and holds a master's in refugee and forced migration studies from the University of Oxford. Madison's research has focused primarily on the integration of children's rights in Canada's Refugee Status Determination procedures, access to justice for newcomers, and the relationship between civil society and refugee resettlement in Canada.

KAYLEE PEREZ is the Refugee Sponsorship and Settlement Associate at Mennonite Central Committee Ontario, and Vice Chair of the National Sponsorship Agreement Holders Council. She has an MA in peace and conflict studies and has worked extensively in the refugee settlement support field.

CRAIG DAMIAN SMITH is a senior research associate at the Canada Excellence Research Chair in Migration and Integration at Ryerson University. He researches the international politics of migration, irregular migration systems, and refugee integration. He is the Principal Investigator of Pairity (www.pairity.ca) – a project to measure the effects of social networks on integration and social cohesion.

PIERRE-ANDRÉ THÉRIAULT is a PhD candidate in law at Osgoode Hall Law School of York University. He practices refugee law and is a co-editor of *Refuge: Canada's Journal on Refugees.*

ANTHEA VOGL is a lecturer in law at the University of Technology, Sydney. Her research addresses refugee and migration law, with a focus on the use of administrative powers to regulate refugees and non-citizens.

JONA ZYFI is a PhD student at the Centre for Criminology & Sociolegal Studies and a junior fellow at Massey College at the University of Toronto. Her research focuses on artificial intelligence and biometrics in relation to migration and refugee processes.

Index

Numbers in italics denote figures and tables

access to justice, 212, 217, 223, 228, 240
additionality: principle of, 51–2, 78, 123, 125, 136, 248, 265, 278, 279n5
Afghan Ismaili refugees, 52, 135
Allen, Clare, 165
Allende, Salvador, 30
Aoki, Eric, 154–6
Approved Church Program, 25, 28–30, 33, 37n28, 46
asylum-seekers: access to legal aid, 241–2n5; Canada's responses to, 75, 82; in European Union, 287, 293–4; obligation of states toward, 67, 88
Australia: approved proposing organisations (APOs), 272; Community Refugee Resettlement Committee, 268, 281n26; community sponsorship, 272–3, 276, 283n50; family reunion pathways in, 276–7; humanitarian visas, 264, 284n61; Indochinese refugees, 266–7; migrant centres, 267; National Population Committee (NPC), 271; private sponsorship programs, 82, 265–6, 272–5; Refugee and Humanitarian Program (RHP), 275; refugee policies, 265, 267, 276–7, 279n14, 310; refugee resettlement statistics, 267; Special Humanitarian Program (SHP), 269, 281n33
Australian Refugee Advisory Council, 268, 280n20
Australia's Community Pilot Program (CPP), 264, 272–3, 279n7
Australia's Community Refugee Settlement Scheme (CRSS): administration of, 268; categories of refugees eligible to, 269; community participation, 271–2; debates about efficiency of, 270–1; difference between the CSP and, 275; duration of, 265; family reunification under, 269–71; government

grants, 268–9; introduction of, 268; mission of, 268, 280n22; named cases problem, 269–71, 278; perception of, 270; sponsor participation in, 268, 282n38
Australia's Community Support Program (CSP), 310; community participation, 265–6, 275–8; comparison to Canadian program, 275; cost of, 278; criticism of, 275; difference between the CRSS and, 275; family reunification under, 276; introduction of, 264, 273–4; language skills requirements, 274–5; legal framework, 273; market-driven nature of, 276–7; principles of, 265; priority applicants, 274–5, 284n59; problem of named refugees, 278; quota of places under, 273, 275; sponsors' expenses, 276; visa fees, 276
Aziza, Michel, 113

Bibeau, Marie-Claude, 85, 91n27
Bier, David, 251
Blake, Louise, 91n27
Blanchard, Marc-André, 91n27
Blended Visa Office-Referred (BVOR) program: benefits of, 137–8, 142, 312; challenges of, 142–3, 146; community role in, 141–2; criticism of, 135, 139–40; evaluation of, 145; funding of, 145–6, 312; geographic distribution of, 134, 137; goals of, 136; government role in, 8, 143–4; groups of refugees covered by, 135–7; history of, 135–7; introduction of, 8, 83, 307; MCC involvement in, 99; participation rate in, 144; post-sponsorship relationship, 139, 142–3; promotion of, 145; as public–private partnership, 141; recommended destination, 144–5; refugee admission targets, 58n31, 143–4; resettlement streams, 135–6; in rural communities, 137–8, 146–7, 311; sponsor participation in, 142–5, 309; sponsor–refugee relationships, 142–3; sustainability problem, 147; UNHCR-referred refugees and, 134, 136; unused resettlement spaces, 144, 146, 150n50
Blume, Claudia, 159
B'nai Brith human rights group, 31–2
Bonser, Michael, 91n27
Boucher, Catherine, 91n27
Bozdag, Cigdem, 163
Bradley, Megan, 136, 298, 309, 311–13
"burden-sharing" regimes, 63

Cambodian refugees, 251
Cameron, Geoffrey, 143, 188, 196n15, 293, 306–7, 310
Canada: acceptance of immigrants, 51; anti-Muslim sentiments, 165; Immigration Levels Plan, 51, 58n31, 304; World Refugee Year in, 28
Canada–US Safe Third Country Agreement, 82, 157
Canada (Prime Minister) v Kadr, 238
Canadian Association of Refugee Lawyers (CARL), 216

Index

Canadian Baptists of Atlantic Canada, 136
Canadian Bar Association (CBA), 216
Canadian Charter of Rights and Freedoms, 237–8
Canadian Christian Council for the Resettlement of Refugees (CCCRR), 22, 23
Canadian Conference of Mennonite Brethren Churches, 98
Canadian Council for Refugees, 50, 136, 144–5, 230, 313
Canadian Council of Churches (CCC), 22–5, 23, 28–9
Canadian immigration policy: Cold War politics and, 30; decision-making process, 34; evolution of, 26–31, 40n71; Green Paper on, 30
Canadian International Development Agency (CIDA), 98
Canadian Jewish Congress (CJC), 20, 22, 23, 24, 30
Canadian Lutheran World Relief (CLWR), 22, 23
Canadian Mennonite Board of Colonization (CMBC), 22, 23, 109n1
Canadian National Committee on Refugees (CNCR), 23
Canadian Rainbow Refugee Assistance Program, 52
Casasola, Michael, 44
Castello, Dario, 271
Catholic Church's Migration Commission, 7, 32
Catholic Immigration Aid Society, 22, 23
Cato Institute, 252

Chilean refugees, 30–2
Chouliaraki, Lilie, 160–1
church sponsorship program, 22, 24–5, 28
Church World Service, 251
Citizens for Public Justice (CPJ), 307
Citizenship and Immigration Canada (CIC), 48–9
Clark, Joe, 32
Coffin-Karlin, Elizabeth, 308–10, 312
Colombian refugees, 103
community sponsorship: benefits of, 141–2, 310; call for privatization of, 141–2; cross-country comparison of, 310; definition of, 9; humanitarian, 265; judicial system and, 236; religious communities and, 310
Comprehensive Refugee Response Framework (CRRF), 77–8, 289
Connecticut: rallies against travel ban, 253; refugee sponsorship in, 248, 252–4, 257–8
constituent groups (CGs), 7, 9, 96, 99, 108, 214
Convention refugees, 9
Crease v Canada, 238–9
Cuban refugees, 251–2, 261n24
Czech refugees, 30–1
Czech Republic: refugee settlement schemes, 295

Dauvergne, Catherine, 308
Deferred Action for Childhood Admission Program (DACA), 250
Department of Citizenship and Immigration: development of

private sponsorship program, 32; planning for refugee resettlement, 34, 40n71; religious groups and, 25, 27–9
diffusion theory, 290
Dion, Stéphane, 91n27
Dirks, Gerald E., 27
D'Orazio, Francesco, 154
Duin, Cate, 136, 298, 309, 311–13
Durham, Meenakshi Gigi, 161
duties: humanitarian *vs.* justice, 66–7
Dyck, Brian, 97, 106, 110n21, 111n22, 142, 145, 155, 307, 310, 312

Eby, Jessica, 252
Employment and Immigration Canada (EIC), 47
Enns, Thea, 97, 306, 308, 311
Epp-Tiessen, Esther, 104, 109n1
Eritrean refugees, 159
European Union: asylum-seekers, 287, 293–4; Canadian sponsorship model and, 291, 294–7; community sponsorships, 295; cultural integration policies, 294; enlargement of, 292; humanitarian corridors, 295; integration programming, 297–8, 312; migration crisis, 287, 296, 304; refugee quota system, 293, 298; refugee resettlement schemes, 294–6; response to global refugee crisis, 293–4; sponsorship schemes, 55, 296–8, 312; supply-side policy transfer, 292
Evangelical Missionary Church of Canada, 97

Fairclough, Ellen, 28
family: in faith communities, 195n8; institution of, 183–4; as metaphor, 183
family class sponsorship: financial obligations, 188; liability, 188–9; privatization of, 190; *vs.* refugee sponsorship, 188–90, *189*, 196n15
family reunification, 56, 188, 313
far-right nationalism: rise of, 3
Fassin, Didier, 194
Federal Court: judicial review of rejected refugee applications, 237; recommendations on changes at, 240–1
Federal Court of Appeal, 238–9
First Mennonite Church in Vineland, 102, 105
Fraser, Malcolm, 266–7
Fratzke, Susan, 51
Freeland, Chrystia, 91n27
Friesen, Chris, 157

George, Chris, 253
German Baptist Immigration and Colonization Society, 23
German Baptist Union, 22
Gibney, Matthew, 67
Gingrich, Luann Good, 306, 308
Giustra Foundation, 145
Global Compact on Refugees (GCR), 77, 274, 288–90, 295
global North, 76–7, 82, 87, 88n1
global refugee crisis, 28, 83–4, 86, 153
Global Refugee Forums, 289
Global Refugee Sponsorship Initiative (GRSI): challenges of, 292–3; as community-based

model, 310; goals of, 286, 293, 296, 303; introduction of, 4, 287; MCC input into, 111n22; promotion of Canadian sponsorship model through, 43, 78, 286–92, 296, 298–9; public events hosted by, 291
Good Gingrich, Luann, 97
Government Assisted Refugee (GAR) program: approval rates, 242n12; economic performance, 54; family reunification aspect of, 49, 56; naming principle and, 55–6; refugee protection aspect of, 56; sustainability of, 55
government-assisted refugees (GARs): criteria of, 134; judicial review of applications, 236; vs. private sponsored refugees, 140–1; resettlement plans, 8; statistics of, 14n27; support for, 140–1
Grandi, Filipo, 303
Grant, Michael, 91n27
Greece, refugee policy, 295
Greenhill, Kelly M., 250
Groups of Five (G5), 9, 214, 221, 236

Hacker, Jacob S., 25
Haines, David W., 249
Harding, Scott, 312
Hayes, Saul, 24
Hebrew Immigrant Aid Society (HIAS), 251
Herzer, T.O.F., 22
Hirsch, Asher, 310
Hoang, Khanh, 310
Howe, C.D., 21
humanitarian duties, 66–7
humanitarianism: principle of, 67

humanitarian organizations, 6, 26
humanitarian sponsorship, 265
Human Rights First, 252
Hungarian refugees, 26–8, 38n32
Hussen, Ahmed, 86, 91n27, 287
Hyndman, Jennifer, 193, 297

Immigration, Refugees and Citizenship Canada (IRCC), 49, 145, 188, 222–3, 229–31
Immigration Act (1976): introduction of, 19, 31, 42, 46, 213; private sponsorship provision in, 6–7, 20, 31, 33–5
Immigration and Refugee Board (IRB), 229
Immigration and Refugee Protection Act (2001): amendments to, 213–14; codification of refugee classes, 45; introduction of, 48, 213; objectives of, 50, 312; references to refugee resettlement, 237
Immigration and Refugee Protection Regulations, 9
Indochinese refugees: Australian aid to, 266–7; resettlement of, 7, 32–3, 120, 312; sponsorship program for, 7, 40n71, 104, 138–9, 306
infantilization of non-white people, 160–1
Integrated Refugee and Immigrant Services (IRIS), 252–5
internally displaced persons (IDPs), 74
International Catholic Migration Commission Europe, 55
International Committee for European Migration (ICEM), 27

International Organization for Migration, 55
International Refugee Assistance Project, 252
International Refugee Organization (IRO), 5, 21, 24
international refugee regime, 75, 79, 81, 86–8, 88n2
Iranian refugees, 252
Iraqi refugees, 135, 214, 216
Italy: resettlement schemes, 295; sponsor referral of refugees, 56
Iverson, Erika, 252

Jallow v Canada, 239
Janzen, William, 31, 95, 99, 104
Jewish Child and Family Services (JCFS), 114
Jewish Family Services Ottawa, 145
Jewish Immigrant Aid Services of Canada, 31
Jewish Immigrant Aid Society (JIAS), 7, 23
Jewish Joint Distribution Committee (JDC), 24
Jewish refugees: obstacle with obtaining visas, 24; private sponsorship of, 20, 31–2, 130n24, 252
Joint Assistance Sponsorship (JAS), 128
Jordan, Grant, 26
judicial review: analysis of, 231–2; decision on the merits, 231; definition of, 227–8; before the Federal Court, 237; as individual redress, 235–6; of inland refugee, 237; leave test, 231; legal barriers to, 239; limitations of, 228, 235; outcomes of, 234; overview of applications, 233; statistics of, 232–5; structural role of, 236–9

Kekic, Erol, 252
Kharay, Suneet, 219
Kumin, Judith, 54–5
Kurdi, Alan: photograph of lifeless body of, 80, 152–3, 164, 255, 288; public reaction to death of, 155
Kyriakides, Christopher, 179, 193, 306, 311

Labman, Shauna, 20, 52–3, 56, 142, 289
La Corte, Matthew, 251
Lange, Kelsey, 309, 312
Laotian refugees, 251
Lehr, Sabine, 142, 145, 307, 310, 312
Lenard, Patti Tamara, 136, 309, 312–13
LGBTQ+ refugees, 135
Libal, Kathryn, 312
low-income cut-off (LICO), 188, 196n17

MacDonald, Flora, 32
MacKellar, Michael, 267
Macklin, Audrey, 140, 239, 306, 310, 313
Madokoro, Laura, 34
Manicom, David, 306
Manion, Jack, 31
Master Agreements, 7, 33, 40n68, 46, 95, 99
McCallum, John, 4, 91n27, 287
McLaughlin, Carly, 161
McNally, Rachel, 309–13
Mennonite Central Committee of Canada (MCC Canada): access to

government funding, 98; foundation of, 95, 109n1; interaction between affiliated churches, 99–101; international cooperation, 98, 102–3, 111n22; leadership in SAH Council, 98–9, 108, 110n21, 308; Master Agreements with, 7, 46, 95, 99; motto of, 105; refugee sponsorship programs, 10, 33, 95–9, 107–8, 306; reputation of, 96, 100–1; self-definition of, 98; "Source Country Class" program, 103; study of, 96–7

Mennonite Central Committee of Ontario (MCC Ontario), 96–7, 103, 111n36

Mennonite refugees, 95–7, 109n1

Mennonites: congregations, 96–8, 102, 108; ethnic background, 97, 104; identity formation, 105, 107; organizations, 109n1; refugee sponsorship, 104–8; theology of, 105–8

Migration Policy Institute: "Engaging Communities in Refugee Protection" report, 304; study of private sponsorship, 298

Miller, Stephen, 250

Mohammad, Rahaf, 152

Molloy, Michael J., 34, 306

Murad, Nadia, 113, 118

Nafziger, Gloria, 110n21

Nagy, Imre, 27

named sponsorships: Australian and Canadian practice of, 278; definition of, 44; family linked, 48; interest of religious groups in, 46; proposal to cease, 270; restrictive caps, 136; statistics of, 47

naming principle: characteristics of, 42; citizens' engagement in, 43; criticism of, 43, 47; cross-country comparison, 42; equity and fairness issue, 52; evaluation of, 61; family reunion and, 54; financial considerations, 44; government's reliance on, 47–8, 53–4; history of, 46–9; intended and unintended consequences of, 49–52; legal framework of, 44, 46; motivations for, 49–50; practical perspective on, 44, 53; sponsors' interest in, 47–8

Naso, Nafiya, 113–15, 120

Neville, Anita, 113

New York Declaration for Refugees and Migrants, 77, 274, 286, 288

New York State, refugee sponsorship in, 257

Niskanen Center, 252

Nova Scotia, refugee sponsorship initiatives, 138–41

O'Connor, Brendan, 264

Operation Ezra: advocacy work, 125; bottom-up model of, 120; challenges of, 115, 118; community engagement, 118, 120–1; criticism of, 115, 127; effects of, 112; establishment of, 113–14; expansion of, 124–5, 128–9; family reunification sponsorship, 115, 119–20; formal committees of, 116; fundraising, 114, 119, 122, 126; government partnership with, 123–4, 126–7; grassroots mobilization, 120;

interviews with members of, 113–14; lobbying activities, 124–5, 132n45; mission of, 114, 118, 311; multifaith solidarity, 118; naming of refugees, 116, 119; partners of, 114–16, 130n23; proposal of public-private partnership, 125–6; resettlement work, 114, 119–20, 123, 125; services to refugees, 121–2, 128; sponsorship initiatives, 114–18, 309; structure of, 117; sustainability of, 117; testimonies before parliamentary committees of members of, 125, 132n44
Oraha v Canada, 238–9
Ott, Brian, 154–6
Ottawa Centre Refugee Action, 131n29
Ottawa Mennonite Church, 101–2

Palestinian refugees, 103
Pearlman, Madison, 142, 289, 308, 310–11
Pence, Mike, 250
Perez, Kaylee, 111n36, 306, 308
Perry, Barbara, 165
Pierson, Paul, 20, 25
Poland: resettlement schemes, 295
policy diffusion, 290
policy transfer, 290–2
Portugal: community sponsorship, 295
private refugee sponsorship: academic discourse around, 4–5; application process, 7–8, 10, 212–15, 220–1, 309; benefits of, 70–1; "bulk labour" movement, 21; case studies, 10; challenges of, 19, 305–7, 311; "close relatives" scheme, 21–2, 25; in comparative perspective, 11, 296–9; cost of, 9; criticism of, 28; decline of, 46–7; definition of, 4; distribution of financial responsibility, 19, 307–8; expansion of, 305–8; funding of, 28, 124; governmental discourse on, 83–7; history of, 4, 19–35, 305–8; integration and, 297, 310–12; legislative basis for, 6–7, 19–20, 34–5, 46; naming principle, 7, 42, 52, 310; for non-family members, 71; origins of, 20, 306; peripheral support of, 308–9; personal relationships in, 177, 310–11; privatization of resettlement through, 308–9; promotion of, 78, 87–8; public debates on, 3, 153; relationship-building and, 304–5, 310–12; religious groups and, 20, 24–5, 30–1, 34–5; risks of, 82; selection criteria, 19, 22–3; sponsoring groups, 4, 7, 9, 22–5, 31–2; statistics of, 12n5, 46; study of, 4–5, 306; as tool for family reunification, 7; training for, 312
private sponsor groups (PSG), 198–9, 204, 207–8
private sponsors: duties of, 4, 67; financial donations to, 205; government agreements with, 7; legal support to, 10, 236; motivations of, 80–1; opposition to, 205–6, 209; refugee naming, 4, 64, 66; visibility of, 204–6
Private Sponsorship of Refugees (PSR) program: application process, 213, 222; approval rates,

213–14; criticism of, 61; development of, 153, 223, 313–14; economic performance of, 54; efforts to export, 75, 82; establishment of, 95; evaluation of, 48–9, 54, 221; as example for other countries, 54–5, 77–8; family reunification and, 49, 54–6; government reliance on, 53; humanitarian aspect of, 222; limitations of, 74; naming principle and, 42–3, 55–6, 61; origin of, 46; popular support of, 74; private sponsors of, 53; promotion of, 71, 208; recommendations on, 49; refugee protection aspect of, 56; resettlement of refugees through, 8, 51–2, 78–80; risks associated with expansion of, 87–8; selection of refugees, 62; Southeast Asian crisis and, 44–5; sponsor-referred cases, 44; statistics of refugees, 14n27; sustainability of, 55; Syrian Refugee Initiative and, 140–1; UNHCR's Agenda for Protection and, 54; visa office-referred cases, 44, 49
pro bono organizations, 217–18
Project FOCUS Afghanistan, 8
public guilt, 155
public sector agencies (PSA), 198

Qarizada v Canada, 238
quasi-governmental entity, 126
Quora forum, 163

Rawls, John, 66
Reddit forum, 163, 164, 166
Refuge: Canada's Refugee Journal, 306

Refugee Appeal Division (RAD), 229
Refugee Convention (1951), 5–6, 48, 88n2, 251, 297
refugee–host relationships. *See* sponsor–refugee relationship
refugee resettlement: accessibility of, 76; in comparative perspective, 34–5, 62–4; cost of, 77, 307–8; critique of, 76–7, 79; definition of, 5–6, 76, 80; fairness in, 64–6, 69; family reunification and, 70–1; funding of, 8, 77; global proliferation of, 289; goals of, 76, 182; government policies on, 8–9, 82, 84–5; historical evolution of the idea of, 5; identity politics and, 87; in international context, 74–5, 87–8; legal framework, 227, 237–40; migration management function of, 76; named *vs.* state-sponsored, 51–2; "One-Year Window" process, 313; as pathway of refugee admission, 5; political and social impact of, 3; popularity of, 76; prioritization in, 86; privatized model of, 78–9; refugee perception of, 199; rejection of applications for, 227–8; responsibilities to other forced migrants and, 81–2; risks of, 10, 75, 78–9, 83, 90n26; spaces for, 72n10, 131n25; statistics of, 4–5, 23, 314; for temporary stays, 72n3; unintended consequences of, 10; urban *vs.* rural, 137–8, 311; vulnerability principle in, 65, 71
refugee resettlement in the United States: community support of,

253–9; co-sponsorship model of, 253–4, 257–9; faith groups and, 257–8; government agencies and, 253, 259; statistics of, 254; volunteer groups and, 253–7

refugees: admission quotas, 20–1, 34, 40n71, 222, 298; application process, 66, 227, 243n27; Assisted Relative Class, 313; community support of, 51; Convention Refugees Abroad Class, 9; Country of Asylum Class, 9, 45, 90n26, 237, 240; distribution of resources for, 28, 64–6; eligibility criteria, 240; in Europe, 20, 51; family reunification, 312–13; financial assistance to, 128, 133n57; from the former Yugoslavia, 135; global distribution of, 288–9; *vs.* immigrants, 25; inadmissibility requirements, 240; integration outcomes, 6, 54; language training, 193; legal aid to, 229; naming principle, 10, 313; oppositional discourses towards, 204–5; in postwar period, 20–1; primary destinations for, 6; protection of, 48–9, 237; public perception of, 160, 311; right to financial independence, 197n27; selection process of, 10, 52, 64, 67–8, 312–13; statistics of, 62; status determination of, 230; survey of, 49; ties with sponsors, 139; UNHCR-referred, 136, 313; voluntary repatriation of, 6

Refugee Sponsorship Support Program (SSP), 236; challenges of, 223; clients of, 216; criticism of, 219–20; development of, 212, 215–16, 308; legal services provided by, 216–17, 309; limitations of, 221; mission of, 217; number of processed applications, 222; online resources, 218; partnership with RSTP, 216, 218; pro bono work, 217–18; reliance on volunteers, 219–20; support to sponsors, 218–19

Refugee Sponsorship Training Program (RSTP): creation of, 212, 214, 308; efficiency of, 61; mission of, 140, 214; partnership with SSP, 216, 218; services provided by, 215

Refugee Studies, 200

Rehaag, Sean, 234

religious groups: denominations and activities of, 23; as humanitarian actors, 26; informal networks, 26–7; Master Agreements with, 33–4, 40n68; refugee sponsorship, 20, 22–5, 29–32, 34–5, 117; relationship with immigration officials, 25–31, 35

Rempel, Michelle, 124

resettlement applications: appeals on rejected, 229, 231; approval rates, 228–30, 230; decision-making procedure, 228–9, 240–1; GAR and PSR streams of, 229; leave grant rates for, 235; *mandamus* applications, 232; outcomes of, 232–3

Resettlement Operations Centre, 214

resettlement programs: establishment of, 6; evaluation of, 50, 54, 61

Ridgeway, Cecelia, 200
Ripple Refugee Project, 153, 158–61, 166
Rohingya refugees, 86, 278
rule of law, 239–40
Running on Empty (Molloy), 306
rural communities: private sponsorship in, 207; reception of refugees in, 206–7
Rural Settlement Society, 23
R v Hape, 238

Sajjran, Harji, 91n27
settlement workers, *vs.* private sponsors, 184
Shapiro Foundation, 145
Shen, Marisa, 165
Sierra Leonean refugees, 52, 135
Singh v Canada, 237–9
Skran, Claudena, 305
Slahi v Canada, 238
Slovakia: refugee resettlement schemes, 295
Slovic, Paul, 156
Smets, Kevin, 163
Smith, Craig Damian, 56, 303, 307, 312
Smyers, Jenifer, 252
social media: comments about refugees on, 152–3, 160–1, 163–5; government reaction to posts on, 156–7; photograph of Alan Kurdi's corpse on, 152; tragic framing on, 154–5; trolls' activities, 164–5
Solaylee, Kamal Al-, 162–3
Source Country Class program, 9, 45
Southeast Asian crisis (1979–80), 44–6

sponsor–refugee relationship: affective bonds in, 185–6; familial tropes in, 139–40, 183–4, 187–8, 310; financial control and, 197n24; kinship analogy of, 177–8, 183, 186–7, 193; language training and, 193; orientalist tone of, 182–3; parentalism in, 182, 193–4; positive aspects of, 181–2; power imbalance in, 180, 191–4, 197n24, 197n27; pre-arrival interactions, 202–3; respect for autonomy in, 182–3, 190–2, 197n27; social media and, 185; sponsors' role in, 179–84, 186, 191; survey of, 195n2; temporal nature of, 190, 192–3; tensions in, 190–1; transactions of worth, 199–201, 203, 206, 208–9
sponsors: charitable actions of, 68–70; duties of justice of, 66–9; legal support for, 218–19, 309; lobby of private sponsorship, 52; matching process for, 138; moral impact of work of, 70; motivations of, 179–80; obligations of, 196n21, 197n24; *vs.* parents, 187; participation in the BVOR program, 142–5; power of select refugees, 44; reflections on sponsorship experience, 180–2, 184–5; refugee advocacy, 56–7; resettlement tasks of, 68; rural, 191; *vs.* settlement workers, 184; survey of, 68–9; training for, 140; view of the GAR program, 140
sponsorship: challenges of, 10, 309; comparison to parenting, 187–8;

family class *vs.* refugee, 188–90, *189*, 196n15; goal of, 182, 190; institutional structure of, 182, 188–90; parentalist foundation of, 182–3; private *vs.* government, 309
Sponsorship Agreement Holder (SAH), 7, 9, 99, 108, 145, 157–8, 213, 223, 308
sponsorship groups, 9, 33–4, 215
"strategic use of resettlement" (SUR), 77
Swedish Red Cross, 156
Syrian refugee crisis: Canada's response to, 155–6; international reaction to, 152–4; media coverage of, 162–3, 166, 255
Syrian refugees: application approval rates, 230; BVOR program and, 134–7; in Canada's public discourse, 86; comments on social media about, 163–6; community reception of, 203–4; eligibility criteria, 215; experiences of, 200; families of, 195n6; government-sponsored, 311–12; hospital experience of, 202–3; legal aid to, 216; loans for resettlement expenses, 307; media portrayal of, 162; in Nova Scotia, 134; perception of resettlement success by, 199–201; perspective on rural lifestyle, 138; post-arrival challenges, 157; pre-arrival contact with sponsors, 201–3; priority placement of, 83; private sponsorship of, 86, 198–9, 200–4, 308, 310–12; projected targets for, 214, 303–4; requirements for status determination documents, 216; resettlement of, 78, 85, 134–7, 155, 214–15, 253, 286, 294, 310; statistics of, 83, 154–5, 198, 214–15, 294, 303; status eligibilities of, 199–201; study of, 198–9, 306; treatment by visa officers, 242n11

Al Tadamon ("solidarity") group, 159
Temple Shalom, 121
Teusaquillo Mennonite Church in Bogota, 103
Thelen, Kathleen, 25
Thériault, Pierre-André, 312
"They Came to Destroy: ISIS Crimes against the Yazidis" (UN report), 113
Toronto Star, 158
tragic images: public reaction to publication of, 155–6
Treviranus, Barbara, 44
Troper, Harold, 27
Trudeau, Justin, 84, 91n27, 155–6, 159, 161
Trudeau, Pierre Elliott, 32
Trudeau government: refugee policy, 81–2, 84–5, 90n27; Syrian Refugee Initiative, 49, 53–4, 140, 178–80, 190, 207, 214, 286, 294, 303–4
Trump, Donald: anti-immigrant rhetoric, 253; election of, 252, 255; executive order on travel ban, 253, 289; immigration and refugee policies, 82, 247, 250–1, 255–6, 259, 289
Turnbull, Malcolm, 274
Tyyska, Vappu, 162

Ugandan refugees, 30
UN High Commissioner for Refugees (UNHCR): Agenda for Protection, 48; called for greater support for refugees, 252; Canada's donations to, 81; definition of resettlement by, 5, 80; lack of institutional memory, 306; recognition of family reunification, 56; refugee referrals, 27, 55, 134
United Jewish Relief Agencies (UJRA), 23
United States: Displaced Persons Act, 249; Refugee Act, 250–1; refugee co-sponsorship, 248–9, 252–3; Resettlement Act, 249; retreat from leadership role in refugee regime, 87; xenophobia in, 247
University of Ottawa Refugee Hub, 145
Urban Justice Center, 252
US Committee for Refugees and Immigrants, 251
US Conference of Catholic Bishops, 251
US refugee policy: admission quota, 247–8, 250; deportation without due process, 250; evolution of, 247, 249–51; experiments with private sponsorship, 252; legislation, 249–50; religious organizations and, 251–2; resettlement program, 63, 248–52; restrictions in, 247–8, 250, 255–6; voluntary agencies and, 248–9, 251–2

Vietnamese refugees, 251–2, 267
Vietnam War, 98
visa office–referred sponsorship, 44
Vi som tar emot flyktingar pa Stockholms central (We Who Welcome Refugees at Stockholm's Central Station) group, 159
Vogl, Anthea, 310
voluntarism/voluntary agencies, 248–9, 253, 255–7, 259, 260n8

Watson, Jim, 216
Weiss, Lorne, 12, 122
#welcomerefugees movement, 155, 158, 162–3, 165–6
Whitlam, Gough, 266
Wilson, Bertha, 238
World Council of Churches (WCC), 22–4
World Refugee Year, 28

Yazidi refugees: Canadian diaspora, 112–14; cultural adaptation of, 122; divisions within, 119; government assistance to, 121–3, 126–7; ISIS attacks on, 112–13; private support of, 126–7; proposal of hybrid program for, 125–6; in public discourse, 86; religious practices, 112; resettlement of, 112, 122–3; vulnerability of, 127–8